Maynooth College is two hundred [years old] and achievement is to be honoured [...] ment will be widely celebrated on the bicentenary. The occasion will see the celebration of Maynooth's original purpose, still continued, the training of priests for Ireland. It will also mark the development of that purpose over two centuries, eventually to include third-level education of men and women in philosophy and theology, in the sciences, and in the arts.

To honour in an appropriate way these two hundred years of teaching, members of the college staff are publishing a series of books in a number of academic disciplines. Edited by members of the College Faculty, these books will range from texts based on standard theology courses to interdisciplinary studies with a theological or religious involvement.

The venture is undertaken with pride in the long Maynooth academic tradition and in modest continuance of it.

Editorial Board:

Patrick Hannon
Ronan Drury
Gerard Watson

If you understand, it is not God ...
(St Augustine)

Martin Henry

On Not
Understanding God

the columba press

First published in 1997 by
the columba press
55A Spruce Avenue, Stillorgan Industrial Park,
Blackrock, Co Dublin

Cover by Bill Bolger
Origination by The Columba Press
Printed in Ireland by
Colour Books, Dublin

ISBN 1 85607 196 0

Copyright © 1997, Martin Henry

Contents

III. BACKGROUND TO THE CONTEMPORARY DEBATE

IV. LOCATING GOD

Preface

It should be admitted right at the outset that this book has been written in direct violation of Lichtenberg's prayer: 'Heaven, please let me not write a book about books.' Little in this book is original. How could it be otherwise if, as has been asserted, whatever does not come from the tradition is a plagiarism? What I have done is to bring together certain ways of approaching the God-question that have struck me as interesting or unusual and worth drawing attention to. There is nothing sacrosanct about the ideas put forward, or about the order in which they have been placed. Someone else would no doubt have chosen a different order and made a different choice of what to include or exclude. In what follows it is therefore almost inevitable that many aspects of the God-question that others judge to be of indispensable importance will be neglected.

While this does not pretend, as the title already concedes, to be a systematic treatment of the doctrine of God, certain long cherished ideas about the subject surface at different points in the course of the book, especially on the question of evil. This may lend it, perhaps, some degree of unity, without, one would hope, making it monotonous.

There is, then, no progressive argument in what follows, but rather a series of essays (in the French sense) or attempts to probe various facets of this question of all questions. However a loose structure, of a largely chronological character, has been imposed on the material. An introductory section, raising recurring features of the topic briefly, is followed by three chapters on the biblical and patristic ages' tussle with God, and on some of the traditional arguments for the existence of God that are associated in the minds of many with the Middle Ages. Obviously, with such a huge sweep, at

most 'only just almost nothing' can be asserted with any confidence. I have sought therefore only to gauge provisionally how
much the patience of former God-seekers (and God-listeners) must
have found, for us to re-discover, and to wonder how much they
must have known to which we may never have access. The third
section deals with the modern period. I have chosen to concentrate
on the two seminal thinkers at the beginning of this period:
Schleiermacher and Hegel, and on Feuerbach, the most influential
interpreter of Hegel's philosophy of religion, because their thought
still determines the parameters within which the God-question is
currently debated. In the period following their immediate dominance I have given special emphasis – inevitably – to Nietzsche
who, it seems to me, demands to be heard. For more recent times
general overviews already exist that deal with the better-known
twentieth-century theologians.[1] An attempt to add one more survey
to the list would add little to the understanding of the thinkers
involved. I considered it possibly more useful to offer an interpretation of how the contemporary vogue of postmodernism relates to
the question of God. In the final part I attempt to tease out how
God's transcendence or 'unavailability', God's eternal attraction for
humanity, which is as unavoidable as death, might be spoken
about, yet again.

I have tried where possible to acknowledge debts, but some may
have escaped my notice, even to the extent of my not 'referencing'
specific verbal echoes of things once read, noted or heard, but
whose precise provenance I no longer recall. Such omissions are as
regrettable as, alas, now incorrigible. In book references I have usually given the publication date of the copy used, which is not
always the date of first publication.

I should like to thank my friend and editor Professor Patrick
Hannon for applying pressure at just the right times, and in just the
right amounts, and Dr Dermot Lane for kindly agreeing to read the
book in manuscript form, at short notice, and in the midst of a variously very busy life. The recommendations of both editors have

---

1   For example, John Macquarrie, *Twentieth-Century Religious Thought*
    (London, 1989[4]); David F. Ford (ed.), *The Modern Theologians. An
    Introduction to Christian Theology in the Twentieth Century* (Oxford,
    1996[2]); Stanley J. Grenz and Roger E. Olson, *Twentieth-Century Theology.
    God and the World in a Transitional Age* (Downers Grove, 1992). These
    works all contain useful information on recent contributions to the
    God-question.

been of great assistance in lightening (and enlightening) the final text. I also wish to record my thanks to Alan Haugh and Dr Vincent Twomey for their helpful suggestions.

In what follows the term 'man' is used in its traditional English inclusive sense. Similarly conventional is the reference to God as 'he'. To attempt to use self-consciously 'inclusive language' for the human race, and asexual language for God, seems to me to lead to stilted, cumbersome English, so wooden as to appear almost ideologically motivated. In trying to avoid this pitfall, I trust that no offence will be taken where none is intended.

Finally, the book is dedicated to the Maynooth students who from 1982 until 1996 have listened quizzically (I hope) to the many stages of its gestation.

PART I

Exploring the terrain

CHAPTER ONE

Approaching the God-question

Theology is a science, but at the same time how many sciences? ...
A town or a landscape from afar off is a town and a landscape, but
as one approaches it becomes houses, trees, tiles, leaves, grass, ants,
ants' legs, and so on ad infinitum. *All that is comprehended in the*
word 'landscape'.

... [T]he end of things and their principles are unattainably hidden
from [man] in impenetrable secrecy.

— Blaise Pascal

View from the middle

A book on the incomprehensibility of God may appear, superficially,
to be a contradiction in terms. For if we truly believe that God is
beyond human understanding, is silence not the only appropriate
way of registering this conviction? However, even silence can have
different dimensions. The silence, for example, which follows the
performance of a piece of music has a different quality from the
silence which precedes it. Similarly, in theology to end with silence
is very different from a premature refusal ever to speak about God.
Only in the former case does some element of comparison exist by
which to assess the significance of the final silence. A legitimate
scepticism about the pretensions of theology should therefore not
be confused with defeatism. To struggle with questions is more difficult, and surely more productive, than to make a lazy peace with
them. Nevertheless, even traditionally noble and flattering terms
like 'struggle' and 'difficulty' can have connotations which render
their use perhaps somewhat ambiguous in Christian theology. That
is to say, if the Christian reality is ultimately a miracle of grace, how
appropriate is it to speak of approaching it through intellectual
striving? Is there possibly a latent pelagianism in all theology?

From a slightly different quarter come, curiously enough, similar warnings about the inability of intellectual endeavour alone to
nourish human beings. Samuel Beckett, for example, spoke in an

early poem about 'a world politely turning/From the loutishness of learning'. This quietly expressed sentiment is still in tune with Nietzsche's much more violent castigation in his day of accurate but, in human terms, not very valuable historical scholarship. Yet such warnings about the acquisition of existentially irrelevant knowledge can be heeded as warnings, without having to be turned into prohibitions against thinking. They can serve as constant reminders of the modesty, ambiguity and final inadequacy of the theological enterprise. In so doing they can highlight the quasi-impossibility, to say nothing of the chutzpah, of any writing claiming to call itself 'theological'. Perhaps the distinction between what is necessary and what is adequate could be applied with special aptness to Christian theology. It is a necessary 'moment' of faith to seek understanding, for otherwise faith can degenerate into fideism,[1] but theological understanding can never be an adequate representation of, or substitute for, faith. Faith always remains a grace which is beyond our reach, because it stems from God.

The 'line' that will be followed in this book is then rather dull, and quite unexciting, because it is the line in the middle of the road, *nel mezzo del cammin*, which is everywhere and always. Mediocrity is our condition, the only golden age we are ever likely to inhabit. This 'vision' of things is old, I also believe it happens to be true. If an old vision is not broken, why mend it? In the light of this vision it becomes easy to see that we are 'incapable of certain knowledge or absolute ignorance' (Pascal).[2] This applies to theology as much as to anything else. Since God is infinite, whether we see a little more or a little less of the truth at any one time is not as important as to realise that we will never know everything, nor will we ever be entirely bereft of sight. Thus, for example, even chaos can only be 'perceived', paradoxically, if some 'order' is at least presumed to exist, in relation to which chaos can make its impact; similarly doubt makes no sense in isolation from certainty, which it thereby reveals; likewise, error points to truth, and even the sense of losing one's bearings presupposes that reality is somehow 'mapped'. We can

---

1 Fideism, which glories in the allegedly irreconcilable antithesis between faith and reason, is resisted by the Catholic tradition for two main reasons: firstly, because it implicitly denies a real connection between our thinking and God, a connection upheld by the doctrine of creation; and, secondly, because it turns the act of faith into an act of self-assertion – a kind of creaturely *creatio ex nihilo* – whereas it is rather, viewed at least from the human side, a response to an objective reality.

2 *Pensées* (fr. 199), tr. A. J. Krailsheimer (Harmondsworth, 1983), p. 92.

therefore be grateful for any understanding of things that we find anywhere, knowing that all truth is interconnected. Thus any tiny fragment of it we come upon will put us in touch with it all.

If moreover we believe God to be omnipresent, then any starting-point for discussion of the God-question is bound to be arbitrary. Indeed, strictly speaking, there can be no absolute starting-point for talking about God. Intellectual enquiries of whatever kind always begin and end in the middle, a point that has been made over and over again. There is no 'square one' to get back to, no absolute Cartesian starting-point: 'There is no absolute beginning in thinking, no absolute language (Plato knew that – witness *Cratylus*), and even no way how we could express in a contingent language – the only one at our disposal – the very concept of the absolute language (and thus the concept of the contingent language as well) or the absolute beginning. Inevitably, we start and end in the middle of our itinerary.'[3]

Perhaps another way of making the same point is to notice how language's own 'original sin', its inborn frailty,[4] its resistance to complete transparency appears to be historically irremovable. And if this is so of spoken language,[5] how much more true is it of written language? Misgivings on this score go back at least as far as Plato,[6] and they are also found in ancient Jewish culture.[7] Yet language,

---

3   Leszek Kolakowski, *Metaphysical Horror* (Oxford, 1988), p. 11.
4   The endlessly fastidious Flaubert wrote: 'Language is a cracked kettle on which we beat out tunes for bears to dance to, while all the time we long to move the stars to pity' (quoted in *The New Penguin Dictionary of Quotations*, ed. J. M. and M. J. Cohen, Harmondsworth, 1993, p. 165).
5   Cf. Peter Brown's comments on one of the ancient masters of the word, Augustine: 'He was a contemplative in the austere tradition of Plotinus. He came near to regarding speech itself as a falling-away of the soul from its inner act of contemplation' (*Augustine of Hippo*, London, 1969, p. 256). Augustine himself wrote: '[I] am saddened that my tongue cannot live up to my heart' (*ibid.*).
6   Specifically in the *Phaedrus*: see F. Overbeck, *Über die Anfänge der patristischen Literatur* (Darmstadt, 1966), p. 40.
7   Cf. James Barr *Holy Scripture: Canon, Authority, Criticism* (Oxford, 1983), p. 12, especially his comments on the practice of Jesus: 'There is not a single point at which Jesus commands that an event or a teaching should be written down so that it would be accurately remembered. The probability lies in the opposite direction: that, in spite of the existence of previous scripture in the form of the Old Testament (as we call it now), the cultural presupposition suggested that committal to writing was an *unworthy* mode of transmission of the profoundest truth.'

despite its evident limitations, does of course help us to express our ideas and to orientate ourselves in the world, but there is no way apparently from within language itself of going beyond it and using it as a completely reliable instrument that could enable us to vault over the limitations of this world so as to reach what is not exhausted by the world, namely God. Our ideas cannot evade or transcend the gravitational pull of language, which is rooted – or at least seems to be rooted – in this world. Moreover, as the story of the 'Tower of Babel' reminds us, language is a great force for confusion as well as for clarification in the world, the two being not of course unlinked. To say nothing of the fact that language can be used for purposes of concealment or obfuscation. 'Language has been given to man', Talleyrand among others is reputed to have said, 'to disguise his thought.' Language may indeed be more a sign of human alienation than an expression of the desire to communicate, though again the one need not exclude the other. Infants start to make sounds when they feel they are being abandoned, indeed as soon as they are expelled from their mothers' wombs, in order to attract attention to their as yet linguistically unarticulated needs.

Being limited, then, we cannot but err, being opaque we cannot achieve perfect clarity, *pace* Descartes. 'Our false philosophy', Lichtenberg wrote, 'is incorporated in our entire language; we can, so to speak, not reason without reasoning falsely. We fail to consider that speaking, regardless of what, is a philosophy ...'[8] Hence the value of suspicion or an attitude of mistrustfulness towards the exercise of our rational and other powers. Hence also the truth of Ved Mehta's observation that 'the Christian distrusting reason even as he reasoned' is nothing new in Christian tradition.[9] However, even distrust and suspicion must be limited, if we as creatures are to remain true to our condition.

All human enquiries then take place between an inaccessible beginning and an unforeseeable end.[10] If for no other reason than this, there will always be a gap between our perception of reality's

---

8 G. Chr. Lichtenberg, *Aphorisms*, tr. R. J. Hollingdale (Harmondsworth, 1990), p. 115 (henceforth quoted as *Aphorisms*).

9 Ved Mehta, *The New Theologian* (London, 1966), p. 172. Mehta adds (writing in 1965): 'Aquinas in the end had no more use for his "Summa" than Barth now has, in a way, for his "Dogmatics"'.

10 Cf. Manès Sperber, *Sein letztes Jahr*, (Munich, 1985), p. 105: 'The end of history: that is a piece of nonsense; there is no such thing. We are always on the move with regard to truth; it can never become our settled possession.'

full truth and that truth itself. This however does not indicate that
the view from the middle is of no value. It is certainly not everything, but neither is it on that account nothing. For the awareness
that what we experience is only part of a larger picture, whose full
comprehension – to repeat – will always elude us, is in itself a valuable piece of knowledge, reinforcing our suspicion that, if even per-
ceptible reality is always more than what we can say about it, how
immeasurably more than, or other than, all we can say about him
must God be. Hence religion's ever-repeated antiphon on the
incomprehensibility of God.

In life we can see many things, but we cannot see God. Gregory
Nazianzen (329–389), writing in his *Second Theological Oration* on
the biblical passage that recounts Moses' attempt to see God, notes
that Moses was only permitted to look on the back of God, and –
Gregory adds – the back of God is the world (and by implication
God's face is his own hidden essence, accessible to God alone,
hence concealed from us). All we ever see of God or can see of God
is the world itself. Although faith teaches that this world is God's
creation, we would need God's eyes to be able actually to *see* that, just
as we would need God's eyes to see fully the goodness of creation.

We cannot therefore see God, we can only see the world and feel
its pressure, and its insufficiency. This leads to a sense of dissatisfaction, once described by Hans Urs von Balthasar as 'that which is
most fundamental in us.'[11] And at least since the time of St
Augustine, dissatisfaction or restlessness has been widely acknowledged as a strong hint of our relatedness to God.

In posing the God-question from this angle, however, one could
evoke the suspicion that 'God' is principally a way of expressing
the hope that human dissatisfaction will eventually be relieved.
And then 'God' might run the risk of being seen as merely an emer-
gency exit from reality, and faith in God as an illusion. This is how
many nineteenth-century sceptics judged the religious situation of
their own times: some – in England – melancholically; others, like
Leopardi, with unrelenting despair; still others, like Marx, contemptuously; and finally, Nietzsche, not so much renouncing as
denouncing Christianity, with occasional flashes of high-spirited
defiance. Religion has of course not disappeared, but neither have
the large questions the nineteenth century asked about it. Is religion
an anaesthetic, dulling the pain of existence (the *'opium* of the peo-

---

11 Quoted by Andrew Louth, *The Origins of the Christian Mystical Tradition*
    (Oxford, 1983), p. 90.

ple'[12])? Is faith cowardice in the face of reality (so, Nietzsche)? Or on the contrary should not religion rather be understood as an 'aesthetic', i.e. a way of helping people not to suppress reality, but to perceive it as it actually is?[13] Assuming the God-question to be still open, the problem of finding a window or windows in the world that open out on to God, or through which God can look in on the human scene, still remains. For the human side of the God-question can never be omitted from the equation, even if it cannot be, as both Barth and Balthasar in this century took great pains to emphasise, and indeed as the mainline Christian tradition has always tenaciously maintained, in the dominant or controlling position, which of course has always been reserved to God and his revelation.

The task

What is especially frustrating about trying to write a book on God is, of course, the intrinsic unknowability of the subject. This is also, perhaps unfairly, what may deprive it entirely of interest for some potential readers. For why should anyone be interested in what will always remain – here and hereafter – unfathomable? It is, moreover, the unknowability of God which makes it impossible to prove that the God-question, the question of ultimate truth, simply has to be faced. And would any demand that it should, not be a form of intellectual bullying?[14] The long European tradition of philosophy and theology, the spiritual and intellectual adventure of the West, just like, say, the European tradition of classical music, may be completely ignored by millions, who do not feel their humanity diminished, or their lives any less valuable, on that account. One may

---

12 To be fair to Marx, one should perhaps recall that the sentences preceding this well-known tag read: '*Religious* suffering is at one and the same time the *expression* of real suffering and a protest against real suffering. Religion is the sigh of the oppressed creature, the heart of a heartless world and the soul of soulless conditions' (K. Marx, *Early Writings*, tr. R. Livingstone and G. Benton, Harmondsworth, 1975, p. 244).

13 We recall that 'aesthetic' is derived from the Greek verb 'to perceive'.

14 Cf. Nietzsche's criticism of Luther on this question: *Daybreak* §82, tr. R. J. Hollingdale (Cambridge, 1983), p. 49: '"This you have to decide within yourself, for your life is at stake": with this cry Luther springs at us and thinks we feel the knife at our throat. But we fend him off with the words of one higher and more considerate than he: "We are free to refrain from forming an opinion about this thing or that, and thus to spare our soul distress. For things themselves are by their nature incapable of forcing us to make judgements."'

lament this fact, but it is hard to deny it. And if still others scoff at
metaphysical questions, who, in the words of William Paley, can
refute their sneers? If it is true, to adapt some words applied by
Seamus Heaney to art, that religion can be refused, but not refuted
or disproved, then if someone is just not interested in religion, all
one's efforts to awaken interest in the God-question are likely to be
in vain. All the more so if one accepts that faith in God can only
arise by an act of grace, over which we have no control. There
appears even to be a certain fittingness in finding that Christianity's
doctrine of grace coexists with a certain amount of indifference to
the God-question. They are two sides of the same coin.

According to Socrates, the unexamined life is not worth living.
But not worth living for whom? Philosophy, the love and pursuit of
wisdom, may be ultimately a matter of taste.[15] This is not just a
question of formal education. It is undoubtedly possible to be perceptive without being learned (and vice versa), and to believe that
the process of living is more important or more valuable than the
desire or ability to examine that process, although it would probably have to be conceded that such a belief is itself the result of some
kind of scrutiny of existence. But be that as it may, it is scarcely
open to debate that, as in Valéry's celebrated line: 'Le vent se lève!
... il faut tenter de vivre!' ('The wind is rising! ... We must try to
live!'), 'to live' is clearly more than what its minute intellectual
examination amounts to or could ever justify, for all that 'living'
includes 'thinking'.

Thus, it is not surprising that in his projected apology on behalf
of Christianity, Pascal should have been concerned first and foremost to *persuade* a potential believer to take an interest in his undertaking. Otherwise all the good arguments in the world are directed
only to the desert air, which is the fate of most 'official' documents
in the Christian churches. What was true for a relatively small number of people in Pascal's time – namely, unbelief – is now true of
vast numbers. One perhaps unexpected sign of the huge shift in
religious sensibility that has occurred between antiquity and our
own times is 'the decline in the potency and frequency of real cursing

---

15 Nietzsche once (with tongue in cheek?) made a connection between
   sophia ('wisdom') and taste, (*Human, All Too Human*, II, §170). Linguistically – though admittedly this is no compelling argument – there
   do in fact seem to be points of contact between the two concepts:
   'knowledge' and 'taste'. One thinks of the French cognate pair 'savoir'
   and 'saveur', or the two senses of the Spanish verb 'saber', ('to know'
   and 'to taste of').

... God and the prophets do a great deal of it in the Old (and to some extent the New) Testament. Judaism and Islam use the curse. So did the ancient Egyptians ... As faith in the supernatural declines, so does the living curse... It takes the form of a curse but is not a true curse: it is just a snarl. Modern cursing, though common, is uninteresting and routine because its soul is dead. We have lost our link with the supernatural.'[16] On a slightly different register, E. R. Dodds, the renowned classical scholar, may be taken as symptomatic of the modern mood when he writes in his autobiography: '[T]o me, as to so many of my generation, the age-old question "Why are we here?" has ceased to be meaningful. It was meaningful once, when the earth was God's theatre and man the tragic hero of a unique and divinely conceived drama. But for a small animal bred we know not how on a third-rate planet in a fourth-rate galaxy even to ask such questions seems to me senseless; to offer confident answers, hybristic. I can only say humbly with Erasmus "Scientiae pars est quaedam nescire" (Not to know certain things is a part of knowledge).'[17]

As the testimony of E. R. Dodds shows vividly, the difficulty with the contemporary God-question is not so much that people no longer have belief in God, but that they do not know what it could possibly even now mean to profess such belief. What difference does it make to life? Little wonder that Yeats asked the question, 'whether the word *belief* belong[s] to our age at all.'[18] At an even earlier stage, Nietzsche, in a letter of 22 October 1879 to his friend Franz Overbeck, had touched in passing on this modern problem when he mentioned his inability to know what was meant by 'believing in something'. The reflection was prompted by a letter Nietzsche himself had received from another friend, Heinrich Romundt, encouraging him to seek through faith a way of overcoming his anxieties. Nietzsche writes: 'Faith in what? I ask ... But perhaps he means *faith in faith.* – I would prefer a slice of bread and butter to anything so vague.'

An approach theologians are sometimes tempted to take in dealing with this problem is to answer it by, as it were, not answering it. For one can simply refuse to enter into dialogue with unbelief, considering it futile, or even dishonest, to seek common ground where

---

16 Matthew Parris, *Scorn: With Added Vitriol* (Harmondsworth, 1996), p. ix.
17 *Missing Persons* (Oxford, 1978), p. 193.
18 Richard Ellmann, *The Identity of Yeats* (London, 1968), p. xviii.

it seems there is none. And if one cannot sincerely argue with, but yet does not wish to ignore, unbelief, one would seem to have no other option but to *confront* positions incompatible with belief, and seek to replace them with something considered better. Initially this approach appears attractive, especially if one accepts that faith is more in the nature of an act of trust or of will, a decision, rather than the conclusion of an argument. In the twentieth century Karl Barth is a representative of such an understanding of the theologian's task. His theological method may be summed up in the assertion: 'Belief cannot argue with unbelief, it can only preach to it.' (One's confidence in this approach may be slightly dented if one recalls Lichtenberg's dictum: 'The fact that sermons are preached in churches makes lightning-conductors on such buildings not unnecessary.')

Preaching to unbelief alone can, then, scarcely function as an answer to the question that was raised by Nietzsche and Yeats. In the first place, to see no common ground between belief and unbelief is to come perilously close to dualism, as if religious faith could find no point of contact with what it believes to be the *created* human condition. If this were truly the case, then the God of creation and the God of redemption would be two different gods, as was Marcion's view. Such a position is clearly incompatible with the monotheism professed by Christianity. And, secondly, to see faith as a pure act of will is to risk glorying in the irrationality of fideism. Now while no one can prove the truth of faith by argument, it would appear nevertheless to be impossible to have faith in God without at least having some idea of what or who is designated by the word 'God'. An intellectual dimension to faith is simply human. Despite occasional lapses Christianity is in the long run never likely to be at ease with fideism, if only out of a residual sense of shame: 'Many have no doubt attained to that humility which says: *credo quia absurdum est* and sacrificed their reason to it: but, so far as I know, no one has yet attained to that humility which says: *credo quia absurdus sum*, though it is only one step further.'[19]

To sacrifice one's intellect for the sake, allegedly, of one's faith is in fact an irrational act of self-assertion. Certainly, human acts of will are in the last analysis non-derivative, but that is not to say that they are arbitrary or irrational. Indeed one of reason's greatest triumphs is not to repudiate itself but to recognise its own limitations. As Jaroslav Pelikan puts it: '[T]he recognition that reason does not

---

19 Nietzsche, *Daybreak*, §417 tr. R. J. Hollingdale (Cambridge, 1983), p. 176.

exhaust the range of meaning in human life is itself an accomplish-ment of reason.'[20] If, on the other hand, one wishes to try to absolve oneself from personal intellectual responsibility for the act of faith, and instead to base one's theology on a willed acceptance of an inscrutable divine truth, ostensibly relayed – without any explana-tion – to the believer by bible or church teaching authority, then one may have taken up an impregnable position; but, as Gerd Theissen points out, not thereby a true position ('a claim is not necessarily true simply because it cannot be refuted').[21]

The ancient rhetorical need to win a hearing is thus still an essential part of the theological trade. For what is the point of speaking about God if no one is listening, indeed if the God-quest-ion itself is felt to be senseless or faith felt to be irrational? And what is the point of speaking about God in a style no one can any longer make sense of?

However, even from the point of view of a religious believer there is, putting it at its mildest, something faintly absurd in the notion of a book on God, as though the creature could take it upon himself to speak about the source and purpose of the universe. So is this just another book to prove (even unwittingly) the shortcomings of books about God? Or is it an attempt to show that the truth about things, assuming such an expression has a meaning, is not to be found in any book, however exalted, however hallowed by tradi-tion, however sacred? Though if that were the case, why, apart from the communication of pressing utilitarian concerns, or the desire to entertain or to earn a living, write anything at all, to say nothing of a book on God?

One might be encouraged to find a partial answer to this depressing question by taking one's cue from a recent work of Kolakowski's. While it is true, as Kolakowski points out,[22] that the main questions in philosophy have remained unresolved since ancient times, their constant recurrence and seeming unwillingness to disappear suggest that they will inevitably continue to be raised by each new generation according to its own idiom. *Mutatis mutandis,*

20 J. Pelikan, *The Melody of Theology* (Cambridge, Mass., 1988), p. 70.
21 G. Theissen, *On Having a Critical Faith,* tr. J. Bowden (London, 1979), p. 5; cf. Nietzsche, *The Will to Power* §535, tr. W. Kaufmann and R. J. Holling-dale (London, 1968), p. 290: 'An assumption that is irrefutable – why should it for that reason be "true"?' 'Irrefutability' may be seen as a nec-essary but not a sufficient condition for 'truth'.
22 *Metaphysical Horror,* pp. 1f.

the same, one may hope, will be true of theology, especially since Christian theology is so closely interwoven with the Western philosophical tradition. But even more to the point, if one believes that there is only one God, then this one God will be related to the past, present and future. And talk about this God will therefore have to take account of the Christian tradition in the past, as well as the malaise of the present, and our hope for the future.

However, even this tentative starting-point itself begs the question of the extent to which communication with the past is possible at all. An act of faith would certainly seem to be an inevitable prelude to any such endeavour. One must assume that there is a continuity in human nature, which makes the thoughts of past generations still accessible to us. Such an assumption may however not be very different from the assumption one makes in trying to understand a contemporary culture foreign to one's own, and perhaps even in trying to understand anyone at all other than oneself, foreigner or not, or even indeed in trying to understand oneself.

Yet it must be admitted that 'human nature' is in contemporary thought a highly controverted notion. Indeed an important aspect of the mood of the modern age is the suspicion, now almost a cliché, that the idea of a fixed human nature is without foundation. For the Spanish philosopher Ortega y Gasset this suspicion was, apparently, an indisputable fact: 'Man has no "nature"; he only has history.'[23] Yet there is perhaps a *via media* between seeing human nature as a completely empty concept and seeing it as an exhaustively definable one. What many modern theologians, such as Wolfhart Pannenberg or Gerd Theissen (and also of course many non-theologians), have argued for is the idea that human nature is 'open to the world', and not entirely determined by its environment, unlike other created (animal) natures. This is perhaps a modern re-interpretation of the old, notoriously slippery, notion of human freedom.

Apart from presupposing the relative stability, coherence and continuity of such a vague notion as 'human nature,' it must also be assumed that thinkers of the past may have important insights to impart which we ourselves, for a variety of reasons, are unable, or no longer able, to reach. Furthermore, if certain thinkers have managed to attract the attention of many generations of human beings, then the presumption that they have delved deeply into some of

23 Quoted by Van A. Harvey, *The Historian and the Believer* (London, 1967), p. 72.

life's enigmas may not be entirely arbitrary, even if it cannot be demonstrated in advance. And just to ignore past thinkers because they are dead, would amount to a kind of discrimination, surely incompatible with an openness to the truth.

Yet when strong interest is shown in the intellectual achievements of a past age, that interest often has its roots in some contemporary difficulty for which a solution is needed. This is spectacularly true of the modern maladjusted age. But, to a greater or lesser extent, it must be true of all ages, since human beings always live in a constantly moving present which they can never grasp, hovering uncertainly between past and future. For knowledge we can look to the past, and for a final resting place we are directed to the future.

In our world, the chief reason which now encourages people to try to re-express what Christianity has to say about God, and to look to the past for some guidance in the matter, is simply that 'God' has become problematic in our culture. Indeed the modern sense of the exhaustion and lack of orientation of Western culture is an expression of what Nietzsche diagnosed as the great event of modern times: the 'death of God', and the advent of nihilism. Although it was Nietzsche, who most dramatically announced the bad news, many others, as for example Jean Paul[24] and, slightly later, many of the so-called Young Hegelians (such as D.F. Strauss, L. Feuerbach and K. Marx) – to speak only of the German tradition – had themselves reached the same conclusion. And ever since, even some of those who consider themselves to be believers in God have become unsettled in their belief, and unsure about just what the nature of this God is in whom they think they still believe. Belief in Christianity's God has for many become elusive, or it has faded away altogether. This prompts people to try to probe once more 'The uncontrollable mystery on the bestial floor'.

It is perhaps worth noting in passing that the atheism of the nineteenth century has a different quality from that of the sometimes smug materialistic atheism of the Enlightenment (e.g. d'Holbach, Helvétius – though not, I think, the Marquis de Sade). The atheism of the nineteenth century often combines rejection of belief in God with an interest in the historical Jesus, abandoned

---

24 Cf. his work *Siebenkäs* (1796/7), with its famous evocation of Jesus' discovery of an empty heaven after the resurrection … (It was of this writer that the North German dramatist Friedrich Hebbel remarked unkindly: I would rather be forgotten with Lichtenberg than immortal with Jean Paul', quoted in the Introduction to *Aphorisms*, p. 16.)

before an empty, silent heaven. This is a fairly common theme in, for example, French Romantic poetry after Jean Paul's time.[25] The Romantics' atheism is often a protest against the cruelty of existence (Schopenhauer), and occasionally Jesus functions as a symbol of inexplicable, pointless, innocent human suffering, and becomes thus – ironically – an argument *against* the existence of God. Nietzsche, characteristically, gives this problematic his own unique twist and, far from seeing the existence of a cruel world as an objection to God, sees 'God' as 'hitherto … the greatest objection to existence'…[26]

To return to the theme mentioned a moment ago, it is a fairly safe generalisation to say that since the end of the Middle Ages the following pattern has become clearly established: the disorientation of the present has acted as a spur to look either into the self, as with Descartes, or into the past, for guidance. Some have looked back to the Christian past itself, as at the Reformation; others to the pre-Christian alternative one might almost say, as with the Renaissance thinkers and their successors. The increasing awareness that there was an alternative to Christianity in Graeco-Roman antiquity, and the suspicion that the culture Christianity defeated may in many respects have been superior to it, is an intensely held conviction in the thought of a key-figure such as Nietzsche, for example, albeit with the ironic complication that Nietzsche's passionate honesty is unthinkable without the Christianity that intervened between the world of antiquity which he venerated and perhaps idealised, and the modern world of decadent late Christian culture that he abominated.

Perhaps the most pressing aspect of contemporary religious disorientation is the seeming inability on the part of believers themselves to agree on what difference belief in God makes to their life, either as regards its conduct or its meaning. Is there any longer a recognisable distinguishing mark between the believer and someone who has consciously rejected belief in God? For while the main beliefs of Christianity can be fairly easily stated, the problem today is that the traditional language seems to have lost touch with the texture of modern experience. Thus, even if Christians say that they believe in God, in the divinity of Jesus, the presence of the Holy Spirit in the church, the forgiveness of sins, grace and redemption, the resurrection of the body and life everlasting, what does all this

---

25 Cf. Baudelaire, *Les Fleurs du Mal*, ed. A. Adam (Paris 1961), p. 420.
26 *Ecce Homo* tr. R. J. Hollingdale (Harmondsworth, 1980), p. 58.

mean, and how does its theoretical meaning manifest itself in practice? For presumably – since human beings are not pure spirits – Christian belief cannot exist only on the plane of pure ideas or consciousness but must also find embodied expression. The difference, therefore, between belief and unbelief cannot be confined to any exclusively intellectual level; if such a difference is genuine, then it will have practical as well as theoretical consequences. Such issues gravitate round the God-question, making it, it would appear, the central question with which religion, and not only theology, has to deal. We can begin to tackle this question by looking briefly at a recent important discussion of the meaning of belief.

Christian believing

In *Discerning the Mystery*[27] Andrew Louth draws a serious distinction between 'believing' and 'finding oneself believing'. The latter 'fatalistic' attitude is exemplified by, for instance, the late Professor Lampe who in Louth's view appears to have capitulated theologically to the historical-critical method.[28] Real Christian believing would seem to be something more immediate, more definite and more intimate. It consists essentially in accepting as true the claim 'that through certain specific events in the past God has revealed himself to men,'[29] and in responding with heart and mind to this revelation: '[B]elief, faith, is not a purely rational exercise; it involves, as an indispensable element, the response of the will or the heart to the One in whom we believe.'[30]

There is no doubt that Louth has put his finger on a sore point in modern Christianity. For a wide gap does indeed appear to have opened up between hesitant believers who worry about what exactly it is they have inherited from the past and how they should now deal with it, and no-nonsense believers who are confident that Christianity speaks for itself, and has a definite meaning, even if that meaning is not fully known to any believer but can always be explored ever more deeply by minds that assent to the basic truths of the Christian faith.

Yet the more robust approach to believing is, clearly, no mere repetition of the idea that faith is the assent of the mind to truths

27 A. Louth, *Discerning the Mystery* (London, 1983).
28 An excerpt from Lampe's contribution to the report *Christian Believing* (London, 1976), p. 100, illustrating Louth's point, is quoted in *Discerning the Mystery*, pp. 15f.
29 Louth, *Discerning the Mystery*, p. 16.
30 *Ibid.*, p. 3.

proposed by the church for our belief and which we should accept
on the church's divinely established authority. Rather, a more
personal note has crept (back?) into 'faith', and the need for loving
contemplation of God on the part of the believer is, if not upper-
most, at least certainly not hidden under a bushel.[31]

Yet even here one is faced with a typically theological 'chicken-
and-egg' question. Do we experience love in life and then attribute
it to God, or are we only capable of experiencing love in the first
place, because God first loved us (1Jn 4:19)? Christianity has indeed
always said: 'God is love, he loves the world and we can only love
God because he first loved us.' This seems straightforward: after all,
we only speak, because we have first been spoken to. But that is an
analogy, and analogies cannot be applied without qualification to
God, as the Fourth Lateran Council (1215) makes crystal-clear.[32]
Since we do not see God directly and cannot have a one-to-one relationship with God as with another human being, we must ask in
what sense is it true to speak of our relationship with God in terms
of love. For could it perhaps be the case that the slackening of traditional communal ties, the atomisation characteristic of modern life,
has forced more and more people into an unwelcome solitary con-
finement, and consequently endowed 'personal relationships' with
an almost redemptive significance that may not in pre-modern
times have been so pronounced? What more natural conclusion
then than to see religion as being essentially about love, and hence
to see God as the unsurpassable partner in the ultimate 'personal
relationship'? And would such a conclusion amount to creating
God in the image of our dearest value, our deepest craving? Before
trying to answer this question, we may look briefly at the possible
relationship between solitude and belief in God.

Solitude and God

It is not good, says the bible, for man to be alone. According to

---

31 See, for example, Hans Urs von Balthasar, *Love Alone: the Way of
   Revelation*, ed. Alexander Dru (London, 1977).
32 'Constitutiones' § 2 *De errore abbatis Ioachim*: 'quia inter creatorem et
   creaturam non potest tanta similitudo notari, quin inter eos maior sit
   dissimilitudo notanda' (For between creator and creature there can be
   noted no similarity so great that a greater dissimilarity cannot be seen
   between them), *Decrees of the Ecumenical Councils*, Vol. I, ed. N. P.
   Tanner, S.J. (London, 1990), pp. 231f.; cf. DS 806 (Barcelona, 1967),
   p. 262, and *The Catechism of the Catholic Church* (Dublin, 1994), p. 18.

Lichtenberg, 'Man loves company, even if it is only that of a smoul-
dering candle.'[33] Even the severe Plotinus was unwilling, after cut-
ting himself off from mundane ambitions, to remain completely
alone; even he, in his contemplative solitude, longed to flee to the
ultimate other Alone ('the flight of the alone to the Alone'). Religion
may perhaps be then the result of what Pascal called man's inability
to remain alone on a chair in a room. Nietzsche himself, for all his
anti-Christianity, in his beautiful and moving poem, 'Gondola
Song'[34] (sometimes also called 'Venice'), in *Ecce Homo*, clearly
longed for a deep connection with something or someone beyond
him. And despite Beckett's claiming somewhere, resiliently, that
there is nothing funnier than unhappiness, much of his own work
(e.g., *Malone Dies, Company, Ghost Trio, Quad I and II*) is so arresting
because it dramatises the harrowing plight of individuals at the end
of their tether, unable either to break out of their solitude or to
render it liveable.

If then religion is arguably, even etymologically – for what *that*
is worth – about connecting with that which is other than oneself,
could God be conceived as the Other than whom there is no
greater? Is believing in God then the desire for the ultimate connection, or recognition or even audience? Why did, for example, St
Augustine abandon a glittering career as a professor of rhetoric?
Was it – dare one suggest? – because he found a better 'public' in
God, the only 'public' that could fully appreciate what he had to
say?[35] And Newman notoriously understood religion as the connection between 'two and two only supreme and luminously self-
evident beings, myself and my Creator.'[36] The corollary of all this
would appear to be that not 'to connect', or to remain isolated, is so

---

33 *Aphorisms*, p. 171.
34 One of the most poignant details of Overbeck's account of Nietzsche's
   breakdown is his recollection of Nietzsche's singing at dead of night
   'das wunderschöne Gondellied' ('the very beautiful Gondola Song') to
   a strange melody, on their train journey through the Gotthard pass on
   the way back from Turin to Basel, in January 1889, following
   Nietzsche's collapse into madness (cf. C.A. Bernoulli, *Franz Overbeck
   und Friedrich Nietzsche. Eine Freundschaft*, Jena, 1908, vol. 2, p. 234).
35 Cioran, suddenly struck one day by the mystery of time, realised, he
   says, how right St Augustine was to enter into debate about it with
   God: with whom could one otherwise enter into a serious debate about
   time? ... (See *Aveux et Anathèmes*, p. 66).
36 J. H. Newman, *Apologia Pro Vita Sua* (London and Glasgow, 1972), p. 98
   (cf. pp. 245, 262, 277).

to speak religion in reverse, with the experience of immense inner turmoil and solitude intact, but not assuaged or transcended by any glimpse of peace. Hell, as well as possibly being in Sartre's famous phrase 'other people', could then also – with at least equal justice – be described as final, eschatological one might say, isolation.

Heaven – on this interpretation of solitude – would be the enjoyment of the right connection or communion with that which is other than oneself, ultimately God. This is a possibility which the Augustinian interpretation of human alienation has indelibly imprinted on the Western psyche as a sometimes tormenting hope.

There are however two pressing questions to be put to Augustine's understanding of human existence, the answers to which should help us to appreciate the *kind* of truth it contains. Firstly, does its vital component come from Christianity, ultimately from what Jesus brought into the world (and which could have come from no other source)? Or is Augustine's vision one that in principle could have been worked out by anyone with a curious and powerful enough mind for the job, like Plotinus – whose vision of reality is not *toto caelo* different from Augustine's? Augustine departed from the way of Plotinus of course when he became a Christian, yet his thought – especially its emphasis on the individual's restless heart – remained deeply imbued with Neoplatonism, and we are told that when he finally withdrew to die, it was with words of Plotinus rather than scripture ringing, or at least purring, in his ears.

Nietzsche once commented on Augustine's *Confessions* in a letter to Overbeck of 31 March 1885, that their philosophical value was 'absolutely zero. Vulgarised Platonism, that is to say, a way of thinking that was meant for the highest spiritual aristocracy, tailored to the needs of slave-natures' (cf. the 'Preface' to *Beyond Good and Evil* written in June 1885, where Christianity is described as 'Platonism for "the people"'). For Nietzsche, therefore, Christianity is simply an ego-trip for slaves and Augustine's Neoplatonising philosophy its intellectual expression.

The question then is: Did Augustine break with the philosophers because he did not wish to be a mere disciple of a philosophical school and because he was himself unable to develop a viable philosophical alternative to Plotinus? Or did he break with the philosophers because he discovered in Christianity something not available elsewhere – which Nietzsche also saw, (mis)understood and repudiated[37] – and which subsequently he could not but

---

37 'Augustine is the deepest ancient name of Nietzsche' according to T. J. J.

try to explicate with the aid of Neoplatonist thought, that being the best and most congenial intellectual vehicle to hand for the task? One could of course simply refuse this question on the grounds that it is too brazen. But if one allows it, it could still be said – at least from within Christianity's (and especially Augustinian Christianity's) own self-understanding – to be in the last analysis unanswerable, since the acceptance of Christian faith is ultimately a grace over which we have no control and about which we cannot therefore speak authoritatively, either in our own case or *a fortiori* in anyone else's. This is another example of Christianity's ability to have things both ways.[38]

All I wish to try to establish at this point, however, is that the resemblance between Augustine's philosophy and Neoplatonism clearly cannot be denied, but neither does it constitute in itself an irrefutable proof that (Augustinian) Christianity is 'nothing but' 'Platonism for "the people"'. This point is of some help in answering the second question raised a moment ago about Augustine's understanding of human existence, which can now be posed: If the Augustinian interpretation of Christianity has been so influential in and on the West, does that mean that it is only of relevance to the West? In adumbrating a possible response to this huge question, one can readily concede that no interpretation of existence can be other than locally coloured, but must that fact in itself constitute an incontrovertible argument against its potential universality? Can a truth be universally damned, as it were, because of its particular origin? Would it not be a form of the genetic fallacy to say that it could? Clearly, of course, to show that something is not necessarily false is not to demonstrate that it is definitely true. We shall return to this question. For the moment, suffice it to say there can be scarcely any doubt that the restlessness inseparable from solitude with its *Splendeurs et misères* is one of the profoundest and most

---

Altizer, *Genesis and Apocalypse: A Theological Voyage toward Authentic Christianity*, 1991, as cited in *Theological Studies*, Vol. 53, No. 3, 1992, p. 564 by S. J. Duffy, who calls this a 'facile fusion[s]'. More than facile it is in fact profoundly misleading, if the differences as well as the undoubted existential resemblances between the two are not kept in mind. It is interesting though that Nietzsche often invites comparison with Christian thinkers; he is indeed in many ways so close to Christianity, and yet finally its quasi-antipode. To call him the complete antipode of Christianity would be going too far, since it would be going into dualism, which Christianity itself forbids us to do.

38 Cf. below, Chapter 5, 'Introduction'.

human of experiences. It is an experience which faith believes – following Augustine's persuasive advocacy – connects us truly with God, but even faith does not say that it *is* God. *Corruptio optimi pessima*[39] applies here too. Christian faith, we recall, has only ever unambiguously identified God in this world with Jesus.

It is, admittedly, always possible to discount the 'Augustinian' interpretation of man's resistance to solitude by saying, with Marx for instance, that man's being is a 'species-being',[40] and therefore by 'nature' he seeks contact with other human beings. In a naturalistic perspective, the human attempt to connect with God can always be interpreted as simply a pathological, thus erroneous, expression of a perfectly 'normal' instinct.

However, if we are now more inclined than at some other times in the past to see God as the ideal friend or lover, this need not of course be an alarming or subversive suggestion, as if faith in God were simply the product of profound human need. (Even if it were, that would not necessarily make the object for which faith absolutely craves imaginary and unreal.) If modernity can be interpreted as a new sojourn in the desert, of which there are examples both in the bible and in the Christian monastic tradition after all, why should God not speak in the desert of modernity as clearly as in the past? The desert has always been the place where one may concentrate on the *unum necessarium* (God) without too many distractions. It has been the place *par excellence* where God has spoken most intimately and unmistakably to human beings. And if modern life can be interpreted as a kind of desert, where traditional existential supports (perhaps even some aspects of inherited religious practice) have weakened, leaving people isolated, uncertain and painfully reminded once again of the constant refrains of the Judaeo-Christian tradition: 'The world is not God', and – slightly more difficult, subjectively at any rate – 'Man is not God', what more natural religious reaction than to see God as the partner who transcends the world and its inability to love, but also continually inspires the search for love in his Creation?

39 'The corruption of what is best is the worst kind of corruption.'
40 Cf. Van A. Harvey, 'Ludwig Feuerbach and Karl Marx', in Ninian Smart et al. (eds.), *Nineteenth Century Religious Thought in the West*, vol. 1 (Cambridge, 1985), p. 302: 'Marx uses the term "species-being" [*Gattungswesen*], as well as its synonyms "species-character" (*Gattungscharakter*), "species-life" (*Gattungsleben*), to refer to those distinctive human capacities the exercise of which constitutes self-realisation.'

Indeed if there were no God, would one feel the insufficiency of the world so acutely, would the world's insufficiency breed such a keen sense of dissatisfaction? Put briefly, where there is dissatisfaction, there is hope, for radical human dissatisfaction points (but only *points*) man beyond himself for his salvation. And indeed, as Joseph Brodsky reminds us, uncertainty, which was evoked above and which is inseparable from dissatisfaction, is not necessarily a bad thing either:

> Uncertainty . . . is the mother of beauty, one of whose definitions is that it's something which isn't yours. At least, this is one of the most frequent sensations accompanying beauty. Therefore, when uncertainty is evoked, then you sense beauty's proximity. Uncertainty is simply a more alert state than certitude, and thus it creates a better lyrical climate. Because beauty is something obtained always from without, not from within.[41]

So it is, Christian faith has always claimed, with God and our redemption. Redemption comes from outside us, not from within us, and no amount of human striving or authenticity can produce it. It comes from without, as grace, or it does not come at all.

To return more specifically to the question of faith, there may be, we are suggesting, good historical grounds to explain why in the modern world faith sometimes takes on the character of a personal relationship between the believer and God, and in this way links up with the much older tradition of Christian mysticism. And while the personal or subjective side of faith is evidently stressed in this approach, the objectivity of faith is kept clearly in view too, as is evidenced by the question Louth himself puts to certain theological responses to the cultural and religious disarray of our age: 'Cut off from the movement of the heart towards God, theology finds itself in a void – for where is its object? Where is the God with whom it concerns itself?'[42] This is indeed a serious question, revealing a deep concern to preserve the objectivity of Christian faith, in the sense of a respect for the object of that faith, God. However, this question, in turn, also raises some counter-questions.

Quite apart from the perhaps not insuperable difficulty of understanding how God could be said to be an 'object' for human beings, there is the further problem that the 'objective' approach to

---

41 From 'On "September 1, 1939" by W. H. Auden', in *Less Than One. Selected Essays* (Harmondsworth, 1987), pp. 339f.
42 *Discerning the Mystery*, p. 2.

faith we have been discussing shows faith to be apparently very
much at home in the element of human consciousness, and hence
open to the suspicion that, no matter how often it stresses the need
to be connected with its supreme object (God), it never really gets
beyond the confines of the theologian's own consciousness, profoundly interesting and informed though that consciousness may
be, as – to speak only of the departed – was undoubtedly the case
with Karl Barth and Hans Urs von Balthasar. For many of his critics,
this problem was notoriously the Achilles' heel of Karl Rahner's
theology, but it may only have been more glaringly in evidence in
his case than in the case of others who were considered, and who
considered themselves, to be more 'objective', and critical of the
theological modernism stemming from Schleiermacher and from
the more historically-conscious thought of Hegel.

If it is true, as we are suggesting, that not only modern theology
but also its most resolute critics move within the orbit of classical
German Idealism (which may, of course, not be the worst or the
least congenial orbit for Christian theology to move in), then the critique which Nietzsche made of the notion of faith within such an
intellectual tradition, may be worth pondering:

> It is false to the point of absurdity to see in a 'belief' ... the distin-
> guishing characteristic of the Christian: only Christian *practice*, a
> life such as he who died on the Cross *lived*, is Christian ... *Not* a
> belief but a doing, above all a *not*-doing of many things, a differ-
> ent *being*. ... States of consciousness, beliefs of any kind, holding
> something to be true for example – every psychologist knows
> this – are a matter of complete indifference and of the fifth rank
> compared with the value of the instincts ... To reduce being a
> Christian, Christianness, to a holding something to be true, to a
> mere phenomenality of consciousness, means to negate
> Christianness. *In fact there have been no Christians at all.* The
> 'Christian', that which has been called Christian for two millen-
> nia, is merely a psychological self-misunderstanding. Regarded
> more closely, that which has ruled in him, *in spite of* all his 'faith',
> has been merely the instincts – and what instincts! 'Faith' has
> been at all times, with Luther for instance, only a cloak, a pretext,
> a screen, behind which the instincts played their game ... one has
> always *spoken* of faith, one has always *acted* from instinct ...[43]

Nietzsche is clearly no defender of Christianity, but he may never-

---

43 *The Anti-Christ* §39, tr. R. J. Hollingdale (Harmondsworth, 1990), p. 161.

theless have seen more clearly than its defenders what it truly entailed – and then rejected it all the more enthusiastically. And if he was right about the radical difference between Jesus and his followers (a difference enshrined in the very creeds of Christianity), may he not also have been right in dismissing 'faith' understood as 'a mere phenomenality of consciousness'? Does not the New Testament itself over and over again draw distinctions between 'doing the will of God' and 'knowing the will of God', according more value to the former?

Yet of some interest to us also, surely, is to enquire whether or not there may be good grounds, within the Christian tradition itself, why a form of faith, which we have described as being of an 'Idealist' cast, should have been instinctively felt by Nietzsche to be suspect? There are, it seems to me, good biblical and theological reasons to support Nietzsche's suspicions.

The only naming or description of God in the bible which is deliberately put into the mouth of God himself (and hence presumably given priority over other descriptions) is the one found in Exodus 3. 13-14: that God is 'He who is'. If one takes this in conjunction with St Thomas Aquinas' teaching that we can say that God is, but not what God is, i.e. that we can affirm the existence, but not comprehend the nature of God, then it would seem to be the case, that when any description of God (for example, 'God is love') is included in the fundamental act of belief, belief is sooner or later, but inexorably, going to be worn away. And this, of course, as has often been stated, is a large part of the story of modern atheism. Christianity, Overbeck wrote, 'undertook to convince the world of God's *love*, and with this undertaking it has failed. Atheism is the price both Christianity and the world must now pay for this failure.'[44] Emmanuel Lévinas, as F.J. van Beeck remarks, has also seen Christianity's promotion of a God of pure love as a no doubt unintentional but real cause of modern atheism: 'He contrasts Judaism's mature, morally responsible faith in the God of the Torah with what

---

44 See Martin Henry, *Franz Overbeck: Theologian?* (Frankfurt a/M, 1995), p. 60, n.91; cf. F. Overbeck, *Christentum und Kultur*, ed. C.A. Bernoulli (Darmstadt, 1963), pp. 64f.: 'Christianity set out to *justify* the Old Testament God, by trying to convince the world that God should not only be feared – something that from the outset it considered to have been established by the Old Testament – but should also be loved. With this undertaking Christianity has failed miserably; up to now it has not succeeded in convincing the world that such a God really exists.

he sees as Christianity's immature, morally evasive reliance on an Incarnate Savior-God – a God of pure comfort and forgiveness. Such a God of unqualified indulgence, he argues, is no more than a "heavenly magician", and as such, a dangerous illusion. People who live by faith in such a God will either remain childishly imma-ture, or they will grow up and discover that this God is wholly ineffectual, and so reject any God as unreal. This puts the seed of humanistic atheism right in the soil of the Christian faith.'[45] One may certainly have excellent grounds for wishing to go beyond a mere statement of belief in the existence of God, in order to say something analogically about God's nature, but Christian faith does not demand it; it only states that in God essence (or nature) and existence are one. Faith is valid without further demands, and one may surmise, perhaps safer also. That God is good, that God is love, that God is the creator of heaven and earth, all of this need not be denied, but it is not as important as saying: God is.[46]

Yet even this minimal affirmation says, of course, already quite a lot. For it does actually go beyond the classical naming of God as 'He who is', in that the very term 'God' suggests the link between 'Him who is' and ourselves, a point not lost on the mystical writers of the Christian tradition: 'Angelus Silesius [1624–77] shocked his readers when he wrote that without the creature God would not be God. Yet in this statement we hear the authentic voice of Christian mysticism. For without the creature God is He who is. Only for his creatures does He adopt the name of God.'[47]

Nevertheless, because of the difficulties Christian faith can fall into by offering hostages to fortune every time it undertakes to *define* its 'object' (God), even with the most sublime descriptions like 'love', it will be suggested throughout this book that it is on the whole better to proceed negatively, and demand only that belief be directed towards the God who is, without further portrayal. The

---

Christianity's Old Testament presuppositions have remained unshaken. In relation to the Old Testament, Christianity can now only appear to any human world view as incredible and sentimental, compared with the sound judgement [of the Old Testament] not to attempt any such theodicy.'

45 Frans Jozef van Beeck, *God Encountered: A Contemporary Catholic Systematic Theology*, Vol, 2/1 (Collegeville, Minnesota, 1993), p. 102, n. [b].

46 I follow here the suggestions of É. Gilson, developed in his *God and Philosophy* (New Haven and London, 1969).

47 Louis Dupré, *The Deeper Life. An Introduction to Christian Mysticism* (New York, 1981), p. 54.

positive side of the picture – as will, it is hoped, gradually emerge – should be filled in by human beings themselves in respect of what they are willing or not to endorse about *this* life. If this sounds like hedging one's bets or having things both ways, it nevertheless seems to me to be fully in line with Christian tradition. For traditional Christianity has, it could be fairly said, always had a knack of having things both ways[48] as for example in its doctrine of the two natures of Jesus, and even in its accommodation of the deepest human experiences of both hope and futility, as the Letter to the Romans (8. 19–21) explicitly states.

Another way of trying to make the same point is to say that Christianity is and always has been, and probably always will be, the most ambiguous, and thus the most human of religions. Naturally – perhaps inevitably, given the prevalence of the effects of 'original sin' – even this truth can be abused, and deliberate obfuscation – what Nietzsche called Christianity's 'art of holy lying'[49] – can for ignoble motives on occasion supplant genuine uncertainty and ambiguity. In the same section of *The Anti-Christ* from which this description comes Nietzsche gives what amounts to a disturbing pen-portrait of Christian power-seekers, which shows all the corruption great ideals are capable of enduring, the frightening ambiguity of our noblest beliefs – especially the most powerful belief of all, belief in 'God' – and the truth Eliot expressed in a more restrained, measured manner when he wrote of 'the shame/Of motives late revealed, and the awareness/Of things ill done and done to others' harm/Which once you took for exercise of virtue.'[50] Nietzsche's denunciation, delivered in the uncompromising, incandescent language of a prophet makes uncomfortable reading:

> By allowing God to judge they themselves judge; by glorifying God they glorify themselves; by *demanding* precisely those virtues of which they themselves are capable – more, which they are in need of to say on top at all – they present a great appearance of contending for virtue, of struggling for the triumph of virtue. 'We live, we die, we sacrifice ourselves *for the good*' (– 'truth', 'the light', the 'kingdom of God'): in reality they do what they cannot help doing. By making their way in a sneaking fash-

---

48 Cf. the interesting brief comments on this theme by Peter Pawlowsky, *Christianity*, tr. J. Bowden (London, 1994), pp. 46f.

49 *The Anti-Christ* § 44, p. 167.

50 'Little Gidding', *The Four Quartets*.

ion, sitting in corners, living out shadowy lives in the shadows, they make a *duty* of it: their life of humility appears to be a duty, as humility it is one more proof of piety ... The reality is that here the most conscious *arrogance of the elect* is posing as modesty: one has placed oneself, the 'community', the 'good and just', once and for all on one side, on the side of 'truth' – and the rest, 'the world', on the other ... *That* has been the most fateful kind of megalomania that has ever existed on earth: little abortions of bigots and liars began to lay claim to the concepts 'God', 'truth', 'light,' 'spirit', 'love', 'wisdom', 'life' as if these were synonyms of themselves so as to divide themselves off from the 'world' ...

However, Christianity's very flexibility may be, humanly speaking, one of the secrets of its durability. This flexibility is not only reflected in its ability to have things both ways, but it is also revealed in its ability to absorb, even if with great reluctance, any criticism because of its final commitment to truth over convenience or success (described, ironically, by Nietzsche as having 'always been the greatest liar'[51]).

But to repeat finally the point at issue: an existential approach to Christian faith and even theology can be welcomed. Talk of a loving relationship with a loving God in faith can be respected. But it should not be given pride of place, which belongs as ever to the incomprehensible God who is, *tout court*. .

We can turn our attention now to filling out negatively, that is by contrast, what we can say about the God of Christianity. This will be done by outlining briefly how Christianity in contrast to other religions or world views interprets what is now, as always, the key existential issue in religion: God's relationship to the world.

God's connection with the world

It may be true, as Hermann Hesse remarked, that: 'Atheism is simply the negation of a thing that never had any substantial, but only ever a verbal, existence,'[52] but the question of what the substance of theism amounts to is still far from clear. However, what is clear is that the meaning of either 'theism' or 'atheism' will include the way one understands the world.

The way Christianity has traditionally understood the world, or rather the link between the world and God, is not shared by all reli-

---

51 *Beyond Good and Evil* §269.
52 Hermann Hesse, *Lektüre für Minuten 2* (Frankfurt a./M, 1976), p. 91.

gions or world views. The basic point to note is that Christianity has always asserted an irremovable distinction between God the creator and the creation, of which we are a part. Christianity also teaches that the creator God, or the ultimate reality on which all of creation depends, is gracious, i.e. well-disposed towards us, is on our side. Not all religions or world views share these beliefs.

(a) Pantheism, for example, sees no distinction between God and the world. Instances of pantheism include Stoicism in the world of antiquity, and in modern times the philosophy of Spinoza (1632-1677), who spoke of 'God or Nature', *Deus sive Natura*. Pantheism is, in fact, a denial of what Christianity has taken God to be. It was Hobbes, as Kolakowski points out, who remarked that 'to say that the world is God amounts to saying that there is no God.'[53] 'Pantheism,' wrote Schopenhauer, 'is only a euphemism for atheism.'[54] For pantheism, the forces governing nature are the supreme expression of reality and whatever happens, no matter how we experience it, no matter whether it strikes us as bad or good, desirable or undesirable, is in fact the final expression of the divine will. Schiller's dictum: 'The world's history is the world's judgement' is a useful summary of what is at stake existentially in this vision of things.

Pantheism cannot make the distinction which Christianity makes between good and evil. Redemption, if it is to have any meaning for a pantheist, can therefore only amount to a stoical or even an exuberant acceptance of the world, exactly as it is. 'Process theology',[55] associated with thinkers like A.N. Whitehead and C. Hartshorne, is often seen – perhaps unfairly – as a milder form of pantheism. The also milder term 'panentheism', coined by the nineteenth-century German Idealist philosopher K. Krause, is sometimes used to describe process theology, since the latter tends to

---

53 *Religion* (Oxford, 1982), p. 110. – The coining of the term pantheism is usually attributed to the Irish writer John Toland (1670-1722) from near Derry, in a work first published in 1720 entitled *Pantheisticon*, although according to D. W. D. Shaw (*A New Dictionary of Christian Theology*, ed. by A. Richardson and J. Bowden, London, 1983, p. 423) it was 'first used, apparently, in 1709 by a critic of the deist John Toland.'

54 A. Schopenhauer, *Parerga und Paralipomena*, 'Fragmente zur Geschichte der Philosophie', *Werke* IV, ed. W. Frhr. von Löhneysen (Darmstadt, 1976), p. 143.

55 Process thought, as developed by Alfred N. Whitehead (1861–1947), saw 'becoming' or 'process', rather than 'being' or 'substance' as the primordial ontological category. Whitehead wished to replace the static

view the world as enclosed, so to speak, in the deity as in a womb, or even as itself the 'body' of God, who is then to the cosmos what our soul or spirit is to our body. However, process theology at least tries to think God and the world together, yet in such a way as to respect the distinct reality of both. But, since it denies the doctrine of creation, it finally seems suspiciously close either to some form of dualism – where God and matter are two ultimate principles – or, as just suggested, to pantheism – where God is everything. Either way, the problem of evil cannot be dealt with. For if one accepts pantheism, the problem of evil can scarcely be taken seriously as a problem from which we need to be redeemed; and if one accepts dualism, the problem of evil remains untreatable, since it lies beyond God's healing reach. Process theology has, moreover, a further difficulty when it speaks about God's enriching himself through his interaction with the world, for this seems hard to square with the Christian understanding of God who does not take from, but gives to, the world.

(b) Another view of the relationship between the world of the divine and the world of human beings is that associated in the ancient world with the philosopher Epicurus (c. 342/41 – c. 271/70 BC) who did not deny the existence of a divine realm but considered the gods to be uninterested in human affairs:

> Gods exist, living a happy life sempiternally in the intercosmic spaces. They take no thought for our cosmos, or for any other; such concern would detract from their perfect Epicurean contentment. It is good for man to respect and admire them, but not to expect favours or punishments from them.[56]

(c) Yet another interpretation of the relationship between God and the world was that taught by the Christian dualist heretic Marcion in the second century. His central conviction was that the creator

conceptions of classical Western thought with the dynamic conceptions of process thought. Thus God too is changing, because he includes all entities within his own life and is enriched by them. 'Process' theologians speak of God as dipolar: he has a 'primordial' nature, corresponding roughly to the traditional notion of divine transcendence, and a 'consequent' nature, according to which he includes the cosmic process within himself. Whitehead and his followers were convinced that the static categories of being and substance were philosophically mistaken, and could not do justice to the God of biblical faith or genuine religious piety.

56 *The Oxford Classical Dictionary* (Oxford, 1970) p. 391.

God, the God of the Old Testament whom he called the 'demiurge', had nothing to do with the God of Jesus Christ. The 'demiurge' whom Jesus came to overthrow was cruel, the God of Jesus Christ was the God of love.[57]

(d) Finally, a thinker like Schopenhauer (1788-1860), often referred to as the philosopher of pessimism, saw the world as the expression of what he called the 'Will to Life' (*Wille zum Leben*).[58] This blind 'Will to Life', to which the intellect is entirely sub-servient, is a dark, irrational, inexhaustible force producing inces-santly a world in which the fundamental experience is suffering. Through aesthetic experience, especially through music, Schopen-hauer felt that some release from the suffering of the human condi-tion was possible, but it was of a temporary nature. The only true release came from renouncing the 'Will to Life' itself, i.e. through self-denial, even though such a move – as a willed act – seems, at least superficially, somewhat incoherent in terms of Schopen-hauer's own philosophy.[59]

Christianity rejects all such ways – Pantheism, and the world views associated with Epicurus, Marcion and Schopenhauer – of understanding the relationship between the world and God. Christian faith affirms on the contrary (1) that there is a real distinc-tion between God and creation; (2) that creation, which is utterly dependent on God, is fundamentally good; (3) that creation in its present historical condition is flawed by human sin; (4) that God is freely interested in our lives, in the sense of being well-disposed towards human beings. This divine benevolence is classically what is meant by grace, which is, to adapt an expression from St Athanasius[60] (c. 296–373) a 'second gift' in addition to the gift of existence itself.

This distinction is referred to in the course of Christian tradition by various other pairs of terms, for example: 'existence and life' (St Augustine), 'creation and new creation', 'creation and covenant or election', or 'creation and redemption', but always with the same underlying meaning. The 'second gift' is the development or fulfil-

---

57 'Demiurge' ('craftsman'), from the Greek *demiourgos*, the term used in Plato's *Timaeus* for the Divine Being charged with the formation of the material world.

58 On this term see the comments of Christopher Janaway, *Schopenhauer* (Oxford, 1994), p. 38.

59 See Janaway, *ibid.*, pp. 91ff. for a brief discussion of this aspect of Schopenhauer's thought.

60 See E. Yarnold, *The Second Gift. A Study of Grace* (Slough, 1974), pp. 2f.

ment of the first, with divine assistance. It is not a development or fulfilment which could have occurred automatically through the dynamic evolution of energies immanent in creation. However, God will not complete his plan without our co-operation. Now, although we can sketch out in theoretical terms how, according to Christian belief, God's reality is interwoven with ours, the practical expressions or consequences of Christian belief, as we shall see, often present a rather more complex picture.

Ambiguities of belief and unbelief

The question of belief in God, as Oscar Wilde remarked about truth, is rarely pure, and never simple. Normally, for example, it is assumed that it is good, desirable and consoling to have faith in God, and sad and distressing not to. However, belief has more than one face. For while some believers find joy and consolation in religion, others are tormented by it and, like St Paul before his conversion, see religion as imposing impossible demands, threatening punishment should the demands not be fulfilled. Such people are condemned by their belief in God to a life of frustration. They would dearly love to be without religion but find that it is, sadly, inescapable. The father of Søren Kierkegaard appears to have been of such a lugubrious disposition and to have passed it on in some measure to his son. This variety of what one might call guilt-edged religious experience Nietzsche diagnosed as flowing from Christianity's 'hangman's metaphysics.'[61] The Christian faith has, then, an ambiguous legacy, a point made long ago by Hegel: 'Every joy in life has been linked with this faith, while the most miserable gloom has found in it its nourishment and its justification.'[62]

Unbelief is also a mixed blessing. For while those who do not or cannot believe in God sometimes envy those who do believe, the opposite is also true. Some unbelievers may consider themselves superior to believers, because *they* are mature and honest enough to be able to dispense with the guidance and consolations afforded by belief in God, whereas believers, in their view, remain prisoners of their fears, needs and uncertainties. In between there is Luis Buñuel who said he was an 'atheist by the grace of God'.

To be convinced that there is no God can be for some a liberating,

---

61 *Twilight of the Idols*, tr. R. J. Hollingdale (Harmondsworth, 1990) p. 63.
62 *On Christianity: Early Theological Writings*, tr. T. M. Knox, intro. R. Kroner (Gloucester, Mass., 1970), p. 169.

even exhilarating, experience which leaves them free to seek a new meaning or direction for their lives. Indeed in the wake of the critique of religion carried out by Feuerbach, Marx, Nietzsche and Freud, one of the major objections to belief in God in the modern world is that it is incompatible with human freedom (whatever that is[63]). If God is the fullness of being, omnipotent and omniscient, how, some wonder, can we really be free and creative? Nietzsche saw a direct connection between the rejection of divinity and the possibility of real human creativity: 'for what would there be to create if gods – existed!'[64] Nietzsche thus experienced religion as an inherited constraint, whose legitimacy he could no longer find any compelling reason to recognise, and which he could see many good reasons for dispensing with: he desired the exhilaration of freedom to create heroically his own values. In this he became a pioneer of modern atheism.

Yet exhilaration is a demanding emotion, and is difficult to maintain indefinitely. Towards the end of his life E. R. Dodds who through his reading of Nietzsche had been liberated from Christianity and its ethics as a young man, considered that the demise of religion led, on balance, to a diminishing of human life: 'At 17 I saw it as a liberation. At 83 I am more often inclined to see it as an impoverishment, the inevitable drying-up of one of the deeper springs from which the human imagination has in time past been

---

63 Cf. Lichtenberg: 'Man is a masterpiece of creation if for no other reason than that, all the weight of evidence for determinism notwithstanding, he believes he has free will' (*Aphorisms*, p. 159). The actual constraints on human 'freedom' by social processes, for example, may mean that what at first sight seems real freedom is simply 'the freedom, as it has been put, of a man to walk east on a boat going west' (Alastair Hannay, *Kierkegaard*, London, 1991, p. 311). Hannay adds (p. 375, n.14): 'The remark is attributed to Samuel Beckett by Peter Mew in "The Liberal University", *Inquiry*, vol. 12 (1978), p. 245. I do not have the original reference.'

64 *Thus Spoke Zarathustra*, tr. R. J. Hollingdale (Harmondsworth, 1986), p. 111. It should be noted, however, that getting rid of God does not necessarily make human beings free. Marxism, for instance, was a deterministic system without God. And of course Nietzsche himself, despite what he said about human creativity without God, did not on that account believe in the existence of 'free will': see, for example, the section entitled 'The Four Great Errors', in *Twilight of the Idols*. It is curious that Christianity has been interpreted as both affirming free will and denying it (cf. 'predestination'), and so has atheism.

nourished.'[65] Dodds, like many modern cultural historians, saw Christianity in particular and religion in general as a strategy for enduring the burden of existence, a strategy that had worked reasonably well in the past but was now regrettably no longer available.

While defiant atheism is nevertheless still a possibility for some, for others it is a disaster to conclude that there is no God. For they then find themselves face to face with meaninglessness, absurdity and moral nihilism. At least that is how the consequences of atheism have often been presented since Dostoevsky (1821–1881): in *The Brothers Karamazov* his character Ivan maintains: 'If God does not exist, everything is permitted.' At a slightly earlier date Kleist's reading of Kant, which convinced him that truth was unattainable, cast him into total despair.[66] The greatest poet of Germany's golden literary age, Hölderlin, experienced similar anguish when critical thought robbed him of his childhood religious faith.

If one moves out from the individual to the social or political sphere, one finds here too that both religion and the rejection or loss of religion have had ambivalent careers. Heavenly goodness and infernal cruelty alike have sought justification in the name of religion.[67] And, similarly, atheists too have proved to be capable of both civilised and barbaric behaviour.

And if one were tempted to generalise about the moral experience of the human race, one would find, I suspect, a similar ambiguous mixture. Morality for believers is sometimes suspected by unbelievers of being a matter of prudential bartering: 'If I keep the rules, I'll go to heaven, if I don't, I'll go to hell.'[68] Hence, so runs the argument, religious believers remain, morally speaking, perennial cunning children, afraid of offending an authority figure, even though they might dearly wish to. They thus never reach moral

---

65 *Missing Persons* (Oxford, 1978), p. 194; cf. *ibid.*, pp. 19f.

66 Cf. Karl Popper, *The Open Society and Its Enemies* (London, 1969), vol. 2, p. 382. Heinrich von Kleist (1777–1811), German playwright and short-story writer, was one of the great writers of the classical period (roughly 1770–1830) of modern German literature.

67 'Men never do evil so completely and cheerfully as when they do it from religious conviction' (Pascal, cited in D. Tracy, *Plurality and Ambiguity*, London, 1988, p. 86).

68 Such a calculating attitude to morality seems to have been behind the remark attributed to Pope Urban VIII on hearing of Cardinal Richelieu's death in 1642: 'If there is a God, Cardinal Richelieu will have much to answer for; if not, he has done very well' (quoted by Arthur Koestler, *The Sleepwalkers*, Harmondsworth, 1969, p. 478).

maturity. Nor do they ever reach the stage of freely enacting the true desires of their heart. (This, if true, might of course not always be a bad thing.) Yet as against this hostile assessment of the effects of religion on morality, one might wish to argue that, historically speaking, the major moral codes of humanity have in fact had religious origins, until, that is to say, the recent advent of widespread atheism, and even here it would be practically impossible to prove, surely, that the ultimate origins of even an atheistic sense of morality do *not* lie in an ancient religious context.

Furthermore, the actual experience of morality, essential to the concept of humanity, is often deemed to have no ultimate foundation if in fact it has no religious, transcendent, root or basis. In that case it could only be interpreted reductively, as resulting from an arbitrary play of forces and energies which different cultures attempt to organise according to their own unpredictable and inscrutable preferences. From a reductionist standpoint reality can have no 'profound nature' below the kaleidoscopic surface of appearances, in which morality or anything else could be grounded. Deep down, things are very superficial. The only meaning to which we have access is the passing show of the moment. In Nietzsche's terminology, 'becoming' (i.e. the natural process) is 'innocent' of any deeper or more sinister meaning. Hence, to continue to believe in morality in such circumstances (i.e. without believing in God) would, from the believer's point of view, be to succumb to an illusion. In short: for atheists, 'God' is the theist's illusion, for theists, morality is the atheist's. Curiously, however, theists officially believe in what they say atheists do not ('morality'), whereas atheists do not believe in what theists officially say they do ('God'). Theists therefore might be perceived as unwilling to share their morality with atheists, whereas atheists could seem to be ascetically declining the belief of theists. Theists could thus appear possessive and selfish, and atheists to be practising mortification, which is an odd reversal of what one might expect. But even Christians were called atheists once.[69] So, presumably the truth of belief and unbelief cannot be reduced to a matter of words, important though words obviously are. On the other hand, if someone did want badly enough to restrict the notion of truth to the linguistic field, it is difficult to see how he could be stopped.

---

69 This was a designation the early Christians were, of course, only willing to accept in a very restricted sense: they did not worship state-gods. Cf. Walter Kasper, *The God of Jesus Christ*, tr. M. J. O'Connell (London, 1983), pp. 16f.

To sum up, religion and atheism can generate different emotions and unleash conflicting drives in their adherents. Religion can be experienced as a liberation or an enslavement, and similarly atheism can mean for some the welcome possibility of real autonomy, and for others despair. Both are capable of war and peace. Hence it would seem that both belief in God and atheism are ambiguous in their psychological effects: both can lead to either serenity or desperation. And the record is mixed too in other spheres. Small wonder if it is difficult to decide whether religion is an illness or a cure or perhaps both.

Yet all such considerations must remain finally unconvincing, not just because of the ambiguous conclusions to which they point, but even more so because the effects of a belief, even were they quite unambiguous, do not constitute in themselves a clinching proof of its truth. With neither theism nor atheism can the question of truth be decided by psychological or other effects alone. Pragmatic considerations are certainly not worthless ('By their fruits shall you know them'), but on their own they do not provide solutions to the question of truth.

The role of theology in Christian tradition

Attention will be given later to the specific notion of God which is encountered at various stages of the Judaeo-Christian tradition, but in this introductory chapter I wish to make a few general remarks about the nature of Christian theology itself, and to insist somewhat on its problematic status within Christianity. For this status is not unrelated, I believe, to the Christian apprehension of God.

Theology was born in the early church as a result of the fusion of biblical and Hellenistic spiritual and intellectual traditions. In this complex process – which was not paralleled in the contemporary Jewish tradition (Philo remained an isolated figure) – one can observe how the Christian idea of God was forged by a process of interaction with the surrounding culture of the time. Popular Hellenistic religious notions were often the object of Christian polemics, but Hellenistic philosophical ideas were taken seriously, and adapted where possible to the Christian idea of God. A not completely dissimilar process had indeed already occurred in the time of the Old Testament, when the notion of God was also hammered out – usually antagonistically – in relation to the views on the deity entertained by Israel's neighbours. However there was also, sometimes, a willingness to see common ground between

Israelite faith and, say, the Wisdom traditions of the ancient Near East.

Such patterns would not appear to be historically accidental. Rather they emerged almost inevitably, or at least naturally enough, from the belief that the Judaeo-Christian God is the creator of the whole world. Hence any truth available in the world at large must be compatible with belief in this God, since truth, like God, is unique. Similarly, God must be relevant to the world at large, if he really is the creator God. Any incompatibility between the truth about God, and the truth available in the world must lead to the conclusion that at least one of the alleged 'truths' is false, for they certainly cannot both be right.

The decision by the early church to use pagan wisdom in the service of theology was thus in line with Christianity's faith that God, as the creator of the human mind, is reflected, albeit finitely, in its structure and discoveries. But it should be noted that the decision to allow Greek wisdom into the church's teaching enterprise did not go uncontested. There has indeed always been, to put it mildly, a certain nervousness in Christian circles about the fittingness of using philosophy to express what is believed to be beyond understanding: 'The intransigent anti-philosophical trend, of which Lactantius' *De Falsa Sapientia* is a classic monument, has never entirely died out in Christian culture and St Paul's letters endow it with a permanent legitimacy.'[70] This nervousness is related to the Christian sense that faith is not a species of knowledge (*gnosis*), but an attitude of mind issuing in a particular way of life, and that without the 'rethink' (*metanoia*) or change of mind Christianity speaks about, all knowledge *about* religion is pointless.[71] Or as Wittgenstein put it: 'I believe that one of the things Christianity says is that sound doctrines are all useless. That you have to change your *life*. (Or the *direction* of your life.)'[72]

---

70 L. Kolakowski, *Metaphysical Horror*, p. 93. The anti-philosophical trend in the Christian tradition should not be confused with the various mystical currents within Christianity which see God in quite uncontroversial terms as lying beyond philosophy. Mystics in fact often use philosophy as a vehicle for their thoughts. In the early church Neoplatonism functioned in this way.

71 As the New Testament itself intimates, we can believe true doctrine about God without being good ourselves: 'You believe that God is one; you do well. Even the demons believe – and shudder' (James 2:19).

72 L. Wittgenstein, *Culture and Value* (Oxford, 1980), p. 53e.

In this connection a rather pointed remark of Emil Cioran's on his fellow-Romanian, the historian of religion, Mircea Eliade, is worth considering: '[R]eligion for him was an object, and not a struggle ... let's say, with God. In my opinion, Eliade was never a religious person. Had he been, he would not have bothered about all those gods. Those who possess a religious sensibility don't spend their lives enumerating the gods, making an inventory of them. It is hard to imagine a scholar kneeling down. I have always seen in the history of religions the very negation of religion. That is certain, I don't think I'm mistaken on that.'[73] This is reminiscent of Franz Overbeck's view that Christian theology itself is a sign of a faith in decline. Theology he once described as the 'Satan of religion' and theologians as the 'grave-diggers' of Christianity.[74] One might conclude from this that theology is not neutral or innocent. It is as much marked by 'original sin' as anything else in human existence. One of Nietzsche's exasperated paradoxes reads: 'Theology, or the corruption of reason by "original sin" (Christianity).'[75] However, if theology can remain persistently mindful of its inherent corruptibility, it may avoid, paradoxically, a premature disappearance.

But apart from the stress on the primacy of faith over understanding, there was also another reason for the church's hesitations about philosophy. For with the introduction of philosophy into the church came the constant danger of an intellectualisation of the Christian faith and the consequent appearance in the church of heresies, and also of an element of intellectual snobbery or vanity arising from the division between the intellectually gifted Christians and the so-called 'simple faithful'. This latter possibility should alert one to the always ambiguous nature of the theological enterprise. Why, one might ask, is so much religious literature anonymous? No doubt, because the writers thought themselves to be only the instruments of the deity, who was the real inspiration behind the writings. Their own names were unimportant. Similarly, all Christian theological writing is supposed to be about the God of Jesus Christ, but it inevitably also directs attention towards its authors, who, if I recall Kierkegaard's wry phrase accurately, are

---

73 From an interview given by Cioran to Gabriel Liiceanu in 1990, and published in Gabriel Liiceanu, *Itinéraires d'une vie: E. M. Cioran, suivi de 'les continents de l'insomnie,' entretien avec E. M. Cioran* (Paris, 1995), p. 129.

74 Franz Overbeck, *Christentum und Kultur*, pp. 13, 20.

75 *Twilight of the Idols*, tr. R. J. Hollingdale (Harmondsworth, 1990), p. 77.

professors of the fact that Christ was crucified. The church has of
course always in principle taught that from the point of view of
faith all are in the same boat, whatever intellectual boats they may
or may not be in.[76]

Yet despite the undoubted risks, Christianity has constantly
striven to make connections between its faith and the changing
cultural constellations in which it finds itself. In this regard it is
interesting to recall Whitehead's remark: 'Christianity ... has always
been a religion seeking a metaphysic, in contrast to Buddhism
which is a metaphysic generating a religion.'[77] This seems true at
least of Christianity, whether one thinks of the early church's effort
to express its faith in terms of Hellenistic, mainly Platonist, thought,
or the mediaeval effort to re-express the Christian faith with the
help of a re-discovered Aristotle, or the nineteenth century's
attempt to express the substance of Christian faith through German
Idealism: 'fides quaerens intellectum' is a permanent feature of
Christianity. And the 'quaerens' stresses the fact that theology,
understood as 'faith thinking', is a search for understanding, not a
statement of the obvious. It is, furthermore, impossible to have faith
in God, without trying to gain some insight into what that means,
or at least without having some idea of what is meant by 'God'.
Faith unaccompanied by any effort to understand is, as mentioned
earlier, ultimately indistinguishable from fideism.

Part of the malaise of modern Christianity no doubt lies in the
fact that there is now no widely accepted philosophical account of
reality with which it can interact. Rather the contemporary philosophical landscape is murky, confused to the point of chaos. Chaos,
however, may not be the worst place in which to start thinking, for
as Wittgenstein wrote: 'When you are philosophising you have to
descend into primeval chaos and feel at home there.'[78] Yet if
Christianity is meant to be the salt of the earth (and not a substitute
for the earth[79]), could its function possibly now be, not to provide a
'Christian philosophy' but to provide intellectual effort with faith in
its value? For such a faith cannot come from philosophy alone.
Philosophy left to its own devices eventually seems to undermine

---

76 Cf. Kolakowski, Religion (Oxford, 1982), p. 60.
77 Religion in the Making, pp. 50f., quoted by Linwood Urban, A Short
    History of Christian Thought (Oxford, 1986), p. 3.
78 Culture and Value, p. 65e.
79 Something, incidentally, which makes the very idea of a Christian cul-
    ture or a Christian nation highly ambiguous, and to be handled with

itself, as do all purely inner-worldly activities, whether intellectual, political or aesthetic.

It might be objected, however, that a disenchanted scepticism is such a widespread mood in the contemporary world, that religious faith would be the last thing to invoke in order to try to re-enchant the world intellectually. But could not scepticism itself, even an exasperated scepticism, be interpreted as a philosophical echo of Christianity's belief in the transcendence of God? This belief relativises all merely worldly powers and human ambitions, but it only relativises them, it does not destroy or seek to destroy them. Thus it might be argued that the philosophical expression of its message with which Christianity could in present conditions be most comfortable is, precisely, scepticism. It seems indeed an odd irony that such a strong champion of freedom in the moral sphere of conscience as Newman should have been so wary of freedom when it manifested itself in what he once termed 'the energy of human scepticism, … the all-corroding, all-dissolving scepticism of the intellect in religious inquiries.'[80] Yet Newman's acute personal awareness of the awesome power of scepticism may have been the menacing, dark side of his own near-solipsistic sense of life, rather than a justified conclusion about the role of critical thought in religion.

Classically, scepticism and doubt have been viewed as the archenemies of Christianity. But this can surely only be so if one has already identified intellectual truth as the heart of the Christian religion. Now while gnosticism may wish to claim that the fullness of truth is intellectual, this can scarcely be so of Christianity. Hence the great fear of doubt and scepticism that has been such a salient characteristic of Christianity since the time of Montaigne may suggest that much Christian apologetics is perhaps crypto-gnostic. If we accept that Christianity is about redemption, accorded to the human race through Jesus by an incomprehensible God, then far from its being undermined by scepticism, it is eminently compatible with, if not positively endorsed by, it. The day scepticism ceases to be welcomed as the shadow-side of Christian faith, may be the day on which faith in the Christian God begins to end.

Historically, however, it must be admitted that Christianity has

care. If the transcendence of God is to be respected, and the relative independence of the created order to be taken seriously, then the Christian reality can never become unambiguously identified with any temporal dispensation, sacred or profane.

80 J. H. Newman, *Apologia Pro Vita Sua*, pp. 281, 279.

often been obsessed with *vera doctrina*. This obsession may be, in part at least, a legacy of Christianity's mortal struggle with gnosticism. Gnosticism, to put the matter very crudely, was a serious rival to Christianity in the early centuries because it too offered salvation to its adherents, caught like everyone else in a world of pain. But the salvation gnosticism proposed was fundamentally intellectual in nature. However the attraction of the gnostic way with its glamorous pessimism could not have been countered by the young Christian church, had it ignored the intellectual challenge gnosticism presented. Here, perhaps, is a classic case of Christianity's being forced on to slightly foreign territory in the effort to defend itself, and in so doing running the risk of subtly distorting its own nature. The same may be true of more recent Christian intellectual history, if one agrees that the modern Christian struggle with rationalism since the days of Descartes has encouraged Christian apologists to try to become better rationalists than the pure rationalists themselves, and in the process to underplay, or underestimate, what it is that makes them Christians in the first place. This may be an example of putting the cart before the horse. For what Descartes was essentially looking for was not rational knowledge for its own sake, but security based on certainty expressed in the form of clear, distinct and indubitable ideas. This is at heart a religious quest pursued in the realm of the mind. Christianity's traditional interpretation of that quest had been to reverse it, and claim that religion was essentially God's quest for us. Although Pascal restated that interpretation, his voice was drowned out by the rising tide of rationalism.

But to return directly to the question of scepticism, one positive advantage which an alliance with scepticism could bring, might be the distancing of Christianity from belligerent forms of modern religion. These are, at least theoretically, although not always from the historical evidence of Christianity's own past,[81] out of harmony with the Christian injunction to love one's enemies, to say nothing of being in conflict with its image of a 'crucified God', to borrow Pascal's terminology.[82] Religious scepticism – which does also have an appropriately modest place in scripture itself – would, moreover, appear to be entirely reconcilable with the demands of a

---

81 'No kingdom has ever had as many civil wars as the kingdom of Christ', wrote Montesquieu in the *Lettres persanes* (quoted in M. Parris, *Scorn*, p. 257).

82 *Pensées* fr. 964, tr. A. J. Krailsheimer (Harmondsworth, 1983), p. 340.

whole-hearted attachment to the Christian faith, especially with Christianity's call to martyrdom in certain circumstances, since the call to faith is a call to a particular way of living, and, if necessary, dying; it is not primarily a call to a particular way of philosophising. And faith, hope and charity can remain wholehearted even when understanding falters.

CHAPTER TWO

The nature of the God-question

After all, is our idea of God anything more than personified incompre-
hensibility? — Georg Chr. Lichtenberg
God is a crude answer, a piece of indelicacy against us thinkers – fun-
damentally even a crude prohibition *to us: you shall not think!*
— Friedrich Nietzsche

Religion or God?

The God-question is in the first instance an inherited question.
Would we raise it, had we not been told about it? Perhaps. What
happened in the past was precisely that. For there must have been
an original poser or posers of what was to become a seemingly
perennial question. However, even if one accepts that the God-
question is endemic to human experience, the way in which any
historically self-conscious group will deal with the question is now
largely a matter of tradition.

This dual aspect of the God-question in the modern world has
been the source of an as yet unresolved debate about the legitimacy
of Christianity's claim to special status in the history of the human
race. The debate turns on the question of whether or not it is justifi-
able to take the step from seeing Christianity as one religion among
others to seeing it, in accordance with its own – at least until recent
times – consistently expressed historical self-understanding, as the
religion of the human race which was called into being and continues to be sustained in existence by a unique and, in principle,
unsurpassable divine revelation. Is Christianity's central incarna-
tional claim – that Jesus is the divine redeemer – still valid? Is it
even meaningful?

In other words, can it be said of Christianity's view of God that it
is uniquely true in a way that no other religion's image of God can
be said to be? Or do all religions provide equally valid expressions
of the human sense of God? Are religions like languages, in short,
which all express the human capacity for communication in different, but similarly (un)reliable ways? For no one would claim that
any particular language is absolutely better than any other. So, on

this analogy, is no specific religion absolutely better or truer than any other?

For the Enlightenment, apparently not, as Lessing's famous 'ring parable' suggests. Indeed for the same Lessing, even the claim to absolute truth was hybristic. At most man could and should entertain the desire to search for truth, but the possession of truth was the prerogative of God alone. For the Enlightenment all historical religions were variously disguised or corrupt forms of a genuine underlying natural religion, in principle common and accessible to all humanity. The titles of such typically Enlightenment works as John Toland's *Christianity not Mysterious* (1696)[1] or Matthew Tindal's *Christianity as Old as the Creation, or the Gospel a Republication of the Religion of Nature* (1730) reflect this deistic interpretation of Christianity. 'Deism' did not necessarily deny the idea of divine immanence in the world, but it did deny that any historical religion (and for the Enlightenment Christianity was in this regard the primary example) offered a privileged access to God not shared by any other. As Gilson observes, however, the deistic re-interpretation of Christianity – inspired, ironically, by the universalist ideal of the Enlightenment that had itself grown out of Christian faith – failed ultimately to carry conviction. It was a form of Christianity without Christ, that is to say, without revelation, without God's direct involvement in human history in the person of Jesus. As such it could function only as a 'philosophical myth,'[2] and its God could be 'but the philosophical ghost of the Christian God,'[3] a reincarnation of Plato's demiurge from the *Timaeus*, who now structured the world in accordance with the theories of Newton.[4] This judgement was anticipated by Pascal for whom 'deism was almost as remote from Christianity as atheism,'[5] while Bossuet saw it as simply 'Atheism in disguise.'[6]

However, while deistic Christianity was not finally accepted as genuine *Christianity*, it did have enormous influence in shaping the way the modern world copes with religion. In so far as one can speak of any consensus emerging on this question in the West, it is

---

1   A title which, according to É. Gilson, *God and Philosophy* (New Haven and London, 1969), p. 106, 'should have become the Deist's slogan.'
2   É. Gilson, *God and Philosophy*, p. 107.
3   *Ibid.*, p. 104.
4   Cf. *ibid.*, p. 107.
5   L. Kolakowski, *Religion* (Oxford, 1982), p. 176.
6   J.B. Bossuet, *The History of the Variations of the Protestant Churches*, Bk. V, ch. xxxi, quoted by É. Gilson, *God and Philosophy*, p. 104.

probably a safe generalisation to claim that those who tolerate or
even look sympathetically on religion regard it as the legitimate
expression of an ineradicable aspect of the human condition. But
they tend to be sceptical about the specific truth-claims of any one
religion. In particular, scepticism about Christianity's traditional
claims to unsurpassable religious authority has increased. This
modern phase of doubt about Christianity's legitimacy has in turn
provoked a bout of Christian self-questioning which many find
unsettling. It can however be seen as a characteristic expression of a
habit of mind that Christianity, theoretically at any rate, has always
espoused, namely to accept the primacy of truth over intellectual
power, comfort, certainty and 'final solutions' to the human
predicament.[7] It may have been such a happy instinct that moved
Cavafy to embrace the lack of any empirical 'solution' to the human
condition in his famous poem 'Waiting for the Barbarians'.

The Enlightenment outlook, then, was not generally hostile to
religion as such, but was hostile to the notion that any particular
tradition could be privileged above any other. This view fed into
Romanticism which, from Schleiermacher to Troeltsch and beyond,
emphasised the human capacity for religious experience that had
given rise to the various religious traditions, but had enormous difficulties in dealing with the question of truth, as between one religion and another. This characteristically modern approach to religion is reflected in such a 'non-professional' commentator as
Benjamin Constant (1767–1830). Constant, in his *De la religion con-
sidérée dans sa source, ses formes et ses développements* (published
1824–31), has a positive view of the phenomenon of religion in
human affairs, but tends towards a relativistic interpretation of various historical expressions of the 'religious sense'. In him, as in
many other subsequent writers, is found an at least tacit acceptance
of the Enlightenment's critique of all positive ('revealed') religions,
together with an acknowledgement of that undeniable 'religious
sense' which was so important to the Enlightenment's foes and successors, the Romantics. In the year 1804 Constant noted in his *Diary*:
'A felicitous distinction that should be preserved, between the religious sense and the positive religions.'[8] Referring specifically to
Schleiermacher in the same year he observes: 'Schleiermacher says
in one place: "God and the immortality of the soul are not ideas that

---

7   Cf. L. Kolakowski, *Modernity on Endless Trial* (Chicago and London,
     1990), pp. 30f.
8   *Oeuvres*, ed. A. Roulin (Paris, 1957), p. 235.

are indispensable to religion," and in another place he says: "A religion without God may be better than a religion with God." These assertions, in appearance so absurd, are true in the sense in which he means them. I said the same thing when I said that the religious sense is very compatible with doubt, and that it is even more compatible with doubt than with any specific religion. But, expressed as Schleiermacher expresses them, these ideas appear those of a madman.'[9]

Rejection of revealed religion amounted in practice to rejection of Christianity with its specific notion of God. One might sum this situation up in the phrase: Religion, yes; the Christian God, no. Nietzsche noted precisely this combination in his own day: '[I]t seems to me that the religious instinct is indeed in vigorous growth – but that it rejects the theistic answer with profound mistrust.'[10] At a slightly earlier date Baudelaire had expressed the modern attitude in the following aphorism: 'God is the only being who, to rule, does not even have to exist.'[11] This phenomenon of respect for the human dimension of religion, coupled with scepticism about 'God', is one that is still alive in the contemporary world. The great Romanian conductor, Sergiu Celibidache, who died in 1996, said on the subject of religion: 'We are all former believers, we are all religious spirits without religion.'[12] Oscar Wilde rather mischievously went to the heart of the modern problematic when he wrote: 'Religion is the fashionable substitute for Belief', thus emphasising how God's identity has now become blurred in a thick fog of religion (or 'spirituality'?). Nevertheless, can one dismiss the 'religious sense' as cavalierly as Wilde's witticism seems to do? For how can one search for God, if one cannot find one's way in this fog?

In more recent times, even some 'professional' theologians have begun to say that the God-question is not so much about 'God' as about the religious dimension of human culture. Bernard Lonergan, for example, observed that 'while theology used to be

9   *Ibid.*, p. 378.

10 *Beyond Good and Evil, Part Three: The Religious Nature,* §53, tr. R.J. Hollingdale (Harmondsworth, 1990), p. 80.

11 'Dieu est le seul être qui, pour régner, n'ait même pas besoin d'exister' (*Oeuvres complètes,* ed. C. Pichois, vol. I (Paris, 1975), p. 649).

12 Quoted in the *Frankfurter Allgemeine Zeitung,* 17 August 1996. 'Religion' I take here to include: 'any specific understanding of God', although in the article in question Celibidache does describe God as: 'the ultimate emanation of music' (*die äusserste Emanation der Musik*).

defined as the science of God, today I believe it is to be defined as reflection on the significance and value of religion in a culture.'[13]

One might raise the question, in passing, whether the Christian religion and church could disappear, yet a (non-specific) belief in God – religion in a non-dogmatic sense, one might say – remain? This was, it would appear, the position of Lichtenberg.[14] For thinkers like Lichtenberg belief in God was, in the Middle Ages, held by ecclesiastical authorities to be tied to membership of the Catholic church. The most serious successful challenge to this belief came with the Reformation, when it was accepted by large numbers of people that belief in God was compatible with rejection of the Catholic church and with membership of one of the Reformed churches. And subsequently with the weakening of the Reformed churches' hold over many of their members, large numbers of people in the modern Western world began to think that they could perfectly well believe in God without belonging to any church whatsoever. Whether, however, such a position is tenable in the long run is debatable. Autonomous believers, i.e. believers attached or affiliated to no church, may in fact be drawing their spiritual sustenance still from past ages of church-organised faith. Could such spiritual nourishment continue to be available if Christianity were to cease being a living cultural, social and indeed even political force?

Yet while large sections of Western society from the Enlightenment onwards have moved from a specific attachment to Christianity to a general interest in, and occasionally even luke-warm respect for, the place of religion in human existence, it can, I think, plausibly be argued that the Enlightenment is itself the child, albeit the wayward child, of Christianity. For although the Enlightenment may have arisen partly in reaction to the religious wars of the sixteenth and seventeenth centuries, in Germany at least its passion for truth seems to have been nourished also by the pietist strain in Reformed Christianity. Certainly the Enlightenment's non-relativistic belief in the uniqueness (or specificity) and universal applicability of truth would seem to owe much to the tradition it sought to uproot. Indeed Nietzsche himself at a later

---

13 *Philosophy of God and Theology* (London, 1973), p. 33. Cf. Sr M. Noelle Ethel Ezeh, *Cosmic Community and Human Community: An Exploratory Essay on the Contemporary Christian Theology of Respect for Creation* (STL Dissertation, Maynooth 1995), pp. viif.

14 Cf. G.Chr. Lichtenberg, *Aphorisms*, p. 11.

stage noted the connection between his own commitment to truth
and that of the tradition he was committed to overthrowing:

> You see what it was that really triumphed over the Christian
> god: Christian morality itself, the concept of truthfulness that
> was understood ever more rigorously, the father confessor's
> refinement of the Christian conscience, translated and sublimat-
> ed into a scientific conscience, into intellectual cleanliness at any
> price.[15]

'Nietzsche,' writes Ernest Gellner, 'attacks and rejects a certain kind
of ethic in the name of honesty and truth, but also sees full well that
the high valuation of honesty and truth which impels him to it is
itself part of that ethic.'[16] In short, the Enlightenment-inspired
scrutiny of, and at times all-out attack on, Christianity in the modern world is arguably a fruit of Christianity's own habit of questioning and even self-questioning, a habit perhaps going right back to
Jesus who distinguished in his own day between God and human
traditions about God. This critical faculty has always been one of
the potential sources or taproots of Christianity's theological tradition, and is connected with its notion of God as incomprehensible
and too holy to be directly experienced. In Christianity the basic
sense of the holiness and otherness of God, a legacy from Judaism,
acquired a sophisticated intellectual means of self-expression when
the Greek philosophical tradition (which also of course had its own
in-built critical element) was given right of residence within the
house of faith. And since all provisional understandings of the
Christian God are and will continue to be incomplete, a permanent,
intellectual and moral or spiritual restlessness thereby arises within
Christian culture which history abundantly documents. This restlessness is clearly visible also in the Old Testament in the way no
historical arrangement between God and the people of the
covenant ever succeeds in becoming permanent. Needless to say, a
religious interpretation of such patterns can always be contested in
the name of a purely naturalistic explanation where the only
imponderables in play are the as yet not fully comprehended
dynamics of the so-called historical process itself.

To call the Enlightenment a child of the Christian tradition is not
to call it the apotheosis of Christianity, or the end of the Christian
line. For the Enlightenment 'as Gadamer aptly observes, is merely a

---

15 *The Gay Science*, §357, tr. Walter Kaufmann (New York, 1974), p. 307.
16 *Thought and Change* (London, 1964), p. 54.

stage in our destiny.'[17] It has however forced Christianity out into the open once again, and obliged it to give an account of itself. However here the differences between Christianity and the Enlightenment start to appear, for Christianity is not simply a philosophy, but a communal faith guided by certain beliefs that can be lived with, even though they are not fully understood. Christianity can thus in principle continue to live, even when understanding is weak. The Enlightenment on the other hand is – again in principle – a courageous ethic of truthfulness and honesty, guided by rational principles, but it must subvert or destroy itself if it cannot find intellectual justification for its ethical steps. The Enlightenment would not seem to have the resources to deal with its intellectual shortfall, on the ethical or existential front. From what other source can it live? If Christianity seems somewhat ironically to have the theoretical edge on the Enlightenment at the level of actual living, that is perhaps because the God-question which is its lifeblood is not only an intellectual question, but is simultaneously an intellectual, moral[18] ('"God" on the lips without a good conduct of life, is but a word,'[19] Plotinus declared), and aesthetic question. The three theological virtues of faith, charity and hope are all interwoven with the Christian God-question, just as it is bound up with the past (where Christian faith has its origin), the present (where charity is to be exercised) and the future (to which the human hope for fulfilment is directed).

While reticence is called for in dealing with the complexities of the God-question, nevertheless in the Judaeo-Christian tradition it is in principle true to say that we are encouraged to err on the side of the question, rather than to be cowed into silence by the traditional size of the answer. All the more so, surely, if we accept Lichtenberg's comment: 'To err is *human* also in so far as animals seldom or never err, or at least only the cleverest of them do so.'[20]

What is knowledge of God?

That the God-question is multi-layered is evident in the way the exploration of any of its many layers leads inevitably into an awareness of the others. To ask, for example, if the God-question is about

---

17 Kolakowski, *Metaphysical Horror*, p. 118.
18 Cf. John 3. 21: ' ... he who does what is true comes to the light ...'
19 Plotinus, *Enneads*, II.ix.15, tr. by S. MacKenna, rev. edn. London, 1969, p. 148, quoted by A. Louth, *Discerning the Mystery* (Oxford, 1983), p. 76.
20 *Aphorisms*, p. 9.

knowledge, is to ask if we are primarily looking for information or for personal knowledge of God? In the twentieth century the Jewish thinker Martin Buber is the writer whose name is above all associated with the difference between objective knowledge and personal knowledge, in the sphere of religious experience. In *Eclipse of God* Buber writes:

> Philosophy errs in thinking of religion as founded in a noetical [i.e. 'confined to the mind only'] act, even if an inadequate one, and in therefore regarding the essence of religion as the knowledge of an object which is indifferent to being known. As a result, philosophy understands faith as an affirmation of truth lying somewhere between clear knowledge and confused opinion. Religion, on the other hand, insofar as it speaks of knowledge at all, does not understand it as a noetic relation of a thinking subject to a neutral object of thought, but rather as mutual contact, as the genuinely reciprocal meeting in the fullness of life between one active existence and another. Similarly, it understands faith as the entrance into this reciprocity, as binding oneself in relationship with an undemonstrable and unprovable, yet even so, in relationship, knowable Being, from whom all meaning comes.[21]

In Christian theology Emil Brunner, under the influence of Buber, also drew the distinction 'between two kinds of truth and knowledge: "it-truth" and "Thou-truth". … Consequently … Brunner asserted that any theology that treats knowledge of God as analogous to knowledge of objects … is fundamentally wrong-headed … Knowledge of God is personal in the sense that it transcends the plane of objects and the subject-object dualism inherent in knowledge of objects, calling instead for personal decision, response and commitment.'[22] There is clearly a difference – marked indeed by some languages, for example French, German, or Irish – between objective and personal knowledge. Knowledge of God is surely more akin to a moral commitment than to propositional knowledge.[23] And this implies that we can only know God to the extent

---

21 Martin Buber, *Eclipse of God: Studies in the Relation Between Religion and Philosophy* (New Jersey, 1979), pp. 32f.

22 Stanley J. Grenz and Roger E. Olson, *Twentieth-Century Theology: God and the World is a Transitional Age* (Downers Grove, 1992), p. 80.

23 Cf. the discussion of 'propositional' versus 'personal' knowledge in J. Barr, *The Bible in the Modern World* (London, 1973), pp. 123ff., *Old and New in Interpretation* (New York, 1966), p. 84.

that we are committed to him. Were anyone tempted to act on this hunch, it would presumably be in the hope of one day 'seeing' God, since God is not visible just at the moment. But who would want to see God, were God not intrinsically attractive or 'agreeable', i.e. beautiful? On this critical issue one may well surmise that Christianity's way of envisioning God as making man in his image will mean that finding God attractive and finding human existence attractive will ultimately stand or fall together. Misanthropists should find the Christian God difficult to warm to.

The pattern we have detected in the God-question – knowledge through moral commitment seeking vision – is reminiscent indeed of the pattern of topics broached successively by Kant in his three *Critiques*: 'What can I know? What should I do? What can I find agreeable?'[24] Since the great difficulty of modern religion is its lack-lustre 'image', its lack of interest for many, we may look briefly at what might prove to be the central aspect of the God-question, its aesthetic dimension.

The aesthetic experience is the experience of the beautiful and the sublime. It is an experience that transcends pure reason (could that be why Wallace Stevens said that 'Beauty is momentary in the mind–/... But in the flesh it is immortal'?). In it we perceive 'the harmony between nature and our faculties,' and are then 'impressed by the purposiveness and intelligibility of everything that surrounds us. This is the sentiment of beauty. At other times, overcome by the infinite greatness of the world, we renounce the attempt to understand and control it. This is the sentiment of the sublime.'[25] The aesthetic experience is thus a further illustration of the *mysterium tremendum et fascinans*: we are both fascinated by the ability of our rational faculties to interact with and thus gain some limited perception of 'the wonders of nature and the majesty of the universe',[26] and yet we are at the same time overwhelmed by the infinite extent to which it transcends us. '[T]he aesthetic *experience,*

---

24 Cf. R. Scruton, *Kant* (Oxford, 1982), p. 24. See also H.J. Störig, *Kleine Weltgeschichte der Philosophie* (Frankfurt a/M, 1995), p. 28, who points out that in a letter written in his old age Kant, looking back on his life's work, had said that it could be summed up as an attempt to answer three questions: 'What can we know? What should we do? What may we believe?'

25 Scruton, *op. cit.*, p. 89.

26 Kant, *Critique of Pure Reason*, B 652.

which involves a perpetual striving to pass beyond the limits of our point of view, seems to "embody" what cannot be thought.'[27]

Against this view of the aesthetic experience arising from the sense of harmony between our minds and the 'external' world could of course be set Newman's view of the world:

> Starting then with the being of a God ... I look out of myself into the world of men, and there I see a sight which fills me with unspeakable distress. ... I look into the living busy world, and see no reflection of its Creator. ... I am far from denying the real force of the arguments in proof of a God, ... but these do not ... take away the winter of my desolation ...
>
> To consider the world in its length and breadth, ... the tokens so faint and broken, of a superintending design, ... – all this is a vision to dizzy and appal; ... I know that even the unaided reason, when correctly exercised, leads to a belief in God, in the immortality of the soul, and in a future retribution; but I am considering it actually and historically; and in this point of view, I do not think I am wrong in saying that its tendency is towards a simple unbelief in matters of religion. No truth, however sacred, can stand against it, in the long run ...[28]

Newman sees no benign creator as the world's source and no benevolent design in its structure. Yet even a frightening vision of the world such as Newman paints is essentially an aesthetic reaction to life, not a purely rational or moral one. It too clearly shows in its own way the *mysterium tremendum et fascinans*, because horror by its overwhelming and seemingly endless power can fascinate as much as beauty.

The aesthetic experience is not a theoretical argument for the existence of God. Rather it gives us an intimation of an order in nature which touches but immeasurably transcends our mind. Taking a hint from Flaubert's famous statement about the relation of an author to his book, we can say that the aesthetic experience of reality gives us a faint, inarticulate sense of the transcendent 'God in his universe, everywhere present and nowhere visible'. This aesthetic experience has parallels moreover with the experience of morality which conveys both the sense that there is an order in reality (even if it can be contravened) and an awareness of how infinitely it transcends us (moral perfection being unrealisable in history). The

---

27 Scruton, *op. cit.*, p. 88.
28 J.H. Newman, *Apologia pro Vita Sua*, pp. 277–279.

moral experience then, like the aesthetic, puts us in touch with the *mysterium tremendum et fascinans*: its attractions we cannot deny, but its demands are awesome.

To refuse the aesthetic experience is to deny the place we occupy in nature and to assume a false autonomy. It is finally 'to say that our point of view on the world is all that the world consists in, and so to make ourselves into gods.'[29] But the fact that we can understand this world at all, however limitedly, the fact that we can grasp it as a world or universe (a single totality) is an aesthetic feat, giving us some slender contact with what transcends us. And since we live with some freedom in an ever changing history, we have scope to try to conform, or to respond, to the transcendent source of our existence. Guided thus by fleeting experiences of meaning, goodness and beauty we can hope that our final destiny will be to participate fully in that transcendent reality which creates the conditions for our lives and marks them with those signs which make us human. But since God has in Christian tradition been taken to be the supreme perfection of truth, goodness, and beauty, this appears to imply – if we accept that only like can know like – that our sense of God will always be inadequate, will always fall short of the truth, to the extent that we ourselves fall short of such perfection. Hence, that we will only see and understand what or who God is, when we have ourselves in some sense become 'God'. As long as history continues, however, this human process of becoming 'God' will always remain incomplete.

To engage with God is then a composite enterprise involving all aspects of the human condition. It is 'the concrete being' (Newman), the existing, acting being (Blondel),[30] the 'man of flesh and blood' (Unamuno), not a thinking automaton, who engages, or refuses to engage, with God.[31] As for pure knowledge, even if it is *of*

---

29 Scruton, *op. cit.*, p. 90.

30 Writing in 1886 Blondel expressed his dissatisfaction with a purely intellectualist approach to truth in the following terms: 'Truth is no longer *adequatio rei et intellectus* and no one lives on "clear ideas" any longer. But there remains the truth, and the truth which remains is living and active; it is *adequatio mentis et vitae*' (quoted in Maurice Blondel, *The Letter on Apologetics and History and Dogma*. Texts presented and translated by Alexander Dru and Illtyd Trethowan, London, 1964, p. 33).

31 It is perhaps wise, therefore, not to pursue any of the various dimensions of the God-question in isolation. Lichtenberg for example shrewdly remarked: 'That God, or whatever it is, has induced man to propagate himself by making him enjoy coition must also be borne in mind in

God it is still not *God*, and if taken for God is only an idol.
Knowledge is only of use as a route to God. It is not – as the bible
from Genesis to St Paul makes monotonously plain – an end in
itself, which is perhaps why it is always double-edged, taking away
with one hand what it gives with the other. 'We have perhaps
looked too deeply into the heart of things,' wrote Franz Overbeck,
'and that is why we have reached a moment in human life when we
know too much about everything, even about the most hidden and
most inaccessible things, above all about ourselves and our end,
which is death. There is no getting away from this knowledge and
we have to live with it.'[32] But knowledge's sobering disappoint-
ments and frustrations can direct us to other resources that may
help us to live, and presumably may help us finally to embody that
which knowledge would love to embrace but never can. For, as
Kierkegaard noted: 'Philosophy can pay attention to but cannot
nourish us.'

The same fundamental lesson emerges from the Christian mystical tradition, which never sees knowledge as of paramount importance in religion. Indeed this tradition has always claimed that since
God is beyond knowledge, ineffable, inexpressible, essentially not
comprehensible in terms of worldly existence – precisely because of
his transcendence of all created things – that therefore what the
creature seeks in trying to approach God is not so much knowledge
of, but rather union with, the divine.[33] Different kinds of awareness
must therefore be distinguished in talk about God, so that it is clear
whether we are speaking about the mere acknowledgement of the
existence of God or about a richer, subtler, more complex and,
above all, lived and living apprehension of the divine.

---

reflecting on Kant's highest principle of morality' (*Aphorisms*, p. 154).
And he qualified even further the enormous respect usually accorded
to dispassionate reason when he wrote: 'May not much of what Herr
Kant teaches, especially in regard to the moral law, not be a consequence of old age, in which passion and inclination have lost their
strength and reason alone remains?' (*ibid.*, p. 198). However pitfalls are,
sadly, easier to imagine than to avoid.

32 *Christentum und Kultur*, ed. C.A. Bernoulli (Darmstadt, 1963), p. 300.
33 For example, pseudo-Dionysius (sixth century): 'Union with the
    Unknown, *theósis*, deification, is the aim of Dionysius' philosophising'
    (G. Watson, *Greek Philosophy and the Christian Notion of God*, Dublin,
    1994, p. 122).

God and creation

If we do come to know God, it is surely not God in himself that we come to know, but God in so far as he can be perceived in relation to the world and to human beings, even if God's reality can be affirmed by faith to be truly (and not simply notionally) distinct from the existence of the world. Indeed Karl Barth went even further and claimed that 'an abstract doctrine of God has no place in the Christian realm, only a "doctrine of God and of man," a doctrine of the commerce and communion between God and man.'[34] And yet Hans Urs von Balthasar can praise Barth precisely for the 'objectivity' of his theology, by which however he means that Barth is more interested in the object of Christian faith (God as revealed to the world in Jesus Christ) than in its subjective reception, and can thus avoid the dangers implicit in a theology consciously seeking to be 'pastoral'.[35] According to Balthasar Luther but not Calvin opted to concentrate on the subjective appropriation of Christian faith, a move repeated later by Schleiermacher, with results that Barth set out to counter.

Yet while it is undoubtedly true that God has been spoken about in ways that presuppose a non-self-interested awareness of him,[36]

---

34 *The Humanity of God* (London and Glasgow, 1971), p. 9. This point Barth repeats in almost identical terms later in the essay 'Evangelical Theology in the Nineteenth Century' from which the above quotation is taken: 'Theology is in reality not only the doctrine of God, but the doctrine of God and man' (*ibid.*, p. 24). In the 1956 lecture which gave the overall title to this small volume Barth had already said: 'Who God is and what He is in His deity He proves and reveals not in a vacuum as a divine being-for-Himself, but precisely and authentically in the fact that He exists, speaks, and acts as the *partner* of man, though of course as the absolutely superior partner. He who does *that* is the living God. And the freedom in which He does *that* is His deity ... It is precisely God's *deity* which, rightly understood, includes his *humanity*' (*The Humanity of God*, p. 42).

35 Cf. H. Urs von Balthasar, *Karl Barth. Darstellung und Deutung seiner Theologie* (Einsiedeln, 1976), p. 35.

36 Cf. the anonymous Golden Age Spanish sonnet 'To Christ Crucified', described as 'one of the finest religious poems in the language' by Arthur Terry (*An Anthology of Spanish Poetry 1500–1700*, Part II 1580–1700, Oxford, 1968, p. 96): 'It is not the heaven that You have promised me, my God, that moves me to love You, nor is it the hell I so fear that moves me to cease sinning against You. / *You* move me, Lord; it moves me to see You nailed to that cross and despised; it moves me to see Your

nevertheless, utilitarian though it may sound, the knowledge of God that really matters in religious terms is surely knowledge that will be of use to human beings. Such knowledge, however, will not necessarily be attained by any direct attempt at being 'relevant', but only (if at all) by speaking about what is substantial and true. For reality cannot be cheated. Barth's theology is of course thoroughly subjective too[37] – how can any human product not be marked by its author's subjectivity? – but its possible relevance to others will be, surely, a by-product, and not the main aim, of its concentration on what Barth felt was objective truth.

Since the Judaeo-Christian tradition itself sees humanity as made in God's image,[38] this would also suggest that real or worthwhile knowledge of God will in fact be knowledge of God in relation to humanity rather than knowledge of what one takes 'God' to be in himself. Thus even if we accept that God exists from himself and not in dependence on anything else, or in theological terminology that God enjoys *aseity*, it seems impossible not to maintain also that we can only understand God from a human point of view and to the extent that God – assuming God to be in some sense personal – may choose to make himself known to us, as indeed all personal knowledge depends on the extent to which the person in question is willing to reveal himself.

God's otherness from his creation is part (but not all) of what is meant by his aseity. If it were all that were meant by divine aseity, that would make God dependent on creation because he would 'define' himself over against his creation, and to speak then of divine aseity would be a nonsense. Yet if we can never fully com-

---

body so wounded; the insults You suffered and Your death move me. / Finally, Your love moves me, and so much that even if there were no heaven, I should love You; and even if there were no hell, I should fear You. / You have not to give me anything to make me love You; for even if I did not hope for what I do hope for, I should love You just as I do' (*The Penguin Book of Spanish Verse*, tr. J.M. Cohen, Harmondsworth, 1988, pp.198ff.).

37 Cf. the comments on Barth and Feuerbach in Chapter 8 below.

38 The same belief is at the root of the crisis of modern atheism. For to deny God is also to deny the traditional meaning of man as made in God's image. Hence in a post-Christian world, the image of man needs to be redefined. In the twentieth century this task was undertaken fanatically by fascism and communism, but no purely naturalistic or this-worldly solution to the problem has yet found universal acceptance.

prehend what is meant by aseity, why talk about it? What is the significance of this doctrine? Divine aseity is significant for at least two good reasons. Firstly, it implies that we can add nothing whatsoever to God, no matter what we do or fail to do. Hence God cannot be understood either as exploiting us for his own greater glory, or needing to frustrate and humiliate us in order to prove who is in charge of existence. Thus the doctrine of God's aseity and otherness implies that our freedom, our room to breathe freely is, so to speak, divinely unhampered, indeed divinely made possible, and constricted only by the inherent reality of the created order itself. The restrictions that we meet with in life come, in other words, not from the existence of God but from the existence of the world in which we find ourselves, even though we believe that the world was created by God. On this question Christianity can have things both ways.

The second reason why the doctrine of God's aseity is important is that it alerts us to the meaning of the God-question for us as *creatures*. For this difficult doctrine illuminates – by shrouding in darkness – both the motive for, and the status of, creation. If God enjoys perfect, infinite bliss in himself, if he has no need of the world, if he was not obliged to create by any force either within his nature or *a fortiori* – since nothing else existed – outside himself, if he was thus under no compulsion to express himself in an alien element (matter, space, time), how can one explain the motive for the creation of the world? Moreover if God is infinite, as his aseity implies, even assuming he wanted to create, where or how could he do so? How can there be anything 'more' than infinity? And if God is immutable, as again his aseity implies, how is it possible to think of creation as not belonging to the very essence of God?[39]

There are, disappointingly or mercifully perhaps, no answers to these questions. Paradoxical though it may sound, if there were, i.e.

---

39 One should perhaps add in passing that creation has been understood not only as an outflowing or overflowing of goodness – *bonum sui diffusivum* – but also, albeit less frequently, as a process of divine self-limitation, a process which allows us a space in which to exist, so to speak. This theory springs from the kabbalistic thinker Isaac Luria, 'who first of all developed these ideas in his doctrine of *zimsum*. ... The kabbalistic doctrine of the self-limitation of God has also found a place in Christian theology. Nicholas of Cusa, J.G. Hamann, Friedrich Oettinger, F.W.J. Schelling, A. von Oettingen, Emil Brunner and others all saw that when God permitted creation, this was the first act in the divine self-humiliation which reached its profoundest point in the cross of Christ' (Jürgen Moltmann, *God in Creation*, London, 1985, p. 87).

if God and his actions were truly comprehensible to us, there would be no religion, and no need of religion. For to comprehend in the deep sense in which we crave to comprehend ultimate answers to ultimate questions, comprehension and being would have to coincide. There is a faint echo of this, it seems to me, in the way we so to speak 'become' anything we have really comprehended. There is an even stronger echo of it in the experience of 'music heard so deeply/That it is not heard at all, but you are the music/While the music lasts,' as Eliot puts it. And of course mystical literature speaks characteristically not of seeking knowledge of, but of seeking union with, God. In other words, all is well so long as ultimate questions do *not* receive ultimate answers, because if they did, they would cease to be *ultimate* questions for us, and we would cease to be human. If we fully understood the answer to the mystery of existence, we would ourselves have to *be* that answer, we would have to be God, which of course is the destiny Christianity promises us through grace. Not being God by nature we simply do not know why God created. We can only surmise. A corollary of this would appear to be that any religion or philosophy offering ultimate intellectual answers to ultimate human questions is fraudulent. A more positive corollary resides in Wittgenstein's feeling about why 'those who have found after a long period of doubt that the sense of life became clear to them have then been unable to say what constituted that sense.'[40] We shall come back to this issue in the final chapter.

So much for the 'God-side' of the coin of creation. The other side of that coin is the acceptance of the incomprehensibility of the world (what God created). So both the divine motive (for creation) and the outcome (creation itself) are unknown and probably unknowable to us. Yet by retaining the doctrine of divine aseity (which, to repeat, is incomprehensible to us), we can with some aptness view and continue to view the existence of the created order (the only partly comprehensible projection of the incomprehensible God) as something which, even though it can furnish vital clues as to the nature of its maker, cannot fully be explained or understood. One understands, as it were, by not understanding. (*Vous comprenez?*) Not for nothing, as Barth noted, is the doctrine of creation a doctrine of faith, contained in the first article of the Creed alongside belief in God.

It should be pointed out in concluding this section that the

---

40 *Tractatus* 6.521, tr. D.F. Pears and B.F. McGuinness (London, 1972), pp. 149f.

Christian notion of *creatio ex nihilo* has been under extreme pressure
from the time of Spinoza and the German Idealists. Fichte, for
instance, ridiculed the incoherence and unintelligibility (from his
point of view) of the idea of creation out of nothing.[41] Both Spinoza
and Fichte, in rejecting the idea of creation, also consistently reject
the idea of God as personal.[42] And a more recent commentator has
found the Christian idea that creation is not only the work of God,
but a willed and a good work, an impossible notion to swallow:
'The world is a divine accident, *accidens Dei*. – How right Albert the
Great's formula appears to be!'[43]

The naming of God

In the light then of the challenges to traditional religious views
implicit in the cultural changes that mark off the modern world
from previous periods in Christian history, the main question to ask
is whether God is a transcendent reality apart from us and our
world, who nevertheless willed to create and sustain the world and
thus is in some incomprehensible sense also immanent in it; or
whether 'God' is just a word, a symbol used perhaps to give morality a silver lining (cf. Matthew Arnold's remark that religion is
'morality touched by emotion'), or an expression conveying our
sense of life's depth and seriousness. If the latter were the case, then
'God' would be a way of talking about our humanity and our
human experience, a way of registering our acknowledgement of
the majesty and awesomeness of life, rather than a way of naming
the unnameable, the hidden source of all reality.

The paradox of 'naming the unnameable' reminds us that

---

41 Cf. A. MacIntyre's article 'Pantheism' in *The Encyclopedia of Philosophy*,
    ed. P. Edwards (New York, 1967), vol. 6, pp. 31–35. The problems with
    the Christian doctrine of creation did not of course begin in the modern
    world. In antiquity the conviction among Graeco-Roman pagan intel-
    lectuals that creation 'out of nothing' was an unthinkable proposition is
    conveyed by for example Lucretius (c.94–55 BC): 'Nothing can ever be
    created by divine power out of nothing' (*De rerum natura*, 1.160, cited by
    Robert L. Wilken, *The Christians as the Romans saw them*, Yale, 1984,
    p. 90), or Persius (AD 34–62): 'De nihilo nihil fit', 'de nihilo nihil, in
    nihilum nil posse reverti', a sentiment that goes back far in Greek
    thought, to Epicurus and Aristotle.
42 Cf. W. Pannenberg, *An Introduction to Systematic Theology* (Edinburgh,
    1991), pp. 34f.
43 'Le monde est un accident de Dieu, *accidens Dei*.— Que la formule
    d'Albert le Grand paraît juste!' (E.M. Cioran, *Aveux et anathèmes*, p. 138).

Christianity has, like Judaism, asserted the reality of the creator God, but has never ventured to spell out precisely in what God's nature consists. It has in fact never sought to name God except in relation to Jesus. For the Judaeo-Christian tradition has always affirmed that God, not being an object – not even the greatest object – alongside other objects, is beyond our understanding, hence beyond our attempts to name him and therefore beyond language itself. The fact, for instance, that so many different names are used for God in the Old Testament would indicate that, for the Old Testament writers, no simple, single naming of God was thought feasible or – and this is perhaps more significant – appropriate,[44] apart from the name given in Exodus, according to the narrative, by God to himself.

According to the witness of the Old Testament then we might conclude that we have no right to name God. Or it might be more accurate to say that how we name anyone is a question that demands tact and sensitivity, since the name we give another person is not simply a way of designating that person, but usually says something also about the relationship between the namer and the named. Standard modes of address that denote various degrees of blood relationship between people, titles, nicknames and pet-names are evidence of this simple fact. It would be strange indeed if, *mutatis mutandis*, similar considerations did not apply to the naming of God.

Moreover, to have someone's name is to have a certain power over that person, as debate about the compulsory carrying of identity-cards, for example, suggests. And it is clearly impossible for us to have power over God. A plurality of names for God, such as one finds in the Old Testament, does not therefore necessarily signify theological richness but may at best be rather a sign of its opposite, a matter of beating about the bush rather than hitting the target dead centre.

Borges' parable 'Everything and Nothing', ostensibly on Shakespeare, captures this idea nicely, but with the added twist that the divine 'target' is unhittable, because it is, in fact, not specifiable or identifiable. Its uniqueness cannot be established. The parable ends with what is perhaps an ironically subversive echo of the ancient problem of the One and the Many:

---

44 Cf. the way that pious Jews from c. 300 BC onwards would not even pronounce the sacred tetragrammaton (YHWH) when reading the scriptures, substituting instead 'Adonai'.

History adds that before or after dying he [Shakespeare] found himself in the presence of God and told Him: 'I who have been so many men in vain want to be one and myself.' The voice of the Lord answered from a whirlwind: 'Neither am I anyone; I have dreamt the world as you dreamt your work, my Shakespeare, and among the forms in my dream are you, who like myself are many and no one.'[45]

The question of naming God, then, is clearly one fraught with difficulties that cannot be resolved intellectually. For this reason, no doubt, a preference for saying what God is not, rather than what he is has long taken root in Christian theology. 'Apophatic (negative) theology' has stressed the unknown side of God, as opposed to 'cataphatic (affirmative) theology' which emphasises what *can* be said about God. Apophaticism thus refers to the human inability to express the reality of God.[46] Yet despite all qualifications about our knowledge of God in himself, the Judaeo-Christian tradition has always affirmed that there is an unbreakable link between God and humanity. An important implication of this is drawn by David Tracy when he claims: 'Every human understanding of God is at the same time an understanding of oneself – and vice versa.'[47] Hence, to reject God is also implicitly to reject a particular image of man. Those who do so may then feel compelled to try to forge a new one. The sense of urgency which Nietzsche's writings convey is surely not unrelated to the obsessive sense of mission he felt on this score. As for the believer's attempt to understand and to name God, it too must include the search for the source of our own identity.

God cannot however be exhaustively identified simply with an explanation of human existence. Indeed, no human understanding of God, not even one that includes an interpretation of our own nature, can be identified 'without remainder' with the reality of God. This belief, which has been a consistent feature of the

---

45 J.L. Borges, *Labyrinths. Selected Stories and Other Writings*, edited by D.A. Yates and J.E. Irby (Harmondsworth, 1970), p. 285; cf. E.M. Cioran: 'it is *unbelievable* that one can be a man ... , that one can have a thousand faces and none, and that one can change one's identity every moment ...' (*La chute dans le temps*, Paris, 1964, p. 27).

46 Cf. A. Louth, *The Origins of the Christian Mystical Tradition* (Oxford, 1983), p. 165: 'Cataphatic and symbolic theology are concerned with what we affirm about God: apophatic theology is concerned with our understanding of God, when, in the presence of God, speech and thought fail us and we are reduced to silence.'

47 David Tracy, *The Analogical Imagination* (London, 1981), p. 429.

Christian tradition, is ultimately rooted both in a general sense of the difference between reality and thought, and – more profoundly – in a more specific acceptance of the Christian doctrines of creation and redemption. For both of these doctrines are unbelievable if they do not presuppose that God, like the possibility and 'motive' of creation and redemption, is incomprehensible. In conclusion, we may recall St Thomas Aquinas' distinction between our knowledge *that* God exists and our ignorance of *what* God is in himself.[48] This mixture of knowledge and ignorance, where the latter is always finally the preponderant element, we shall see appearing over and over again throughout the history of Judaeo-Christian thought on God.

---

48 See, for example, (a) *STh* 1a. 1, 7; (b) *STh* 1a 2, 2 ad 3 ('God's effects, therefore, can serve to demonstrate that God exists, even though they cannot help us to know him comprehensively for what he is'); (c) *STh* 1a. 3 ('Now we cannot know what God is, but only what he is not; we must therefore consider the ways in which God does not exist, rather than the ways in which he does' – both tr. T. McDermott). Aquinas spells out his reasons for saying that we cannot comprehend God's essence in *STh* 1a. 12.

PART II

Theological sources

CHAPTER THREE

God and the bible

Experience proves surely that the bible does not answer a purpose, for which it was never intended... [A] book, after all, cannot make a stand against the wild living intellect of man ...
— John Henry Newman

Our theologians want to make of the bible a book in which there is no human understanding. — Georg Chr. Lichtenberg

Introduction

In the heyday of the historical-critical method, it was firmly believed that the bible should be investigated 'like any other book'. This starting-point ignored the fact that the bible was, historically, not 'like any other book'. For it had functioned as a foundational document, or charter almost, for the Jewish and Christian communities throughout the centuries. This fact belongs as much to the 'meaning' of the bible as do the words it contains. A historical-critical reading of the bible is, of course, both legitimate and instructive. Indeed an implication of Christianity's anti-docetic interpretation of Jesus is precisely that the New Testament should *not* be regarded as a body of literature that deals with an only apparently real historical personage. However, beyond this specific historical dimension of the New Testament one must also take into account the undeniable weight of the Jewish and Christian traditions themselves. For these traditions give the bible its world-historical claim on our attention.

The bible is thus important in itself, for what it intrinsically contains. But it is also important because two major and interconnected historical traditions saw in what it contains a unique account of God and God's relation to the world. These accounts – for as Christianity's breaking-off from Judaism shows, they were finally judged to be different – were taken to be permanently valid, and from them both Judaism and Christianity have continued to draw sustenance, insight, and hope. In this wider, human sense, more than in any narrow historical sense, Jews and Christians see their scriptures as true.

In this chapter, therefore, an attempt will be made to restate the abiding truth and, consequently, interest of the bible's varied teaching on God.

The Old Testament

Given the Hebrews' prohibition of images, it is hardly surprising to find an absence of intellectual icons or images of God in their scriptures. For the Old Testament the existence of God is not a problem, as it has become in the modern age. No discussion was thought necessary to demonstrate God's existence. God is simply assumed to exist before the bible opens. This point is made implicitly by the Enlightenment thinker Lessing, who argued that there was religion before there was an Old Testament, just as there was Christianity before there was a New Testament.[1] In short the Old Testament does not set out to prove or argue for the existence of God.[2] What the bible does is to develop what can be said about a God already assumed to exist.

This is not to say that the nature or the purposes of God do not cause any problem for the authors of the Old Testament. Nothing could be further from the truth. One only has to think of the Book of Job or Ecclesiastes or the writings of the great prophets to be convinced of that. However, if one were to make a large generalisation, one might say that in the Old Testament the God-question is bound up with the human quest for salvation, and hence with the question of God's interest in the human race. It is, from the human point of view, an existential question, and it is this existential question that in turn motivates the Old Testament's concern with creation. The implicit contrast here is with an approach to the God-question that is based more on a sense of wonder before the mystery of existence or even a sense of curiosity about the meaning of existence.

---

1 Yet for Lessing to say that what is written in the Gospels is true not because the Evangelists wrote it, but that the Evangelists wrote it because it is true, is only valid up to a point, and ignores the question of the inevitable particularity of all historically mediated truth.

2 In this section, as indeed elsewhere in this book, the reader will undoubtedly recognise debts to many scholars, debts so pervasive that it is not worthwhile enumerating every instance of an influence. Suffice it to say at this point that, for what is said about the bible, I have, in particular, found the works of James Barr indispensable.

Admittedly, these two broad approaches to the God-question over-lap at many points, but they seem sufficiently different from each other to be regarded as two fundamentally separate ways of deal-ing with what, from a human point of view at least, are ultimate questions.

If one wishes to retain the concept of 'revelation' for what one finds in the bible, then revelation should be understood not as something that is initiated by the Old Testament, but rather some-thing by which the Old Testament is initiated. The Old Testament's very existence, indeed, presupposes the possibility of revelation in this sense, and revelation in turn presupposes the ever present pos-sibility that God can and wishes to communicate with human beings. Revelation, in short, does not begin with the Old Testament but is presupposed by it. It should be possible moreover to main-tain this position without claiming in advance to know how revela-tion is going to develop. In other words, both the permanent possi-bility and intelligibility of revelation, and its unforeseeable content would appear to be helpful principles of interpretation when deal-ing with this highly contested theological category.[3]

The Old Testament gives therefore deeper insight into a God already known before the biblical tradition (by definition a written tradition as the name bible[4] itself suggests) opens. This deeper insight was gained over the centuries of the formation of the Old Testament in the context of Israel's religious experience. To this extent it is perhaps more helpful to see the Old Testament as the record of Israel's religion or religious faith, rather than as a record of revelation through divine intervention in history. There are dif-ferent reasons for this assessment of the Old Testament evidence.

The idea of the deity intervening in history is, in the first place, not something that differentiates Israel from her neighbours but, on the contrary, something she has in common with them.[5] Secondly, large sections of the Old Testament, notably the Wisdom Literature and much of the Psalms, are not most immediately or exclusively

---

3   For us who are always *in medias res* it would seem to be impossible to foreclose discussion of the ultimate meaning of any human experience. One can, for example, and no doubt always should, refuse to condone what diminishes human life. Such negative judgements can be defini-tive. But no positive claim about the ultimate meaning of history can be justified, so long as history lasts.

4   Derived from the Greek *biblia*, meaning 'books'.

5   Cf. Bertil Albrektson, *History and the Gods* (Lund, 1967).

comprehensible at all as records of God's mighty acts in history. Thirdly, and finally, the one single most frequently quoted piece of evidence for seeing Israel's God as revealing himself by his mighty acts in history, namely the exodus from Egypt, cannot be interpreted simply and straightforwardly as a divine act from which significant knowledge of God can be deduced. As it stands, the text depicts God as communicating with men before, during and after the events. Only God's previous communication with Moses, indeed, made the exodus event intelligible or even possible. The conversation at the burning bush,[6] far from being an interpretation of the divine acts, is a precondition of those acts.

What must be emphasised is that the understanding of God that emerges from the Old Testament cannot be based exclusively on an interpretation of events. Without entering into the complex question of what constitutes an 'event', it is surely uncontroversial to claim that no event can be understood in complete isolation from the rest of history. Newness can never be absolute. If it were, it would be incomprehensible, indeed unnoticeable. Hence to speak of certain events as revealing God cannot mean that before the events God was completely unknown. To speak of divine revelation in history presupposes always that even before the revelatory events took place some genuine human understanding of God already existed. Without such prior understanding of God, the events would be indecipherable as revelatory of God. We could go further and say that, just as sight is necessary if we are to understand painting, a pre-understanding or sense of God must be taken for granted in human beings, if we are to make sense of any religious claims, biblical or otherwise.

At this point a brief excursus on the large question of the relationship between the bible and history may be useful. The bible is not interested in history in the sense of accurately recording things as they actually happened in the past.[7] The narrative books of the

---

6 Exodus 3-4.
7 Sometimes the difference between Hebrew and Greek thought, especially with respect to history, is advanced as a reason for the difference between Hebrew and Greek views of God. That there were undoubtedly differences between Hebrew and Greek culture seems uncontentious, but that the differences should be looked for in their respective views of history is less so. For the difference between the Greek and the Hebrew view of history, see James Barr, *Biblical Words for Time*, and *The Semantics of Biblical Language*; Hannah Arendt, 'The Concept of History: Ancient and Modern', in *Between Past and Future* (Harmondsworth, 1977), p. 52.

bible are rather, to use Hans Frei's term, 'history-like'.[8] For their
interest is in God's engagement with human history; hence these
books do clearly have points of contact with real historical events
and personages. But their essential purpose is to discern patterns of
interpretation in the religious sphere which will be as valid for the
future as they once were for the past. One could even see part of the
meaning of the immutability, or the uniqueness, of God as lying in
the belief that God's purpose in creating and redeeming is vaguely
discernible in the historical process, and is always the same, always
seeking the one and same ultimate end or goal. Is God then perhaps
essentially Will? The Will to the End, which is traditionally called
salvation?

At the outset it was said that God is not a problem in the Old
Testament, or at least not a problem in the same way as he seems to
be for many moderns. In this respect ancient Israel's religion resembles that of her neighbours for whom the reality of the divine was
taken for granted. Where Israel differed from her neighbours was
on the question of the identity or nature of God, not on the question
of whether or not God existed. As regards the nature of God, the
Old Testament sees the God of Israel as being different from the
gods of other peoples, and furthermore as being, in his transcendence, different from human beings. Yet although transcendent, the
God of the Old Testament is also immanent in creation to the extent
that he can communicate with human beings within the world.

However, in saying that the Old Testament acknowledges a difference both between the God of Israel and other gods, and
between God and man, it is important to add that every difference
implies a similarity. Hence, while Israel's God is different from
other gods, he also in some sense resembles them, and while God is
different from man, man must also be in some sense similar to God.
Indeed the bible implies precisely this in claiming that God made
man in his own image.

To maintain that there is a difference and similarity between the
God of Israel and other gods mentioned in the bible, is to affirm that
the ancient Hebrews gradually elaborated and refined their understanding of God in conflict with the religions of their neighbours[9]

---

8   See Hans Frei, *The Eclipse of Biblical Narrative* (Yale, 1974), ch 1; cf. J. Barr,
    Explorations in Theology 7 (London, 1980), p. 5.
9   See Henri Frankfort et al., *Before Philosophy: The Intellectual Adventure of
    Ancient Man* (Harmondsworth, 1971), for the Near Eastern intellectual
    background to the bible.

and also through their own internal conflicts. This pattern – of internal conflict within Israel and external conflict with other peoples –
is a pattern that has continued in the religious tradition of the West
right down to the present day. Indeed some of the most intense,
even acrimonious, debates about God have taken place not between
Christians and those outside the Christian tradition, but among
Christians themselves.[10]

The Old Testament, then, can be seen not as presenting a clear-
cut doctrine of God, but rather as presenting a series of conflicting
views about the identity of God, all of which claim to be valid even
though the tensions among them remain unresolved within the
bible itself and hence can continue to generate new meanings
throughout history: 'The working out of the biblical model for the
understanding of God was not an intellectual process so much as a
personal conflict, in which men struggled with their God, and with
each other about their God. It was, in Old Testament terms, a *rîbh* or
dispute, a controversy to which the public attention is drawn so
that men can learn from it'.[11] This aspect of Old Testament faith
seems to have passed over into Christianity, where the lack of a
clear-cut understanding of God has been, arguably, one of its great
strengths. If – and for some this may be an unacceptably large 'if' –
but if one accepts, as has been recently asserted, that Christianity's
'influence seems to derive from the fact that it brings liberation
from prejudices and ideological fixations, and escapes being taken
over by any side,'[12] then surely this freedom is not unrelated to the
incomprehensibility of God that is at the heart of Judaeo-Christian
faith.

The Mesopotamian context

In the Mesopotamian (Babylonian) or ancient Near Eastern vision
of the cosmos there existed a unity or fusion between the world of

---

10 A. H. Armstrong, 'On Not Knowing Too Much About God' in Godfrey
    Vesey (ed.), *The Philosophy in Christianity* (Cambridge, 1989) p. 129, n.1,
    quotes the remarks made in the period of late antiquity by the historian
    Ammianus Marcellinus, who, speaking on Julian the Apostate's views
    on the Christians, observed: '"Julian knew from experience that no wild
    beasts are such enemies of humanity as most Christians are deadly
    dangerous (*ferales*) to each other" (Ammianus XXII, 5.4)'.
11 J. Barr, *The Bible in the Modern World* (London, 1973), p. 119.
12 Peter Pawlowsky, *Christianity*, tr. J. Bowden (London, 1995), p. 12.

the divine and the world of man.[13] Jean Bottéro points out that there
was only one universe for the Babylonians, encompassing both
gods and men, whereas in the bible one finds two distinct spheres,
totally different from one another.[14] The Babylonian gods are in fact
too like human beings – they even have their foibles – to be considered transcendent in any strong sense,[15] despite the fact that they
were, as in all ancient Semitic religious thought, considered to be
superior to human beings in some fashion. As well as being thoroughly anthropomorphic, Babylonian religion was also clearly
polytheistic, another fact differentiating it from the religion of
Israel, which tried as far as possible to reduce anthropomorphic
conceptions of the deity and to resist (through the prophets) the
intrusion of polytheistic tendencies whenever they surfaced in their
culture. Israel's religious ideas did not therefore remain static in the
course of her history, but a sense of the superiority of their own
God, combined with a consequent lack of interest in other gods led
the Israelites eventually to assert the transcendence and uniqueness
of their God and the non-existence of any others.[16]

Another major difference between Babylonian and biblical
views of God lies in the primacy of ethical conduct – for all, without
exception – in the religion of Israel.[17] One must bear in mind that
Mesopotamian religion was one aspect of a Mesopotamian culture
that evolved over the centuries in a natural fashion, so to speak, i.e.
without any sacred scripture or official (orthodox) religious authorities,[18] whereas in Israel the religion in question was founded (by

---

13 The same indeed is true of the Greeks: see Jean Bottéro, *Naissance de
   Dieu* (Paris, 1992), p. 283: '[T]he first philosophy in our world, as developed by the Greeks, came, as is well known, directly from their mythology. In their mythological theogonies, whose model is Hesiod's, in the
   eighth century BC, one can already discern not only the great questions
   and the essential problematic that will occupy all later Greek philosophers, but even the general spirit in which each will make his response:
   the notion of the integral unity of the Universe: divine and human; the
   uniqueness of the principle of things; the fundamental importance of
   becoming, whereby the question of an absolute beginning is never considered ... '

14 J. Bottéro, *Babylone et la bible* (Paris, 1994), pp. 253f.; cf. further J. Bottéro,
   Naissance de Dieu, pp. 278, 290, for other references to the radical difference between creator and creature in biblical thought.

15 Bottéro, *Babylone et la bible*, p. 252.

16 Bottéro, *Babylone et la bible*, pp. 248f., 253.

17 *Ibid*, p. 254.

18 *Ibid*., p. 251.

Moses) at a specific period, and based on a certain number of definite religious doctrines and moral precepts that were codified (orally
and in written form), and thus handed on in a fairly specific form.[19]

Monotheism versus polytheism

One important similarity between Israel and her neighbours lies in
the question of monotheism-versus-polytheism. For monotheistic
and polytheistic tendencies can be found in the religious traditions
of both Israel and her neighbours. In ancient Egypt, with the short-
lived reforms of Akhnaton,[20] and in the Babylonian religion of
Mesopotamia where the deity Marduk was honoured as 'King', and
in Canaan where El came to be regarded as 'Father of the gods',
there were clear attempts to move religion in a monotheistic direction, even though such attempts did not lead to an explicit denial of
other gods.

On the other side of the debate there were clearly polytheistic
tendencies within Israel. Monotheism, as a clear affirmation, is not
to be found in the earlier narrative books of the bible. Nor is there
an unambiguous denial of the reality of other gods (*Elohim*) before
Second Isaiah in the sixth century BC. However it is important to
remember in this debate that, as Ronald Clements remarks,[21]
'Polytheism and monotheism do not represent distinct stages in a
progressive intellectual development, but rather indicate contrasting
emphases in a very complex pattern of religious traditions.' Hence the
assumption that monotheism represents the culmination of a

---

19 *Ibid*, p. 252.
20 This was the name of Amenophis IV (ruled 1375–1358) who proposed
    that only the sun (Aton being the name of the solar disk) should be wor-
    shipped as the sole god.
21 Art. 'Henotheism', *A New Dictionary of Christian Theology*, ed. A.
    Richardson and J. Bowden (London, 1983), p. 249. Henotheism is the
    technical term referring to belief in one god without however denying
    the possibility of the existence of others. As regards its appropriateness
    to the case of Israel, R. Clements points out (*ibid.*), nevertheless, that it
    has been argued by H. H. Rowley (*From Moses to Qumran*, 1963, pp. 35-
    66) that the accepted notion of henotheism fails to do justice to the
    prominent sense in Israel that Yahweh was *superior* to all other divini-
    ties. Clements adds that this sense of Yahweh's superiority to other
    deities has been shown by C. J. Labuschagne (*The Incomparability of
    Yahweh in the Old Testament*, 1966, esp. pp. 64ff.) to have emerged in
    Israel at a very early stage, certainly long before Second Isaiah (i.e. long
    before the sixth century BC).

process that began with animism, and passed through polytheism and possibly henotheism before reaching its climax, seems to owe more to the preconceived notions of an earlier, rationalistically-minded generation of students of religion, than to the historical evidence.

It should perhaps be emphasised that any easy assumption of the superiority of monotheism over polytheism is almost certainly erroneous. Indeed the fact that human experience is so varied would make monotheism at first sight a much less likely explanation for the existence of the kind of world we live in, than polytheism. For it seems, superficially at any rate, more plausible to assume that the different aspects of reality point to different ultimate transcendent causes, rather than to just one. Certainly the presence of evil in the world seems initially more compatible with dualism than with monotheism.

One possible way, however, of retaining belief in monotheism despite the presence of evil might be, as Kolakowski in his tongue-in-cheek manner suggests,[22] to assume that the Devil could have made out of divinely given matter his own evil creatures; in which case any supposed link between creation and goodness would become incredible. Such diabolical creation would not, of course be creation *ex nihilo*. The link between creation and goodness could then only be retained, properly speaking, for divine (*ex nihilo*) creation. Yet this poses two further questions: firstly, how far is the philosophically defined doctrine of creation *ex nihilo* itself compatible with the biblical evidence? And, secondly and perhaps more seriously, how valid is the biblical tradition or assumption which equates 'the ability to create with goodness'?[23] As Kolakowski points out: 'this tradition is not exclusively biblical; it appears in various, not necessarily monotheistic, mythologies. It is far from being omnipresent, though; in old Iranian myths and their Manichean off-shoots the malevolent God is a creator too, and one may argue that apart from the strength of the biblical heritage there are no firm grounds for such an equation.'[24]

A God whose nature was dual (good and evil) could obviously not be monotheistic in the traditional Christian understanding of the term, because for Christianity God is not only the only God, but in God, conceived of as perfectly good, there is no darkness, no evil, no hatred, no chaos, no destructive will. Thus, polytheism or dual-

---

22 *Metaphysical Horror*, pp. 82f.
23 *Op. cit.*, p. 82.
24 *Ibid.*

ism seems a much more obviously attractive solution to the enigma of existence than monotheism, and places upon monotheism the onus of proof to the contrary.

The complexity of the monotheism-versus-polytheism problem however deepens if one accepts that monotheism and polytheism are in fact only understandable and definable in relation to each other,[25] and this must be borne in mind in any attempt to reconstruct the history of the perception of the divine in ancient Israel, or in any attempt to tackle the question of the extent to which developments in religions foreign to Israel may have influenced Israel herself in reaching the notion of the uniqueness of Yahweh. In any case, as regards monotheism in the proper sense of the term, i.e. implying the denial of the reality of other deities, received wisdom appears still to favour the idea that such a belief is not to be found firmly established in Israel before the sixth century BC, even though Yahweh had been known from about the early seventh century BC as the 'creator of heaven and earth' and hence as the creator of all peoples.

This received view seems plausible when one considers the fact that the destiny of Israel was so obviously intertwined with that of her neighbours in the sixth century BC during the Babylonian exile, and indeed for centuries before that. This fact, one may suppose, must have helped the Israelites to realise that their God who, they believed, was guiding their destiny must, in order to do so, also have been guiding the destiny of other nations.[26] That is to say, Israel's historical experience from (roughly) the eighth to the sixth centuries BC may have been the key which unlocked the truth of the uniqueness of Israel's God and his sovereign control over the destinies of all nations. The key-belief in the covenant between God and Israel could also be retained in a credible form and transformed through this hard-won theology of history, since it could obviously, after the Babylonian exile, no longer be upheld in its older form as including Israel's uninterrupted possession of the 'Promised Land'.

The notion, moreover, that it was only during the Babylonian exile that Israel acquired, through the efforts of the prophets, a new and firmer conviction concerning an exclusive type of monotheism, becomes even more plausible, when one recalls that it was, significantly, this period, referred to by Karl Jaspers as an 'Axial Age', that witnessed an important number of religious reforms not only in the

25 R. Clements, art. 'Monotheism', *op. cit.* (1983), p. 381.
26 Cf. William McNeill, *The Rise of the West* (Chicago, 1963), pp. 158ff.

ancient Near East but also further afield. In the sixth century, Zoroaster reformed the ancient religion of Persia, declaring *Ahura Mazda* as the sole High God: this was a monotheism based on revelation.[27] In the same period Buddha was active in India, Confucius in China, and the pre-Socratics in Asia Minor and southern Italy.[28] As for Israel herself, it was during the Babylonian exile (587–538 BC) that the writer of Deuteronomy and the prophets of this same period gave definitive shape to Israel's monotheism.[29]

However it should not be forgotten that even biblical monothe-

---

27 According to J. R. Hinnells (ed.), *Dictionary of Religions* (Harmondsworth, 1984), pp. 361ff., this date has been disputed. Some would place Zoroaster's dates much earlier, between c. 1700–1400 BC. However the history of Zoroastrianism before, roughly, the sixth century BC is little known. If the earlier date be accepted, this would make Zoroaster the first prophet in the history of religions. He has indeed been termed the first monotheist.

28 As exceptions to this general pattern one could cite Egypt and Assyria-Babylonia, where no renewal of religious vision occurred in the course of the first millennium BC. Not surprisingly, in the course of the next millennium these old cultures were to be taken over by Christianity and subsequently, and more thoroughly, by Islam.

29 It would be beyond the scope of this book to attempt to investigate the extent to which the experience of exile is conducive to the forging of new ideas. Given that in the sixth century BC the Ionian philosophers and the thinkers of Israel experienced exile, it seems plausible to suggest that exile can act as a spur to a renewed vision of reality, once the former reality is perceived as obsolete or lost. Perhaps one could go further and ask oneself whether all serious religious and metaphysical thought is a product of exile. For at the basis of religion and of the metaphysical search for 'reality' is the sense of the strangeness or 'foreignness' of the world, the sense that our real home, which is intuited as being elsewhere (*La vraie vie est absente*, as Rimbaud would have it), wherever it may be, is most certainly not here. As Kolakowski puts it: 'The crucial insight we find in religious experience, repeatedly recurring in various sacred books, may be summed up in one single word: alibi – elsewhere' (*Metaphysical Horror*, p. 28; cf. also *Religion*, pp. 50f.). It is interesting to reflect on the number of writers, especially in the nineteenth and twentieth centuries, who have at some point known the experience of exile, even if exile was not, strictly speaking, always forced upon them: for instance, Heine, Dostoevsky, Roth (Joseph), Pound, Joyce, Conrad, Nabokov, Solzhenitsyn, Alberti, Beckett, Canetti, Cioran, Ionesco, Kolakowski. It would be no doubt difficult to prove an infallible link between exile and literary creativity, but to suggest the existence of such a link appears to be not too far-fetched.

ism itself could be interpreted with differing emphases. It could be understood narrowly and exclusively as implying a complete denial of the validity of non-biblical religious traditions. Or again, as against this, it could be interpreted more widely and inclusively to accord some truth to non-biblical religions, with the claim that God had revealed himself in other ways through them (cf. Mal 1:11) or that he had been partly understood, albeit imperfectly within them (cf. Acts 17:23–28; Rom 1:18–23). This same tendency, i.e. to see some validity in non-biblical religion, is to be observed in the biblical use of concepts such as wisdom (cf. Wis 13:1ff.), and in the post-biblical period in the patristic notion of the *logoi spermatikoi*, i.e. the various reflections, scattered throughout world history, of the truth of the *logos* believed by Christians to be incarnate in Jesus.

As regards wisdom, the concept is not one that is restricted to the Old Testament. It links rather the Old Testament with the broader context of the ancient Near East. In Egypt and Mesopotamia, for instance, gods venerated for their wisdom can be found. However in Israel, the concept of wisdom was related exclusively to Yahweh, and within this perspective the highest form of wisdom was believed to be manifest in creation and, more inscrutably, in the course of human history. Moreover in Israel wisdom was never seen as exclusively speculative or intellectual, but its connection with piety was always kept to the forefront: the beginning of wisdom was *timor domini*.[30]

Summary

The Old Testament view of God is therefore rather paradoxical, presenting a notion of great complexity and elusiveness. God is personal, hence close to man and accessible, but he is so only by his own gracious will, not out of any necessity, since he is not part of our world, but transcends it and in no sense depends on it, while everything is dependent on God. Israel's God furthermore is specific and unique. He is associated in a special way with Israel from the time of Abraham onwards, but unlike the specific gods of other nations, Israel's God is claimed to be the God of all other peoples, and not just of Israel, and to be in fact the God of the whole universe and of the whole human race.

The New Testament

The New Testament, although based on what was from the orthodox Jewish point of view a heretical modification of the Old

---

30 Cf. Kolakowski, *Metaphysical Horror*, p. 92.

Testament tradition, nowhere repudiates the God of Judaism. The unity and transcendence of God, his creative role regarding the world, his governance of the world and ability to reveal himself within it, are taken over by the New Testament. But, in the words of Walter Kaufmann which paint at least half of the picture: 'Christianity was born of the denial that God could not possibly be seen… Christians were those who believed that God could become visible, an object of sight and experience, of knowledge and belief.'[31] God was re-defined in Jesus who, in Colossians 1:15, is described as 'the image of the invisible God'. Jesus, according to St John (Jn 1:18), is 'the only Son, who is in the bosom of the Father,' who 'has made him [the Father] known.' Names of God from the Old Testament (e.g. 'Lord' [*kyrios*]) were applied to Jesus, who was also identified as the Messiah promised to Israel. Post-biblical Judaism, being unable to abandon the notion of a Messiah still to come or to accept the doctrine of the incarnation, logically had to slough off the Christians as heterodox.

In the language of the Letter to the Hebrews (Heb 1:3) Jesus 'reflects the glory of God and bears the very stamp of his nature.' Jesus, however, does not supplant God, but is associated uniquely with him; and furthermore, in the New Testament witness he promises to send the Spirit who proceeds from the Father and comes to the church in the name of Jesus. Hence the Old Testament question regarding the name of God is answered in the New Testament in Jesus. God, in short, is for the Judaeo-Christian tradition not an impersonal force but a personal reality, who can and does communicate with man.

Moreover, just as in the time of the Old Testament the notion of wisdom was employed to forge connections between the religion of Israel and non-biblical religions, so too in the early Christian period wisdom – still regarded as inseparable from piety – came to be seen as one of the ways of interpreting Jesus and his relationship to God for the Hellenistic world. However for Christians the interpretation of wisdom itself shifted definitively when it incorporated the reality of Christ's crucifixion and resurrection. According to St Paul true wisdom is not the intellectual wisdom of the philosophers, but Christ crucified (cf. 1Cor 1:18, 22; 2:2).[32]

---

31 'Prologue' to Martin Buber, *I and Thou* (Edinburgh, 1970), p. 34; the first part of the above passage is quoted by Nicholas Lash, *Easter in Ordinary* (London, 1988), p. 207.

32 In modern times wisdom has again become a subject of speculation in

It is worth noting that the self-abasement or self-emptying of Christ to the point of death on the cross, expressed in Philippians 2:5–11, has also been understood as a prolongation and deepening of the same attitude of self-limitation manifest, according to some thinkers, in the divine act of creation itself.[33] This is of considerable interest to our main theme. For to speak of the self-limitation of God is a possible way of trying to imagine what is meant by the incomprehensibility or hiddenness of God, or God's withdrawal from direct human perception. As for our own sense of God's incomprehensibility or hiddenness, one vitally important way in which this arises in us, is in the reality of our freedom. Paradoxical though it may sound, to the extent that God remains hidden through his own self-limitation, and thus cannot be perceived by us in any straightforward, unmistakable way, he actually becomes a condition of our freedom, rather than a threat to it, as some modern critics of religion claim.

But to return to the New Testament descriptions of Jesus, in addition to being identified with divine wisdom, Jesus is also spoken of as the divine *logos* ('Word'). In the prologue to the fourth Gospel Jesus is described as the *logos* of God; the *logos* is the agent of creation, and in Jesus the same *logos* becomes the incarnate revelation of God. In the Greek philosophical tradition the *logos* ('reason') was the link between God and the universe, and the source and manifestation of order in the world. In the patristic period the *logos* was a title that could be exploited by Christian writers to forge links between biblical and Hellenistic thought, since the concept was deeply embedded in both traditions. The religious *logos* of Judaism and the rational *logos* of Hellenistic philosophy were in fact fused in order to try to convey the universal claims of the Christian faith in the then intellectually appropriate and most compelling way. The common ground between the two traditions, however, should not, and indeed could not, mask the differences between Greek rationalism and Christian faith in Jesus, the incarnate *logos*, whose sacrifice was believed to have redeemed suffering and sinful mankind.

With the New Testament dispensation came, then, new ideas about God. In the Old Testament God was seen as creator,

---

connection with the deity in the thought of Russian authors such as Soloviev and Bulgakov. These writers distinguish a created from an uncreated wisdom, which together form the unity of God and the world.

33 See Chapter 2, n.39.

redeemer, lawgiver, author of Messianic hope and source of wisdom; in the New Testament terms like Son, *logos*, incarnation, atonement, and Holy Spirit are used to describe the relationship between the God of the Old Testament and Jesus, the central figure in the New Testament. The understanding of God hinted at by this new terminology was to lead in the fifth century to the formulation of the classical Christian definition of God as a Trinity of three divine persons in one divine nature and it is belief in the Trinity that distinguishes Christianity from the religion that nurtured it, namely Judaism. However the old problem still remained: how can the transcendent God of the Old Testament be the God who is so present in the world that he can be said to be incarnate in Jesus Christ?

Transcendence and immanence

Two features of the biblical view of God that are of indispensable importance for Christianity are the already mentioned notions of God's transcendence *vis-à-vis* the world and his immanence in the world, and these must now be dealt with in some more detail.

Transcendence implies that the creator God of the Old Testament is the unique being who is over against the whole cosmos, the whole created order, both physical and spiritual. God is other than the world, other than man even in the latter's spiritual constitution. God is not identical with human consciousness. Moreover, because of God's transcendence man does not confront God as one unique centre of consciousness over against another. God is not simply a kind of super-being. Rather God is that reality without which nothing would exist, the reality presupposed by each existing thing or person. As Kafka writes somewhere, punning on the German word *sein* (at once the verb 'to be', and the third person possessive adjective), 'to be' means 'his', i.e. 'to belong to him [God]'.

To say that each person is grounded in the transcendent and unique God on whom everything depends is, however, a potentially misleading way of trying to express the relationship between God and man. It is misleading because it is suggestive of pantheism or monism. God can scarcely be, as Tillich would have it, the ground of our being. The ground of our being must itself surely also be a created reality, unless we wish to believe that we ourselves are in some sense divine by nature. This admittedly rudimentary line of argument does still leave unsettled the question of the connection between God and the ground of all created being. But perhaps it may always have to remain philosophically unsettled, since otherwise God would be 'known' and hence become our possession. Then of course God would no longer be God. But to the eyes of faith the connection can be described by the theological terms 'creation' and 'redemption'.

God's immanence in the world is a unique kind of immanence. It is certainly not to be understood primarily in terms of matter, time and space, as if it were the case that God is in, even if not contained in or confined by, all matter, time and space. Nor is immanence to be understood in any pantheistic sense, as if it referred to God's ontological immanence in the world, as if – after the model of the human soul and body – God were, so to speak, the world's soul, and the world God's body. If this were the case, the world would be necessary to God's being, or at least to the divine self-articulation or self-expression or self-development or self-becoming. Yet, as Kolakowski points out, some Christian thinkers have not shrunk from affirming precisely this. Thus in *Sermon on Luke*, 2:42 Meister Eckhart asserts: 'you are a thousand times more necessary to [God] than He is to you.'[34] Hegel too believed that the cosmos was a necessary stage through which Spirit [God] had to pass in order to become finally Itself. And for 'process thought' it is as true to say that God needs the world as it is to say that the world needs God.

However the traditional Christian understanding of divine transcendence and immanence seems to have been aimed at excluding two unacceptable ways of conceiving the relationship between God and the world. These possibilities are: (1) that God is completely separate from the world, and (2) that God is completely identical with the world. The former possibility would make the world altogether independent of God, and this would be a form of dualism. In this perspective, the notion of creation does not arise as a way of conceiving the relationship between God and the world, and furthermore redemption would appear to be unthinkable: for how can God redeem what he can have no contact with? The second possibility would be monism or pantheism, which again, as well as making creation a redundant concept, would also rule out any substantial notion of redemption, since God, being identical with the world, would be in as much need of being redeemed as the world itself – assuming always of course that the world is experienced as being in need of redemption. For how can that which is in need of redemption be itself the author of redemption? If Hegel is right in thinking that God and the world can only be notionally but not

---

34 Quoted in *Metaphysical Horror*, p. 94.

ontologically held apart, and hence that they belong together in an unbreakable union, then the term 'creation' becomes a misnomer for the link between God and the world, and 'redemption' can only be used to describe a necessary process of cosmic and human evolution.[35] But again, how could we know?

Yet in this latter model, there is perhaps a way out of the dilemma that afflicts traditional Christianity when it speaks of an infinite, absolutely perfect, immutable God who nevertheless creates a world that is not intrinsically divine, is not part of the definition of God and adds nothing to God's being. For this way of conceiving of God's relationship to the world appears to the eye of a perhaps naïve logic quite simply self-contradictory and intellectually untenable, making any personal relationship between God and us unthinkable. How can there be anything alongside of God? How can there be anything 'more than' infinity? Above all, if God is unchanging and unchangeable, how could he create, how could 'creation' not belong to the unchanging being of God, and hence not be creation at all, as traditionally understood? If God is, by definition, *actus purus*, all that he ever could be, incapable of any increase or decrease, what is the status of his putative creation? It seems, by definition, to be precisely 'nothing'.[36]

Christianity, in seeing the cosmos as creation *ex nihilo*, appears indeed to have harboured a constant suspicion that if it accepted a strong interpretation of the concept of divine transcendence *vis-à-vis* the world, a nihilistic evaluation of the world was always going to be the likely outcome of its theology. Small wonder that classical expressions of Christianity have tended to be world-renouncing and focused sharply on God.

However, the expression 'creation *ex nihilo*' seems to be itself perilously close to wordplay. For the term *nihil* is, strictly speaking, itself inconceivable, since the very concept of nothing, being something, would seem to be in flagrant and permanent contradiction to that which it is attempting to conceive. Hence, is the expression creation *ex nihilo* perhaps just another example of negative theology, that is to say a matter of ruling out, like the terms transcendence and immanence, unacceptable ways – such as dualism or pantheistic

---

35 Just in passing, one might advert to the connection between monism and fatalism that has often been commented on, for instance by John Updike, *Hugging the Shore* (Harmondsworth, 1985), p. 799.

36 Cf. Kolakowski's discussion of this quandary in *Metaphysical Horror*, pp. 82ff.

monism – of describing the God/world relationship, rather than being a positive statement of what in fact is the case?

To return to the notion of divine transcendence itself, one of its important implications is that God is not tied down to any particular aspect or aspects of the world. God transcends the limits and distinctions or differences of his creatures, indeed of his whole creation. The reason for this lies simply in the fact that God is the source of such limits and distinctions and characteristics: as their source and origin, he cannot simply be one more instance of them. As the source of all finite realities and of their interrelations he transcends all experienced substances and all ordinary relations and interrelations and causes. Thus he is not bound to any particular place or time, but he is free to make himself available to all existence and to all human beings at all times.

The transcendent God of the bible is 'totally other' than the world, and it is in fact only in virtue of this that he is at the same time the 'not-other' (Nicholas of Cusa), who in his own specific otherness transcends the differences that exist between one object and another, and between one human individual and another. Differences between distinct objects and people are necessary for the maintaining of all their separate identities; but the difference between God and any created reality is of another kind. It is what we mean by his transcendence, his otherness. And it is because his otherness from his creation is of such a unique kind that he can be present to, or immanent in, his creation in a unique way. This is what Hans Urs von Balthasar appears to mean when he writes: 'It is only because he [God] is transcendent and above the world that he is in it.'[37] In other words, it is actually – paradoxical though it may sound – God's transcendence that makes him relevant to the world rather than remote from the world. It is his transcendence that allows him to overcome and not be restricted by the world's differences, and to be present to, or immanent in, creation in a unique way. By the term immanence we imply furthermore that nothing exists outside of God or without God or independently of God. Yet the world, to repeat, is not itself God and adds nothing to God.

The notion of the transcendence and immanence of God must surely be invoked if we are to believe that in God omnipotence and goodness, justice and mercy, can co-exist.[38] This is the problem that

---

37 *Love Alone: The Way of Revelation*, ed. A. Dru (London, 1977), p. 122.
38 Cf. Edward Young, 'A God all mercy is a God unjust.' *The Complaint*: *Night Thoughts*. 'Night', iv, I. 233.

Dostoevsky raises through the character of Ivan Karamazov in *The Brothers Karamazov*. In purely human terms, it is difficult to see how someone could be absolutely just, and yet merciful enough to forgive sin and evil. The one would seem to contradict the other. It is only belief in the transcendence of God, in the fact that he is wholly other than man, that allows us, not to understand or know how, for example, the two attributes justice and mercy are not mutually incompatible in God, but at least to have faith and hope in the conviction that they are not. If God were not transcendent, not completely other than man, we could not even begin to believe that a combination of such qualities in God could be possible. And were God not immanent in the world and hence in human life, it is hard to see how one could believe that his justice and mercy could touch our lives, or be in any way relevant to them.

The difficulty with the modern attempt (since the time of Hegel) to see the relationship between God and the world as one of ultimate sameness, is that it must lead to a drastic modification of the Christian faith. The modification in question would be the abandonment of one of Christianity's deepest convictions, perhaps even its most essential tenet, namely the long-established and until recently non-negotiable distinction, inherited from ancient Israel, between God and the universe. That a Karl Barth felt compelled to reassert this doctrine so forcefully in this century is a sign that it had become insecure and no longer self-evident. Not, of course, that such a situation is unique, for arguments about the true nature of God, and about the nature of God's connection with the universe, are an inalienable part of the Judaeo-Christian tradition. One has only to think of the classical prophets of the Old Testament,[39] or the Arian controversy, or the Reformation, to be convinced of this.

If however one were to abandon the essential difference between God and the world, or, in other words, if one were to sacrifice the Christian doctrine of creation, one should not underestimate the magnitude of the change involved. For this change would make the traditional approach to the problem of evil, and the doctrine of redemption, henceforth untenable. It was the sense of the radical difference between the human and divine spheres, together with a corresponding belief in the transcendent otherness, holiness, absolute justice and perfection of God, emerging first in Israel and subsequently inherited by Christianity, it was this faith that gave

---

39 Cf. J. Bottéro, *Babylone et la bible*, pp. 254f.

coherence to the claim that evil could not possibly have its origin in God, but must have originated in man.

On the other hand, since God was not evil, but was the creator, it was not impossible that he could, should he wish, be the redeemer of the human race. For evil and the devastation it brings could not, as an aspect of the created order, be put on a level with God, but must, at least in theory, fall within the potentially healing ambit of God's power. The belief that God is truly transcendent to man means, however, that we can never know for sure how God can deal with the problem of evil, and hence any proposed solutions to this problem will – or at least should – always leave lingering doubts in the minds of the 'faithful'. In Mesopotamia belief in the superiority of the divine sphere to the human bred finally a sense of pessimism and resignation. The Babylonians were satisfied that this was the only 'solution' available to the question of evil and suffering; the gods, who knew the meaning of existence, were simply superior to human beings, who would always remain ignorant of it. But in Israel such satisfaction was resisted. Why? The reason suggested by Jean Bottéro[40] is that such a 'satisfying' solution to the problem of evil was in fact incompatible with Israel's belief in God's radical transcendence, for this belief precluded forever any humanly comprehensible (or satisfactory) solution to the problem of evil, (even the Babylonian 'solution' of resignation), but it did at the same time leave open a possibility that a solution did exist, albeit in the world of the divine, to which human intelligence has, however, no truly adequate access.

But if God's radical otherness is sacrificed, and, no matter how one tries to explain it, if God and the world are fitted under the one roof, so to speak, then evil, like everything else, becomes part, inalienably so, of the totality, that is to say, of God. Should such a change be made in the Judaeo-Christian tradition? Would it not be an even greater departure from Christianity than was Christianity's own early separation from Judaism? Would it not mean the end of Christianity?

---

40 If I have correctly interpreted his argument in *Babylone et la bible*, pp. 244ff., and especially pp. 248f.

CHAPTER FOUR

God in the early church

The abbot Allois said, 'Unless a man shall say in his heart, "I alone and God are in this world," he shall not find quiet.'
— The Sayings of the Fathers

The extreme of the known in the presence of the extreme
Of the unknown. — Wallace Stevens

Introduction

When the first Christians moved beyond the religious world of Judaism into the sphere of Graeco-Roman culture, they had to speak about the God of the bible to a world formed entirely outside the experience of Israel. The Christians' God was for this culture an unknown quantity, a fact consciously acknowledged in Acts 7:23, even if the world of Hellenism was not exactly unknown to Jews of the first century, as the language of the New Testament itself amply demonstrates.[1] In facing up to the difficulties inherent in what one might term the intellectual dimension of their missionary task, the early Christians had to deal with two basic problems. One resided in the difficulties inherent in the Christian idea of God itself, and the other lay in the problem of trying to express this view of God to a non-biblical culture.

How, in other words, were Christians to build bridges between the world of biblical faith and the outside world? How, to echo a famous phrase of Tertullian's, were they to build bridges between Jerusalem and Athens, between the church and the academy?

The Christians' need to understand the God they had inherited from Judaism brought into sharper focus difficulties that were already present in the Old Testament view of God. For the Old Testament presents a God who is unique, omnipotent, sovereign,

---

1 On the influence of Hellenism on Judaism, cf. generally the works of Martin Hengel. Arnoldo Momigliano in *Alien Wisdom* discusses the evidence for Hellenistic awareness of the Jewish tradition.

transcendent and eternal, and yet at the same time, a God who has created the world, cares for man, enters freely into relationship with him, and through the Jews, the people of the covenant, offers all mankind forgiveness and salvation. An obvious question which the Old Testament raises but does not answer is: how can God be transcendent to all the limited and specific forces and powers of our experience of nature, history and the self, and yet be related to history?

Leszek Kolakowski's answer to this quandary is to deny that the terms of the problem – in the traditional form outlined above – have been correctly stated. It may be indeed the case, he writes, that 'from the standpoint of Christian-Platonist orthodoxy' one must accept the doctrine of 'God's perfect actuality, omnipotence' and 'his uniquely privileged power of creation.'[2] However the bible tells a different story:

> The Bible's God is victim of all emotions, he is angry at, and frustrated with, the wayward manners of his subjects, but he loves them and he rejoices at seeing the kindness and obedience they display – albeit infrequently – in their lives. He is a god of love and he is a person in the same sense as we are... Within the language of the biblical myth in which God, though hidden, appears as a loving, if occasionally rather severe, protector, it is proper to say that his sadness in the face of our iniquities is no less real than his joy at the sight of the little good we prove to be capable of doing. If so, he is not a perfectly immutable Absolute, he is really growing through his creatures, he is, in other words, a historical god; it even appears that the very idea of the diffusion of divine love is not compatible with the absolute non-historicity and impassibility of the Creator, at least as long as those ideas of love and of impassibility retain the meaning we usually have in mind – and what other meaning could we construct? ... In fact, not only the Bible – as well as sacred scriptures of other civilizations – offers us the image of God who is not a total plenitude of being but enjoys the good deeds of the denizens of this universe and thus presumably becomes richer as a result. This speculation about God, who, in the act of self-alienation or even self-mutilation is growing in the body of the universe and in the painful toil of human creatures, is not absent in Platonizing currents of Christian theology: in Scotus Erigena, in Eckhart, in Cusanus, in the German pantheists of the sixteenth and seven-

teenth centuries. It seems as if God, in this view, had to smash the impenetrable shell of his aseity, to break out of his unity, to expand and to venture into the universe in order to become what he was only potentially: a person. His self-supported subsistence 'before' time is then inaccessible to us, inexpressible and even indifferent; it can really be thrust into the pale realm of negativity, of Nothingness. It is by becoming 'something' as a creator, lover and legislator, that God can be addressed or loved.[3]

One could ask whether Kolakowski perhaps overlooks the significance of the doctrine of the Trinity for understanding how God could be thought of as personal, even without the world.[4] Nevertheless, even accepting the classical doctrine of God as Trinity, one still has no easy intellectual answers to the question of how God and the world are related. For the bible nowhere explains how God can be transcendent, and yet related to history. Similarly it assumes but does not explain how God can be moral and just, the source of the law, and not slow to punish those who disobey it, and yet at the same time a God who shows mercy, patience, faithfulness and grace to his chosen people, and despite their infidelities promises them redemption. The New Testament compounds the problem of trying to reconcile God's justice with his mercy by pointing out that God allows his sun to shine and his rain to fall on all indiscriminately. And the Good News that Christ's death takes away the sins of the world still leaves in uneasy abeyance the question of what finally happens to those who continue to do evil.

The God the Christians had to persuade the Hellenistic world to accept was, therefore, a God full of apparent contradictions or, at least, tensions. God was, it was argued, transcendent but yet – as the doctrines of creation and redemption implied – related to human beings and their world. He was eternal – i.e. having no beginning outside of, and *a fortiori* within, time – and yet in some way temporal since he could deal with specific individuals like Abraham and Moses, and was incarnate in Jesus. He was changeless but somehow changing as well; actual yet in some sense potential; self-sufficient, and yet somehow dependent.

The Christians' task of explaining their view of God to outsiders was, it would appear, closely connected to their task of explaining it to insiders. For of course they had to try to understand it them-

---

3   *Ibid*, pp. 87–91.
4   Cf. below, Chapter 7, nn.113, 115.

selves before attempting to explain it to anyone else. In their efforts to make sense of their own experience of God they borrowed from the intellectual traditions of the Hellenistic culture of their day, the same culture which the Jewish thinker Philo (c. 20 BC–c. AD 50) had exploited in interpreting the Hebrew scriptures.

It could also be plausibly claimed that the early missionary zeal of Christianity, a zeal perhaps fuelled by the belief in the imminence of the parousia, was what brought the first Christians face to face with the need to put their beliefs about God into a form that would make sense to people of Hellenistic culture. At the same time this task enabled them to find the intellectual means of explaining their beliefs to themselves. The existential awareness of a non-Christian world, in short, forced the Christians to give an intellectual account of their faith to themselves as well as to outsiders.

The bridge between Jerusalem and Athens would seem then to have been constructed not only for the benefit of outsiders who were enabled by it to hear about Christianity, but also for the benefit of Christians themselves, in so far as they were enabled by it to find a medium through which their faith could be expressed intellectually, an element in which it could culturally survive and even thrive.

As has already been said, the possibility of using Hellenistic intellectual traditions for the purpose of interpreting biblical ideas had occurred to Jewish intellectuals such as Philo before the advent of Christianity. As a Jew living in a great cosmopolitan centre in the Hellenistic world, Alexandria, he was confronted with the problem of how to reconcile his Jewish faith with a prestigious non-Jewish culture. He was faced with the problem of deciding how much of his faith as mediated by the Jewish scriptures he could literally endorse, and how much did not make literal sense any longer, and would have to be reinterpreted to fit in with the standards of rationality established by the Hellenistic intellectuals who in his environment set the tone in these matters. Philo chose not to turn his back on pagan learning but to use it, where appropriate, in order to express his own Jewish faith. His example was to be followed enthusiastically by Christian intellectuals in their turn although, as it happened and for whatever reason, not by Jewish intellectuals in the same period.

Plato's doctrine of God

Since Christian thinkers of the early period (and of many later periods too) found the Platonist tradition most compatible with their own religious preoccupations, it might be helpful at this stage to mention briefly some aspects of Platonist thought which may provide a clue as to why Christian theologians have so often thought to detect in this current of philosophy a kindred spirit. In what follows I rely almost entirely on Andrew Louth's lucid book *The Origins of the Christian Mystical Tradition*, which, conveniently for our purposes, looks at Plato's thought with a view to the influence it subsequently exercised on Christian thinkers.

In Plato the comprehension of ultimate reality is governed by the belief that this reality is beyond knowledge and can only, if at all, be 'known' to the extent that it reveals itself to the soul, which receives this revelation in ecstasy or rapture. Knowledge of God is therefore not simply intellectual knowledge, but a knowledge which involves intimate communication with that which is known. Hence knowledge of God is more like union with God[5] or sharing in the divine life, than simply knowledge *about* God. In a somewhat similar sense the Socratic idea that virtue is knowledge should not be taken in a narrowly intellectual or cerebral sense, but should be seen to include the practical living out of the virtuous life which alone brings real knowledge of virtue. It is perhaps interesting in this context to note Nietzsche's understanding (misunderstanding?) of the ancients' placing of virtue above knowledge as something that has been finally and, from his point of view, not regrettably overcome: 'In antiquity the dignity and recognition of science were diminished by the fact that even her most zealous disciples placed the striving for *virtue* first, and one felt that knowledge had received the highest praise when one celebrated it as the best means to virtue. It is something new in history that knowledge wants to be more than a mere means.'[6]

From a rather different angle Louth writes: 'Knowledge (*episteme, noesis*) is for Plato more than knowledge *about*: it implies identity with, participation in, that which is known ... For Plato real knowledge is more than intellectual awareness – it implies the orientation of the whole person so that one participates in the realm of Ideas or Forms.'[7] Indeed the contemplation of the Forms of the Good and the Beautiful (see the *Republic* and the *Symposium*) is dif-

---

5   A. Louth, *The Origins of the Christian Mystical Tradition* (Oxford, 1981), p. 13.

6   *The Gay Science*, III, 123, tr. W. Kaufmann (New York, 1974) p. 180.

7   *Op. cit.*, p. 2.

ferent from that of the other Forms, and 'cannot be simply called knowledge (*episteme*).'[8]

Transcendent knowledge moreover cannot, as has been indicated, be gained by the soul's unaided exercise of its own powers. Ultimate reality – which is what Plato seems to mean by such expressions as the Form of the Good, or the Form of the Beautiful – is beyond knowledge since it is itself the cause of all reality and the source of the conditions which make knowledge of reality possible in the first place.

Thus the Form of the Good is not simply that which is most truly real but, further, it is the source of all true reality, the source of both being[9] (in *The Republic* Plato sees Goodness as being beyond being) and knowledge, and hence the source of all perception in the realm of the understanding. To the extent, therefore, that it is the 'cause of knowledge and truth', it is beyond knowledge and truth, and in consequence must be itself unknowable.[10]

'Knowledge' of eternal truth is difficult to attain in this world of 'change and illusion'[11] because the soul is here cut off from the world it used to inhabit, and hence it can no longer remember the vision of truth and beauty it once contemplated. For before being joined at birth to a body, the soul lived in the world beyond the heavens, where the Forms are located. Consequently there is a kinship between the soul and the world of the divine, the soul's real home to which it longs to return during its time on earth.

---

8 *Op. cit.*, p. 13.
9 The assertion of a causal relationship between the 'ultimately (transcendently) real' and empirically experienced reality raises the perennial question of the precise nature of this relation: is it necessary, accidental, or freely willed (on the part of the ultimately real)? Is there, moreover, an absolute, radical difference between the two spheres, so that even the use of a univocal term like 'sphere' should be avoided? Or do the two spheres exist within a common, all-encompassing context? Is 'reality', in a word, all of a piece, or is there an indestructible line of demarcation between the world human beings experience, and the world of the 'divine'? Platonists of various hues will always come down on the side of monism or the indivisibility of being, if one may so put it. Christians (and gnostics?), on the other hand, believe in a real and unchanging distinction in status between creator and creation, and are thus constantly open to the charge of dualism. Christians vehemently deny this charge (while insisting nonetheless on the radical difference in status between creator and creation), whereas gnostics willingly accept it.
10 Cf. Louth, *op.cit.*, pp. 12f.
11 *Op. cit.*, p. 1.

The knowledge the soul can have of this earthly world of change and appearance is not, for Plato, true knowledge at all but mere 'conjecture and opinion'.[12] For real knowledge is 'certain, and the object of knowledge must therefore ... be immutable, eternal.'[13] Contemplation of the Forms of Truth, Beauty and Goodness is alone real knowledge, and in this world the soul can only regain such knowledge, albeit imperfectly, through a process of remembering, whereby what the soul knew before its descent into time at birth is recalled. What memory remembers thus preceded time. Within the limits of this earthly life the full regaining of knowledge of the truly Real is not possible. Hence the aim of philosophy – which is to seek such knowledge – is one that transcends this life and can only be satisfied after death.

The bible and Greek wisdom

What was, we may now ask more specifically, the Greek wisdom that the Christians absorbed in order to express their idea of God? The first thing to note is that they did not attempt to explicate their beliefs by borrowing from the religious heritage of the Hellenistic world. Rather they turned away completely from 'the gods of the various religions' and concentrated their attention on 'the God of the philosophers'.[14] It is worth recalling that in similar circumstances the Israelites had always refused to assimilate their God to the gods of the surrounding religions, but they had, as the Wisdom Literature of the Old Testament shows, seen a valid link between the worship of Yahweh and the pursuit of authentic human wisdom; and in the New Testament itself the link between Israel's God and human rationality is ratified in the *logos* doctrine.

In other words, the Christians were clear that the God of Jesus Christ had nothing to do with the gods of the pagan Graeco-Roman world but – despite what Pascal was to say later – they had no difficulty in claiming that their God and the God of the philosophers were one and the same. The early church rejected therefore the whole spectrum of ancient Mediterranean religions, regarding

---

12 *Ibid.* Plato here follows Parmenides (c. 500 BC), who described all approximate knowledge of the changing world of daily experience as not real knowledge at all, but simply 'opinion' (*doxa*), a term hovering uneasily between true knowledge and sheer error (cf. Jeanne Hersch, *L'étonnement philosophique. Une histoire de la philosophie*, Paris, 1993, pp. 19f.).

13 Louth, *op. cit.*, p. 1.

14 J. Ratzinger, *Introduction to Christianity* tr. J. R. Foster (London, 1968), p. 94.

them all as untrue and illusory. The Christians chose instead to explain their faith by saying that their God was Being itself – that which the philosophers described as the God above all the forces of the created order. The God of the philosophers, the God reached by the human *logos* rather than by the beautiful and profound myths of ancient religions: this was the God the Christians recognised as their own. In so doing they 'desacralised' the world of the time and its religious traditions.[15]

One should however point out that a 'demythologising' process, to use a modern term, had in the Greek world itself long been carried out by the philosophers themselves. At about roughly the same time as the great Hebrew prophets were active, Greek thought quite independently of the prophets' achievements had for its part come to discover the existence of a supreme being transcending the world. This was the discovery that Aristotle in fact eventually made. But even before Aristotle the mythical gods of Greek religion had been demythologised by the philosophers from the pre-Socratics down to Plato. In Greece the meeting of faith and reason, myth and *logos*, led finally – among the admittedly tiny band of 'intellectuals' only, of course – to the defeat of mythical religion and to the triumph of reason or critical thinking.

By the time of Christianity, therefore, and indeed long before it, the gods of Greek traditional religion had become incredible to the eyes of philosophical reason. The Greek *logos* had destroyed the gods of mythology, just as the classical Hebrew prophets had destroyed and demythologised the gods of their world in favour of the one and only God, Yahweh. The gods of the Greeks weakened and disappeared because the gulf between them and the God of the philosophers became simply too wide, as piety and reason diverged totally.

Historically, it is true, the ancient religions, although inwardly defunct as far as thinking people were concerned, lingered on well into the Christian era and were held in veneration even by intellectuals like Origen's famous adversary Celsus, as part of an immemorial social and cultural tradition. The outward trappings of the ancestral religions were therefore maintained even when their inner soul had long since died.

It is of some interest to note that one of the main objections the

15 This assertion would seem to be supported by the fact that the Catholic church is often seen from a Protestant perspective to represent a 'paganisation' of Christianity. Cf. F. Overbeck, *Über die Christlichkeit unserer heutigen Theologie* (Darmstadt, 1974), p. 92.

pagan intellectuals of classical antiquity made against Christianity
was that, unlike their traditional religions, Christianity was what
from a contemporary perspective might be called a very modern
phenomenon. Yet although pagan intellectuals such as Celsus saw
in Christianity's only recent appearance a reason for abhorring it, it
was precisely this feature of the new faith that made it attractive for
others. In the words of A. N. Whitehead: ' ... Democracy in modern
times, and Christianity in the Roman Empire, exemplify articulated
beliefs issuing from aspirations, and issuing into aspirations. Their
force was that of consciously formulated ideals at odds with the
ancestral pieties which had preserved and modulated existing
social institutions. For example, we find the Christian theologian,
Clement of Alexandria, exhorting his contemporaries to shun custom ... Those Christian ideals were among the persuasive agencies
refashioning their respective ages.'[16] It is slightly curious to see the
old objections to Christianity surfacing once again in such a modern
figure as Nietzsche. Yet his admiration for the pre-Christian culture
of antiquity – undoubtedly due in part to the nostalgia for (an idealised?) Greece that was such a conspicuous feature of the German
intellectual tradition from the eighteenth century onwards – seems
to have been fired less by love for ancient Greece than by loathing
of contemporary Christianity.[17]

But to return to the early church, the Christians countered the
objection against the newness of their faith by claiming that truth
was more important than tradition, a point of view implied in
Tertullian's statement: 'Christ called himself truth, not custom.'[18]
The general point Tertullian is making is echoed much later by
Newman in his *Apologia Pro Vita Sua*. Newman argued that the
church of his own day could not appeal to the witness of the early
church as true simply on the grounds of its antiquity, because in
that period the church was not itself antique. The appeal to the early
church could only be persuasive if what the early church had to say
was actually true.

This fundamental preference for truth over tradition is, at least

---

16 *Adventures of Ideas* (Cambridge, 1943), pp. 6f.
17 Cf. the following statements from *The Anti-Christ*: 'Christianity was the
     vampire of the *Imperium Romanum* ... (§58) ... The whole labour of the
     ancient world in vain ... (§59) ... Christianity robbed us of the harvest
     of the culture of the ancient world ... (§60)' (tr. R. J. Hollingdale,
     Harmondsworth, 1990, pp. 190,192,193).
18 *De virginibus velandis* I,1, in *Corpus Christianorum seu nova Patrum collec-
     tio* (C. Chr.), II, p. 1209. Quoted by J. Ratzinger, *op. cit.*, p. 97.

in theory, a hallmark of Christianity, and any abandonment of this characteristic of what is authentically Christian would lead eventually to the disintegration of the Christian faith. The early Christians made a choice for the truth, for the *logos*, for the God of the philosophers, over the gods or the piety of traditional Graeco-Roman religion, even when this choice brought them into political conflict with the state. In short, they declared that their religion was a religion of the truth, that their God was the truth, and in so doing they, implicitly and often explicitly, let it be known that ancient religious tradition by itself, or considerations of political pragmatism alone, could not be the truth.[19] In thus casting aside the option of making common cause with the religious world of the Roman Empire in favour of the God of the philosophers, the early Christians aligned themselves with something that was not regarded by the ancient world as having any obvious religious significance at all.

It is worth recalling at this point that the history of Greek philosophical thought is rich and complex. It lasted for over one thousand years, from the time of the pre-Socratics to the closing of the famous philosophical schools in Athens by order of the Christian Emperor Justinian in the sixth century. In this long tradition there developed two quite contrasting ways of interpreting the nature of the divinity and its relation to the world. On the one hand, there was the conception of the deity as the supreme, sublime and ineffable principle of truth, beauty and goodness, the One about which nothing, strictly speaking, could be said, but which was the origin of all things, though itself timeless. In Neoplatonism 'the One, though sometimes spoken of as God, is not a person. It is unknowable. The Intellect knows that there is a One, but not what it is like. Hence it ... can be spoken of only by way of negation.'[20] On the other hand, the deity could be conceived as a ruling soul or *demi-*

---

19 It was perhaps because of their agreement on the importance of truth that Christianity and Platonism were able to draw so close together, as Nietzsche was much later to suspect (cf. *The Gay Science* §344). However, in the context of Nietzsche's suspicion about the value of 'truth', it should be pointed out that there has in fact always been in the Christian tradition a reluctance to identify God too simplistically with 'truth'. In this regard one could mention Pascal: 'We make an idol of truth itself; for truth without charity is not God, but his image and idol, which we must neither love nor worship' (quoted by Aldous Huxley, *The Devils of Loudun*, Harmondsworth, 1971, p. 326).

20 D. J. O'Connor (ed.), *A Critical History of Western Philosophy* (New York, 1985), p. 76.

urge who moulds and fashions the world in the light of ultimate principles or forms. (One curious, though in fact quite logical, consequence of this belief was that Plato, according to Pascal Quignard, strictly disapproved of landscaping, since it involved for him an implicit rivalry with the *demiurge* who had shaped the world in which we find ourselves.[21])

Although theoretically both of these possibilities – i.e. seeing God either as the remote 'One' or the involved 'demiurge' – lay open to Christian theologians, as they sought to explicate their biblical notion of God with the help of Greek philosophy, in practice they chose to identify their God with the first, more sublime conception of the deity. Hence God 'was conceived as the utterly transcendent, timeless, changeless absolute which, like Plato's Form of the Good, was "beyond being in dignity and power", so that very little could be predicated of it. The attributes of this One were largely negatively defined. "He" was absolutely simple (containing no complexity or distinctions, except those of the Trinity), immutable (in no sense capable of change), eternal (in no sense subject to time), ubiquitous or omnipresent (in no sense subject to space), infinite (in no sense limited), omnipotent (in no sense limited in power) and uncaused (possessing aseity).'[22]

The God of the philosophers, the supreme being transcending the world, was ultimately the discovery of Aristotle; it was a God who was remote, severe and almost inaccessible. He was 'more a supreme thought ("A thought which thinks itself") than a sovereign existence.'[23] Furthermore, he will not initiate personal relations or enter into a covenant with human beings. The God of Aristotle is indifferent to mankind. In the tradition of Greek rationalism to which Aristotle belongs there is no equivalent to the Book of Job or to the Psalms,[24] to say nothing of a crucified redeemer. Nietzsche was to look, revealingly, in the culture of Greek antiquity, to 'Dionysus', not to Aristotle's God, as an alternative to Christ. Moreover, Aristotle's God exercised hardly any influence at all on everyday life in the Greek cities; he remained confined to the attentions of a few intellectuals.[25]

---

21 Cf. P. Quignard, *Le sexe et l'effroi* (Paris, 1994), pp. 69f.
22 Van A. Harvey, *A Handbook of Theological Terms* (London, 1964), p. 92.
23 Jean Milet, *God or Christ?* tr. J. Bowden (London, 1981), p. 7.
24 Oedipus, for instance, is pitted against a destiny he can neither evade nor hope to be redeemed from.
25 Cf. Milet, *op. cit.*, pp. 7f.

Yet such general statements cannot stand without qualification. As A. H. Armstrong points out: 'It would be an entirely misleading generalization to say that the Greek philosophical conception of God is impersonal; rather, there is a continual tension and interplay between personal and impersonal ways of thinking about God, between thinking about him in terms of human thought and action and thinking about him in terms of natural forces or abstract concepts, which appears as crude, if rather likeable, inconsistency in the Stoics, but is also present in subtler forms in the thought of Plato and Aristotle.'[26]

Despite such qualifications it is still a tolerable generalisation to state that Aristotle's God was not only remote from the various gods of the Roman Empire, but that he also appeared remote from the God of the bible. In taking over the God of the philosophers therefore, and in identifying him with the God of biblical faith, the Christians could not but alter radically the significance of the philosophers' God. This God had previously been understood as pure being or pure thought. He was impersonal, eternal, immutable. Now those who identified him with the God of the Christians saw him as a God concerned with mankind. He was no longer seen simply as the ultimate source of the order in the universe, or as truth, but now he was also perceived as love. And the measure of that love was declared to be Jesus Christ, the 'crucified God', to repeat a phrase of Pascal's.[27]

The Christian philosophical tradition

We can now examine more closely the process whereby the early Christian Church sought to express its faith in a sophisticated philosophical idiom. The attempt to forge a new understanding of the biblical God in the thought categories of Greek philosophy was made difficult for two quite specific reasons which, by reinforcing the concept of God's transcendence, exacerbated some of the problems already inherent in the biblical understanding of God. In the first place, the main Greek philosophical notion of God had stressed the absoluteness, transcendence and immutability of God. Whether Christian theologians found Platonist ideas about the divinity compatible with the gospel or not they all were agreed that their understanding of the relation between creator and creature required 'the

---

26 A. H. Armstrong and R. A. Markus, *Christian Faith and Greek Philosophy*, (London, 1964), p. 14.
27 *Pensées* fr. 964.

concept of an entirely static God, with eminent reality, in relation to an entirely fluent world, with deficient reality.'[28] Not surprisingly therefore, when biblical faith was expressed with the assistance of Greek philosophical categories, the biblical view of divine transcendence emerged stronger and clearer than ever.

Secondly, in the formative period of Christian theology, and indeed in the entire later Hellenistic stages of the Graeco-Roman philosophical tradition (i.e. from c. 200 BC-AD 400) the sense of the reality, value and ultimate meaning of the changing, temporal, material world, and of earthly, human, historical life grew ever weaker.[29] This cultural and, above all, psychological fact worked likewise to reinforce the importance of the transcendent aspect of God in the philosophical, and hence ultimately in the Christian, view of God.

The upshot of all this was that the divine came to be interpreted as that which infinitely transcends change, time, matter, and history. As a perfectly natural consequence, those transcendent and absolute aspects of the creator God of the bible were intensified and extended in the conceptualisation of God that developed from about 150 to 400. God came to be seen as eternal, in the sense of utterly non-temporal; necessary, in the sense of absolutely non-contingent; self-sufficient, in the sense of absolutely independent; changeless, in the sense of participating in and relating to no change; purely spiritual, in the sense of having no contact with material reality, and of being thus unaffected by and apparently unrelated, and even unrelatable, to the world.

The absoluteness of this conception of God did not flow, therefore, entirely from the philosophy that the patristic writers had inherited. It flowed equally from the nature of their spirituality which stressed, as most Hellenistic – pagan and Christian – spirituality did, the victory of the incorruptible, immortal and changeless principle of deity over the corruptible, mortal and transient character of creaturely life. Transience was thus seen as man's greatest problem. In such circumstances the divine is and must be that which transcends and wins the ultimate, eternal victory over the transience of human, mortal flesh.

As recently as the First Vatican Council the same basic notion of

---

28 A. N. Whitehead, *Process and Reality* (New York, 1929), p. 526.

29 Cf. E. R. Dodds, *Pagan and Christian in an Age of Anxiety: Some Aspects of Religious Experience from Marcus Aurelius to Constantine* (Cambridge, 1965).

God was restated in the Dogmatic Constitution on the Catholic
Faith *Dei Filius* (1870), in order to confront the threats posed to the
Christian concept of God by the various materialistic and pantheistic
currents of thought that were influential in the nineteenth century.[30]
The notion of the transcendence and immutability of God is thus
one that has had a very long history, from the patristic period down
to modern times, although it has recently, as we shall see, come in
for much criticism. For it is difficult to see how the immutable God
can be related to history.

But it should not be forgotten that, in transforming the philosophical notion of God, the early Christians challenged a way of
thinking about God that is deeply anchored in human nature: this is
to think of God as great by our standards and thus to lose sight of
the fact that those standards cannot be used to measure God. We
might, for example, want to think of God as so great that he could
not possibly be concerned about human beings. God's transcendence, however, implies that he can be present completely to the
tiniest fragment of his creation, and hence to human beings. An epi-
taph composed for St Ignatius of Loyola by an anonymous Jesuit
contains the line (used by Hölderlin as the epigraph for his novel
Hyperion): *Non coerceri maximo, contineri tamen a minimo, divinum est*
('Not to be encompassed by the greatest, but to let oneself be
encompassed by the smallest – that is divine').[31] This gives a neat

---

30 'The Holy, Catholic Roman Church believes and confesses: there is one
God, true and living, Creator and Lord of heaven and earth, mighty,
eternal, immense, incomprehensible, infinite in his intellect and will
and in all perfection. As he is one unique and spiritual substance,
entirely simple and unchangeable, we must proclaim him distinct from
the world in existence and essence, blissful in himself and from himself,
ineffably exalted above all things that exist or can be conceived besides
him.' Among the condemnations appended to the decree the following
two are noteworthy for the emphasis they place on divine transcendence: (1) 'If anyone says that the substance and essence of God and all
things is one and the same, *anathema sit*.' (2) 'If anyone says that finite
beings, the corporeal as well as the spiritual, or at least the spiritual
ones, have emanated from the divine substance; or that the divine
essence becomes all things by self-manifestation or self-evolution; or
lastly that God is the universal or indefinite being which, by self-deter-
mination, constitutes the universality of beings, differentiated in genus,
species and individuals, *anathema sit*.' (Quoted from *The Christian Faith*
ed. J. Neuner and J. Dupuis, Dublin and Cork, 1973, pp. 108f.)
31 Cited by J. Ratzinger, *op. cit.*, p. 101.

summary of what Christian faith understands by 'God'. For God's greatness lies in the fact that he who has created and sustains all being reaches also beyond the totality of created being, and hence to him it is, even in its totality, 'small'. At the same time he can reach down to the smallest part of his creation because to him nothing is small or insignificant as it often seems to us. In the words of Dionysius the Areopagite: '[I]t must be borne in mind that no single existing thing is entirely deprived of participation in the beautiful, for, as the true word says, all things are very beautiful'.[32]

The overturning of conventional notions of greatness, especially as regards our idea of God, is central to the Christian faith, and can be found in other religions and cultures equally.[33] The transcendent creator and redeemer God of Christianity is simply incommensurable with our universe. Since he is not part of the universe, nor the whole of it, since he is infinite, he cannot be measured by our inner-worldly notions of great and small. This is one way in which his unknowability becomes palpable.

The question still remains, however, of how we are to know this God. If God is truly absolute, truly transcendent, wholly other than we are, there can be nothing in our experience with which to compare him, hence he must remain unknown and unknowable, and cease to be the personal God of the bible. If, on the other hand, we think of God rather in terms of his relation to the world, do we not run the risk of anthropomorphism? Yet how is this risk to be avoided, given that we cannot but think in human terms?

To put the matter in slightly different language: 'God' is a term referring to religion's central concern, to the reality believers worship, to whom they pray, to whom they look for guidance, redemption, enlightenment, happiness. This is, one might say, the existential buzz the term possesses. But 'God' refers also, historically, to the ultimate intellectual explanation, source, meaning and goal of all life, the elusive reality pursued by philosophers and historians of religion. Now if God can bear these two differing meanings (as a focus for personal piety, and as the ultimate philosophical explanation of the world), how can these two senses be combined? The problem becomes even more difficult if the deity, the absolute power originating and sustaining all life, is taken to be either absolutely incomprehensible or an unchangeable, infinite, impassible,

---

32 *The Celestial Hierarchies*, Chapter II, (Surrey, 1965), pp. 25f.
33 Cf. Chuang Tzu: 'Achievement is the beginning of failure, / Fame is the beginning of disgrace.'

omniscient and omnipotent being. How can the faith in God that comes to expression in personal symbols be reconciled with the belief reflected in the symbol of the incomprehensible *One* of mystical experience, or the impassible, omniscient, omnipotent Absolute of abstract theology and philosophy? For if the personal symbols (God as father, shepherd, lover) are taken seriously, Christianity seems to degenerate into anthropomorphism; if, on the other hand, the symbols of absoluteness are taken as primary, the heart of biblical religion seems to be destroyed.

But what is historically curious in the Christian tradition is that it is not those who have insisted on the absoluteness of God who have tended to argue for his unknowability. Rather it is those who have stressed the more biblical view of God as personal and involved in the world who have asserted his unknowability and man's need for revelation in order to know him. Those, on the other hand, who have stressed God's absoluteness and immutability have been quite insistent about claiming that God's existence can be demonstrated by reason. What no one seems to have achieved is a view of God that holds on to the personal, biblical language about God while retaining the classical philosophical insistence on the divine absoluteness, immutability and perfection.

The dehellenisation of dogma?

The process by which the church Fathers thought through their belief in God with the help of Greek philosophical ideas has often been termed the hellenisation of dogma. Since at least the time of Adolf von Harnack (1851–1930)[34] the idea has been popular that the simple Galilean gospel was corrupted, or at least obscured and unnecessarily complicated, by Hellenistic metaphysics, and hence that Christianity urgently needs to dehellenise itself in order to recover its pristine purity and thus presumably become relevant to the modern age. In Catholic circles a conspicuous champion of this cause has been Leslie Dewart, who claims that 'the integration of theism with today's everyday experience requires not merely the *demythologisation of scripture* but the more comprehensive *dehellenisation of dogma*, and specifically that of the Christian doctrine of God.'[35] One might just remark in passing that it is difficult to see

---

34 Harnack described the dogma formulated by the Catholic tradition 'in its conception and development ... a work of the Greek spirit on the soil of the Gospel' (*History of Dogma*, tr. N. Buchanan, London, 1905, vol. 1, p. 17).
35 L. Dewart, *The Future of Belief: Theism in a World Come of Age* (London, 1966), p. 49.

why it is now regarded as a good thing to try to make Christianity intelligible to the modern age, and yet it is often regarded as a bad thing for the early Fathers to have adapted Christianity to the intellectual traditions of Hellenistic culture.

Behind modern calls for the dehellenisation of doctrine is a variety of considerations. It is claimed, for example, that the traditional Christian dogmatic view of God was worked out in an ahistorical fashion. Man is however a historical being, and hence all his utterances concerning the meaning of human existence and, by implication, concerning God, are all radically historical too and can never have any absolute but only a relative validity. Indeed in a historicist perspective, the very notion of absoluteness is suspect, and would appear to have only a verbal existence. Moreover, it is argued, an ahistorical, 'absolute' God would be irrelevant to historical man's concerns. A further reason for dissatisfaction with the traditional understanding of God is, it is alleged, that this traditional view yields a static God, whereas what man really needs is an involved, dynamic God.

Historically this seems a very shaky thesis. If the early Christians had not attempted to make their faith available for a wider public by developing a philosophical theology, it is likely that Christianity would never have become a distinct world religion, but would have remained a sect of Judaism and, like the Jewish-Christian sect of the Ebionites – a branch of Christianity that refused to compromise with the 'world' – would eventually have disappeared.

Moreover, the modern hostility to the Christian dogmatic tradition seems to ignore the extent to which the theologians who created this tradition did not take over Greek philosophical ideas lock, stock, and barrel, but often modified these ideas on the basis of the biblical witness. Hence, rather than talking of a hellenisation of dogma, it might be more accurate to speak about a christianisation of Greek philosophy. Nevertheless, it would probably have to be conceded that the 'folly of the cross', which in some modern theology has been more deliberately thematised, was somewhat toned down in the early centuries as the result of the development of a philosophical theology. Certainly Yeats' evocative lines: 'Odour of blood when Christ was slain/Made all Platonic tolerance vain/And vain all Doric discipline',[36] could scarcely serve to characterise the general spirit of the patristic theological enterprise. On the other hand,

36 W. B. Yeats, *Collected Poems* (London, 1977), p. 240.

it should not be overlooked that the 'dogmatic' efforts of the early
Christian thinkers often served as a protection against an intellectualisation or rationalisation of Christian truth. For, in the development
of both the Trinitarian and Christological controversies, the main
place to look for a hellenisation of Christianity is in the heresies
against which the dogmatic creeds and councils were directed,
assuming that orthodoxy itself is not, as is sometimes said, simply a
successful heresy. One might make this mistaken assumption, were
one to imagine that dogmas were ever supposed to be ultimate and
exhaustive explanations of the mysteries of Christianity, whereas,
as Balthasar pointed out, dogmas are, on the contrary, rather like
fences around the mysteries. They draw attention to where the
mysteries lie but refuse ever to try to spell out their meaning definitively. In short, the church's dogmatic tradition is a tangible sign of
how God is believed by Christian faith to lie beyond our comprehension.

In the early centuries it was those theologians who had too
philosophically uncompromising a view of the unity and absolute
transcendence of God who were, then, regarded as heretical by the
church. The subordinationists – strains of whose ideas can be found
in Justin and Origen and most explicitly in Arius – maintained, for
example, the absolute transcendence of God by subordinating the
Son and the Holy Spirit to the Father. This was the most rational
interpretation of Christianity, but it was rejected. A related tendency
that was declared heretical was the monarchianism whose interpretation of monotheism tried to take as rigorously as possible the
notion of the absolute unity of God.

The attempt to express the Christian understanding of God with
the help of Greek philosophy undoubtedly produced tensions in
writers like Origen and Augustine, who wrote both apologetic
works addressed to pagans and biblical expositions for Christians.
However, the liveliness of the God-question is surely not unrelated
to the tension that undoubtedly exists in the Christian understanding of God and which was explicitly present from the beginning, in
the New Testament itself, and then subsequently in the first sustained efforts made by the patristic writers to explicate their vision
of God with the assistance of Greek thought.

This tension is probably not capable of being resolved, thus
ensuring the permanent attraction of the Christian idea of God,
given that the unknown and inaccessible, that from which we are
excluded, is always more alluring than the known (as Swann in

Proust's famous novel was irresistibly attracted by the 'vie incon-
nue' of Odette), and represents thus a perennial challenge to the
mind. Dogma, paradoxically, rather than being a prohibition on
rational enquiry into the meaning of the Christian faith, and especially into the meaning of the Christian doctrine of God, is in fact a
spur to the human intellect to seek ever new ways of elucidating the
redemptive mystery of faith. If that mystery were ever to be entirely
rationalised or understood, it would become an item of knowledge
and thereby cease to be of continuing intellectual interest. If, in
other words, the unknowability of God were to be overcome – a
move that would, implicitly, offer an intellectual solution to the
problem of evil – the Christian faith would perish.

The unsettled nature of the Christian notion of God

To sum up: the Christian view of God revolutionised the concept of
God of Greek philosophy in two principal ways. Firstly, whereas
the God of the philosophers is absolute, separate from the world
and self-contained, the God of Christian faith can and does enter
into relationship with human beings; secondly, whereas the God of
the philosophers is based on the conviction that thought or the
mind alone is divine, the Christian God is love as well as thought or
reason or *logos*. The *logos* or *raison d'être* of the world is at the same
time love. The ultimate truth about reality, in short, according to
Christianity and its view of God, is love, love as revealed in Jesus
Christ.

However, the primacy of the God of the bible, the God of faith,
over the intellectual concept of God is, it is essential to note, a primacy that cannot be regarded as fixed once and for all, or gained in
the ancient world, never again to be lost. It is true that the early
Christians revolutionised the philosophical notion of God by insisting that God is love and loves mankind, hence that love is higher
than pure thought. However that revolution in the human understanding of God is one that constantly has to be remade.

In the modern age, for instance, many find the idea that God is
love, incarnate in Jesus, and that he cares for human beings, hope-
lessly and helplessly naïve and incredible. One might note in passing the remark on God in Samuel Beckett's play *Fin de partie*: 'Le
salaud! Il n'existe pas!' Indeed the vision of life central to Beckett's
work, evoked in the title: *I Gave up before Birth*, presents an almost
Calvinistic version of atheism, where the dominant note is a fatalistic one, as if the hopeless predicament of Beckett's protagonists (if

that is not too energetic a term) were settled from all eternity, and had nothing specifically to do with their lives. In this sense, for Beckett life is not 'The vale of Soul-making', as for Keats, but a place of torment where no improvement in the human lot can be worked for, and from which only death offers a final, but still inconclusive, still inscrutable release.

The Christian notion that God is love might be seen therefore as offering hostages to fortune, and ultimately, in the fullness of time, as providing, ironically, ammunition to those who would wish to undermine belief in a good God altogether. In the light of the suffering and evil of existence the idea that man on his little planet is the apple of God's eye, indeed that the whole vast cosmos was made by, through and for the Son of God who became man in Jesus Christ – all of this seems to be the height of wishful thinking or even of human conceit.

Yet while the God of love is a difficult God for the modern – or any – age to accept, a God vaguely intuited as a 'supreme being' one could intellectually grope towards, may be acceptable enough to those who still feel that there must be 'something'[37] behind the vast cosmos we inhabit, sustaining and directing it, and that they might be willing to refer to as 'God'. However the Christian view of God insists that it is the God of love, not the God of pure thought, who is at the heart of reality, that love is therefore higher than thought. But none of this is said in order to give us an easier path to God than the philosophers can offer, with their austere processes of reasoning. On the contrary, since love is claimed to be higher than pure thought, the God of love should be seen as even more difficult to speak about and to understand than the God of philosophy. This conviction is already enshrined in the New Testament teaching that the peace of God is beyond understanding. All philosophically guided attempts to overturn that basic insight, Christian tradition has until now resisted.

---

37 Cf. the ironic expression that occurs somewhere in Joyce's writings: 'Oh vague something behind everything!'

CHAPTER FIVE

Arguments for God

Man is to be found in reason, God in the passions.
— Georg Chr. Lichtenberg

Most religious teachers spend their time trying to prove the unproven by the unprovable. – Religions die when they are proved to be true.

— Oscar Wilde

I see philosophy and science as in the same boat – a boat which, to revert to Neurath's figure as I so often do, we can rebuild only at sea while staying afloat in it. There is no external vantage point, no first philosophy.
— Willard V. O. Quine

Introduction

Despite the fact that God is believed to be beyond our understanding, there has been in Christianity a long tradition, going back to the early church, of arguing in favour of the existence of God from the existence and nature of the world. This tradition of 'natural theology' has, however, not always been universally accepted within the Christian fold. And it is easy to guess why. For surely divine revelation makes all merely human enquiry into the God-question redundant, or even rather impertinent. To say nothing of the apparent impossibility of reaching God, who is infinite, by starting from the world, which is finite.

It would seem, nevertheless, that natural theology has a legitimate, indeed a necessary role within Christianity. For since God is believed to be the sole source of the world's existence, the world must reflect in some finite, but real, measure the truth about God. And so must our minds. Moreover, if faith and understanding truly flow from the one source, faith cannot be a brake on understanding, but can only be a spur to it. Indeed if there were any final incompatibility between faith (in God) and understanding (of God), faith would be terminally wounded. But far from seeing any such incompatibility, Catholic Christianity at least has rather regarded faith as, in a way, the condition of possibility for understanding. That is to say, faith and understanding have not been thought of as two different, though equally valid approaches to the same mystery. Rather faith has been considered to exist at a different level from understanding, with understanding presupposing faith in order to begin and sustain its search. Without faith it would have no dynamism, no direction, no purpose. Furthermore, that understanding should happen at all is a ratification of faith's fundamental hunch that there really is order and meaning in life.

It is, admittedly, also true that the relationship between faith and understanding (or reason) has been interpreted in very different terms from those proposed here. Faith and reason have also been viewed as antagonists, locked in mortal combat. But, as has already been often mentioned, Christianity can have things both ways. This expression is, of course, usually seen as pejorative, suggesting acquiescence in intellectual dishonesty or laziness. However, Christianity consistently has things both ways simply because there are two 'perspectives' on every important religious question, both of which must be respected: God's and ours. It is important, however, not to confuse this with believing in two kinds of truth, a theological and a philosophical, as if something could be theologically true, but philosophically false, and vice versa. On the contrary, for Christianity truth is believed to be indivisible, but from our limited, human perspective we cannot see or know, as God can, how truth in fact is ultimately indivisible. Consequently, whenever a dispute has arisen in traditionally controversial areas, such as the relationship between grace and law, providence and free will, being and becoming, eternity and time, or faith and reason, Christian tradition has, in the main, resisted the temptation to go for clean, final solutions by suppressing some element of the problem, and instead has tried to maintain, usually somewhat messily, the claims of both 'perspectives' to be taken seriously. In this way, Christianity manages both 'to care and not to care'.

In this chapter we shall take up some of the better-known traditional arguments for God, in order to discuss both their strengths and their limitations, and to suggest above all why they should not be cheaply dismissed, even if one were tempted to disregard them.

An easy argument, indeed, against arguments for God is to point to their ultimate pointlessness by saying: 'Either God exists, in which case arguments will not make that existence any more real than it already is, or else God does not exist, in which case no amount of argument is going to bring him into existence now.' Yet, as against this deceptively simple stratagem, which could conceivably even be invoked to head off difficult questions, one can say that the so-called proofs for the existence of God, elaborated in the mediaeval period, can now be seen – in retrospect admittedly – not so much as proofs but more as a series of clarifications by believers of what in fact they mean by the word 'God'. The arguments for the existence of God can then perhaps best be seen as different ways of trying to 'elucidate the meaning of God' – if such a potentially absurd expression is provisionally permissible – in human existence, or to suggest where God impinges on human existence in specific ways. They deal with what faith in God implies, but they do not produce that faith, just as, one might perhaps add, the bible was written not to prove the existence of God but because the authors already believed in God. Nevertheless, for the mediaeval thinkers whose names are still wedded to the best-known of these arguments, thinkers like St Anselm or St Thomas Aquinas, it is probably true to claim both that they themselves never seriously doubted the existence of God, and also that they considered their arguments for the existence of God to be fairly watertight.

Saint Anselm

The first of the traditional arguments for the existence of God that were mulled over in the Middle Ages is the so-called 'ontological argument',[1] a piece of reasoning that has turned out to be of endless fascination. It was first developed by St Anselm (born c. 1033), who was archbishop of Canterbury from 1093 until his death in 1109.

The point of Anselm's ontological argument, according to Jeanne Hersch,[2] is to enable us to see what is actually implied when we pose the question of God's existence. The argument is not meant to be a proof of God's existence, indeed it could not be, 'because his existence only makes sense from the point of view of faith,'[3] even

---

1 It may be worth noting that the actual 'term *ontologia* was coined by scholastic writers in the seventeenth century', according to Alasdair MacIntyre, in P. Edwards (ed.), *The Encyclopedia of Philosophy* (New York, 1967), vol. 5, p. 542. The 'subject matter of ontology was being as such' (*ibid.*).

2 *L'étonnement philosophique. Une histoire de la philosophie* (Paris 1993), pp. 108–111.

3 *Ibid.*, p. 110.

though we do not know by faith what the nature of God is, or what the term 'existence' fully means when applied to God.[4] But what the argument does seek to do is to place us before the only two possibilities that confront us when we think about 'God': either we believe in God, and the only God we could possibly believe in is one who actually exists; or else we use the term 'God' as an abstract concept which may or may not designate a God who really exists. In the latter case we are not talking about the existing (or, in biblical terms, the 'living') God of faith, and whether or not existence could be attributed to what such an abstract concept may stand for, is – from the viewpoint of faith – neither here nor there. And indeed if we were to claim to have weighed up the usual arguments for and against the existence of God, and to have come down on the negative side, of what or of whom would we then be said to be denying the existence?

Thus there are, to repeat, only two possibilities on the God-question: either we believe in the existence of the God we are talking about, or we do not. There is simply no third possibility in the matter. This line of thinking resembles the plausible argument mentioned at the start of this chapter: either God exists, so trying to 'prove' his existence will not make him exist any more than he already does, or God does not exist, so no amount of trying to 'prove' his existence will bring that existence about. Historically, the experience of the Judaeo-Christian tradition has certainly been that God is believed in *before* theology begins, from the time of the bible itself right down to moderns like Karl Barth or Karl Rahner.

It is important to note, however, that Anselm's argument is not weakened by the objection that we could in fact be mistaken about God's existence; no matter how strongly we believe in him, our 'God' may not after all exist. Now it is certainly true that God's existence cannot be made to depend on the intensity and sincerity of our belief in it, but the point of Anselm's argument is that in the case of our belief in God, and only in that case, the assumption that God really exists is necessarily part of the belief, whereas we can reason about, for example, the properties of a circle, without having to believe that any circle exists in fact. Hence the 'objection' that we could be mistaken about God's existence Anselm would simply rule out as impossible: the notion of a non-existent God is for

4   The term 'existence' clearly has different meanings. Thus a mathematical idea, the notion of truth, the concept of time, a debt, a tree, a human being, to say nothing of God – all 'exist' in different ways.

Anselm literally and logically unthinkable, and thus, he concludes, the non-existence of 'God' is ontologically impossible.

Anselm's argument, to repeat, is of permanent significance in helping us to realise what we mean when we talk about 'God'. It is the content of the concept that interests Anselm, not the allegedly as yet undecided question of whether the term refers to a truly existing being (outside our minds) or not. In brief, to use the term 'God' in a meaningful sense, existence must be already included or implied in the term's definition. A position of interminable doubt on this question (i.e. of the form: '"God" may or may not exist, I don't know, how *can* I ever know?') is, Anselm is claiming, in fact impossible and thus untenable. It is a non-position, once we consider what the term means. The impossibility of what I have called an 'undecided position', however, only holds true in the case of 'God', just as the word 'exist' has a unique meaning in God's case too. (The same idea may be behind Newman's conviction that probability is incompatible with real belief. If it were not, then 'the highest measure of devotion' would be 'the celebrated saying, "O God, if there be a God, save my soul, if I have a soul!"' But, asks Newman, 'who can really pray to a being, about whose existence he is seriously in doubt?'[5])

It may be noted in this context that if creation did in fact 'add' something to God, then the ontological argument would be null and void, as it would then be possible to conceive something greater than God, namely God plus his creation.[6] In Sokolowski's words: 'God . . . is not considered to be simply the best and greatest of all, but the God who could be all that he is, in undiminished goodness and greatness, even if the whole which we call the world, the place where mind and reason are at home, did not exist.'[7] Anselm himself does not explicitly state this aspect of his argument, but it is implicit in what he does say. Moreover, as Sokolowski points out,[8] Anselm remarks in Chapter 20 of the *Proslogion*, the work in which the ontological argument is set out: 'You [i.e. "God"] are in no way less, even if they [i.e. "creatures"] should return to nothing.'

Yet, whatever the merits of this possible challenge to the onto-

---

5 See *Apologia*, p. 109.

6 See Robert Sokolowski, *The God of Faith and Reason* (Notre Dame, 1982), pp. 8–9. I am indebted to Professor James McEvoy for bringing Sokolowski's interpretation of Anselm's argument to my attention.

7 *Op. cit.*, p. 163.

8 *Op. cit.*, p. 10, n.2.

logical argument (i.e. that God plus creation could be considered greater than God alone), it must be said that as Sokolowski raises it in relation to Anselm, it can only be an apparent and not a real challenge. For in Anselm's theology created things already existed in the thought of the creator before they made an appearance in creation as we now perceive and experience it: 'Hence, although it is clear that the beings that were created were nothing before their creation, to this extent, that they were not what they now are, nor was there anything whence they should be created, yet they were not nothing, so far as the creator's thought is concerned, through which, and according to which, they were created.'[9] How this is compatible with *creatio ex nihilo* is a nice question. And if it is finally incompatible with the doctrine of *creatio ex nihilo*, does that then mean that Anselm's thought represents a form of emanationism where creation at all levels participates in the divine being? This neoplatonising view of Christianity may have been what won Anselm a sympathetic hearing from Hegel.[10]

To return to the challenge and put it in a different form: 'If creation is radically *creatio ex nihilo*, and not a projection of divine thoughts (which would be pantheism or at least panentheism), could God plus creation then be considered greater than God, and if so, would that undermine Anselm's ontological argument?' According to Christian faith this cannot be the case, because creation cannot be seen as adding anything to God. God remains God with or without creation. Creation is not necessary to God, nor is it a natural expression or 'offspring', as it were, of God. Creation is not for Christian faith intrinsically divine. How this can be is impossible for us to say. It would be rationally easier to see the world as

---

9 *Monologium* ch. 9, in *Saint Anselm. Basic Writings*, tr. S. N. Deane (La Salle, 1974), p. 56.

10 Pannenberg points out (*Basic Questions in Theology* vol. 3 (London, 1973), pp. 85f.) that Hegel accepted the validity of the ontological argument, but insisted that 'the concept of God, as the assumption of the ontological proof, must itself be shown to be a necessary and not a merely arbitrary idea.' Anselm's argument was weak in this regard in Hegel's eyes, for it 'presupposes the pure concept, the concept in and for itself, the concept of God, but it also presupposes that this concept at the same time *is*, that it has being. The unity of concept and being is a presupposition, and the deficiency consists in the very fact that it is a mere presupposition, which is not proved but only adopted immediately' (*Lectures on the Philosophy of Religion*, ed. P. C. Hodgson, Berkeley and Los Angeles, 1988, p. 187).

necessary to God and somehow itself divine, but faith forbids us from taking this route. To take it would, however, solve the problem of evil and make redemption unnecessary and hence redundant: for everything would then be an expression of God, including what we call 'evil'. But the inhuman price to pay for such an option (i.e. cold-bloodedly approving and willing and doing 'evil') convinces Christian faith that it is a false route. Faith simply says: 'God is, and the world is not God.'

It is then vitally important to see that God's fundamental description is 'He who is', rather than even: 'He who creates', still less 'He who emanates'. That God is the creator is, of course, part of Christian belief, but this is not the most profound or important thing that we can say about God. Or, as Étienne Gilson puts it: 'Now it is quite true that a Creator is an eminently Christian God, but a God whose very essence is to be a creator is not a Christian God at all. The essence of the true Christian God is not to create but to be.'[11] Hence when Descartes identified God's creative role with respect to the world with God's essence, he had unintentionally taken the decisive step in modern times towards undermining belief in the Christian God. For God was henceforth only a philosophical first principle, the ultimate cause and orderer of nature.

Descartes himself anticipated where this move would lead to: 'By Nature, considered in general, I am now understanding nothing else than either God, or the order and the disposition established by God in created things.'[12] Hence Pascal's rejection of Descartes' natural theology as no better than atheism: 'The God of Christians is not a God who is simply the author of mathematical truths, or of the order of the elements; that is the view of heathens and Epicureans ...; but the God of Abraham, the God of Isaac, the God of Jacob, and the God of Christians, is a God of love and of comfort, a God who fills the soul and heart of those whom he possesses.'[13] Needless to say, Pascal did not derive this view of God from the ontological argument. But accepting the primacy of God's existence over our ability to understand him and his relation to the

---

11 É. Gilson, *God and Philosophy* (New Haven and London, 1969), p. 88. Presumably, had God to create, creation would be no longer free, but necessary.

12 Descartes, *Méditations*, VI, ed. Adam-Tannery, IX, 64; quoted by Gilson, *op. cit.*, p. 90.

13 Pascal, *Pensées*, trans. W.F. Trotter, Everyman's Library, pp. 153-154, quoted by Gilson, *op. cit.*, p. 90.

created order, as the ontological argument (though not, as we have seen, all aspects of Anselm's theology) allows us to do, at least leaves the door open to the possibility of finding Pascal's God eventually, whereas Cartesian rationalism keeps it closed.

To return to the ontological argument proper, in Anselm's discussion about God's existence, God is understood as: 'a being than which nothing greater can be conceived.' 'Greater' here means 'more perfect'. The most perfect conceivable being does not mean the most perfect being in existence. For while the greatest being must exist, this in itself is not what Anselm means by the word 'God'. For Anselm God is so perfect that a more perfect being is inconceivable, whereas in principle the greatest being in existence could always have added to it something that would make it even greater than it is, even though it is already greater than anything else that exists.

In the next stage in the argument, Anselm draws a distinction between something that merely exists in the mind, and that same thing existing both in the mind and in reality. He concludes that God must exist both in reality as well as in the mind, for otherwise the mind would be obliged to harbour a logical contradiction, namely to accept that 'God' is both 'that than which a greater cannot be thought' (i.e. 'God' as an idea in the mind only), and 'that than which a greater can be thought' (i.e. 'God' as an idea in the mind and existing in reality also). This clearly violates the rule of non-contradiction, and Anselm rejects it.

The main criticism of the ontological argument – an argument which in mediaeval times Aquinas, for example, did not accept – was brought by Kant who argued that its basic assumption, namely the assumption that existence is a predicate, or a characteristic that something can either have or not have, was false. According to Kant, the idea of existence adds nothing to the concept of a particular thing. To say something exists, therefore, is to assert that there is something in the world which is an instantiation of what the name of the thing describes. But if 'existence' is a predicate or attribute that can suitably be included in a definition and which, as an appropriate attribute, has to be included in the definition of God, then the ontological argument is valid. For it could not be maintained that the most perfect conceivable being lacks the attribute of existence.

However, if 'existence' is not a predicate but simply asserts that a particular description applies in fact to something known independently to exist in reality, then the ontological argument, considered as a proof of the existence of God, is unsuccessful. Hence the question of whether anything in fact corresponds to the concept of the most perfect conceivable being remains undecided. A definition of 'God' may help us to understand what the name could mean, but it cannot prove God's existence, much less bring it about.

Anselm's elegant argument seems indeed too good to be true, and yet it is difficult to pin-point its defect. The conflicting reactions it provokes are arguably a measure of its depth. It has been claimed[14] that the argument rests on 'realist' – ultimately Platonist – presuppositions, and therein lies its weakness, for these presuppositions are not universally accepted. In mediaeval discussion 'realism' refers to the belief that 'universal substances', so-called abstract concepts (e.g., humanity, wisdom, colour) have a 'real' existence (hence the designation 'realism') which is independent of, and ontologically more secure than, their manifestations in individual things. God is the most universal essence or substance which alone has – or rather *is* – unoriginate being, and which alone is therefore really 'real'; all else only exists by participation (another Platonist concept) in being which God is. God is the only being the thought of which implies its full reality. According to the principles of realism, God's being is the highest being imaginable. Hence to speak as Anselm does of a possible distinction existing between God as a mere thought in our minds (an impossibility from his point of view) and God as really existing apart from our minds is – from Anselm's own perspective – to set up only an apparent argument based on a phoney distinction which he himself cannot for a moment really have taken seriously, but just uses for rhetorical effect. His argument is in fact a tautology. The answer to his riddle pre-exists its statement, which of course his confession *credo ut intelligam* readily concedes. What his confession implies, furthermore, is that for Anselm understanding not only begins with faith but also remains indissolubly wedded to it. This appears however to be the case with all human understanding, theological or otherwise.

Continuing appeal of the ontological argument

Despite the force of the traditional objections to Anselm's argument, it has nevertheless continued down through the ages to seem persuasive to many, for example Descartes and Hegel, to name but two major figures. What is the secret of its attraction? One aspect of

---

14 See F. Overbeck, *Vorgeschichte und Jugend der mittelalterlichen Scholastik*, ed. C.A. Bernoulli (Darmstadt, 1971), pp. 218-222.

the answer to this question may be that Anselm's argument rests on the belief that existence is better than non-existence, or rather, less abstractly, that existence is essentially good rather than evil. Perhaps those who agree with Anselm do so partly as a result of this shared belief in the incommensurable value of existence.

A further part of the answer to the question raised would seem to be bound up with a second assumption Anselm makes, and which his admirers possibly share with him. For the ontological argument rests on the belief that the intellectual processes or operations of the human mind have the ability to comprehend, to a limited but real extent, all reality. It rests, in short, on the assumption that logic and ontology are intimately related, indeed ultimately identical, or in other words, that what can be thought logically must correspond to reality; and, if this be accepted, that the corollary then also holds, namely that what is illogical cannot exist in reality. As Jeanne Hersch points out,[15] the problematic implicit in this assertion goes back (at least) as far as Heraclitus and Parmenides (in, roughly, the sixth century BC). For Heraclitus the flux of things manifestly contradicted such apparently necessary logical rules of language as the law of identity or of non-contradiction, because in changing, things clearly did not remain self-identical (hence his famous saying that one cannot step twice into the same river), whereas for Parmenides only that which obeyed the necessary rules of logic could truly be said to be. This is an early illustration in Western thought of the difficulty of understanding the relationship between being and time, or permanence and change (or God and creation?).

Anselm's ontological argument places him firmly on the side of Parmenides, and indeed most orthodox Christian thinkers have tended to find Parmenides,[16] and the intellectual option he championed, more congenial than Heraclitus.[17] For the basic assumption of

---

15 *L'étonnement philosophique*, pp. 14ff.

16 Parmenides' follower, Plato, was of course to become *the* great intellectual example for Christian theologians. Cf. Sokolowski, *op. cit.*, pp. 49f.: 'The Christian tradition has ... generally thought of the Platonic form of philosophy as more congenial to its own convictions ... Aquinas even mentions Plato's account of creation as being an interpretation of the book of Genesis.'

17 It was however, ironically, Heraclitus who first popularised the notion of *logos* – with which Jesus was to be identified, as early as New Testament times – as the fundamental principle behind all reality and, specifically, as the principle of human intelligence.

Anselm's argument involves accepting, as was intimated above, that the scope of human rationality not only is not confined to the empirical realm of the cosmos – where all is inconstancy, change and uncertainty, the realm of mere opinion – but that, strange though it may seem, human rationality is in fact more 'at home' with non-empirical reality.

If this is so, then we can have a more genuine 'knowledge' of what lies beyond the empirically observable cosmos, namely of the divine itself, than of what appears to lie so obviously within our intellectual grasp, but in fact always eludes it.[18] Not to accept this is to believe that the scope of human rationality is confined to this-worldly reality or that it is purely functional or pragmatic. It is to believe that human rationality can only operate in the empirical, inner-worldly realm, that it has no licence to transcend this world. But to admit this would be to renounce the possibility of ever 'knowing' even the empirical order of reality, to say nothing of God. God would then be irrelevant to our intellectual life and would sooner or later also become irrelevant to everything else, so that it would not much matter whether anyone believed he existed or not.

Anselm's ontological argument must, I think, contain such hidden assumptions, if we are to account for its fascination. Not that all who came after him agreed with him, but they all must have felt that he had touched on matters of great moment: the status of 'existence' and the question of the relationship between thought and reality. What Anselm may have been endeavouring to convey is that human beings who think about God will see that in 'God' reality and thought coincide. God is in fact reality, God is the ultimately real.

The way one might reach such a large conclusion would seem to be somewhat as follows. With our minds we can, albeit imperfectly (*quodammodo*), grasp reality as a whole. 'According to Thomas, who follows Aristotle, even the finite spirit is "*quodammodo omnia* (in a way all things)"; it is directed without limit to the whole of reali-

---

18 It is odd that we have words for what we cannot directly experience (general ideas or terms: e.g. 'lion'), and no words for what we can directly experience (individual examples of general ideas or terms: e.g. 'this specific lion'). Cf. J. Hersch, *op. cit.*, p. 111. This is closely related to 'Aristotle's idea that the individual is unknowable, that only universals can be known' (A. Louth, *The Origins of the Christian Mystical Tradition*, Oxford, 1981, pp. 20f.; the reference to Aristotle is to *Metaphysics* III. 1003 a13 ff.).

ty.'[19] One finds the same fundamental idea expressed more 'existentially' by Pascal.[20] Now although we can only somehow understand reality as a whole with our minds, we can nevertheless intuit or postulate that the totality which we can only intellectually perceive, must be sustained in being by that which is simultaneously its perfect comprehension, namely: God. Kolakowski in fact notes that the expression *quodammodo omnia* was, not surprisingly, applied by St Thomas to God, as well as to our finite minds: *'Deus est quodammodo omnia,'*[21] 'since to perceive a thing "from outside" means to be limited by it' – something one could not say of God, who 'perceives everything, as it were, "from within" and therefore He *is* everything.'[22]

The perceived connection between our minds and the structure and indeed very being of reality, perhaps explains to some extent why Anselm's argument was taken up again much later by Hegel, not in its original form, but for the sake of its basic intuition, namely that human thought can trace the nature of things to its ultimate source.

Saint Thomas Aquinas

The first thing to notice about Aquinas' proofs for the existence of God is the way they differ from Anselm's ontological argument. Whereas Anselm begins arguing from the idea of God, Aquinas starts from a consideration of general features of the actual world we live in and argues that such a world could not be, if the ultimate reality we call God did not exist. In arguing for the existence of God from a general consideration of the world itself, Aquinas is taking up an idea that goes back at least as far as Plato; as Andrew Louth shows, the idea of perceiving God through contemplation of the cosmos, rather than in flight from the world (a view that can also be found in Plato, e.g. in the *Theaetetus* [176 B]), is found in the *Timaeus* (90 A–D).[23]

Most Aquinas experts assure us that while the 'five ways' – as Aquinas' 'proofs' are usually known – are not irresistible, they do have, taken together, a cumulative effect that can be persuasive,

---

19 Walter Kasper, *The God of Jesus Christ*, tr. M. J. O'Connell (London, 1983), p. 154.

20 See *Pensées* (fr. 113), tr. A. J. Krailsheimer, p. 59.

21 'God is in a certain way everything'.

22 *Religion*, p. 29.

23 A. Louth, *op. cit.*, pp. 14f.

even if not devastating, in moving us to accept the reasonableness of theistic belief. John Hick summarises the 'five ways' thus: 'The first way argues from the fact of motion to a Prime Mover; the second from causation to a First Cause; the third from contingent beings to a Necessary Being; the fourth from degrees of value to Absolute Value; and the fifth from evidences of purposiveness in nature to a Divine Designer.'[24]

The first cause argument

The second of these 'five ways', known as the 'first cause argument' runs as follows: 'everything that happens has a cause, and this cause in turn has a cause and so on in a series that must either be infinite or have its starting point in a first cause. Aquinas excludes the possibility of an infinite regress of causes, and so concludes that there must be a First Cause, which we call God.'[25] The weakness of this argument is simply that it is difficult to rule out as impossible an endless regress of events, with no beginning.

This proof however can be looked at in a different way, which is not open to the difficulty just mentioned. Some interpret the endless series which Aquinas evokes as referring not to an endless series of events backwards in time, but to an endless and hence inconclusive series of explanations. Thus if a fact – assuming it could be defined – is made intelligible by its relation to other facts, underlying all of this there must be a reality which is itself self-explanatory, and which contains the ultimate explanation of what one is seeking to understand. To argue in this fashion means of course presupposing the validity of what Leibniz termed the 'principle of sufficient reason', i.e. the principle 'stating that for every fact there is a reason why it is so and not otherwise.'[26] Not all, however, will accept the principle of sufficient reason, and if not, is there any compelling reason which definitively rules out the conclusion that 'the universe is a mere unintelligible brute fact'?[27] Such was Nietzsche's conclusion, even though it too has its problems. One might for instance advance against it Kolakowski's subtle 'suspicion that if "to be" were pointless and the universe void of mean-

---

24 J. Hick, *Philosophy of Religion* (Englewood Cliffs, N.J., 1983), p. 20.
25 *Ibid.*
26 *A Dictionary of Philosophy*, ed. A. Flew (London, 1984), p. 344. The principle of sufficient reason is usually associated with Leibniz, but it is older, being found in mediaeval thought, especially that of Abelard.
27 Hick, *op. cit.*, p. 21.

ing, we would never have achieved not only the ability to imagine otherwise but even the ability to think precisely this: that "to be" is indeed pointless and the universe void of meaning.'[28]

However, quite apart from the Nietzschean objection to traditional metaphysics, the interpretation of Aquinas' argument just outlined, which seeks to find an ultimate metaphysical cause for things, depends still on a view of causality that many would challenge. While causality may make sense for explaining inner-worldly events and facts, it cannot be shown that the same principle operates between the universe as such (assuming – which not all would – that this is an intelligible concept to begin with) and the universe's putative transcendent source. 'It is truly astonishing,' wrote Lichtenberg, 'that we have erected our belief in God upon vague ideas of causation. We know nothing of Him, and can know nothing, for to conclude that the world must have a creator is never anything but anthropomorphism.'[29]

Finally, to the 'first cause argument' for God's existence we can put the question: 'If everything must have a cause, what caused the creator of the universe? What caused God?' May one exempt 'God' from the sway of the 'principle of causality' merely by declaring him to be an 'uncaused cause'? If it is objected that this is an absurd question, which only shows that the asker has no idea of what is meant by the word 'God', are we not back with Anselm's ontological argument, with which even such a strong-minded believer in God's existence as Aquinas himself was uneasy?

The cosmological argument

Aquinas' 'third way' – often referred to as the 'cosmological argument' – argues from the so-called contingency of the world. This argument seems to owe its popularity, at least in theistically slanted literature, to the persistence of what otherwise (i.e. if theism were false) one would have to describe as an odd quirk in many minds. The quirk in question is quite simply the ability to experience a sense of wonderment, even bafflement, before the apparently inexplicable or 'unnecessary' reality of the world, what John Cage once referred to rather optimistically, if I recall correctly, as the 'benign randomness of the universe'. According to the cosmological argument everything in the world is contingent – i.e. it is true of each thing in the world that it might never have existed at all. For proof

---

28 *Metaphysical Horror* (Oxford, 1988), p. 120.
29 *Aphorisms*, p. 151.

one can point to the fact that there was a time when it did not actually exist. Everything points beyond itself to other things. Aquinas argues that were everything contingent, there must have been a time when nothing existed. Hence, nothing could ever have begun to exist, there being nothing to have caused it. But since things do in fact exist, there must be some non-contingent, causal being, namely God. One can strengthen this argument by omitting the time-reference and concentrating on the logical connection between a contingent world and its non-contingent ground. 'Only a self-existent reality, containing in itself the source of its own being, can constitute an ultimate ground of the existence of anything else. Therefore, if there is an ultimate ground of anything, there must be a "necessary being," and this being we call God.'[30]

Aquinas' 'third way' is saying therefore that since the universe exists, even though no intrinsic reason can be adduced for its existence as an ontological necessity, then this state of affairs could encourage one to suppose that it must be grounded in something beyond itself, it must have a willed source or cause, which itself needs no explanation; and this cause is more popularly known as God. The attraction of the argument from contingency even for those who finally reject its cogency is illustrated vividly by Kant:

> Unconditional necessity, which we so indispensably require as the last bearer of all things, is for human reason the veritable abyss. Eternity itself, in all its terrible sublimity ... is far from making the same overwhelming impression upon the mind; for it only *measures* the duration of things, it does not *support* them. We cannot put aside, and yet also cannot endure the thought, that a being, which we represent to ourselves as supreme amongst all possible beings, should, as it were, say to itself: 'I am from eternity to eternity, and outside me there is nothing save what is through my will, *but whence then am I?*' All support here fails us ... [31]

Given the emotional power of the notion of contingency, as expressed so memorably by Kant, it is not surprising that historically its intellectual significance is also huge. For it is, as Kolakowski argues, 'the "contingency" of human existence' – in the terminology

---

30 Hick, *op. cit.*, p. 22.
31 *Critique of Pure Reason*, A613, B641, quoted by R.W. Hepburn, art. 'Cosmological Argument for the Existence of God', in P. Edwards (ed.), *Encyclopedia of Philosophy*, vol. 2 (New York, 1967), p. 237.

of 'medieval Christian philosophy' – that is at the root of 'the aspi-
ration of philosophy … to comprehend intellectually the whole of
Being.'[32] This sense of radical human imperfection – or metaphysical insufficiency – has stimulated the long Western tradition of
dialectical speculation stretching from Plato, through Plotinus,
Proclus, Dionysius, Eriugena, Eckhart, Nicholas of Cusa, Böhme
right into the modern world to the Enlightenment, Hegel and the
German Idealists and their successors.

However, despite the undoubted historical importance of the
notion of contingency in philosophical and theological speculation,
the belief that it points to a necessary, self-sufficient, uncaused
being who is the universe's cause and support has not been universally accepted. The 'metaphysical insufficiency' attaching to human
beings as such clings also remorselessly to our speculations.
Objections have been raised against the cosmological argument, in
common with all the others. As with the 'first cause argument', it
has been pointed out from the time of Hume onwards, Kolakowski
notes, that the notion of the Whole (universe, cosmos) is not an
empirically grounded idea. Nor indeed is the idea of contingency:
'we perceive the contingency of things once God's existence is
known to us and not before.'[33] The religious thinker F. H. Jacobi
(1743–1819) attacked all proofs for the existence of God as absurd,
since they all attempted to go from data which could not but be
finite to an infinite conclusion.[34] As for Newman, were it not, he
wrote in his *Apologia*, for the voice of God 'speaking so clearly in my
conscience and my heart, I should be an atheist, or a pantheist, or a
polytheist when I looked into the world.'[35]

Furthermore, does the argument for the existence of God from
contingency, and indeed from order too, not lead perhaps more
naturally to the demiurge of Plato's *Timaeus* – who is specifically
not an 'uncaused cause' despite being, after a fashion, the creator of
the world – than to the God of Christianity?

The argument from contingency has long been locked in indeci-
sive conflict with its rival, namely the claim that the world itself
exists as a self-supporting system of matter, time and space. For this
view the world of appearances, to use a slightly loaded term, is the
only world. The so-called battle of gods and giants, to borrow

32 *Main Currents of Marxism* (Oxford, 1978), vol. I, p. 11.
33 *Religion*, p. 70.
34 Cf. W. Pannenberg, *Basic Questions in Theology*, vol. 3, p. 85.
35 *Apologia Pro Vita Sua*, p. 278.

Plato's image in the *Sophist*, or the battle between those who seek the explanation for things beyond the empirically experienced order, and those who are resolute empiricists and believe in the reality of the empirically experienced order only, is seemingly one that no side can definitively win. For both sides begin from two different and incompatible starting-points, between which there seems little possibility of mediation. And in their beginning seems also to be their end.

If defenders of the cosmological argument cannot show in what way God's eternal existence would be more necessary, more self-explanatory, than the everlasting existence of matter with a natural indestructibility, then their case is considerably weakened. The only difference between the two positions then would seem to be that God's eternal existence could be claimed by theists to be a logically necessary truth, whereas the eternal existence of matter could only be claimed by sceptical materialists to be naturally necessary (perhaps a dubious concept). But that would appear to make the cosmological argument (like the 'first cause argument') ultimately dependent upon the ontological argument: i.e. deriving God's necessary factual existence from a mere concept of his existence as 'logically necessary', and indeed Kant criticises it on this precise score. 'Necessary' is a predicate of propositions only, not of things. A 'logically necessary being', which is how God is perceived both by the cosmological and ontological arguments, is an untenable, if not unintelligible, concept for much modern philosophy – which does not of course necessarily mean that it is untrue.

However a strength of the cosmological argument – as also of the 'first cause argument' – lies, it would appear, in its ability to place a dramatic choice before a potential sceptic: either there is a Necessary Being or the universe is absurd, i.e. bereft of any ultimate and for us ultimately satisfying explanation. But a corresponding weakness lies in the fact that the option favoured by the theist is not inevitably the one that must be chosen. If the second alternative cannot be shown decisively to be not a real option, then clearly the proof for God's existence has failed. If the sceptic remains unconvinced, the proof has not worked, no matter how much satisfaction it may bring to those who already believe in God's existence without it.

There seems thus to be no final objection that can be raised against those who see no compelling reason for looking beneath, or behind, or beyond the surface of things to what is considered by some to be the 'really real'. Those who do look, but find nothing, are sometimes filled in consequence with an acute sense of absurdity, as was Albert Camus; others experience an overwhelming feeling of disgust and boredom. Roquentin, the hero of Sartre's celebrated novel, *La Nausée*, expresses this latter mode of modern meaninglessness. Such tormented souls are presumably, from the point of view of a radical empiricist, either socially maladjusted or philosophical masochists.

At best, therefore, the argument from contingency appears to be compatible with at least three views of reality: Christian theism, belief in the Platonic demiurge, and belief in the absurd. For the last-mentioned position, indeed, the argument from contingency is liable, just – as we shall see later – like the argument from moral experience, to be reckoned as evidence against, rather than for, belief in an all-powerful, all-good, and all-merciful God.

However even worse can happen: the concept of contingency can be dismissed as portentous verbiage, with no purchase whatsoever on reality. In fact the main difficulty that the contemporary world appears to encounter with traditional expressions of the cosmological argument for the existence of God, is not that they are seen as intellectually suspect – though they are indeed frequently so viewed – but rather that they are felt to be ineffectual, because not in contact with the human condition. They are perceived as simply free-floating ideas, even if elaborated with exquisite intricacy and patience, but yet ideas, with no existential urgency or relevance.

Who has not felt that arguments for the existence of God are, for all their occasional subtlety and cleverness, existentially hollow and destined, if for anyone, only for the converted? Hearing them is, at best, like witnessing an intriguing game of chess, at worst, rather like watching a football team playing against an 'opposition' that has gone home. In the latter case, many goals may be scored, but *cui bono*? For it is not our mere existence that demands to be explained, but the nature of that existence. Why is it characterised by suffering and inevitable death? Why does the cosmos seem so indifferent to our fate?

Here however we must be careful. For to speak of a disjunction between ourselves and the cosmos or 'nature' is to fall into the 'pathetic fallacy', attributing, or at least wanting to attribute, human feelings to the forces of nature. Such anthropomorphisms, as is well known, have by now been mercilessly unmasked by, among others, Nietzsche:

The total character of the world ... is in all eternity chaos – in the sense not of a lack of necessity but of a lack of order, arrangement, form, beauty, wisdom, and whatever other names there are for our aesthetic anthropomorphisms... But how could we reproach or praise the universe? Let us beware of attributing to it heartlessness and unreason or their opposites: it is neither perfect nor beautiful, nor noble, nor does it wish to become any of these things; it does not by any means strive to imitate man. None of our aesthetic and moral judgments apply to it.[36]

Thus, when one asks how much explanatory power still resides in the cosmological argument, Christian theology may presumably at most hope that there is at least a correspondence between the unspeakable predicament of humanity – philosophically and rather coyly described as our 'contingency' – and the incomprehensibility of God. Christianity's message of redemption claims of course that there is such a correspondence and moreover that it is compatible with the human sense of the world's indifference to our plight. For according to Christian faith it is not the cosmos ultimately that cares for us, but God himself. And just as no man can have two masters, neither can he have two redeemers.

When the redemptive soul has been removed from theological language it sounds hollow, nowhere more so than in the area with which we are now dealing. Part of the meaning, surely, of the neo-orthodox reaction of Karl Barth in the early part of this century was the realisation that the theologians he attacked seemed (in their writings at any rate) to show little awareness of what it is like to be human, let alone what it is like to be divine. Franz Overbeck, in his day, turned away in disgust from the mindless triviality of what passed for 'theology'. Perhaps one should not even draw the line at theology. As Adorno wrote:

The only form of philosophy which could be justified in the face of despair, is the attempt to see everything in the perspective of redemption. Knowledge has no light other than that which shines from redemption onto the world. Everything else is empty and imitative, sheer technical effects.[37]

Non-theological writers are often more sensitive to the potentially fatal weaknesses of God-talk than theologians themselves: Lucky's

---

36 *The Gay Science*, III, 109, tr. W. Kaufmann, (New York, 1974), p. 168.
37 T. W. Adorno, *Minima Moralia*, 1970, p. 333, cited by W. Kasper, *Jesus the Christ*, 1977, p. 56.

mad theological-sounding rant in the first act of *Waiting for Godot*, for instance, is a moving parody of high-minded theological cant, oblivious of its own futility. Hölderlin spoke of 'professional theologians' as the 'scribes and pharisees of our time.'[38]

Given the difficulties facing the traditional philosophical arguments for the existence of God that theologians had often used before him, it is instructive to note that Pascal should have given no place to such arguments in his projected apology for Christianity.[39] Even in the seventeenth century, therefore, the obsolescence *ad extra*, so to speak, of such arguments was tacitly assumed, their worthlessness in religious argumentation taken for granted, except of course for those who believed anyway, and for whom they were merely superfluous.

There is an amusing short 'parable' by Borges (perhaps inspired by an intentionally playful interpretation of *Pensées*, fr. 3: '"Why, do you not say yourself that the sky and the birds prove God?"') that illustrates the precarious status these arguments now enjoy. It is called *Argumentum ornithologicum*, from the collection *El Hacedor* (1960), and worth quoting in full:

> I close my eyes and see a flock of birds. The vision lasts a second or perhaps less; I don't know how many birds I saw. Was their number definite or indefinite? The problem involves the question of the existence of God. If God exists, the number is definite, because God knows how many birds I saw. If God does not exist, the number is indefinite, because no one could keep count. If that were so, I saw (let us say) less than ten birds and more than one, but I did not see nine, eight, seven, six, five, four, three or two birds. I saw a number between ten and one, which is not nine, eight, seven, six, five, etc. That integer is inconceivable; *ergo*, God exists.

Clearly something more than proofs for the existence of God is needed to make the idea of God credible (again). For, even if such 'proofs' could illuminate more powerfully than they often do the creaturely status of man, this would not necessarily yield the God of Christianity, to Christian faith the one and only God. And according to that same faith, human beings cannot finally reach the Christian God by any process of intellectual and/or mystical ascent

---

38 Quoted by H. Urs von Balthasar, *Herrlichkeit*, Vol. III/I, Part I (Einsiedeln, 1965), p. 7.

39 Cf. *Pensées*, fr. 3, tr. A. J. Krailsheimer (Harmondsworth, 1983), p. 33.

or by following the promptings of their restless hearts. God must descend to us.[40]

Moreover, the suspicion that we can never *know* the intrinsic nature of external reality, except to the extent that it reflects the nature of our own minds, has been a kind of running sore in all arguments for the existence of God based on the order of the external world. For the suspicion always lingers, after the proofs have been spelled out, that the order in question, though real, is at best only an accurate description of empirical reality, at worst a simple reflection of the structure of our own minds. It is this latter possibility that Lichtenberg envisaged when he wrote: 'We can do no other than recognise order and judicious direction in the world, but this, however, is a consequence of the structure of our intellect. It does not follow, though, that something we are obliged to think is necessarily really so, for we have no conception at all of the true nature of the external world: from the nature of the external world alone, therefore, it is impossible to demonstrate the existence of God ... '[41] He added elsewhere: 'There exists no bridge that leads beyond our thoughts to the objects of them.'[42] However, even if we could be

---

40 See A. Louth's insightful treatment of the differences between Neo-platonist and Christian mysticism in *The Origins of the Christian Mystical Tradition*.

41 G. Chr. Lichtenberg, *Aphorisms*, p. 153. (Cf. Kant: 'Thus the order and regularity in the appearances, which we entitle *nature*, we ourselves introduce' [*Critique of Pure Reason*, A 125].) The First Vatican Council wisely taught 'that God, the beginning and end of all things, *can* [my emphasis] be known with certainty ["certo cognosci posse"] from the things that were created through the natural light of human reason ... but that it pleased his wisdom and bounty to reveal himself and his eternal decrees in another and supernatural way ... ' (J. Neuner, S.J. and J. Dupuis, S.J., *The Christian Faith*, Dublin and Cork, 1973, p. 43; cf. *Decrees of the Ecumenical Councils*, Vol. II, ed. N. P. Tanner, S.J., London, 1990, p. 806). The Council did not teach that anyone had in fact ever proved the existence of God by argument. Once again one must admire official or orthodox Christianity's ability to be fair to all sides of a question, and in a certain sense to have things both ways. This is a feature of the Christian faith one can observe at great length in, for example, the tortuous controversies that have characterized treatment of the nature/grace debate over the centuries. In general, and not only in the nature/grace dilemma, those who wished to decide questions on the meaning of Christianity with total clarity usually became heresiarchs.

42 *Aphorisms*, p. 196.

sure that our minds do perceive an objectively real order in the cosmos, would that order in itself be a strong enough argument to take us beyond the world to God who, Christianity claims, is totally other than this world?

Value of the arguments for God

Nearly two hundred years ago Hegel, who was far from being ill-disposed towards religion, referred quite unpolemically to the 'now somewhat obsolete metaphysical proofs of God's existence'.[43] If the traditional arguments for God's existence are weak or, as some would say, worthless, why are they still discussed? What is the secret of their attraction? It is, I think, fair to say that they are not seriously considered any longer, if they ever were, as proofs for God. In fact it would be disastrous for Christian faith if they were successful as rational proofs, for that would then mean that the link between God and creation was one of rational necessity, something Christianity through its doctrine of *creatio ex nihilo* has always refused to say, mainly I suspect because of the consequences it would have for the problem of evil. But the fact that the arguments we have reviewed cannot perform one task does not mean that they may not be able to perform another. They continue to be important surely, as was hinted at the start of the discussion on the cosmological argument, as a way of alerting us to the strange status of the world, to the fact that its existence – and hence our own – is problematic. This is a lesson one can learn supremely well from Aquinas. For one of the consistent, indeed almost relentless strengths of his theology is its lack of simple-mindedness, its sensitivity to the ambiguous nature of the world, an ambiguity mirrored in the light and shade of his typical argumentative procedures where the objections to belief are always given an airing and truth, as Aquinas perceives it, is hammered out in relation to them.

The problematic nature of existence springs naturally from even the simplest question. If I ask for example why does the table at which I am writing exist, I can reply: because someone made it. To question the reply itself, and the reply to the reply is possible, but I can never find a fully satisfactory answer. I cannot jump *logically* from any factual, contingent explanation to a necessary metaphysical, ultimate one. All the answers we ever attain always have about them what Nietzsche called the 'melancholy of fulfilment', the

---

43 *The Logic of Hegel*, tr. from the *Encyclopaedia of the Philosophical Sciences*, with Prolegomena, by William Wallace (Oxford, 1874), p. 3.

sense of disappointment that often attends the successful conclusion of some line of reasoning. Conclusions turn stale with the realisation that they are in no sense final. It is merely that in the treadmill of intellectual existence, old horizons give way to new ones. Conclusions never satisfy, but only provoke new questions. We might therefore simply have to reconcile ourselves to the possibility that no definitive, absolute knowledge about anything is ever attainable for the very unexceptionable reason that ultimate truth, with which all intermediate truths are finally connected, is itself beyond knowledge.

The wider question, not just why does any particular object exist, but why does anything exist might prompt the flippant reply: why not? Any grander, metaphysical, supposedly final answer can be cut to pieces by critical reason. If however no real answer to such an enduring human question as: Why does anything exist? can be found, one might begin to wonder whether the question is a real one after all.

It certainly has the form of a question, but it is more a way of registering wonder and awe in the face of the existence of the world, just as Leibniz's question: 'Why is there something, rather than nothing?', which Heidegger later latched on to, is not a real question, but an expression of wonderment. This wonder and awe at existence is what Aristotle defined as the starting-point of philosophy,[44] an idea echoed by St Thomas in the term *admiratio* (STh 1a 12, 1). Descartes, referring to it as 'l'admiration', saw it as the first of the passions.[45] Questions, therefore, such as: 'Why should anything exist at all?' or: 'Has the world a final cause or a necessary ground or foundation?' or even: 'Does God exist?' – these kinds of questions are not real questions at all, but that is not to say they are meaningless.[46] However they only have depth and urgency for those who are already in some sense religiously moved. They are signs of religion, the effects of religion, rather than steps that will lead someone to religion. Even if one accepted, say, St Thomas' 'five ways', the God produced by such philosophical argument might simply be an infinite brain or computer, rather than the God of Christian faith who is believed to be interested in the world.

---

44 'It is because of wonderment that men ... start to study philosophy' (quoted by Jonathan Barnes, *Aristotle*, Oxford, 1986, p. 65).
45 In his *Traité des passions* (art. 53); *cf.* H. T. Barnwell, *The Tragic in French Tragedy* (Belfast, 1966, p. 23).
46 Cf. Kolakowski's comments on 'meaning' ('Reading The World') in *Metaphysical Horror*, pp. 113–120.

In religion things operate according to a 'logic' of recognition rather than demonstration. One does not have questions in religion which are pressed until an answer is forthcoming. The presence of questions in religion – fundamental, ultimate questions – does not point forward to an answer, but backward to the source of the questions. Hence religion talks characteristically not about proof, but about conversion or turning round, *metanoia* or re-thinking, having what Germans call an 'aha-experience', recognition or discovery rather than invention or demonstration. Religious questions that occur to us are like shadows that we project ahead of us. The meaning of the questions is not found ultimately by looking forward and scrutinising those shadows but by turning round and being blinded by the realisation of what is causing them. That is of course merely an analogy, comparing God to the sun at our backs. But the point of the analogy is, I think, valid. Religion does not find answers to questions by pursuing them relentlessly on and on. Rather, it sees that questions eventually point away from themselves to their source which we *believe* is God. In religion, in short, whatever about anything else, the answer pre-exists the question. We would indeed not seek God, to echo Pascal's paradox, if we had not already found him.[47]

---

47 See *Pensées* (fr. 919, 929), tr. A. J. Krailsheimer, pp. 314, 320.

PART III

Background to the contemporary debate

CHAPTER SIX

The origins of modern theology

Knowing the world means knowing that one doesn't signify much in it, means believing that no philosophical dream can be realised in it, and means hoping that it will never be otherwise, or at best only somewhat flimsier.

[I]t is folly to make a distinction between this world and the next.

The divine wisdom is the ground in virtue of which the world, as the scene of redemption, is also the absolute revelation of the supreme being, and is therefore good.

— Friedrich Schleiermacher

Introduction

The modern period is characterised by a certain novelty and even urgency missing from most other periods in Christian history. For example, in the early church the Arians and their opponents, whatever their disagreements, never doubted God's existence. At the Reformation, Catholics and Reformers may have argued about the true nature of Christianity, but none of them dreamt of denying God's existence. However, the changes attendant on the rise of the modern world, including the phenomenon of widespread atheism in the West, have forced Christianity to rethink and reinterpret its doctrine of God in the light of modern knowledge and experience. This is clearly an enterprise fraught with danger and risk, as the 'Modernist' crisis at the turn of this century shows.

In this and the following two chapters I wish to discuss three figures who are at the fountainhead of the modern debate about God, or who are the poisoners of the theological wells, as some prefer to see them: Schleiermacher, Hegel and Feuerbach, the 'Father of Modern Atheism'. All did their epoch-making work in the first half of the nineteenth century.[1] On account of his historical importance in the second half of the last century some attention will be paid also in the present chapter to Ritschl, the founder of Liberal Protestantism, for Ritschl was convinced he had rectified, and created a replacement for, the modernised version of Christian theology developed by his great predecessor, Schleiermacher. And since Feuerbach's critique of religion had an important influence on Barth's attempt to divert the movement of modern theology in the twentieth century, brief reference will also be made in Chapter Eight to neo-orthodoxy's use of Feuerbach's thought. A short excursus on the problem of modernism within the Catholic Church at the turn of this century has been appended to that chapter. However, before speaking about the shapers of the modern God-question, something should be said about the temper of the age in which they forged their ideas.

The modern age

In a preliminary list of typical elements that make up the texture of the modern age[2] and militate against any unproblematic or simplistic endorsement of traditional religious notions, the following four factors – which we present with some critical comment – could be included:[3]

(a) *An emphasis on experience as the sole valid source for arriving at true concepts and testing them.* Related to this is the prestige enjoyed in the modern age by scientific methods of investigating reality. These points were urged against theology most flamboyantly by A. J. Ayer in his famous 'Tract for the Times': *Language, Truth and Logic* (1936). Theology, in contrast, cannot turn religious faith into a series of hypothetical claims about the reality

---

1 To be precise, from 1799 onwards, that being the publication date of Schleiermacher's famous *On Religion: Speeches to Its Cultured Despisers*.

2 Cf. the concise remarks of Roger Scruton's on the meaning of the term 'modern': '"Modern" I take to be a term of social and intellectual history. In the realm of ideas, the modern age began with Bacon (1561-1626), was armed by Descartes (1596-1650), attained self-consciousness through the *Philosophes* and self-doubt through Kant, and thereafter lived in mourning for the home that it had destroyed, becoming wistful, iconoclastic and murderous by turns' (*TLS* Dec 18, 1992, p. 3).

3 For what follows I am indebted to L. Gilkey in P. Hodgson and R. King (eds.), *Christian Theology. An Introduction to its Traditions and Tasks* (London, 1983), pp. 70f.

of God open in principle to verification or falsification.[4] On the other hand, the presumption that thought based on experience is superior to flabby a priori theorising – a charge frequently brought against theology – ignores the fact that 'experience' is itself by no means an innocent concept. All experience is *interpreted* experience. To try to bypass all the interpretative categories through which we experience the world in order to see it 'purely', seems impossible: 'every sentence we utter presupposes the entire history of culture of which the language we use is an aspect... Spoken of, the world is never naked.'[5]

(b) *A shift to the subject as the only source of authority in matters of intellectual and moral truth.* This shift, which is part of the Cartesian legacy, appears questionable and unrealistic if it is not balanced by a sense of the indispensable social factors involved in the emergence of any individual human subjectivity in the first place. As for the *cogito* itself, to the extent that existence – or being – precedes or is presupposed by thought, one may perhaps safely say that *cogito, ergo sum* is the most basic truth one can be *aware* of, but that could turn out to be a shaky enough basis for reaching doubt-free, transcendent 'truth'.

(c) *A rejection or severe calling into question of the value of external authority.* This is a corollary of the previous point, with wide-ranging implications for a religion whose legitimacy is so intimately intertwined with tradition. For while scripture or the Christian doctrinal tradition might still be seen as historically interesting in the new enlightened dispensation, they will not be regarded any longer as authoritatively binding, without prior intellectual justification. The clash between tradition and independent thought which so characterises modernity is not, of course, in itself an entirely new phenomenon in Western culture. When the pre-Socratics, for example, decided to investigate the world rationally, they thereby challenged traditional views about the gods, thus revealing that it was possible to stand back critically from one's culture and to reassess it. As Kolakowski notes: 'Whatever mat-

---

4   To those positivists who say that religion is not empirically graspable and is thus no concern of ours, we could perhaps reply, with Elias Canetti: 'Confine oneself to what is of some real personal concern? Precisely what constitutes the misery and glory of man is that he must care about was does not concern him' (*Die Fliegenpein*, Frankfurt a/M, 1995, p. 143).

5   L. Kolakowski, *Metaphysical Horror*, pp. 58f.

ters in philosophy – and this means: whatever makes philosophy matter at all in life – is subject to the same options that have persisted since the unidentifiable moment when independent thought, disregarding the mythological legacy as a source of authority, arose in our civilisation.'[6] Kolakowski's remarks are clearly relevant to the problem of tradition and modernity as it affects contemporary Christianity.

The Enlightenment's option to reject the authority of tradition has profoundly marked the modern Western world and is an almost omnipresent article of faith in the writings of its leading intellectuals – who have emerged as a new caste in the past two hundred years.[7] Freedom from the authority of the past has however its price. The price in the contemporary world is the slackening of hope in a transcendent destiny for the human race, and consequent confusion about the meaning of the future. As Alexis de Tocqueville wrote nearly two centuries ago: 'Since the past has ceased to throw its light upon the future, the mind of man wanders in obscurity.'[8]

(d) *The rise of a new historicist appreciation of human consciousness over roughly the past two hundred years.* This has given rise to the problem of historical or cultural relativism, i.e. the conviction that concepts or moral regulations for instance only relate to particular epochs, are mere reflections of ever-changing circumstances but have no abiding or universal meaning. There can therefore be no absolute standards of truth or goodness or beauty. The world has become a cultural 'ad-hocracy'. In Ortega y Gasset's rather melodramatic formulation, the modern world, saturated with relativism, has become 'scandalously provisional'. Inflexible relativists however, in a move at odds with their own philosophy, do in fact absolutise a particular cultural view of reality, namely their own, and thus ultimately undermine the very point they wish to make. The question of historicism was not directly faced by the Catholic church until the Second Vatican Council,[9] which perhaps shows that the problem of rela-

---

6 *Metaphysical Horror*, p. 2.
7 Cf. Paul Johnson, *Intellectuals* (London, 1993); Christophe Charle, *Les Intellectuels en Europe au xixe Siècle* (Paris, 1996).
8 *Democracy in America* (New York, 1945), vol. II, p. 331.
9 Speaking of the cultural change that marks our age M. J. Farrelly wrote: 'One may say that the council relates the problem of faith in our time largely to this change of culture and, more specifically, a modern historical consciousness' (*Belief in God in Our Time*, Collegeville, 1992, p. 20, n. 2).

tivism had by that time, somewhat paradoxically, assumed an air of permanence.

In dealing with relativism Christianity cannot renounce the question of the ultimate truth about its God. If we were to seek a pragmatic solution to the challenge of relativism by shelving the truth-question and agreeing to look on Christian faith as a kind of social cement, containing well-tried guidelines for moral and social behaviour, we would be admitting that Christianity had already entered the stage of its history corresponding to that reached by the official and socially important Graeco-Roman religion of the ancient world, before it was itself ousted and replaced by Christianity. That is to say, Christianity would be respected still (for how long?) as part of the cultural fabric of the West, but it would no longer be taken seriously as 'true'.

Schleiermacher (1768–1834)

One thinker at the beginning of the modern period who was not prepared to see Christianity retreat into a ghetto or collapse into irrelevance before the onset of modernity was Friedrich Schleiermacher, the founder of modern theology. He was dissatisfied with both traditional Protestant orthodoxy and a purely rationalistic natural theology. And he had a much keener sense than the Enlightenment of the historical nature of religious traditions. In his eyes the 'natural', deistic religion of the *Aufklärung* was an abstraction that had never had any 'positive' existence. Moreover, through his contacts with literary figures in Berlin in the 1790s who were to become famous as leading lights in the German Romantic movement, he became confirmed in his belief that true religion was being dismissed by large sections of the cultural élite of the day, because they were, in his view, confusing the genuine article with its caricature. He was not impressed, any more than they were, by 'theologians of the letter who believe the salvation of the world and the light of wisdom are to be found in a new vesture of formulas, or a new arrangement of ingenious proofs.'[10] Schleiermacher, like Pascal in an earlier age in this respect, realised that traditional apologetical techniques had little or no purchase on modern culture, and thus felt compelled to seek a new way forward.

Reacting against the approach to religion favoured by the

---

10 *On Religion: Speeches to Its Cultured Despisers*, tr. J. Oman (New York, 1958) p. 17; cf. B. M. G. Reardon, *Religion in the Age of Romanticism* (Cambridge, 1985), p. 33.

Enlightenment which produced a deist God, remote from the God of the Judaeo-Christian tradition, Schleiermacher made an appeal to religious experience. In his famous *On Religion: Speeches to Its Cultured Despisers* (1799), which he was encouraged by Friedrich von Schlegel to publish,[11] he claimed that religion was not a matter of the mind's adherence to doctrines (as traditional Protestant orthodoxy claimed). Nor was it rooted in the moral will, as rationalists like Kant affirmed: this was simply to reduce God and religion to a support for morality. On the contrary Schleiermacher held that the heart of religion is intuition and feeling (*Anschauung und Gefühl*). By 'feeling' he did not of course mean sheer subjectivity or private emotion, nor did he wish to empty religion of all intellectual content. By 'feeling' he meant a sort of existential self-awareness which conveys an understanding or intuition of the human condition in a relation of total – ontological, one might say – dependence on God or the Absolute. 'Feeling' for him is a matter of 'knowledge through participation'. The basic human situation for Schleiermacher is one where awareness of God is mediated to us through our participation in a world that transcends us at many levels. Knowledge of God is thus mediated to us through the world we live in; it is not given to us in a pure, direct, unmediated way.

The meaning of religion is to be sought therefore not primarily in scripture or tradition or in the theological speculations of human reason,[12] but in the inner consciousness of the genuinely religious person: 'You must transport yourself into the interior of a pious soul and seek to understand its inspiration.'[13] What you find in such a pious soul is 'sense and taste for the Infinite',[14] Schleiermacher's definition of true religion. Religious doctrines therefore are 'a knowledge about feeling, and in no way an immediate knowledge about the operations of the Universe, that gave rise to the feeling.'[15] However Schleiermacher did not think he was teaching pure subjectivism. Religion he explicitly described as 'an affec-

---

11 Cf. Livingston, *Modern Christian Thought. From the Enlightenment to Vatican II* (New York and London, 1971), p. 97.

12 '[B]elief must be something different from a mixture of opinions about God and the world, and of precepts for one life or for two. Piety cannot be an instinct craving for a mess of metaphysical and ethical crumbs' (*On Religion*, p. 31).

13 *On Religion*, p. 18.

14 *Ibid.*, p. 39.

15 *Ibid.*, p. 61.

tion, a revelation of the Infinite in the finite, God being seen in it and it in God.'[16] Hence, what the pious soul contemplates 'is the immediate consciousness of the universal existence of all finite things, in and through the Infinite, and of all temporal things in and through the Eternal.'[17] Furthermore, as Paul Tillich pointed out 'in reference to Schleiermacher, feeling may be subjective, but it is also the impact of the universe upon us and the universe is not subjective!'[18]

In his later, more systematic work, *The Christian Faith* (1821-2), the heart of religious faith was claimed to be 'the feeling of absolute dependence,' an expression that replaced the earlier one ('sense and taste for the Infinite'). Doctrinal statements though are still seen as verbalisations of religious states of mind. Schleiermacher at this later stage was, however, anxious to avoid any impression of pantheism or of suggesting that religion was a purely subjective matter. Thus he claims that the sense of absolute dependence is at the same time 'a co-existence of God in the self-consciousness.'[19] Moreover in both his early and late work Schleiermacher, in speaking of religious experience, is thinking of corporate, not individual or isolated experience. He believed also that religious experience, the 'feeling of absolute dependence, in which our self-consciousness in general represents the finitude of our being' was 'a universal element of life; and the recognition of this fact entirely takes the place, for the system of doctrine, of all the so-called proofs of the existence of God.'[20]

Schleiermacher was able to make such large claims for religious experience because he assumed that the human sense or feeling of absolute dependence was universal and carried with it a consciousness of God so vivid and undeniable as to amount to a co-existence of God in the soul. This, for Schleiermacher, unproblematic correlation between religious experience and God was however subjected to damaging criticism within his own lifetime (notably by Hegel, who made the facetious remark that if the feeling of absolute dependence were the touchstone of religion then a dog would be the most religious of beings[21]), and even more so after his death. However he did convincingly show that God cannot be seen directly

16 *Ibid.*, p. 36.

17 *Ibid.*; cf. Reardon, *op. cit.*, p. 34.

18 Livingston, *op. cit.*, p. 100.

19 *The Christian Faith*, ed. H. R. Mackintosh and J. S. Stewart (Edinburgh, 1968), p. 126.

20 *Ibid.*, pp. 133f.

21 Cf. Stephen Sykes, *Friedrich Schleiermacher* (London, 1971), p. 28.

but only, so to speak, through the prism of the world. If we believe that God is the creator of the world, and since we ('thinking matter') know that we are all in fact part of the world, then it follows that God cannot be glimpsed in isolation from the world. For the 'glimpse' always has its feet firmly on the ground, anchored in the material world. The option of pantheism is therefore omnipresent. As Lichtenberg remarked: '[A]s soon as one believes . . . that God makes matter think one can no longer demonstrate that a god exists apart from matter.'[22]

In this regard, it is interesting to note that the first article of the two most important ancient Christian Creeds[23] (the *Niceno-Constantinopolitan Creed* and the *Apostles' Creed*) holds together belief in God and belief in God, creator of heaven and earth, an implicit admission, surely, that the God-question and the question of the origin, meaning and destiny of the material order are for Christianity inseparable. The fact that in its primary article of faith Christianity holds together, but yet makes a distinction between 'God' and 'God the creator', in order precisely to rule out the option of pantheism, is, it seems to me, an admission that pantheism cannot be dismissed by argument but only resisted by faith (faith ultimately in the victory of God over the evil now present in creation).

Schleiermacher based his view of God on experience or, as he called it, 'feeling', and his theology has been open to criticism on that account ever since, on the grounds that 'feeling' is too subjective to be wholesome. Yet by raising, perhaps unwittingly, the question of the relationship between feeling and thought Schleiermacher gave renewed prominence to the central issue in any discussion of belief in God. For such belief hangs, not so much on how one *answers* the God-question (which cannot in fact be done), as on how one *decides* it. As Lichtenberg noted: 'In the end everything comes down to the question: does thought originate in feeling or feeling in thought? . . . This is the ultimate principle of religion, and the answer to the question "is the power of feeling or the power of thought the ultimate reality?" draws the final frontier between theism and atheism.'[24]

---

22 *Aphorisms*, p. 24.
23 See J. N. D. Kelly, *Early Christian Creeds* (Essex, 1972), Chapters X and XII.
24 *Aphorisms*, p. 135.

Assessment

In trying to assess the validity of Schleiermacher's account of how we come to know God, we may ask whether he succeeds in showing convincingly that religious experience is indeed a universal feature of the human condition, and if so, whether it is self-authenticating and can be interpreted in a way that finds broad agreement. None of these questions can be answered affirmatively with any confidence, especially if Schleiermacher's theology of experience is interpreted as an instance of what R.C. Solomon calls 'the transcendental pretence',[25] which has 'two central components: first, the remarkable inner riches and expanse of the self, ultimately encompassing everything; and secondly, the consequent right to project from the subjective structures of one's own mind, and ascertain the nature of humanity as such.'[26]

In the modern critique of religion the movement from the eighteenth to the nineteenth century witnessed the shift from, as it were, 'fraud' to 'Freud'. That is to say, the eighteenth century (as in the French *philosophe* Nicolas-Antoine Boulanger [1722–59] or the German deist Hermann Samuel Reimarus [1694–1768]) specialised in 'unmasking' what was assumed to be deliberate deception in the field of religion, whereas the nineteenth took pleasure in 'unmasking' the unwitting self-deception of pious 'wishful thinkers'. Hence it is not surprising to learn that Schleiermacher's theology was received by and large negatively, if not contemptuously, by the cultured world he sought to reach. '[I]t was a bad omen,' Barth wrote, 'that Goethe either ignored or viewed with displeasure what was happening. He disliked Schleiermacher's *Speeches*, quite apart from their romantic garb.' [27] One might be inclined to say: 'He would, wouldn't he?' But in the course of the nineteenth century the rejection of Schleiermacher's overtures to the cultured despisers of religion only hardened. The negative answers to the questions raised by his theory of religion were adumbrated by Feuerbach[28] and

---

25 *Continental Philosophy since 1750* (Oxford, 1988), p. 1 and *passim*.

26 *Ibid.*, pp. 1f.

27 *The Humanity of God*, p. 21.

28 Cf. Alister McGrath's remarks, for example: ' ... Feuerbach ... had argued that the Schleiermacherian type of Christology from below (beginning from human experience) was little more than the objectification of human feelings and their projection onto the figure of Jesus' (*The Blackwell Encyclopedia of Modern Christian Thought*, ed. A. McGrath, Oxford, 1993, p. 421).

fleshed out by the other modern so-called 'masters of suspicion' –
Marx, Nietzsche and Freud. Yet while Schleiermacher's theory of
religion manifestly does not prove the existence of God, it surely
describes what one would expect to be the case, were a religious
interpretation of reality in fact true.

However the projectionist critique of Schleiermacher's theory of
religion is worth pursuing a little further. This critique attempts to
discredit his theology on the grounds that it deals only with the
psychological basis of religion. But such an objection might itself
fall into the trap of the so-called genetic fallacy, i.e. confusing the
intrinsic truth of a theory with its genesis. A naturalistic or reductionist account of religious convictions – e.g. in terms of a projection
of one's longing for a perfection not experienced on earth, or a need
for security, or a desire for self-aggrandisement, or eventual compensation for wrongs suffered in this life – leaves too much unex-
plained to be persuasive. For it fails to explain how, in a naturalistically conceived universe, creatures like us could possibly ever have
appeared, with desires for what is beyond the material, and project-
ing our needs and cravings on to what a materialist must deem to
be an empty heaven. If, in short, the world can be understood naturalistically and is in fact comprehensible in purely rational terms,
how did religion, which is not completely rational, ever emerge? In
terms of strict rationalism religion should not exist.

The limitations of a rational account of religion are fairly clear.
To refuse to acknowledge them is surely only to bury one's head in
the sand of one's own rationalism. How, for instance, can we
explain rationally, and without recourse to religion, the fact that we
are, in Kant's phrase, cut from 'crooked timber'? For surely religion
alone can permit us to speak of two wills – ours and God's – at work
within the world, and to go on to say that it is the frequent clash
between the two that produces the warp in our condition? As
against a religious explanation of our predicament, one might prefer to argue that even the strange feature of the human condition
that so impressed Kant can be accounted for naturalistically by saying that the 'warp' in humanity represents Nature's (whatever that
is) mechanism for keeping us on our evolutionary toes, or is the
result of the clash of irreconcilable human wills within history. But
if the latter explanation were true, why do we feel such clashes as
not only tragic, but as the way things should not be. A warp can
only be a warp, if we have some idea of what perfection might be.
And where can the idea of perfection come from, if it nowhere

exists or can exist? Moreover if the world is to be explained materi-alistically, then why should we regard human beings as anything more than flesh and blood? Where does our sense of the limitation of what we can do to other human beings or ourselves come from? To explain human existence naturalistically, therefore, would indeed be to offer a, so to speak, 'internal solution' to the problem of explaining our twisted world. And yet, since no one can predict how the world-process is to continue, let alone culminate, even such an 'internal solution' rests on a substantial act of faith. Who can claim that a *Weltanschauung* that depends on such 'worldly' faith is superior, or preferable, to the description of the world that rests on religious faith?

It is surely just as reasonable, perhaps even more reasonable, to assume that religion, as well as being partly a matter of projection, is, as Gerd Theissen argues, 'also "reflection", the reflection of objective reality'.[29] That is to say, it is at least as reasonable to argue that religion exists because God elicits responses from us, as to claim that we simply project our needs on to nothingness. The fact that our responses to God do not include the achievement of an adequate understanding of God does not undermine faith in God, let alone prove God does not exist. Furthermore, while the human desire that God should exist is admittedly not a convincing argu-ment for his existence, neither is it, logically, a cogent argument against it. If one is well-disposed towards religion, one will speak of it as being a legitimate human response to God, if one is hostile towards religion one will see it as a series of projections of human needs on to what we are not, on to what lies beyond us. But the evi-dence from the human side is ambiguous, and certainly not con-trary to belief in God's existence.

Moreover the fact that we realise our ignorance and uncertainty and doubts in so many areas would appear to point dialectically to a natural link between ourselves and truth. Where there is no truth, neither can there be ignorance or doubt or error. Our search for truth or God, and the perennial ambiguity of the answers we arrive at, are compatible with our status as creatures who are connected with, but in important ways still distinct from, God. Similarly pes-simism, or despair, or disappointment, points to the durability of goodness, otherwise why are we so instinctively disturbed when things turn out badly, and not when they turn out well? We speak naturally of the 'problem of evil', not of the 'problem of good'. This

29 *On Having a Critical Faith*, p. 28.

is certainly no clinching proof of the superiority of good over evil, but it points in that direction. Of course, an Augustine could also see 'good' as problematic and in need of explanation, but that does not undermine belief in the supremacy of good.

Finally, we might reverse the original question and ask naturalist critics why they are so keen to de-divinise religion and to 'unmask' it as a merely human, all too human illusion? Where does such a commitment to truth come from? Is it itself perhaps a projection, just wilful and wishful thinking? So, to sum up this part of our discussion, while the projectionist critique of religious experience should certainly engender caution in making claims about 'God' based on the evidence from the human side, on the other hand this critique is neither necessarily destructive of religion, nor – more seriously – is it self-justifying on its own terms.

Right into the early part of this century Schleiermacher's influence in theology was still strong. The most celebrated exponent of the tradition he initiated was Rudolf Otto (1869-1937) who re-edited the *Speeches on Religion* in 1899, the centenary of its first appearance, and whose own classic work, *Das Heilige* (*The Idea of the Holy*), was published in 1917. This work seems in retrospect to have marked the end of an era rather than the start of a new one, for the years following the appearance of Otto's book were dominated in fact by neo-orthodoxy.

However in more recent times there has been a renewal of interest in the older theory of religion. Some contemporary writers consider that Otto's ideas were too peremptorily dismissed in the early part of this century. For example Gerd Theissen for whom 'the experience of the holy that is accessible to us is a matter of being driven to and fro by experiences of resonance and absurdity, being affected by overwhelming meaning and oppressive meaninglessness, by the *mysterium fascinosum et tremendum* of reality', regrets 'that this approach has not been continued in the theology of the last fifty years.'[30] Similarly Ninian Smart considers that Otto's 'emphasis on the numinous is good in characterising the feel of various kinds of theism, where God is the Other', even if 'it does not work so well in characterising non-theistic mystical experience, especially Buddhist', but he does not see this drawback as invalidating Otto's basic approach.[31]

When modern religious thinkers appeal to experience to sup-

---

30 *On Having a Critical Faith*, pp. 34, 100, n. 9
31 *The World's Religions* (Cambridge, 1993), pp. 349f.

port belief in God, usually their appeal to experience is not in fact restricted to a specifically 'religious' or haunting type of experience in the tradition of Schleiermacher and Otto. Rather it has a broad range of reference that includes an appeal to elements of ultimacy or transcendence in everyday secular experience. The sense of transcendence is usually dialectically perceived: i.e., it is in sensing reality as something we are situated or caught or trapped in, or thrown into, that we realise how little control we ourselves have over our own destiny. This in turn points to God as the ultimate source of our limitations, an expression one may interpret as a restatement of Schleiermacher's 'feeling of absolute dependence'.

Modern religious thinkers who work from the notion of experience but widen the scope of this concept would include Langdon Gilkey and Wolfhart Pannenberg, or the sociologist of religion Peter Berger. With such writers, especially Pannenberg, man's indeterminacy or openness to the world becomes the starting-point for speculation about the religious meaning of experience. Theissen locates the putative connection between the human and the divine in what he and many religious theorists take to be the correspondence between the 'indeterminacy of man' and the transcendence ('transparency') of God who only 'appears through' the world, but is not identical with it:

> The specific appeals presented by the reality of his environment do not affect man as a summons to a specific pattern of behaviour; they are an indefinite demand. Man does not know how to respond... The more consciously he perceives the indeterminate demand, the more strongly he emphasises the transcendence of the deity over its concrete manifestation... [T]he basic theme of all prophetic criticism of religion is that God is greater than particular manifestations of him, that every specific form of the holy can be superseded... [T]he transparency of the holy derives from the human condition, from man's sensitivity towards an indeterminate obligation which transcends all specific forms of the holy.[32]

However while religious believers interpret the experience of 'indeterminacy' as pointing to the transcendent God, for others it points only to the *immanent* forces of the cosmos that govern our existence. Ironically the aspect of Christianity that Schleiermacher wished to recover was precisely belief in God's *immanence* in the world.

If one wished to locate the strengths of Schleiermacher's

32 *On Having a Critical Faith*, p. 16.

approach, one could no doubt stress that he brought back to prominence an aspect of the God-question which was not entirely new,[33]
but had been somewhat neglected by the Enlightenment (with its
'watchmaker' God[34]) and to a lesser extent by Protestant orthodoxy,
though not by pietism. This aspect was what one could term the
immanence of God in the world and the corresponding emphasis
on the human experience of God. Christianity tries to avoid, and
Western culture seems always to have remained unconvinced by,
either extreme transcendence or extreme immanence in regard to
God's relationship to the world, and when emphasis on either
divine transcendence or divine immanence has been exclusive, this
has provoked a reaction. Schleiermacher's enterprise can be understood as the reassertion of the importance of divine immanence and
religious experience.

Not infrequently, however, the recovery or rediscovery of an old
truth blinds one to the reality and importance of other truths.
Schleiermacher's discovery of a new way of speaking about God
led him perhaps to dismiss in too cavalier a fashion other, better-
known arguments for theism that even today still continue to be

33 As he himself was well aware. It is interesting to note that as an epigraph to his major theological text *The Christian Faith* (1821-22) he chose
two brief extracts from the works of Anselm (*Proslogion* ch. 1, and *de fide
trin*. ch. 2) which stressed the need for the experience of faith as a necessary precondition for understanding: 'Neque enim quaero intelligere ut
credam, sed credo ut intelligam. – Nam qui non crediderit, non experi-
etur, et qui expertus non fuerit, non intelliget.' ('For I do not seek to
understand so that I may believe; but I believe so that I may understand. – He who will not have believed, will not know by experience,
and he who will not have known by experience, will not understand.')
34 The 'watchmaker' notion of God goes back to William Paley
(1743–1805), who in his argument drew upon 'virtually all the sciences
of his day' (Hick, *Philosophy of Religion*, p. 24), an early example of theology's (possibly unsolicited) exploitation of science. Paley was not quite
so keen to listen to Hume's objections to the design argument for the
existence of God, even though Hume had expressed his views twenty-
three years previously (Hick, *op. cit.*, p. 25). In Paley's analogical
description God is seen as the agent responsible for the marvellous
design of the cosmos, much as a watchmaker would be responsible for
designing a complex timepiece. Paley's argument is now not often considered sophisticated enough to be convincing. However, his basic
notion of God may have hidden strengths. On realising what the atom
bomb could do Einstein said: 'If only I had known, I should have
become a watchmaker.'

important.[35] Does he underestimate the persuasiveness of the traditional metaphysical arguments, or the moral argument, for the existence of God? How, for example, without God, can one perceive, or
recognise abiding meaning in, the distinction between good and
evil?

However an ultimately more serious problem for Schleiermacher's theology is that in attempting to mediate between
Christianity and culture (always a hazardous undertaking) he had
rather lost sight of, or had side-stepped, the 'scandal' of Christianity. This is perhaps not unconnected with the sometimes scornful rejection of his theology by many nineteenth-century figures
such as Schopenhauer,[36] Kierkegaard,[37] Lagarde,[38] Nietzsche[39] and
Overbeck who were of course not only critical of Schleiermacher
but also generally critical of, and disaffected towards, the culture of

---

35 Cf. W. Barrett's comment on Heidegger: '[I]t often happens with a
philosopher who has had an original perception that he rides it too
intensely and exclusively, while shutting off other and more usual
points of view' (*Death of the Soul*, Oxford, 1987, p. 139).

36 Schopenhauer saw in 'the great Schleiermacher' only a 'German philosophical windbag'; cf. A. Schopenhauer, *Werke* V (Darmstadt, 1976),
p. 330.

37 Kierkegaard noted in 1836 (when he was twenty-three): 'What
Schleiermacher calls "Religion" and the Hegelians "Faith" is at the bottom only the first condition for everything – the vital fluidum – the
atmosphere we breathe in – which does not really deserve this name'
(quoted in Louis Dupré, *Kierkegaard as Theologian*, London, 1964, p. 118).

38 Referring to Schleiermacher's mediating theology Lagarde wrote scorn-
fully: 'In the mornings Schleiermacher played religion on the G string
and in the afternoons philosophy on the D string; on request the other
way around … Schleiermacher's death did not so much create a gap as it
showed that the abyss which even then was yawning had not been
bridged by him for the educated classes but had merely been veiled [*ver-
schleiert*: a pun on Schleiermacher's name] by him' (quoted in Fritz Stern,
The Politics of Cultural Despair: A Study in the Rise of the Germanic Ideology,
Berkeley and Los Angeles, 1974, pp. 36f.). The importance of the rather
sinister figure Paul de Lagarde (1827–91), an orientalist and noted
Septuagint specialist (professor at Göttingen from 1869 until his death),
is treated by Fritz Stern in Part One of his excellent study.

39 'He who has once contracted Hegelism and Schleiermacherism is never
quite cured of them' (*Untimely Meditations*, tr. R. J. Hollingdale, Cambridge, 1983, p. 27; Nietzsche made the inevitable pun on Schleiermacher's name [*veil-maker*] in *Ecce Homo*, tr. R. J. Hollingdale, Harmondsworth, 1979, p. 122).

their own times and, like Newman in England, deeply suspicious of liberalism.[40]

Overbeck's critique was more humane in that he recoiled from what he took to be Schleiermacher's subtle or covert exploitation of human fear as a basis for justifying Christianity: for Overbeck this is ultimately inhuman,[41] as is the threat contained in theology's 'general terroristic rejection of atheism', which in fact only serves to mask its own 'will to power'. Overbeck, however, may have been viewing Schleiermacher through the cruder lens of the dominant Ritschlian theology of his own times. Nonetheless, his instinct to question any theology presenting Christianity, in however qualified a sense, as a response to a threat is surely worth taking seriously. Could such a theology point to a form of dualism (God as a saviour from, rather than of, the world), and be therefore an implicit denial of the doctrine of creation?

The critical rejection of Schleiermacher's enterprise in the nineteenth century was enthusiastically echoed by Karl Barth. Schleiermacher was felt to have either domesticated or overlooked the profound drama of human existence and the often agonising nature of the religious quest. Schleiermacher's 'sense and taste for the Infinite' or 'feeling of absolute dependence' proved to be no match for Kierkegaard's 'Fear and Trembling' and 'Sickness unto Death'.[42] In other words, the aspect of the religious question alluded to by Whitehead when he 'once suggested that a religious sensibility begins with a sense that "something is awry,"'[43] or by Newman when he felt 'the human race' to be 'implicated in some terrible

---

40 Newman saw in 'Liberalism' (in religion: cf. *Apologia*, p. 123) only 'the halfway house' to 'Atheism' (*ibid.*, p. 251). To Newman writing in the 1860s 'Liberalism' seemed to have entirely permeated the English intelligentsia: 'The Liberalism which gives a colour to society now, is very different from that character of thought which bore the name thirty or forty years ago. It is scarcely now a party; it is the educated lay world' (*ibid.*, p. 293).

41 Cf. *Christentum und Kultur*, p. 264: 'For what else is ... Schleiermacher's definition of religion as a product of the human feeling of dependence, other than a sophistically sublimated form of the Epicurean reduction of religion to *deisidaimonia* ["superstitious fear"]'; (cf. Schopenhauer, *Werke* III, p. 359, n.1).

42 Cf. Siegbert Prawer (ed.), *The Romantic Period in Germany* (London, 1970), pp. 7f.

43 David Tracy, *Plurality and Ambiguity* (London, 1988), p. 111.

aboriginal calamity'[44] is not very conspicuous in the actual substance of Schleiermacher's thought (as opposed to his clear initial perception that something was wrong with the traditional presentation of religion in his culture, and that a new approach was called for). The thought of Schleiermacher, in short, has 'an insufficient appreciation of the fallen condition of man, of guilt and sin,'[45] it neglects one of the striking features of the Christian understanding of God and his engagement in our lives. For, as Peter Pawlowsky has expressed it, Christianity 'preserves something of the endtime expectation of its early days, in the awareness that the drama of one's own life is caught up in the drama of salvation history.'[46] And the drama of everyone's own life is marked, as human life from the beginning always has been, with the scourge of evil and suffering, and the ever-present threat of death, shadows which continually darken the encounter with intellectual truth, beauty and love.

Whether one accepts Schleiermacher's theory of religion or not, it is still important to note that the religious experience of which he speaks, is not direct experience by the believer of God, but rather experience of the divine as mediated through the world and the world's impact on human consciousness, i.e. it is impersonal, and apparently morally neutral. It is not clear how this type of experience is related to the Judaeo-Christian experience of God recorded in the bible and continued for Christians in the life of the church, for this experience is of a personal and moral character. Karl Barth may have had this issue in mind when he wrote: 'The God of Schleiermacher cannot show mercy. The God of Abraham, Isaac, and Jacob can and does.'[47]

The church claims that we experience – in the sense of: 'have to do with' – God directly in Christ. This is not quite the same as saying that Christ had religious experience which we should strive to emulate, even though there is surely some degree of overlap in the two meanings of 'experience'. For the gospels clearly speak about Jesus' awareness of God, his relationship to God in prayer, his 'religious experience', if you will. And this fact can hardly be ignored by those who believe in the divinity of Jesus. But in preserving the distinction between humanity and divinity in Jesus it is unnecessary to go so far as, say, Lessing, who saw a complete dichotomy

44 *Apologia*, p. 279.
45 S. Prawer (ed.), *op. cit.*, p. 7.
46 P. Pawlowsky, *Christianity*, tr. J. Bowden (London, 1994), p. 103.
47 *The Humanity of God*, p. 49.

between Jesus' own 'religious experience', and the 'religious experience' of those who believe him to be the divine redeemer. Lessing widened the genuine distinction between the two meanings of the expression into an unbridgeable gulf, when he wrote: '[T]he religion of Christ and the Christian religion are two quite different things. The former, the religion of Christ, is that religion which as a man he himself recognised and practised; which every man has in common with him ... The latter, the Christian religion, is that religion which accepts it as true that he was more than a man, and makes Christ himself, as such, the object of its worship.'[48] For Lessing only the former definition of Christianity has now any authentic meaning.

Lessing, as a man of the Enlightenment, could only accept the humanity of Jesus, which is of course part of Christianity; he could not accept Jesus' divinity. But can it be ruled out in principle that belief in the divinity of Jesus is excluded by acceptance of his full humanity? Lessing clearly thought it could, or he assumed that the notion of the divinity of Jesus was in any case incredible. This assumption is, however, what Christianity has always challenged, while rejecting also the possibility that divinity and humanity are identical. If the Enlightenment through its spokesman Lessing rejected the divinity of Jesus, and retained the humanity, Schleiermacher, for his part, presented the divinity of Jesus as a modification of human consciousness. In trying to express Jesus' divinity in this way Schleiermacher, as we have already suggested, rather lost sight of the scandal of Christianity, which cannot be contained within any intellectual system.

This puts, I think, a question-mark over the persuasiveness for belief in the God of Christianity of the approach to the God-question associated with Schleiermacher and Otto, because in the light of their theory one would tend to see Jesus as an exemplar of a kind of religious possibility that is still, in principle, available to all. It is true that Schleiermacher accords a position to Christ in relation to all other human beings which is unique, in that in Christ God-consciousness, as Schleiermacher calls it, is so unclouded as to repre-

---

48 *The Religion of Christ* [1780], in H. Chadwick, *Lessing's Theological Writings* (London, 1956), p. 106. Cf. F. Overbeck, *Christentum und Kultur*, p. 28: 'Christianity means nothing other than Christ and his followers' faith in him, it is something supratemporal, in Jesus' own lifetime it did not yet exist.' For Overbeck himself neither of Lessing's interpretations of Christianity is credible in the modern world.

sent what was traditionally referred to as Christ's divine nature. However, to spell out divinity in terms of human consciousness, however sublime, seems to make Christ, finally, different in degree, not in kind from the rest of humanity. If Christianity is to retain its savour, Christ must remain as incomprehensible as God.

Yet Schleiermacher's major importance is undeniable. For he gave modern theology its starting-points. He put at the top of the theological agenda items which are still there, even if they are understood in radically different ways by different writers. These questions are so simple, so fundamental and so difficult to deal with that one might be forgiven for thinking they were always the staple diet of Christian theology. In fact for a long time before Schleiermacher they were taken for granted, and theologians presumed they knew the answers to them, whether in a Catholic or a Reformed sense. But Schleiermacher forced both the question of the very nature and meaning of religion – and hence how the term 'God' should be interpreted – and that of the essence and meaning of Christianity itself to the forefront of theological thinking once again. The origins of both the modern God-question and of modern Christology go back to him.

It is a measure of the power of his basic theological conception that even those who most trenchantly reject what he has to say cannot ignore and in fact have to adopt the terms in which he posed the central questions of religion in the modern world. No one would wish to claim that theology began in 1799, but it would be difficult to overestimate the innovative quality of Schleiermacher's approach to religion and theology. Yet on one issue he did not change the direction initiated by the major thinkers of the modern period such as Luther, Descartes and Kant. Like them, he also took a subject-centred starting-point for his theology, so to that extent his work marks not the beginning of an absolutely new current of thought, but the continuation of what is perhaps the main intellectual habit of modernity. However, it is not subjectivity as such that is problematic in Schleiermacher's thought. For subjectivity gives undoubtedly one valid perspective on truth. It is rather his exclusive attachment to subjectivity, which appears to rule out the divine possibility that the radically unknown, incomprehensible, and unexpected may occur, that is Schleiermacher's Achilles' heel.

However desperate times call for bold initiatives, and as the title of his most famous work (*On Religion: Speeches to Its Cultured Despisers*) testifies, Schleiermacher was worried about the risk of the disappearance of the religious question from general public awareness and interest, and wanted to put it back forcefully at the centre of thinking people's concerns. Whether one agrees or not with his method of trying to do this is not as important as to realise how right he was to see that Christian faith must debate with the best elements of whatever culture it finds itself in contact with, if it is not to face extinction or a future of public irrelevance.

Albrecht Ritschl (1822–1889)

Finally, brief mention should be made of Albrecht Ritschl who in his own day was seen as the first theologian since Schleiermacher to have given birth to a new epoch. But as Barth points out, 'Ritschl has the significance of an episode in more recent theology.'[49] He saw himself of course as correcting and overcoming Schleiermacher's baneful influence on modern religion,[50] but Schleiermacher's quest-ions outlived Ritschl, whereas Ritschl's answers disappeared with the demise of his system. Overbeck, who saw in Ritschl a theologi-cal Sisyphus, was appropriately enough – given the importance accorded in Ritschl's theology to the moral will – more impressed by his will-power than by his intellect. It is as if, to quote Gracián, Ritschl's works 'were written to exercise the arms rather than the wits.'[51] Above all Ritschl's repudiation of metaphysics appeared to Overbeck foolish on two grounds: firstly because theology has no proprietorial claim on metaphysics to begin with, and secondly because metaphysics has its own intrinsic value which others are at liberty to appreciate even if theologians cannot.[52] Ritschl's concept of religion appeared indeed to Overbeck to be only a coarser ver-sion of Schleiermacher's.[53] Ritschl's self-assurance now seems dated.

His theology is characterised by the following two features: (a) the denial of speculative metaphysics as a basis for religious faith, and (b) the exaltation of practical reason and the value-judgements (*Werturteile*) proceeding from it as a way of justifying religion. In both of these respects Ritschl followed closely the path marked out much earlier by Kant. But his theologically motivated interest in history came from his time as a disciple of F.C. Baur's (1792-1860), the founder of the famous Tübingen School of historical theology.

---

49 K. Barth, *Protestant Theology in the Nineteenth Century* (London, 1972), p. 654.
50 Cf. F. Overbeck, *Christentum und Kultur*, p. 165.
51 Baltasar Gracián, *The Oracle* §27, tr. L. B. Walton (London, 1953), p. 69.
52 *Christentum und Kultur*, pp. 160, 162f.
53 *Op. cit.*, p. 264.

For Ritschl, the founder of the Liberal Protestant movement, God's significance in human life was established through value-judgements. He taught that religion is fundamentally a practical matter. It is neither mystical feeling nor intuition, nor is it a species of metaphysical knowledge ('natural theology'). It is the experience of moral freedom, of being liberated from slavery to nature's blind necessity. In a world unsettled by evolutionary theory and positivistic natural science Ritschl's theology presented Christianity as the power promising believers 'domination over the world'. God is thus posited as a moral need and a guarantee for the attainment of our spiritual victory over the world. 'Knowledge of God can be demonstrated as religious knowledge only when He is conceived as securing to the believer such a position in the world as more than counterbalances its restrictions. Apart from this value-judgment of faith, there exists no knowledge of God worthy of this content.'[54] It is the impact of the historical Jesus on him that produces in Ritschl the value-judgement of faith that in Jesus he is in touch with this power which overcomes the world. The Ritschlian tradition, represented by such figures as W. Herrmann and A. Harnack, faded towards the end of the nineteenth century. However the formal shape of Ritschl's theology, though not of course its dispiritingly tedious content, lived on in an unlikely quarter, in the thought of Karl Barth. For Barth too repudiated metaphysics and religious experience as foundations for Christian theology, and made scriptural revelation and Christology his central theological concern.

---

54 *Justification and Reconciliation* (Edinburgh, 1900), vol. III, p. 212.

CHAPTER SEVEN

Hegel

God himself sees in things only himself.
— Georg Chr. Lichtenberg

The question of how Reason is determined in itself and what its relation is to the world coincides with the question What is the ultimate purpose of the world? — Georg W. F. Hegel

The fact that one can annihilate a philosophy ... or that one can prove that a philosophy annihilates itself is of little consequence. If it's really philosophy, then, like a phoenix, it will always rise again from its own ashes. — Friedrich von Schlegel

Introduction

Another German thinker and contemporary of Schleiermacher's who has had incalculable influence in the last two hundred years on the approach to the God-question is Hegel (1770–1831). Hegel is important for modern theology, in the first place, because he has played such a dominant role in creating the intellectual self-understanding of the modern world in which theology has to exist, and to which it must speak. 'History', said Alexandre Kojève, 'can never refute Hegelianism; it can only choose between conflicting interpretations of it.' But he is important for the more specific reason that he remained throughout his life passionately concerned with religion and its meaning in modern culture. Indeed he considered his own philosophy to be the only viable modern presentation of the Christian faith.

What makes Hegel a perhaps uniquely difficult thinker to get to grips with is the potent combination in his writings of passion and seemingly abstruse intellectual complexity often verging on obscurity[1] which has provoked such widely and even wildly diverging

---

1   'I cannot tell whether he is brilliant or mad. He seems to me to be an unclear thinker,' was one reaction to Hegel's table talk (see Jonathan Glover, I: *the Philosophy and Psychology of Personal Identity*, Harmondsworth, 1991, p. 134).

opinions about the status of his philosophy. They range from Kojève's conviction that Hegel in one form or another is here to stay, to Schopenhauer's untiring disparagement of him as a 'windbag'. But J. N. Findlay's comment that in reading Hegel one is 'at times only sure that he is saying something immeasurably profound and important, but not exactly what it is,'[2] will surely resonate with anyone who has tried sympathetically to make sense of Hegel. In the light of his own judgement 'that only one man had understood him and he had understood him wrongly,'[3] we may surmise that not much is to be gained by asking: 'Was he right, or was he wrong?' What is, it seems to me, more fruitful, is to accept that Hegel managed to find a path through the chaos of human consciousness, a path which will undoubtedly appear to most readers as puzzling, even arbitrary. But the lightning-flashes of Hegel's visionary genius illuminate the path in so many places, jolting the reader with shocks of recognition, that the question: 'Was he ultimately right or wrong?' seems 'almost indecent'.[4] To quote one of Hegel's own aphorisms, 'The condemnation which a great man lays upon the world, is to force it to explain him.'[5] This has certainly proved true in Hegel's own case.

As might be expected, there are many different judgements on his philosophy of religion,[6] which range from seeing him as a credi-

2   From the 'Foreword' to G. W. F. Hegel, *Phenomenology of Spirit*, tr. A. V. Miller, with Analysis of the Text and Foreword by J. N. Findlay (Oxford, 1979), p. xiii.

3   Mentioned by L. Kolakowski, *Metaphysical Horror*, p. 101; (see also F. Overbeck, *Christentum und Kultur*, pp. 218f.).

4   Cf. Arnaldo Momigliano, *Essays in Ancient and Modern Historiography* (Oxford, 1977), p. 10: 'Our instinctive sympathy is for the human beings who by meditation and spiritual search freed themselves from the conventions within which they were born and reoriented the activities of other men. Though questions of "truth" can never be avoided entirely, we feel that it is almost indecent (and in any case too embarrassing) to ask whether what Zoroaster or Isaiah or Aeschylus had to say was true or false.'

5   Quoted by William Wallace (tr.) in his 'Prolegomena' to *The Logic of Hegel*, p. xiii (this is a translation of the 'Lesser Logic' from the *Encyclopaedia*).

6   It is worth noting that the 'philosophy of religion', as B. M. G. Reardon points out (*Hegel's Philosophy of Religion*, London, 1977, pp. xiii, 123) is 'a comparatively modern discipline', the term itself not being used, apparently, before 1793. Among its founding fathers Reardon places Lessing, Herder, Kant, Schleiermacher and Hegel.

ble intellectual defender of Christianity in the modern world, to seeing him as a pantheist or even an atheist,[7] hence a – no doubt unwitting – gravedigger of Christianity. But few would dispute the genuineness of his interest in religion.

The beginnings of Hegel's intellectual odyssey confirm this impression. For he entered the famous *Tübinger Stift* as a student of theology in 1788 with the intention of becoming a pastor in the Lutheran church. However he found the theological teaching he received at Tübingen so unattractive[8] that he abandoned both official theology and his desire to be a pastor. Thenceforth he attempted to work out his own understanding of Christianity. In this Hegel resembles many celebrated figures in modern German intellectual and literary history who began their academic life as students of theology, subsequently abandoned or were dismissed from the official study of theology, but retained a lifelong interest in theological or religious questions, writers like Schelling, Hölderlin, Strauss, Bauer,[9] Feuerbach, Burckhardt, or Overbeck. Even Nietzsche, who

---

7   Bruno Bauer (see below n.9), for example, in his anonymous pamphlet of 1841, *Die Posaune des jüngsten Gerichts über Hegel den Atheisten und Antichristen* (The trumpet of the Last Judgment on Hegel the atheist and anti-Christian), 'cleverly exhibits how atheistic Hegel's doctrines must appear to a naive but devout Christian' (Van A. Harvey, 'Ludwig Feuerbach and Karl Marx', in Ninian Smart et al., *Nineteenth Century Religious Thought in the West*, vol. 1, Cambridge, 1985, p. 293).

8   Reardon (*op. cit.*, p. 1) writes that by the time Hegel went to Tübingen 'he had attained an unusual degree of intellectual maturity ... and with the independence of judgement which this brought he found the conventional academic routine uncongenial, if not a waste of time. Nor could he discover much to admire in his teachers themselves, who struck him as unimaginative and uninspiring.'

9   Bruno Bauer (1809–82), German theologian and historian. Bauer moved early from a conservative Hegelianism to an increasingly critical position, especially on New Testament scholarship, as one of the left-wing or 'Young Hegelians', and friend of Karl Marx. Unlike D. F. Strauss he thought the Gospels were not the products of the religious consciousness of the early Christian community but were the literary creations of individual writers. Discounting the possibility of a historical Jesus, he concluded that Christianity could be explained as a product of second-century Graeco-Roman culture. Not surprisingly for one who regarded Christianity as 'the misfortune of the world', i.e. a radically anti-human force, he was referred to positively by Nietzsche in *Ecce Homo* (p. 85) as 'one of my most attentive readers.' While rejecting his answers, Albert Schweitzer nevertheless valued highly the quality of his questions, to

saw a close connection between Christian theology and the modern
German philosophical tradition,[10] had studied theology officially
for a short time at Bonn university,[11] and, until his breakdown,
remained obsessed with Christianity.

Early writings

Hegel's early writings between 1795 and 1800 (published only in
1907 [ET 1948]) are in fact mainly concerned with questions of theology. Of these early writings *The Positivity of the Christian Religion*
was composed when Hegel was about twenty-five, and still deeply
under the influence of *Aufklärung* rationalism, as typified by Kant.
It presents a view of Christianity very much like that found in
Kant's late work, *Religion within the Limits of Reason Alone* (1793).
'Positivity', in this context (which has no connection with Auguste
Comte's notion of 'positivism' that was developed later in the nineteenth century) means simply everything that constitutes
Christianity as a specific, concrete, historical religion, with its insti-
tutional structures and authority, scripture, liturgy, creeds, doctrine and pastoral organisation. 'Jesus,' Hegel writes, 'was the
teacher of a purely moral religion, not a positive one. Miracles and
so forth ... were perhaps simply meant to awaken the attention of a
people deaf to morality.'[12] In its pristine form Christianity was,
according to Hegel, concerned basically with moral duties and the
pursuit of the good, like all genuine, 'natural' religion. Like most
rationalists of his time, Hegel was unaware of how little historical
evidence was available to support such a contention. Jesus' disciples, Hegel argued, transformed Christianity from a purely moral,

---

New Testament studies ('his eccentricity concealed a penetrating
   insight', A. Schweitzer, *The Quest of the Historical Jesus*, London, 1963,
   p. 160).

10 Cf. *The Anti-Christ* §10: 'Among Germans one will understand immediately when I say that philosophy has been corrupted by theologian
   blood. The Protestant pastor is the grandfather of German philosophy,
   Protestantism itself is its *peccatum originale*. ... One has only to say the
   words 'College of Tübingen' [*Tübinger Stift*] to grasp what German
   philosophy is at bottom – a cunning theology ...' (Cf. *Beyond Good and
   Evil* §11.)

11 See R. J. Hollingdale, *Nietzsche. The Man and His Philosophy* (London,
   1965), p. 38; id., *Nietzsche* (London and Boston, 1973), p. 43.

12 *On Christianity: Early Theological Writings*, tr. T. M. Knox, intro. R. Kroner
   (Gloucester, Mass., 1970), p. 71.

rational religion into a positive one,[13] out of harmony with its original laudable aims. Hegel was to advance far beyond this early rational-istic assessment of the Christian religion, but he always retained a strong bias towards stringent rational thought on religious ques-tions.

Hegel's next important attempt to work out a theory of religion was in *The Spirit of Christianity and Its Fate*, written around 1798/99. This work marked a distinct change in Hegel's understanding of Christianity. It is now made clear that spiritual truth is not to be grasped by the intellect alone, but that it has what might nowadays be called an experiential or existential dimension: 'Nowhere', Hegel writes, 'more than in the communication of the divine is it neces-sary for the recipient to grasp the communication with the depths of his own spirit.'[14] For Hegel the divine is spirit. Hence, assuming only like can know like: 'Faith in the divine is only possible if in the believer himself there is a divine element which rediscovers itself, its own nature, in that on which it believes, even if it be unconscious that what it has found *is* its own nature ... The middle state between darkness (remoteness from the divine, imprisonment in the mun-dane) and a wholly divine life of one's own, a trust in one's self, is faith in the divine... [F]aith in the divine grows out of the divinity of the believer's own nature; only a modification of the Godhead can know the Godhead.'[15]

By this stage Hegel is quite clearly moving away from a purely rationalistic view of Christianity to a view that is not too distant from Schleiermacher's. There is no doubt that Hegel was influenced by the great current of thought and sensibility known as Romanticism, for which religion could never be a purely or exclu-sively intellectual affair. Yet Hegel – and here he differed from Schleiermacher – was always keenly aware of the danger of appeal-ing directly to feeling in religion.[16] For him the problem with feel-

---

13 It is interesting to note how enduring the basic thesis of a radical break (however interpreted) between Jesus and his followers proved to be in modern German thought, from Reimarus by way of Hegel right down to Nietzsche.

14 *On Christianity: Early Theological Writings*, p. 256.

15 *Ibid.*, p. 266.

16 In this respect Hegel somewhat resembles Newman from whom he is otherwise so distinct. For Newman too was aware of 'the danger of being swayed by our sympathy rather than our reason in religious inquiry,' or as he put it on another occasion: 'I have a great dread of going by my own feelings, lest they mislead me' (*Apologia*, pp. 222, 271).

ing was that it did not go beyond the immediacy of 'religious experience'. Hegel was unwilling to rest content with merely subjective
convictions, but sought to transcend feeling and demonstrate the
universal, intellectual defensibility of religious truth. Hence,
although he now accepted that both feeling and thought were
involved in religion, he still continued to attach more weight to
rational thought than to feeling in his philosophy of religion.

In *The Spirit of Christianity and Its Fate* Hegel also broached the
question of human 'estrangement' or 'alienation', a recurrent theme
in his writings to which we shall return when dealing with his
interpretation of the Fall. In the religion of the Old Testament Hegel
saw a vision of human alienation. Alienation is the consciousness of
separation between the self and the world. Normally, for Hegel,
everything that is particular or separated or isolated seeks to be
completed in a larger totality, and this is especially true of the isolated human individual. By contrast the Hebrews saw the world as
a place of exile and were unwilling or unable to find reconciliation
with nature or other human beings, because they sought a relation
only with their transcendent God. In the figure of Abraham Hegel
saw a powerful symbol of the problem that obsessed him. For
Abraham wanted to be an isolated individual. Abraham's career is
therefore, according to Hegel, no object of admiration. By leaving
his original home in Ur he disowned his own community.
Henceforth he lived among foreigners as a self-sufficient individual, holding himself aloof from his surroundings:

> The first act which made Abraham the progenitor of a nation is a
> disseverance which snaps the bonds of communal life and love.
> The entirety of the relationships in which he had hitherto lived
> with men and nature, these beautiful relationships of his youth
> (Joshua xxiv. 2), he spurned... Abraham wanted *not* to love,
> wanted to be free by not loving... He was a stranger on earth, a
> stranger to the soil and to men alike... The whole world
> Abraham regarded as simply his opposite; if he did not take it to
> be a nullity he looked on it as sustained by the God who was
> alien to it. Nothing in nature was supposed to have any part in
> God; everything was simply under God's mastery.[17]

Newman's sense of the objectivity of truth is behind his refusal to
equate sincerity with truth *tout court* (*ibid.*, p. 252). In trying to deal with
subjectivism in religion Newman, of course, chose a vastly different
path from Hegel.

17 *Early Theological Writings*, pp. 185ff. There is no doubt a connection

The source of Abraham's anti-social isolationism lies, in Hegel's interpretation of the story, in his transcendent monotheism. And Abraham's 'spirit is the unity, the soul, regulating the entire fate of his posterity.'[18] Hegel's negative evaluation of Abraham contrasts vividly with Kierkegaard's interpretation of Abraham's saga in *Fear and Trembling*. To Kierkegaard Abraham is a hero, the knight of faith, precisely because he is an individual who dares to break with traditional attitudes and behaviour. 'For Kierkegaard, it is the individual human being who is the concrete reality, and society an abstraction.'[19] He sees God's call to man as 'something incommensurable with the universal demands of rational will.'[20] But for Hegel God's ways are ultimately our ways, provided only that we can think through the meaning of our experience philosophically to the end. For Kierkegaard, by contrast, 'God's salvation must be an "incomprehensible reconciling" in Barth's phrase,[21] or else lose its character as radical giving, as free initiative.'[22]

The contrast between Hegel's and Kierkegaard's interpretation of Abraham is instructive about Hegel's view of God. For Hegel's emphasis on society and the world as against the concrete individual, as the 'place' where the individual overcomes his isolation and finds union with 'God' – an emphasis Kierkegaard strongly resists – corresponds to his view of God as ultimately open and transparent to man's enquiring intelligence. Kierkegaard, however, sees the human individual as a much more problematic reality than does Hegel, and correspondingly views God as more problematic, more inscrutable, more impenetrable to human reason than the God presented by Hegel. It is interesting to note, though, how in both Hegel and Kierkegaard the images of God and man closely determine each another.

Abraham, in this early work of Hegel's, is of course a symbol for what Hegel takes to be the human predicament of alienation in the

between Hegel's negative evaluation of Abraham and his similarly negative view of monasticism, which he shares with the whole liberal-Protestant tradition (cf. Charles Taylor, *Hegel*, Cambridge, 1977, p. 504, n. 1).

18 *Early Theological Writings*, p. 182.
19 John Macquarrie, *In Search of Deity* (London, 1984), p. 129.
20 Taylor, *Hegel*, p. 494.
21 Karl Barth, *Protestant Theology in the Nineteenth Century*, tr. B. Cozens and J. Bowden (London, 1972), p. 418.
22 Taylor, *Hegel*, p. 494.

world. Alienation is painfully felt when the individual trespasses against a law and because of his bad action experiences a split within his own life, yet this very problem prompts the search for an appropriate solution: 'When the trespasser feels the disruption of his own life (suffers punishment) or knows himself (in his bad conscience) as disrupted, then the working of his fate commences, and this feeling of a life disrupted must become a longing for what has been lost. The deficiency is recognised as a part of himself, as what was to have been in him and is not.'[23] The search for the solution to this existential problem was to engross Hegel in his mature philosophy.

Between his earliest writings on Christianity and his later famous works Hegel obviously found reason to abandon, not the Enlightenment's commitment to rational thought, but the unimaginative side of that rationalism (for instance its failure to see the profound human significance of the story of the Fall). For it was this side of the Enlightenment that blinded it to the deeper meaning that Hegel was eventually to reconstruct for himself out of the Christian doctrinal tradition. He came to believe that it was incredible to conclude with the *Aufklärung* that historical Christianity represented only stupid superstition. Rather its theology could be shown to contain the most profound truth about the human condition, but a truth that now had to be expressed in a different idiom. Hegel's new project then 'would derive that now discarded theology from what we now know as a need of human nature and would thus exhibit its naturalness and inevitability.'[24] To attempt such a project would of course mean assuming that 'the convictions of many centuries, regarded as sacrosanct, true, and obligatory by the millions who lived and died by them in those centuries, were not, at least on their subjective side, downright folly (*barer Unsinn*) or plain immorality.'[25] But what historical Christianity had hitherto, i.e. up until modern times, expressed in a symbolic or representational (*Vorstellung*) mode had now to be transcended (*aufgehoben*), or translated out into conceptual form (*Begriff*), a task which Hegel was convinced could and should be carried through 'without remainder'.

---

23 *Early Theological Writings*, pp. 230f.
24 *Early Theological Writings*, p. 172 (from a revised form, written in 1800, of early sections of *The Positivity of the Christian Religion*).
25 *Ibid.*; cf. J. C. Livingston, *op. cit.*, pp. 149f.

Later writings

In 1807 Hegel published his first major work: *The Phenomenology of Spirit* (*Die Phänomenologie des Geistes*), one of only four books that he actually published in his own lifetime.[26] It presents a comprehensive account of his system. In German *Geist* means 'spirit' (the translation used here) and 'mind'. That is to say, it has both an intellectual and a more 'religious' or 'spiritual' sense (the English word *ghost* that is cognate with *Geist* is not much help here), which in English neither 'mind' nor 'spirit' alone can capture. It is useful to bear this in mind, when trying to grapple with Hegel's excruciatingly difficult thought and style. In an effort to try to understand Hegel, we could think of spirit as being what he means by 'God', provided we remember that Hegel's 'God' is not the God of traditional Christian theism. Indeed for Hegel 'Christianity ... must give up its traditional theistic view, for such a view still conceives of God as a personal, transcendent Being "out there."'[27]

The *Phenomenology*, if one dared to try to sum it up in one sentence, is the story of the self-realisation or self-becoming of Absolute Spirit as a result of its journey through the dramatic history of human consciousness, 'without which it would be lifeless and alone.'[28] H. B. Acton described it as 'an account of how various human attitudes – reliance on sense experience, the belief in substance, otherworldliness, strenuous moralism, and so on – all have some point and are yet contradictory, leading to the conclusion that "truth is a bacchanalian revel where not a member is sober," as Hegel put it in the Preface.'[29] The book itself is built around three

26 The other three being: *Science of Logic* (1812–16), *Encyclopaedia* (1817; rewritten ed. 1827; rev. ed. 1830), and *Philosophy of Right* (1821).

27 Livingston, *op. cit.*, p. 155. Cf. the comments of Franklin L. Baumer, *Modern European Thought* (New York and London, 1977), p. 317: 'Traditional theism, Hegel believed, had grown up in response to the devaluation of man and his social life in the ancient world. Man, despairing of his earthly state, created a transcendent God, static and wholly other, to whom he stood in the relation of slave to master. But now, having outgrown the wretched conditions of the ancient world, man could see himself for what he really is, a facet of the Absolute, and thus overcome the sharp distinction between God and man.'

28 *Phenomenology of Spirit*, p. 493 (changing 'he' to 'it').

29 In Paul Edwards (ed.), *The Encyclopedia of Philosophy*, vol. 3 (New York, 1967), p. 436. Michael Inwood (*A Hegel Dictionary*, Oxford, 1992, p. 274) points out that one of the meanings of *Geist* is 'alcohol' and suggests,

key-terms[30]: spirit/dialectic/concept,[31] which we shall attempt to elucidate presently. But in order to grasp the sense of Hegel's project it is necessary to see what he wished to avoid or transcend, as well as to see what he was himself endeavouring to say.

In the 'Preface' to the *Phenomenology of Spirit* Hegel had writers such as Schleiermacher[32] in his sights when he wrote with evident disapproval: 'For the Absolute is not supposed to be comprehended, it is to be felt and intuited; not the Concept [*Begriff*] of the Absolute, but the feeling and intuition [*Gefühl und Anschauung*] of it, must govern what is said, and must be expressed by it.'[33] On the contrary, for Hegel feeling is only the beginning of the knowledge of God; the immediacy, and particularity, of feeling has to be transcended (*aufgehoben*) and its content conceptualised and hence universalised by the mind's rational effort. And Hegel's intellectual optimism allows him to absorb even the Owl of Minerva's melancholic wisdom with composure. There is in Hegel no Faustian despair[34] at the shortcomings of human knowledge, no suspicion that 'knowledge increases unreality' (Yeats), no Nietzschean sense of the destructiveness of the equation of knowledge and 'truth' (*Tout comprendre – c'est tout mépriser*, as the 'Epilogue' to *Nietzsche Contra Wagner* has it).[35] In his lectures on the *Philosophy of History* Hegel expresses his ambition as follows:

---

with reference to the above-quoted passage in the *Phenomenology*, that this 'accounts in part for Hegel's occasional suggestions that truth involves intoxication.'

30 Cf. Macquarrie, *op. cit.*, p. 130.

31 For consistency 'concept' will always be used to translate *Begriff*, even when using translations or references which prefer 'notion'.

32 In the *Phenomenology*, Taylor writes, Hegel is critical of 'the theology of contemporary thinkers like Jacobi and Schleiermacher, who had felt the weight of the Enlightenment critique, and tried to find another path to God through sentiment and intuition' (Taylor, *Hegel*, p. 184).

33 *Phenomenology of Spirit*, p. 4; cf. Findlay's comments, *ibid.*, p. 495. Hegel returned to the attack in the 'Introduction' to his *Encyclopaedia* (1817): '[The] comfortable view of what constitutes a philosopher has recently received a fresh corroboration from the theory of immediate or intuitive knowledge [*die Lehre vom unmittelbaren Wissen, Wissen durch Anschauen*]' (tr. W. Wallace).

34 See the famous opening lines of Faust's monologue in Goethe, *Faust* Pt. 1, tr. P. Wayne (Harmondsworth, 1971), p. 43 (e.g.: 'And well I know that ignorance is our fate,/And this I hate').

35 See also the fable about the 'Don Juan of knowledge', *Daybreak* §327, p. 161.

In the Christian religion God has revealed himself, i.e., he has given men to understand what he is, so that he is no longer a concealment, a secret. This possibility to know God lays upon us the duty to do so; and the development of thinking Spirit which has proceeded from this basis, from the revelation of the divine Being, must finally proceed to grasp in thought (*mit dem Gedanken zu erfassen*) that which has at first been exhibited to Spirit in feeling and representation (*was dem fühlenden und vorstellenden Geiste zunächst vorgelegt worden*).[36]

It is worth noting that Hegel apparently did not like secrets, especially not divine secrets,[37] but wanted knowledge of God, believing that this was what God too wanted us to have. Indeed, according to Hegel, we have 'the duty' to understand now what God is.[38] This may be a question of 'projection' on Hegel's part, of course, which, if true, would be an odd irony. But it may just have been the enormity of Hegel's ambition that prompted Milan Kundera's caustic remark: 'The nineteenth century invented the locomotive, and Hegel was convinced he had grasped the very spirit of universal history. But Flaubert discovered stupidity. I daresay that is the greatest discovery of a century so proud of its scientific thought.'[39] In any case, the age ushered in by Christianity Hegel views as the period in which 'the final purpose of the world has at last passed into actuality in a universally valid and conscious way.'[40] In this

> ... absolute epoch in world history ... we know as Christians what God is; now God is no longer unknown: if we still say that, we are not Christians. The Christian religion demands the humility ... to apprehend God, not on its own terms, but on the

---

36 Quoted by Livingston, *op. cit.*, p. 150 (German text used: *Vorlesungen über die Philosophie der Geschichte* [*Werke* 12], ed. E. Moldenhauer and K. M. Michel, Frankfurt a/M, 1970, p. 28).

37 The contrast with Nietzsche, again, is striking: 'One should have more respect for the *bashfulness* with which nature has hidden behind riddles and iridescent uncertainties' (*Nietzsche Contra Wagner*, in *The Portable Nietzsche*, ed. and tr. Walter Kaufmann, Harmondsworth, 1981, p. 683).

38 Hegel had no time for what he saw as the lazy and arrogant mock-humility of those who said: 'How shall I, a poor worm of the dust, be able to know the truth? And we have now to contend with the vanity and arrogance of those, who claim, without any trouble on their part, to breathe the very atmosphere of truth' (*The Logic of Hegel*, tr. W. Wallace, pp. 26f.).

39 M. Kundera, *The Art of the Novel* (London, 1990), p. 162.

40 Quoted by Livingston, *op. cit.*, p. 150.

terms of God's own knowledge and apprehension. Christians are initiated into the mysteries of God and so the key to world history is also given to us. Here is given a definite apprehension of providence and its plan.[41]

Though it may be ultimately a matter of temperament or sensibility whether or not we like secrets to remain secrets, in the case of our belief in God secrecy or mystery would seem to be essential. This is a point to which we shall return in connection with Barth's assessment of Hegel's thought. For the moment it is enough to say that, could Hegel's dialectic demonstrate both the rational necessity of evil and the rational necessity of redemption from evil, then the rational possibility of *believing* that a mysterious God can cope with evil and redeem the world, rather than *knowing* how this can be, would appear to be excluded. For to comprehend both evil and redemption would entail showing the necessity of evil, the necessity of the world's existence, and therefore the real impossibility of continuing to see evil as in fact evil. Hegel is right then to say that, in such circumstances, belief becomes obsolete, and knowledge can reveal all. But everything hinges on whether or not we can stomach such a conclusion. And that might be finally a matter of taste, a conclusion which, if accepted, would be a vindication of Schleiermacher's instinct that religion is 'sense and taste for the Infinite', (even though not everyone will interpret 'the Infinite' as Schleiermacher does). However on the basic point here at issue, even the Psalmist seems to make 'taste' a last court of appeal ('Taste and see that the Lord is good'). And the basic point appears to be that Christian belief – though not Hegel – has always resisted the temptation to exchange faith for knowledge, or as St Ambrose put it, faith's sense is that: 'It hath not pleased God to save his people by dialectic.'[42]

However what Hegel, as a rigorous and stringent thinker, objected to in 'the Romantic spirituality of a Jacobi or a Schleiermacher, who wanted to displace the centre of religion onto the devotion of the worshipper, and stressed the unknowability of God,' was that such faith 'remains focussed on the finite subject and his freedom, and it accepts the conclusions of Enlightenment epistemology that nothing can be known about God. Hence it turns to a

---

41 *Ibid.*

42 'Non in dialecticâ complacuit Deo salvum facere populum suum', a favourite maxim of Newman's (cf. *Apologia Pro Vita Sua*, p. 225; he uses it also as an epigraph for the *Grammar of Assent*).

worship of God which is pure feeling, a God about whom nothing can be known but that he is.'[43] Yet Hegel's own transcending of Romantic religion by allegedly transforming faith into knowledge may ironically have failed to carry conviction for the same *reason* as the theology of Schleiermacher failed to win back the 'cultured despisers', namely that both 'theologies', for all their power, failed to find convincing answers to the problem of evil and suffering.

Traditionally Christian faith has taken the problem of evil in conjunction with the doctrine of the Fall, and claimed that Christ's redemptive act has overcome sin and reconciled man to God. Hegel's thought retains many formal aspects of the Christian Story, but with a radically new content. This can be seen particularly clearly in his treatment of the Fall, an idea anticipated in his early writings by the notion of alienation but much more fully developed in his later works.[44] The Fall is a central part of Hegel's thinking because it gives him the specific starting-point for his journey towards God. The Fall for Hegel is in fact nothing other than the actual emergence of self-consciousness which enables the individual to distinguish between self and the rest of reality:

> This is a deep truth, that evil lies in consciousness: for the brutes are neither evil nor good; the merely Natural Man quite as little. Consciousness occasions the separation of the Ego, in its boundless freedom as arbitrary choice, from the pure essence of the Will – *i.e.* from the Good. Knowledge, as the disannulling of the unity of mere Nature, is the 'Fall,' which is no casual conception, but the eternal history of Spirit. For the state of innocence, the paradisaical condition, is that of the brute. Paradise is a park, where only brutes, not men, can remain. For the brute is one with God only implicitly [not consciously]. Only Man's Spirit (that is) has a self-cognisant existence. This existence for self, this consciousness, is at the same time separation from the Universal and Divine Spirit. If I hold to my abstract Freedom, in contraposition to the Good, I adopt the standpoint of Evil. The Fall is therefore the eternal Mythus of Man – in fact, the very transition by which he becomes man. Persistence in this standpoint is, however, Evil, and the feeling of pain at such a condition, and of longing to transcend it, we find in David, when he says: 'Lord, create for me a pure heart, a new *steadfast* Spirit.'[45]

43 Taylor, *Hegel*, pp. 480f.
44 Cf. Livingston, *op. cit.*, p. 169, n.23.
45 *The Philosophy of History*, tr. J. Sibree (New York, 1956), pp. 321f.

Man's 'original sin', that which makes him human is therefore knowledge itself.[46] Once the disjunction between the individual and God is consciously known, however, the individual can set out on the path leading to reconciliation with God. Without the Fall which leads to the separation[47] between man and reality, however, the journey to God would never get started. In this sense, as Hegel puts it in the so-called 'Lesser Logic', 'The hand that inflicts the wound is also the hand which heals it.'[48] The Fall is thus also in Hegel a *felix culpa*, a necessary evil leading to the acquisition of a greater good (than what was lost). For the projected reconciliation will not simply be a return to the pre-conscious unity with God which is what the brute beasts enjoy, but which can no longer satisfy man; rather it will be a consciously achieved, conceptually articulated and hence universalisable reconciliation.[49] The reconciliation with God is charted in the various stages of the *Phenomenology*, in the epic adventure by which God or Absolute Spirit, through its embodiment in the history of human consciousness, achieves the fullness of its own reality. But the human condition whose truth is mythically contained in the story of the Fall is one of wretchedness, because of the many dimensions of man's alienation from God. The texture of human alienation Hegel anatomises in a famous section of the *Phenomenology* (pp. 119–138) in which he discusses the 'unhappy consciousness' (*das unglückliche Bewusstsein*):

---

46 '[T]he very notion of spirit is enough to show that man is evil by nature, and that it is an error to imagine that he could ever be otherwise … Nature is for man only the starting-point which he must transform into something better' (*The Logic of Hegel*, tr. W. Wallace, p. 47).

47 'The beasts never get so far as this separation, and they feel no shame', as Hegel puts it in the *Encyclopaedia* (*The Logic of Hegel*, p. 46).

48 *The Logic of Hegel*, p. 46.

49 Nietzsche, not surprisingly, takes a different tack, and resists what he calls this 'Pride in the spirit' in a passage of *Daybreak* where he writes: 'During the great prehistoric age of mankind, spirit was presumed to exist everywhere and was not held in honour as a privilege of man. Because, on the contrary, the spiritual [*das Geistige*] (together with all drives, wickedness, inclinations) had been rendered common property, and thus common, one was not ashamed to have descended from animals or trees (the *noble* races thought themselves honoured by such fables), and saw in the spirit that which unites us with nature, not that which sunders us from it' (*Daybreak*, tr. R. J. Hollingdale, Cambridge, 1983, p. 23). Characteristically, Nietzsche sees both positions as resting on *prejudices* …

The pages on the unhappy consciousness introduce us to some
of the fundamental ideas of Hegel's philosophy of religion. We
recognise the themes of Hegel's writings on religion of the
1790s, in particular the theme of separation, where man projects
his lost unity into a transcendent spirit to whom he subjects himself absolutely, as in the religion of Abraham.[50]

In the unhappy consciousness, then, the self is torn between its
embeddedness in the mutable world and its longing for union with
a projected, immutable transcendent reality where it can be 'at
home', since in its depths it feels itself to be an 'immutable self-identical subject of thought.'[51] Taylor notes that we can see in Hegel's
reflections on the unhappy consciousness 'the origin of the
Feuerbachian and Marxian conception of religious consciousness as
alienated.'[52] For Hegel, however, God will be seen as not apart from
the world ultimately and hence the possibility of overcoming alienation can be actualised; but a God who remained apart from the
world would always leave the human spirit alienated.

Spirit/dialectic/concept

We can now look more closely at the three key-terms of the
Phenomenology: spirit/dialectic/concept beginning with spirit
(*Geist*). Spirit is, for Hegel, the ultimate reality, 'the substance of
things'.[53] Matter too is real, it is not an illusion; but ultimately what
matter itself is, is spirit. For spirit projects itself necessarily into the
alien element of matter, but is destined to return finally to itself,
having enriched itself with the experience gained during its 'exile'
in matter. As spirit moves into matter, man – embodied spirit –
emerges from matter as self-consciousness. This double movement
of exit and return (*exitus* and *reditus*) is reminiscent of
Neoplatonism.[54] History, building upon nature, is the necessary
process by which the Absolute (Spirit) becomes itself or achieves its

50 Taylor, *Hegel*, p. 160.
51 *Ibid.*
52 *Hegel*, p. 160, n.1. Taylor adds: 'Not that Feuerbach and Marx had the
    same notion of religion as Hegel, of course. These successors "anthro-
    pologised" Hegel's Spirit.'
53 *Ibid.*, p. 209. I follow Macquarrie (cf. *op. cit.* p. 130) on the basic structure of
    the *Phenomenology* (cf. above n. 30).
54 Cf. Macquarrie, *op. cit.*, p. 130. The enthusiasm of the German Romantics
    of the 1790s for Plotinus has been commented on by scholars of the period:
    cf. Arthur O. Lovejoy, *The Great Chain of Being* (Cambridge, Mass., 1974),
    pp. 298, 371, n.18.

complete self-realisation. It is a necessary process because it is the only way spirit can become or realise itself, something which in Hegel's system it must do. There is no going behind this process, as it were, to ask: 'Why?' To understand it seems to be, for Hegel, to know why it could not be otherwise. Real difference, real otherness is thus, finally, a fiction. It is absorbed by the ultimate sameness or monism of spirit. Hegel defines the meaning of spirit in the 'Preface' to the *Phenomenology* in the following difficult terms:

> That the True is actual only as system, or that Substance is essentially Subject, is expressed in the representation of the Absolute as *Spirit* – the most sublime Concept and the one which belongs to the modern age and its religion. The spiritual alone is the *actual*; it is essence, or that which has *being in itself*; it is that which *relates itself to itself* and is *determinate*, it is *other-being* and *being-for-itself* [das *Anderssein* und *Fürsichsein*], and in this determinateness, or in its self-externality, abides within itself; in other words, it is *in and for itself*.[55]

The essence of spirit is dynamic form, the creativity which constructs an ordered universe out of matter. Spirit goes out from itself, yet continues to be itself in a mutual relationship of itself (as 'pure' spirit, so to speak) to itself (as materialised or embodied spirit). This may be Hegel's way of developing an idea of Meister Eckhart's, whom he quotes in the lectures on the *Philosophy of Religion*: 'The eye with which God sees me, is the eye with which I see him; my eye and his eye are one... If God were not, I would not be; if I were not, neither would he be.'[56] 'As subject', spirit 'knows itself as reflected in the object, while the object in turn knows spirit as the original subject.'[57] In other words spirit as subject and spirit as object are somehow the same, even if in its alienated state nature is not (yet) cognisant of its true nature, so to speak, though in man it is destined to be so eventually thanks to the labour of the 'concept' (*Begriff*), which seems to be *Geist* in action in human self-consciousness. Nature[58] is 'self-alienated spirit', but 'in nature, the unity of

---

55 *Phenomenology*, p. 14.

56 *Vorlesungen über die Philosophie der Religion* [*Werke* 16], ed. E. Moldenhauer and K. M. Michel (Frankfurt a/M, 1969), p. 209 (cf. B. M. G. Reardon, *Religion in the Age of Romanticism*, Cambridge, 1985, p. 65).

57 Macquarrie, *op. cit.*, p. 130. Cf. perhaps Goethe's line in *Faust* Pt. 1, 'Nacht': 'Du gleichst dem Geist, den Du begreifst' (You are like the spirit that you understand).

58 Nature is the second of the 'three main phases in the construction of the

the Concept conceals itself.'[59] In the process whereby spirit goes out from itself into the world, 'spirit and matter, God and world, are not separate but correlative'[60]: 'Now nature is, however, far from being so fixed and complete, as to subsist even without spirit: in spirit it first attains its aim and its truth. And similarly, spirit on its part is not merely an abstract world beyond nature and nothing more: it *is* really, and with full proof, seen to be spirit, only when it contains nature as absorbed [*aufgehoben*] in itself.'[61]

Thought ('mind', 'spirit', 'consciousness', 'God') and material reality are therefore, if I am right, ultimately identical for Hegel (hence, the 'identity of identity and non-identity'[62]): material reality is the expression of mind in exile (its being-other), of spirit outside itself. Hegel overcomes, then, the traditional subject/object dichotomy by what often appears as a ruse, asserting the final identity of mind and matter. Spirit is the creative energy shaping the world, or looked at from a slightly different angle, spirit is that power which comes to knowledge of itself, and can only come to knowledge of itself, in and through the necessary process of world-history. The final justification of the world is that it enables Absolute Spirit to achieve its own absolute self-knowledge.

---

life of the Absolute', the 'logical Idea ... and Spirit' being the other two (F. Copleston, *A History of Philosophy*, Vol. 7, Part 1, New York, 1965, p. 215). A logical idea, for Hegel, 'is not a subjective or mental entity ... [It] is the full realization or actualization of a concept (which, too, is not a mental entity): an idea is thus true or the truth. An idea is not transcendent and separate from particulars: it is fully realized in certain types of particular' (M. Inwood, *A Hegel Dictionary*, p. 124). The Absolute (or 'God') comes, seemingly then, to full self-realisation through actualising itself as ideas in the alien element of matter (nature), where both ideas and nature are expressions of Absolute Spirit, the former as concepts, the latter as self-alienated spirit. For Hegel 'the world is a process, each phase of which conditions, but is sublated by, the next phase. Of its main phases, for example, the logical idea conditions nature, which in turn conditions spirit, which then conditions the logical idea; the world is a circle of successively sublated conditions' (M. Inwood, *ibid.*; 'sublated' is the usual translation of the key-Hegelian term *aufgehoben* (from *aufheben*), meaning both 'cancelled' or 'annulled' *and* preserved (literally: 'lifted up'), thus 'transcended but not entirely discarded', as it were).

59 *The Encyclopaedia*, Pt. II, §247, quoted by Taylor, *op. cit.*, p. 353.
60 Macquarrie, *op. cit.*, p. 130.
61 *The Logic of Hegel*, pp. 154f. (amended).
62 Quoted in Taylor, *Hegel*, p. 48.

Mallarmé's dictum ('... *Tout, au monde, existe pour aboutir à un livre.* ...')[63] could perhaps serve as a restrained, clarified, purified crystallisation of Hegel's heady vision.

We come now to dialectic (*Dialektik*). The process 'whereby spirit unfolds and realises itself in material nature and in history is a dialectical one, characterised by the clash of opposites which are then reconciled in a higher synthesis'[64] or at a higher level. Historical movements provoke antagonism or criticism and the result of the conflict is *change* which brings about a new state of affairs incorporating at a higher level (*Aufhebung*) what was 'true' about the previous historical stage; it too in turn eventually provokes dissatisfaction and so history develops, changes and advances. However in trying to understand what Hegel means by dialectic, one common misconception should be avoided. As Walter Kaufmann points out: '[I]t is a commonplace' to suppose 'mistakenly, that all of Hegel is reducible to the three-step Thesis, Antithesis, and Synthesis. As a matter of fact, he does not speak of theses, antitheses, and syntheses at all, although his immediate predecessors, Fichte and Schelling, did; and neither his analyses in the *Logic* nor his dialectic in general can be reduced to any such three-step.'[65] In Kaufmann's interpretation, Hegel's vision of history is that 'different outlooks correspond to different states of mind, different stages in the development of the spirit,'[66] so that one age improves on and develops from its predecessor, none is right or wrong, but all are on the way towards an ever fuller grasp of the truth. The assumption of such a linear progress, which inspires the *Phenomenology*, remains unproved and is surely unprovable. But what moves the whole process along – its inner soul, so to speak – is what Hegel seems to mean by 'dialectic'.

We turn finally to the term 'concept' (*Begriff*). What Hegel means by the 'concept' (*Begriff*) is best seen in contrast with his use of another important term, 'representation' or 'image' (*Vorstellung*). For Hegel the concept 'goes beyond simple representation and is a thinking of something in depth or in several dimensions.'[67] The

---

63 'Everything in the world exists to end in a book', quoted in *Mallarmé*, intro. and ed. by Anthony Hartley (Harmondsworth, 1965), p. ix.

64 Macquarrie, *op. cit.*, pp. 130f.

65 In J. O. Urmson and J. Rée (eds.), *The Concise Encyclopedia of Western Philosophy and Philosophers* (London and New York, 1991), p. 127.

66 *Ibid.*

67 Macquarrie, *op. cit.*, p. 131.

concept, therefore, 'grasps something not just as it immediately presents itself, but as it has come to be in the course of its dialectical
development.'[68] This is of central importance for Hegel in his
mature attempt to understand Christianity, since he sees truth as
being conveyed representationally or symbolically in the 'religious'
stage of human development, whereas the movement beyond the
religious stage will be the philosophical conceptualisation of this
absolute truth offered by his own system of thought.[69]

The 'absolute Concept' would, then, for Hegel be the whole of
reality, thinking and knowing itself in all its moments:[70] '[S]imple
infinity or the absolute Concept is the simple essence of life, the soul
of the world, the universal blood, whose omnipresence is neither
disturbed nor interrupted by any difference, but rather is itself
every difference, as also their supersession [*Aufgehobensein*]; it pul-
sates within itself but does not move, inwardly vibrates, yet is at
rest. It is *self-identical*, for the differences are tautological; they are
differences that are none.'[71]

God in Hegel

How in the light of these three conceptions can we understand
Hegel's view of God? It is fairly clear that what Hegel presents us
with is not in unambiguous continuity with the classical Christian
understanding of God. Yet his philosophy could be said to offer an
interpretation of the traditional Christian idea that God both transcends and is immanent in the world. But in Hegel the classical
notion of God's self-sufficiency and absoluteness – i.e. that God is in
no sense dependent on the world – is explicitly rejected: '"God is
not God without the world" (*ohne Welt ist Gott nicht Gott*).'[72] Rather
for Hegel God or Absolute Spirit has always been 'in the process of
realising its constitutive concept,' and is 'passing over into a form in
which it exists for another.'[73] It is true that 'Hegel speaks of the

---

68 *Ibid*.
69 Cf. Livingston, *op. cit.*, p. 150: 'Historical Christianity had grasped the
    truth in representational form, but philosophy grasps this same truth in
    its rational necessity.'
70 This is reminiscent of Aristotle's idea of God as 'a thought which thinks
    itself', except that for Hegel 'God' becomes the process of life itself.
71 *Phenomenology*, p. 100 (amended).
72 Quoted in Taylor, *op. cit.*, p. 490.
73 *Phenomenology*, pp. 554f. (quoted by Macquarrie, *op. cit.*, p. 132, referring
    to a 1931 translation of *The Phenomenology of Mind*).

absolute Spirit as the first and foremost moment in the world-process, "Spirit absolutely self-contained,"' but 'this is an abstraction ... the transcendent self-subsistent and self-sufficient God is simply a hypothesis, posited at the "beginning" of an eternal process which had therefore no beginning.'[74] Absolute Spirit in the sense of a self-subsistent deity is at best in Hegel only an intellectual construct enabling us to grasp the interaction between God and the world, and it is this interaction, rather than any understanding of God as existing in a strongly transcendent sense (i.e. enjoying, in traditional terminology, aseity) that is the heart of the matter, as far as Hegel is concerned. 'Absolute spirit needs the finite spirits in and through which it knows itself and eventually returns to itself'[75]:

> God is God only insofar as he knows himself; his self-knowledge of himself is moreover his self-consciousness in man, it is man's knowledge *of* God that goes on to become the self-knowledge of man *in* God.[76]

Yet it is not that the Absolute Spirit empties, or exhausts, or dissolves, or loses itself totally in finite spirits: rather the Absolute Spirit comes to know itself in and through the finite spirits, without losing its own identity: 'Spirit is the being which is in the process of retaining identity with itself in its otherness.'[77] Thus God for Hegel is not a self-sufficient, isolated God existing prior to or apart from or at the beginning of the world-process, nor is God 'simply the sum of the finite spirits existing at any moment of the process', nor does God come 'into being only at the end of the process.'[78] God appears in Hegel's thought to be the unifying force that blends spirit and nature together, the governing principle in control of this whole process, in which 'spirit rises above nature,'[79] the dynamic force shaping the course of the cosmic process, and whose essence is rational necessity, striving paradoxically for ever greater freedom. Or, as Van Harvey puts it: 'The Infinite perpetually pours out (objectifies) its life in the finite (creation), struggles with the resulting externality (self-alienation) until finally overcoming it in self-knowledge (freedom).'[80]

---

74 Macquarrie, *op. cit.*, p. 132.

75 *Ibid.*

76 *Encyclopaedia*, Pt. III, §564, quoted in Taylor, *op. cit.*, p. 481.

77 *Phenomenology* , p. 758 (quoted in Macquarrie, *op. cit.*, p. 132).

78 Macquarrie, *ibid.*

79 *Ibid.*

80 Van A. Harvey, 'Ludwig Feuerbach and Karl Marx', in Ninian Smart et al.,

The progressive self-knowledge of Absolute Spirit is, therefore, also the story of freedom. In knowing itself progressively in history, spirit is also continually freeing itself from what eventually come to be understood as inadequate embodiments of itself and moving on to ever more adequate ones, until finally Absolute Spirit's full self-knowledge will coincide with its full freedom. One can see why Hegel's philosophy is politically Janus-faced in that it could be seen as an endorsement of any existing state of affairs (the *real*, i.e. what is actually now existing, is the rational and so should be maintained) or as a call to radical revolution (only what is *rational* should be regarded as real and so, if any given state of affairs is deemed to harbour irrationality and inconsistency within its bosom, it should be overthrown).[81]

In the famous closing section of the *Phenomenology* Hegel visualises powerfully the self-realisation of the truth of Absolute Spirit emerging out of history, which has to happen and die so that its truth can be 're-membered' conceptually and thus preserved, in a 'speculative' form of resurrection. The whole process of history is thus the story of the evolution of God. God had to 'alienate' himself in time, space and matter, in order eventually to become himself fully as 'Absolute Spirit': 'Only from the chalice of this realm of spirits/ foams forth for Him his own infinitude.'[82]

Yet bearing in mind the Christian theological background to Hegel's thought, how did he, in more specific detail, comprehend the process of divine self-becoming within, or rather beneath, the mask provided by the figurative language of traditional Christianity?

In Hegel's system God, man and world are all intrinsically inter-related. This is borne out by the way in which he understands God as Absolute Truth. For God can only be Absolute Truth if the truth in question be historically and concretely manifest. Hence the incarnation is not, for example, simply a symbolic expression of the divinity of all humanity, but it refers specifically to the fundamental change in the history of both God and man that occurred with Jesus Christ, because with Christ God ceased to be an abstract idea for humanity and became a historical individual. This change in God

Nineteenth Century Religious Thought in the West, vol. 1, p. 293.
81 Cf. *ibid.*
82 *Phenomenology of Spirit*, p. 493.

was a necessary step in the process of God's becoming fully himself.[83]

The death of Christ is a vitally important aspect of this process. Hegel interprets the 'speculative Good Friday' as the Spirit's taking on the most complete form of finitude, which is nowhere more radical than in death. If God was to be truly revealed in human existence, which is finite, the path leading to and including death had to be taken. However in submitting to the radical finitude of death and moving beyond it, God destroys and hence overcomes death and thus makes possible the coming of the Universal Kingdom of the Spirit. The death of God on the cross is thus a transitional moment in the emergence of Absolute Spirit: 'Death then ceases to signify what it means directly – the nonexistence of *this* individual – and becomes transfigured into the universality of spirit which lives in its own communion.'[84] In the death of Christ Hegel sees the end of the radically transcendent God of traditional theism who previously had stood as an individual over against human beings.

Hegel therefore accepts that there is a fundamental truth in the Christian teaching on the death, resurrection and ascension of Jesus Christ, but he of course reserves the right to interpret these doctrines as imaginative, particular representations of implicitly conceptual – and hence universally valid – truths that must now be explicitly formulated. The conceptual meaning of the resurrection and ascension of Jesus is that God maintains himself in death and thus his death is the overcoming or destruction of death (radical finitude), the negation of the negativity which death is. In sacrificing, in death, its particular instantiation, the Spirit ushers in the age of Absolute Spirit, the advent of the Holy or Universal Spirit. Without the death of Jesus the true and new Spiritual Community could not possibly have been born, even though the possibility of the universal reconciliation of the divine and the human was implicit in the process of existence from the beginning (in so far as one can speak here of a 'beginning').[85]

'Christianity is the Absolute Religion, for in Christianity alone do we see the actual dialectical process by which Spirit (God) works itself out to full expression in history.'[86] In the Kingdom of the Spirit, which is the goal of the whole historical process, God is no

---

83 Cf. Livingston, *op. cit.*, p., 153.
84 *Phenomenology* (tr. Baillie), p. 780 (quoted in Livingston, *op. cit.*, p. 154).
85 Cf. Livingston, *op. cit.*, p. 154.
86 Livingston, *op. cit.*, p. 155.

longer an object for us, but has revealed himself tangibly to us by coming to consciousness in and through the finite, historical world. Thus for Hegel God is only 'realisable in a community of finite human minds.'[87]

The upshot of this is that Christianity, for Hegel, must abandon its traditional theistic notion of God as a transcendent, personal being, existing strictly apart from us, because such a notion maintains the abyss between God and man and does not take account of the new fact that the absolute religion is the one in which 'man knows God only in so far as God knows himself in man. This knowledge is God's self-consciousness but also God's knowledge of man. God's knowledge of man is also man's knowledge of God. The spirit of man which is to know God is only the spirit of God Himself.'[88] As Charles Taylor puts it: 'God is like a flame which passes from mortal candle to mortal candle, each destined to light and go out, but the flame to be eternal.'[89]

Hegel was convinced that failure to carry out the vital task of translating the spiritual or religious truth of Christianity into conceptual or philosophical truth, would leave the historically contingent, representational forms, in which alone Christian truth had hitherto been expressed, wide open to 'a rational and historical critique'[90] that would lead to Christianity's demise.

Although Hegel's thought has often been seen as incompatible with the Christian faith, he himself saw his philosophy as being a rational account of the deepest meaning of the distinctive Christian doctrine of the Trinity. In his system the Father corresponds to the first moment where spirit is 'absolutely self-contained. But this absolute spirit has already from eternity determined to sacrifice itself.'[91] In Christian terms this determination corresponds to the doctrine of the pre-existence of Christ and God's eternal plan to send Christ into the world for our redemption (cf. Rev 13:8; 1 Pet 1:20). 'So spirit goes out into [or alienates itself in] the realm of finite existence, where the actual historical sacrifice and reconciliation take place. Finally, spirit which has thus abased itself returns to its origin and is now fully manifested and unfolded as spirit.'[92]

---

87 Ibid.
88 Philosophy of Religion (tr. Speirs and Sanderson), III, quoted in Livingston, op. cit., p. 156; cf. above n.76.
89 Taylor, op. cit., p. 495.
90 Livingston, op. cit., p. 156.
91 Macquarrie, op. cit., p. 133.
92 Ibid.

Unquestionably, there is here a clear formal similarity between Christian Trinitarian theology and Hegel's philosophy of spirit. God in Hegel is not to be identified with any of the three basic moments in the unfolding of absolute spirit but is their unity, just as in the Trinitarian understanding of God there is a unity encompassing a threefold diversity. However it is hard to escape the impression that Christian doctrines are not being adequately re-expressed in Hegel's philosophy but are rather seen as vivid, graphic illustrations of universal truths which are then more fully and more adequately spelled out by Hegel.

Hegel tended to see his absolute philosophy as in fact higher than religion. He did not of course see his philosophical interpretation of religion as aridly rationalistic or divorced from 'real life', and indeed he criticised 'the emptiness of a merely philosophical faith, which he called "nothing but a sapless abstract", and he warned that "it ought never to be confused or identified with the spiritual fullness of Christian faith."'[93] However when he makes explicit what this spiritual fullness consists in, he 'tends to identify it with feeling, and to regard feeling in turn as an immediate awareness which is only the beginning of knowledge.'[94]

Religious feeling, in short, is the beginning of knowledge for Hegel: '[T]he immediate consciousness of God goes no further than to tell us *that* he is: to tell us *what* he is would be an act of cognition, involving mediation.'[95] Religion, therefore, 'remains in the realm of the idea (*Vorstellung*), in the sense of "representation" or "image", an immediate and therefore partial view of something in one of its moments. Philosophy pushes on to the concept (*Begriff*), the sum of the moments in their necessary unity. For instance, religion represents God as Father, Son and Holy Spirit, philosophy goes beyond this to grasp the dialectical unfolding of spirit.'[96]

Hegel seems to have assumed the omnicompetence of reason in religion, as in life generally, and not to have considered that religious intuitions might lie not on this side of reason but beyond reason's grasp altogether,[97] as Kierkegaard, Hegel's conscious adversary, always maintained. However for Hegel even mystical experi-

---

93 Macquarrie, *ibid.*, quoting *Logic* (from *The Encyclopaedia of the Philosophical Sciences* [ET, Oxford, 1892]), p. 125.

94 Macquarrie, *op. cit.*, p. 134.

95 *Logic*, p. 136 (quoted in Macquarrie, *ibid.*).

96 Macquarrie, *ibid.*

97 Cf. Macquarrie, *ibid.*

ence can be translated into intellectual terms; not, to be sure, by the workings of an 'abstract rationalism – the "understanding", in Hegel's terminology – '[98] but by the workings of speculative reason. Thought, he wrote, 'is the highest and, in strict accuracy, the sole mode of apprehending the eternal and absolute.'[99] Against the claims of Hegel's ambitious philosophy one might wish to raise the question: 'For whom is reason's own self-decreed legitimation and omnicompetence truly valid?' This question is implicit in remarks made by W. B. Yeats, in a letter written a few weeks before his death: 'It seems to me that I have found what I wanted. When I try to put all into a phrase I say, "Man can embody truth but he cannot know it." I must embody it in the completion of my life. The abstract is not life and everywhere draws out its contradictions. You can refute Hegel but not the Saint or the Song of Sixpence.'[100] If, however, one were to dismiss the question: 'For whom is reason omnicompetent?' on the grounds that it is *ad hominem*, and claim that reason alone can decide about reason's competence, this merely highlights the inescapable problem of Hegel. 'Reason' is rooted in humanity, not the other way round. The eternal question of humanity's own self-understanding arises with consciousness but transcends it, and so can never be answered from within it.

This brings us to an aspect of Hegel's view of the Christian God to which Charles Taylor draws attention. In summing up of the claims of Hegel's philosophy, Taylor locates the weak point in his system in its neglect of the central, if slippery and indefinable, Christian doctrine of grace:

> Lacking the idea of God as giver, Hegel cannot accommodate the relations of God and man as they must be for Christian faith. He has no place for grace in the properly Christian sense. As Karl Barth puts it, 'Hegel, in making the dialectical method of logic the essential nature of God, made impossible the knowledge of the actual dialectic of grace, which has its foundation in the freedom of God.'[101] And he has no place for divine love in the Christian sense, for God's love for his creatures is inseparable from its expression in giving. And what can be said about God's relation to man must be said about the fully developed

---

98   Macquarrie, *op. cit.*, pp. 134f.
99   *Logic*, p. 34 (quoted in Macquarrie, *op. cit.*, p. 135).
100 Letter to Lady Elizabeth Pelham, cited in Joseph Hone, *W.B. Yeats* (Harmondsworth, 1971), p. 480.
101 *Protestant Theology in the Nineteenth Century*, p. 420.

human relation to God, in which man comes to recognise his identity with the divine.[102]

There can be awe before Hegel's God, but no gratitude, no real prayer to such a God, for everything happens according to rational necessity.[103] Thus even the fact of evil would seem to be accommodated by the Hegelian system. Barth concludes on Hegel's system of thought:

> If theology's basis of knowledge is supposed to be revelation – the revelation however of God to man who is lost in his sin – and if the revelation is supposed to be of God's incomprehensible reconciling, then here, where we seem to be permitted to think beyond the mystery of evil and salvation, and where it seems to be permitted and possible to get behind this dual mystery, we have another basis of knowledge, a concept of truth that theology cannot accept.[104]

What may, nevertheless, account for Hegel's fascination for theologians is the fact that, as Taylor has persuasively argued, his system is not any straightforward theism, nor can it be caricatured and dismissed as atheistic, but it is something else which can easily be taken for Christianity:

> Thus the Hegelian ontology itself in which everything can be grasped by reason because everything is founded on rational necessity is ultimately incompatible with Christian faith. Hegel's philosophy is an extraordinary transposition which 'saves the phenomena' (that is, the dogmas) of Christianity, while abandoning its essence. It is not a theism, but it is not an atheist doctrine either, in which man as a natural being is at the spiritual summit of things. It is a genuine third position, which is why it is so easy to misinterpret.[105]

Peter Hodgson points out, however, that Hegel's God does not enjoy the prerogative of real transcendence, and herein lies the weakness that eventually led to the downfall of his system:

> Although transcendence clearly is present in Hegel's thought –

---

102 Taylor, *Hegel*, pp. 493f.
103 *Op. cit.*, p. 494.
104 *Protestant Theology in the Nineteenth Century*, p. 418 (translation amended: cf. *Die protestantische Theologie in 19. Jahrhundert*, vol. 1, Hamburg, 1975, p. 348).
105 Taylor, *op. cit.*, p. 494.

transcendence of the logical idea vis-à-vis nature and finite spirit, the transcendence of God as Absolute Spirit vis-à-vis the rise
of consciousness to the Absolute – the great stress on the
revealedness of the Absolute, its rational comprehensibility, its
implicit identity with the human subject, means that Hegel
inevitably downplays the mysterious, violating, numinous,
revealing/concealing power of Being vis-à-vis human consciousness. Hegel does not forget the Absolute, but he tends to
forget the transcendence of the Absolute, confident that the
Absolute can be known *absolutely*. Thus as Ricoeur suggests, he
ultimately sacrifices faith in the sacred to absolute knowledge of
the Absolute, and this in turn led to 'the collapse of the Hegelian
system itself – by this I mean the absolute incredibility of the
notion of absolute knowledge in a time of a hermeneutics of suspicion.'[106]

In abandoning any non-conceptualisable sense of God's transcendence over against the universe Hegel surely abolishes the difference between God and human beings, without which the notion of
'meaning' loses its savour. Hegel thus anticipates the Nietzschean
vision of recurrence where in the last analysis everything is eternally
the same.

Continuing significance of Hegel

While it is true that the success of Hegel's system as a complete
explanation of existence was short-lived, many aspects of his
thought have continued to be of incalculable importance in the
modern world. Above all his notion of the inter-connectedness of
God, man and world, his sense that history is not just the décor or
scenario of our spiritual lives but constitutes the very substance of
reality itself, is almost a leitmotiv of modern theology, and indeed
has marked even secular modern consciousness indelibly. Truth is
now conceived by many as no longer timeless, complete and
immutable and existing apart from us, but rather it is conceived as
continually developing and, in some sense, being fashioned by the
historical process itself. Hegel's vision of the odyssey of the human
spirit as the story of the generation of God has profoundly marked
the modern understanding of the history of religion. His influence
has continued to be very great in modern theology, in for example
'process theology' (Whitehead, Hartshorne), and in modern German

---

106   P. C. Hodgson, in N. Smart et al. (eds.), *op. cit.*, vol. 1, pp. 111f.

eschatological theology, sometimes called the 'theology of hope' (Pannenberg, Moltmann).[107]

However for many Hegelianism equals pantheism and pantheism equals atheism, since it leads to a merging of God and the world, and whether one calls the resulting compound 'God' or 'world' does not matter very much. Hegel himself certainly considered that his philosophy avoided both pantheism (of which he was accused) and deism (which he thought was Christianity's fate in the Enlightenment). Whatever his intentions, he can now be seen as contributing, along with the theory of evolution, to contemporary pantheistic doctrines as developed by process theologians and perhaps even Kolakowski,[108] for whom God is himself subject to becoming, and hence in some sense finite and temporal. In short God is a historical God.

Kolakowski appears to adopt a quasi-Hegelian approach to the apprehension of God when he argues that, for a certain 'admittedly heretical'[109] strand of Western religious thought, by our moral choices we can affect what he calls 'the being' (God?), by either enhancing or diminishing it, and that thus 'we actually open the avenue to its understanding and thereby to an understanding of existence.'[110] This perspective on the God-question assumes from the outset 'that purely speculative knowledge *in divinis* is not only worthless in terms of our salvation – which no Christian may deny, of course – but is no knowledge at all.'[111]

Kolakowski's ideas at this point seem to echo Hegel's and even Marx's. For Hegel and Marx truth does not exist objectively in a realm transcending ours and waiting to be discovered by metaphysical enquiry, but truth inheres rather in the historical process and has to be actually *created* or made in history before it can be intellectually grasped. Yet if Kolakowski appears to be going down a slightly odd road, it is because he wishes to safeguard the reality of human freedom. For as he says: 'If goodness is by definition always actual – which the dogma of the perfect actuality of God and of God's being the fullness of the good entails – the idea of human free choice is not tenable any longer.'[112] This points us back once

---

107 Cf. Livingston, *op. cit.*, pp. 167f.; Macquarrie, *op. cit.*, p. 125.
108 See *Metaphysical Horror*, pp. 89ff.
109 *Ibid.*, p. 91.
110 *Ibid.*, p. 92.
111 *Ibid.*, p. 93.
112 *Ibid.*, p. 90.

more to the insoluble problem of what exactly creation is, how it was possible, what God's relation to it really is . . .

The doctrine of the Trinity has been the traditional Christian answer to the conundrum: If God 'is perfect in personality he must also be perfect in love; but love implies an object of love that is external to the lover; so God cannot be self-sufficient.'[113] That is to say, for God to be 'personal' does he not need the world, as Hegel taught? Or as Kolakowski puts it: '[I]s it not in keeping with common sense to admit with Hegel, that personal life (or self-consciousness) is conceivable only in contact and exchange – love or struggle, no matter – between persons, in other words, that there is no secluded self-contained personal mind? There is no way we could understand a divine person that would not face, and commune with, other person-like, and not necessarily divine, beings like ourselves.'[114] But behind such questions is there not, implicitly, a monarchian and modalist view of the Godhead? Whereas according to the doctrine of the Trinity, 'God enjoys an infinite life of love within himself through the mutual indwelling of the Father, the Son and the Holy Spirit.'[115] Such a conviction however can only be stated in the language of Christian faith. It clearly cannot be reached by the exploratory power of reason.

Yet if truth could actually somehow be constructed or enacted by us, would this open up a third possible answer to the God-question? For beyond the possibility that God either does or does not exist, there would be the new possibility: God does *not yet* exist for us, but in the future he will.[116] Many will, understandably, balk at such a claim. However that is not a rebuttal of the claim. The claim cannot in fact be rebutted, since it rests on faith, just as it cannot be proved to be true either, for it will only be true when it happens. Nevertheless, the idea that God may only at some future point

---

113 Huw P. Owen, *Christian Theism* (Edinburgh, 1984), p. 24.

114 Kolakowski, *op. cit.*, p. 91.

115 Owen, *op. cit.*, p. 24.

116 'Ernest Renan approximated Hegel's conception when he said, in his *Philosophical Dialogues*, that God (the ideal) will be realised through man's search for knowledge. "You think then, like Hegel, that God *is* not, but that he *will be*?" asks one of the interlocutors. "Not precisely," was the reply. "The ideal exists, it is eternal; but it has not yet been materially realised; it will be some day"' (Baumer, *op. cit.*, p. 317). Renan stops short of recommending unreservedly the novel idea of the futurity of God, offering instead the paradox of what one might call a materialised Platonism.

come into existence will strike most people as philosophically extravagant. What is more plausible is to claim that *our own* final destiny is not yet decided, a view that is not at all at odds with the traditional teaching that, while God may create us without our co-operation, he can only redeem us with our co-operation.

This conviction is bolstered by the realisation that people often suspect they are at no point in time all that they could possibly still become. They feel an 'openness to the future' that invites them, as it were, to try to transform their lives. However this experience, so runs the argument, would be entirely illusory, were there not some transcendent reality beyond the here and now which, in a way we cannot grasp, already in some sense inhabits that future (Pannenberg), thus guaranteeing the connection between it and our present. While we can only partly glimpse this reality now, we may see it 'face to face' in the future, depending on the choices we make in the meantime. Salvation, in this view, is thus not something finished and only existing metaphysically apart from us, but it has to be achieved in part by our own contribution. Hegelianism may thus perhaps be seen as an attempt to express the divinely guided process of human salvation in intellectually accessible but ultimately secularised terms. However, since Hegel can scarcely be said to have expressed the innermost truth of God himself, how reliable finally can his account of salvation truly be? To say nothing of the suspicion that 'openness to the future' may simply be openness to 'the great Void into which all things tumble, to use Alfred North Whitehead's phrase,'[117] or openness to the 'eternal recurrence' of an intrinsically self-enclosed system, as with Nietzsche...

Yet on one point Hegel will always remain alive. For he raises for theology the vital, but unanswerable, question of the meaning of history in the light of eternity. The difference between Schleiermacher and Hegel is that Schleiermacher sees history as the locus where religious experience is available to human beings. Hegel, by contrast, sees all historical experience as itself the process whereby God's being unfolds in and through us. The grandeur of Hegel's vision should not blind us to its unprovability, but neither can its unprovability destroy the power of the implicit question it contains: 'If history is not the process of the self-realisation of God, what is it? And whatever it is, how can it be connected with the transcendent God of traditional Christian faith, and with the drama

---

117   Van A. Harvey, *Feuerbach and the Interpretation of Religion* (Cambridge, 1995), p. 196.

of redemption he is believed to have set in train by creating the world?'

Even though these questions may not be intellectually answerable, certainly not from within Hegel's own philosophy, it must nevertheless be said that, in harmony with the major part of the Western tradition, Hegel is affirmative about the reality of life itself. Unlike Schopenhauer, his most relentless critic in the nineteenth century, he did not consider existence to be an irredeemable catastrophe. Pessimism about the human condition has certainly always had powerful advocates. For pessimism is always proved right in the short run, since everyone finally dies. The process of life continually creates beauty and love and continually destroys them. Pessimists in the past abound. One thinks of the Manichaeans, Bogomils or Albigensians. And since the Renaissance the Western world, despite the wonder of human achievements, has been unable to shake off a mood of impending doom or at least disenchantment. A suspicion of ultimate meaninglessness haunts the contemporary scene. However, from the Renaissance onwards, as before then indeed, total pessimism has also always been resisted by the sheer continuity of human communities, and by the intellectual effort of those writers who, like the Spanish poet Francisco de Quevedo (1580–1645) in his splendid sonnet: *Cerrar podrá mis ojos la postrera/ sombra* ... (The final shade may close my eyes in death ... [tr. A. Terry]), have asserted the power of life and love to transcend death. Hegel's thought, for all its ambiguity and seeming endorsement of evil, stands in a tradition that is committed to life and to truth.

But his philosophy is not simply a needlessly complex way of explicating the truth of the old Latin adage: *primum vivere, deinde philosophari* ('first live, then philosophise'). For he was convinced that history was a goal-directed process rising from lower to ever higher stages, whose meaning would be gradually elaborated by philosophical reflection. This view finds few supporters today. But Hegel's magnificent belief in the transience of truth and the truth of transience does justice, if not to God, at least to the fact that the world is real and has a meaning that transcends it. The world, however, could never have attained that meaning, had it not come into existence and passed away again. In that sense meaning and time are, humanly speaking, interdependent. And the passage of time which separates us gently from experience, permitting us eventually to perceive something of its meaning, is a constant foretaste of death which separates us from life more drastically, but may grant us eventually, we hope, access to a meaning transcending earthly experience; and transcending it at least to the extent that the reality of death transcends the reality of time's passage. For the 'sweet sorrow' of history's passing is an indication that what has passed was at least not nothing,[118] and so may serve as a token of what may still be possible for us. Memory is the power that transforms and preserves the meaning of experience *sub specie mundi*; to transform and preserve the meaning of human experience *sub specie aeternitatis* requires something more, which is manifestly not at our disposal. The name traditionally given to this power by faith is 'God'.

---

118 Cf. F. Overbeck, *Christentum und Kultur*, p. 296.

CHAPTER EIGHT

Feuerbach

The dream of reason produces monsters. — Francisco de Goya

Religion is the dream of the human mind. — Ludwig Feuerbach

Even if God did not exist, religion would still be Holy and divine.
— Charles Baudelaire

Feuerbach and his times

On his deathbed the utopian political and social theorist Saint-Simon (1760–1825) is reported to have said: 'Religion can never disappear from the world; it can only be transformed.'[1] As if to confirm this intuition, attempts to transform Christianity were in fact made in the nineteenth century by thinkers such as Strauss (1808–1874) and Feuerbach (1804–1872) in Germany, and in France by Auguste Comte (1798-1857), a disciple of Saint-Simon's. The transformation such writers aimed at was radically this-worldly. Whereas Christianity had traditionally stressed both transcendence and immanence when speaking about God's relationship to the world, the new 'religions' concentrated solely on inner-worldly realities. Humanity and its welfare became their unique focus of concern; indeed 'humanity' was identified with 'the sacred'.

While the idea of a *Humanitätsreligion* ('Religion of Humanity'[2]) occurs in Strauss, Comte actually took practical steps to develop a secular 'religion of humanity', complete with cult, priests, sacraments and a calendar of secular saints. Feuerbach believed atheism would be the religion of the future ('What yesterday was still religion is no longer such to-day; and what to-day is atheism, tomor-

---

1 Quoted by F. L. Baumer, *Modern European Thought*, p. 314. Saint-Simon's last book was, appropriately, entitled: 'New Christianity' (*Nouveau Christianisme* [1825]).

2 See *ibid.*, p. 314, n.20.

row will be religion')[3]. The new proposals for what one might call,
paradoxically, 'secularist religion' were of interest chiefly to intellectuals, such as the writer George Eliot in England, the celebrated
translator of both Strauss' *Life of Jesus* and Feuerbach's *Essence of
Christianity*. The force of Strauss' historical criticism of the bible and
Christian doctrine, combined with Feuerbach's psychological
undermining of confidence in traditional religion, had left many
intellectuals like George Eliot convinced that faith in Christianity
was no longer possible.[4] They were consequently concerned to find
some credible substitute. The appeal of socialism, perhaps even
Marxism, may be due at least in some measure to the intellectual
need for a new kind of 'opium' which such secular, quasi-religious
movements seemed to offer.

Feuerbach, more than Strauss or Comte, is of continuing interest
to theology both because of the still active seeds of suspicion he
sowed concerning the 'objective' truth of Christianity, and also
because of the power of his own passionately argued re-interpretation of the human condition. His vision of life struck many in the
nineteenth century as more compelling and more 'human' than that
of traditional Christianity.

Already as a teenager Feuerbach began to be preoccupied by
religious questions, and even took private Hebrew lessons from a
rabbi.[5] Like his mentor Hegel, whom he had initially idolised,[6] his
original aim, when he began his studies of theology in Heidelberg,
was ordination to the ministry. He subsequently moved to Berlin in
order to attend Hegel's lectures, and soon found purely theological
lectures unendurable. As B. A. Gerrish put it:

His transfer to Berlin certainly sprang from a desire to sit at the

---

3   *The Essence of Christianity*, tr. George Eliot (New York, 1957), p. 32;
    henceforth cited as *Essence*.
4   'My faith was destroyed', wrote Ernest Renan in his memoirs (c. 1871),
    'by historical criticism, not by scholasticism or logic' (quoted by
    Baumer, *ibid.*, p. 315).
5   Bernd Lutz (ed.), *Metzler Philosophen Lexikon* (Stuttgart and Weimar,
    1995), p. 269.
6   'He was my second father ... the only person who caused me to feel and
    experience what a teacher was' (Karl Grün, *Ludwig Feuerbach in seinem
    Briefwechsel und Nachlass sowie in seiner philosophischen Charakter-
    entwicklung*, Leipzig and Heidelberg, 1874, vol. 1, p. 387, quoted by Van
    A. Harvey, 'Ludwig Feuerbach and Karl Marx', in Ninian Smart et al.
    (eds.), *Nineteenth Century Religious Thought in the West*, vol. 1, Cambridge,
    1984, p. 323, n.1).

feet of Hegel. He reassured his father by pointing out, among other things, that in Berlin he could hear the living word of the Spirit, not in the classroom alone, but from the pulpit of the great Schleiermacher. Once there, however, he attended the classes of Hegel, and he later testified that he found utterly repellent the mishmash of reason and faith served up in the neighboring theological halls of Schleiermacher and Neander.[7] In a year's time he had transferred to the faculty of philosophy.[8]

Feuerbach later moved to Erlangen where he obtained his degree in 1828 and one year later was appointed lecturer. In his doctoral dissertation *On Reason: One, Universal, Infinite* (1828), a copy of which he sent to Hegel, one of the key-ideas of his later philosophy is already clear, namely that 'Christianity ... is not the absolute religion (as Hegel thought), but the religion of misguided individualism.'[9] Feuerbach's conviction that traditional Christianity encouraged individual selfishness was further developed in his later writings, including a work that appeared anonymously in 1830, *Gedanken über Tod und Unsterblichkeit* (Thoughts on Death and Immortality). It was this work, soon discovered by the censor to be by Feuerbach, that ruined his academic career. After marrying in 1837 he retired from the university. Apart from giving – at the invitation of students – a course of lectures on *The Essence of Religion* in the winter of 1848-49 (the lectures were held in the Town Hall in Heidelberg, since the university refused permission for the use of a lecture-hall), Feuerbach lived as a private scholar until his death in 1872.

Thoughts on Death and Immortality

In *Thoughts on Death and Immortality* Feuerbach outlined the history of belief in immortality. The roots of the modern concern with personal immortality he found to lie in the individualism which, he considered, had been encouraged by Protestantism. The 'most virulent forms' of 'modern individualism' lay, for him, 'in pietism and rationalism.'[10] It was the realisation that individual perfection was unattainable in this life which gave rise to the desire to achieve such

---

7   J. A. W. Neander (1789–1850), a pietist theologian, whose original name was David Mendel, was from 1813 professor of church history at Berlin.

8   B. A. Gerrish, *Tradition and the Modern World. Reformed Theology in the Nineteenth Century* (Chicago and London, 1978), p. 162.

9   Gerrish, *ibid.*

10 Gerrish, *ibid.*, p. 163.

perfection beyond the grave. For this reason Feuerbach, in a witty (elegiac) couplet, describes religion as a kind of 'life insurance' institution. We deny ourselves happiness in this life, in the hope of a great reward in the next.[11] Such theologically motivated self-denial is, for Feuerbach, an obvious fraud. Moreover, the misguided desire for a perfect life after death has had the unfortunate effect, he argues, of reducing the importance of life before death. Historical life becomes 'a mere shadow and vision of the future.'[12] This state of affairs cannot, Feuerbach believes, continue, and in the new stage of world history about to open, it can indeed be 'overcome', if man genuinely accepts death as final:

> Only when he accepts the truth of death, no longer denies death, will he become capable of true happiness, true self-denial... Man is eternal, Spirit is eternal ... but in your place a new, fresh person comes into the world of consciousness... The true belief in immortality is belief in the Spirit itself. ... Your belief in immortality is therefore only true belief if it is belief in the infinity of Spirit and the unfading youth of Humanity,[13] ... It is true belief only if it is belief that Truth, Being, Spirit have an existence wholly independent of the existence of individuals, that Humanity has an existence independent of the existence of these particular, present individuals; if, accordingly, it is belief that these present, particular individuals are not immortal and imperishable – that is, not in truth the final individuals in whom the essence of humanity is exhausted and done with.[14]

Feuerbach adduces several arguments why belief in personal, indi-

---

11 See Gerrish, *ibid.*, p. 229, n.30.

12 Gerrish, *ibid.*, p. 163.

13 Feuerbach's replacement of belief in the eternity of God with belief in 'the unfading youth of humanity' was later echoed almost verbally by another 'theological anti-theological' writer, Franz Overbeck (cf. his expression 'the eternal youth of mankind' cited in M. Henry, *Franz Overbeck: Theologian?*, p. 167, n.46). Overbeck's meditations on death, reproduced in the final section of *Christentum und Kultur*, are in many respects close to Feuerbach's, except that in Overbeck's case the all-pervading mood is much bleaker. Feuerbach's influence in fostering what might be called a resolutely this-worldly 'spirituality' among, especially, the German-speaking intelligentsia of the nineteenth century can be seen also in the work of a writer like Gottfried Keller, who in fact attended Feuerbach's lectures on *The Essence of Religion*.

14 Quoted in Gerrish, *op. cit.*, p. 163–165.

vidual immortality is illusory.[15] As individuals, for instance, we are all embedded in the system of nature of which we are merely a part. Immortality belongs to the system, not to the individual elements, taken in isolation. Furthermore, we can only exist in time and space. These coordinates of our being allow us to have a specifically human existence, but by the same token they cannot be prolonged indefinitely. Our existence thus has a limited span. And finally, we are not pure spirits; our existence is embodied existence, and consequently has a limited time to run: 'The soul is not a thing, a substance fixed and at rest, sitting in its body like the oyster. It is pure life, pure activity ... It only *becomes*, never *is*.'[16]

Feuerbach, however, does not draw from his materialistic philosophy of life a message of hopelessness and despair. Quite the contrary. The abandonment of belief in immortality, as guaranteed by the transcendent God of Christianity, is for him a prelude to liberation. Finite, earthly man is now free to put all his energies into loving his fellow-man without having to be concerned about his own personal, 'immortal' fate. Feuerbach's thought, strange though it may at first appear, is thus still profoundly marked by 'religious' motifs. For he also wishes to face up to the fact of death and to counteract individual self-assertion, two obstacles to human happiness that religion has traditionally targeted. Feuerbach too wishes, in his own religiously anti-theological way, if one may so express it, to conquer death and to encourage selflessness:

> For death can only be overcome before death. But death is only overcome by true and complete surrender of the self and – necessarily bound up with it – by the recognition and perception of death in its essence and its truth.[17]

Feuerbach's final aim is not to lead humanity to a supernatural heaven but to unlock human energies for the improvement and 'humanisation' of earthly existence.[18] The substitute he proposes

---

15 See Gerrish, *ibid.*, p. 164.
16 Quoted by Gerrish, *ibid.*
17 From a section of *Thoughts on Death and Immortality* entitled 'The ethical significance of death', quoted in Gerrish, *ibid.*, p. 164.
18 At the end of his lectures on *The Essence of Religion*, Feuerbach stated that the task he had hoped to fulfil in them was 'to turn friends of God into friends of man, believers into thinkers, prayers into workers, candidates for the next world into students of this world, Christians, who on their own admission claim to be "half animal, half angel", into human beings, full human beings.'

for the loss of the eternal life promised by Christianity is reminiscent of the ancient idea of a purely historical afterlife. This will be brief or long, favourable or unfavourable, depending on the impact and quality of one's life. But, like Hegel, he also has a general sense of the contribution all make, whether remembered by posterity or not, to the great unfolding of humanity.[19]

The Essence of Cristianity

Feuerbach's fame rests on his *Essence of Christianity* (1841), the book which caused a 'sensation' on its first publication and in the modern period was *the* work that sowed undying suspicion about the very existence of the Christian God. Strauss wrote that it 'was the truth of our time' and Engels, looking back in later years, said that 'at once we all became Feuerbachians.'[20] Marx himself, who eventually went on to criticise Feuerbach, was initially enthusiastic about his critique of religion. He expressed his admiration for Feuerbach in the pun that was later taken up by Karl Barth, when he wrote:

> There is no other road for you to *truth* and *freedom*, except that leading *through* the stream of fire [the *Feuer-bach*]. Feuerbach is the *purgatory* of the present times.[21]

Atheists existed, of course, long before Feuerbach, indeed as far back as classical antiquity. But Feuerbach touched a sensitive nerve in modern times by suggesting that God was not merely compatible with, but was actually the product of, human desire and need. Lichtenberg had already written: 'Of all the inventions of man I doubt whether any was more easily accomplished than that of a Heaven.'[22] Feuerbach, for his part, sought to spell out in his writings the exclusively anthropological meaning or 'secret' underlying the phenomenon of religion: 'Theology is anthropology', as his famous dictum has it. This perspective on religion has been seen by one commentator as the culmination of a much older process, going back right to the Reformation when salvation was taken as the heart of Christian faith: 'It is ... not entirely fanciful to trace Feuerbach's atheistic interpretation of Christianity back, ultimately, to the

---

19 Cf. Gerrish, *ibid*., p. 166. See also *ibid*., p. 230, n.40.
20 Quoted by Van A. Harvey, *Feuerbach and the Interpretation of Religion* (Cambridge, 1995), p. 26.
21 *Writings of the Young Marx on Philosophy and Society*, tr. and ed. L.D. Easton and K. H. Guddat (New York, 1967), p. 95, quoted in Gerrish, *op. cit.*, p. 168.
22 G. Chr. Lichtenberg, *Aphorisms*, p. 189.

reduction of Christianity to an anthropology with a doctrine of human salvation for its center-piece – that is, to the liberal-Evangelical version of the Reformation's choice of sin and salvation as the central theme of the Christian faith.'[23] This may well be true. But that does not make Feuerbach's claim false. Human salvation is, after all, a large part of what Christianity means. Perhaps one might say that the human side of Christianity must be acknowledged, but not to the exclusion of the divine side. Feuerbach would say, of course, that there is no difference. So if one wishes to refute Feuerbach, one must try to show that there is a genuine, not an imagined, difference between the 'divine' and the 'human' sides of Christianity. We shall return to this question.

Like Hegel, Feuerbach had a historical and developmental view of religion, seeing its various stages as reflecting the changing patterns of the human race's self-understanding. The deity whom Old Testament religion placed outside man, Christianity placed within man. The third stage is to see that what Christianity placed in man is not an awareness of God, but is an awareness of man's own nature.[24] Feuerbach, thus, applied what he termed 'transformational criticism'[25] to Hegel's thought in order to extract from it what it really meant. Hegel had seen 'God' as expressing himself in man. But what this really means, according to Feuerbach, is that in religion man's own alienated self-consciousness comes to expression. Hence to understand the true meaning of Hegel, one only has to reverse everything he said about religion:

> It suffices to put the predicate in place of the subject everywhere, i.e. *to turn speculative philosophy upside down*, and we arrive at the truth in its unconcealed, pure, manifest form.[26]

Feuerbach accordingly substituted for Hegel's Absolute Spirit the Spirit of Humanity, which individual human beings had objectified

---

23 Frans Jozef van Beeck, *God Encountered: A Contemporary Catholic Systematic Theology*, Vol, 2/1 (Collegeville, Minnesota, 1993), p. 102, n. [b]. This implicit critique of Feuerbach's exclusively anthropological interpretation of Christianity was anticipated by Hans Urs von Balthasar when he wrote: '[M]an cannot be the measure of God, nor man's answer the measure of the word addressed to him' (*Love Alone: the Way of Revelation*, p. 119).

24 *Essence*, pp. 31f.

25 See Robert Tucker, *Philosophy and Myth in Karl Marx* (Cambridge, 1972), p. 86.

26 L. Feuerbach, *Kleine Philosophische Schriften*, p. 56, quoted in Tucker, *op. cit.*, p. 86.

and projected beyond themselves, as an ideal self, on to a non-existent 'God', thus alienating their own substance: 'Man – this is the
mystery of religion – projects[27] his being into objectivity, and then
again makes himself an object to this projected image of himself
thus converted into a subject; he is and thinks of himself as an object
to himself, but as the object of an object, of another being than himself. Thus here. Man is an object to God.'[28] Feuerbach saw 'the origins and function of religion as the objectification of the attributes
of the human spirit.'[29] Because, however, of the alienating effects of
religion in its historical career, Feuerbach interpreted the religious
development of humanity up until his own time in negative terms:
'To enrich God, man must become poor; that God may be all, man
must be nothing.'[30] However, the damage done by traditional religion could now, he thought, be reversed if people only realised the
truth – that 'God' was an illusion – and took back to themselves
what they had for so long mistakenly given away to an alienating
beyond.

There is a strong moral, even crusading, thrust in Feuerbach's
argument about the 'true' meaning of religion. For he is concerned
that the damage done by falsely understood religion in the past
should be avoided in the future and that the vast human resources
squandered in religion in the past should be reclaimed for the purpose of human betterment. This is implicit in the following comment:

> Religion is the relation of man to his own nature, – therein lies its
> truth and its power of moral amelioration; – but to his nature not
> recognised as his own, but regarded as another nature, separate,
> nay, contradistinguished from his own: herein lies its untruth,
> its limitation, its contradiction to reason and morality; herein
> lies the noxious source of religious fanaticism.[31]

---

27 It is perhaps worth noting that Feuerbach himself does not actually use
    the term *project* in this context, but *objectify* ('Der Mensch ... vergegen-
    ständlicht sein Wesen und macht dann wieder sich zum *Gegenstand*
    dieses vergegenständlichten ... Wesens,' *Das Wesen des Christentums*,
    Stuttgart, 1974, p. 76). The linking of Feuerbach's name with a 'projec-
    tionist' critique of religion – which of course is not entirely misleading –
    is due, in part, to George Eliot's translation; see Harvey, in N. Smart et
    al. (eds.), *op. cit.*, pp. 294f.
28 *Essence*, p. 29f (amended).
29 Harvey, in N. Smart et al. (eds.), *op. cit.*, p. 294.
30 *Essence*, p. 26 (quoted by Baumer, *op. cit.*, p. 316).
31 *Essence*, p. 197 (quoted by Harvey, *Feuerbach and the Interpretation of
    Religion*, pp. 28f.; cf. also *ibid.*, p. 197).

While Hegel had tried, albeit in an attenuated and, as things turned out, highly ambiguous sense, to retain some distinction between divine and human spirit, with Feuerbach the last vestiges of any such distinction disappeared. In Feuerbach divinity and humanity merged, or – what amounted to the same thing – divinity disappeared and only humanity remained as the Absolute:

> [T]he historical progress of religion consists in this: that what by an earlier religion was regarded as objective, is now recognised as subjective; that is, what was formerly contemplated and worshipped as God is now perceived to be something *human*.[32]

Christianity's doctrine of the incarnation had of course claimed that God became man in Jesus, but for Hegel's disciples Strauss and Feuerbach, two of the group known as the 'Young Hegelians',[33] universal humanity itself was seen as intrinsically divine. Incarnation is not particular but universal. Divinity which had been slumbering within humanity from the beginning was at last waking up to its true nature. Hence alienation, the tragic split between 'man' and 'God', which traditional religion with its belief in a transcendent God had, no doubt unwittingly, fostered, had finally been overcome, and man would no longer be plagued with the problem of divided loyalties. Or so Feuerbach, in his more rapt moments, appeared to think.

But in what, more precisely, did the humanity consist, that Feuerbach extolled so relentlessly? In the opening chapter of *The Essence of Christianity* Feuerbach, like Hegel before him, distinguished man from the animals; he assumed, moreover, that humanity was a universal constant. This was perhaps an unconscious reminiscence of the Christian notion of divine immutability, now applied by Feuerbach to humanity. The distinguishing mark of humanity is of course 'consciousness' which permits man to objectify his own nature, his own 'not finite and limited, but infinite nature.'[34] Taking his cue from Cicero, Feuerbach claims that man 'can conceive no form more beautiful, more sublime than the human,'[35] adding intriguingly that 'only the absolute, the perfect form, can delight without envy in the forms of other beings.'[36] As

---

32 *Essence*, p. 13; cf. Baumer, *op. cit.*, p. 317.
33 Cf. below, n.63.
34 Quoted by Baumer, *op. cit.*, p. 318.
35 *Essence*, pp. 6f. (quoted by Baumer, *ibid.*).
36 *Essence*, p. 7, n.1.

for the substance of human nature, this consists in what Feuerbach called the 'divine trinity in man', Reason, Will and Affection (or Love), the dispensers of human 'power'.[37] Of these three aspects of human nature, 'Love' seemed to be most important to Feuerbach. Once religion had been unmasked as an illusion, 'unalienated man, according to Feuerbach,' would 'be able to love humanity, an "affection" which was palpably impossible so long as one loved God.'[38]

Feuerbach's argument on this latter point is worth looking at in a little more detail. The reason he finds Christianity ultimately anti-human is simply that it is a religion; it cannot, therefore, with a good conscience preach love alone. Christianity, of course, teaches that 'God is love'. But precisely therein lies, for Feuerbach, its problem. For to teach that 'God is love' is to preach faith (in God) and love at the same time, and hence to set up a possible antagonism between them. Christianity, Feuerbach writes, 'has not made love free; it has not raised itself to the height of accepting love as absolute. And it has not given this freedom, nay, cannot give it, because it is a religion, – and hence subjects love to the dominion of faith.'[39] In Christianity, therefore, 'love is tainted by faith.'[40] Feuerbach concludes: 'A love which is limited by faith is an untrue love.'[41]

The distinction he draws between God (the subject) and love (the predicate) may at first sight appear to rest on specious, not to say perverse, logic. But Feuerbach supports his belief in the evil effects of faith by evoking 'the horrors of Christian religious history',[42] which, he implies, would not have occurred without the distinction Christianity made between faith and love. For to make room for faith alongside love is inevitably to accept that, 'Love does not alone fill my soul.'[43] In consequence, 'I leave a place open for my uncharitableness by thinking of God as a subject in distinction from the predicate [i.e. "love"].'[44] The fatal distinction between faith and love is, for Feuerbach, only possible because faith 'clings to the self-

---

37 Cf. Baumer, *op. cit.*, p. 318.
38 *Ibid.*, p. 320.
39 *Essence*, p. 263.
40 *Ibid.*, p. 264.
41 *Ibid.*
42 *Ibid.*, p. 263.
43 *Ibid.*, p. 264.
44 *Ibid.*

subsistence of God', whereas 'love does away with it.'[45] As a result Christian love, since it is 'bound by faith is a narrow-hearted, false love, ... a love which has only a semblance of holiness, for it hides in itself the hatred that belongs to faith; it is only benevolent so long as faith is not injured.'[46] In accents which anticipate Nietzsche's indignant denunciations of Christian hypocrisy, Feuerbach writes:

> [I]n order to retain the semblance of love, [faith] falls into the most diabolical sophisms, as we see in Augustine's apology for the persecution of heretics. Love is limited by faith; hence it does not regard even the uncharitable actions which faith suggests as in contradiction with itself; it interprets the deeds of hatred which are committed for the sake of faith as deeds of love. And it necessarily falls into such contradictions, because the limitation of love by faith is itself a contradiction. If it once is subjected to this limitation, it has given up its own judgment, its inherent measure and criterion, its self-subsistence; it is delivered up without power of resistance to the promptings of faith... We find the same contradictions in the Bible as in Augustine, as in Catholicism generally; ... The Bible curses through faith, blesses through love. But the only love it knows is a love founded on faith. Thus here already it is a love which curses, an unreliable love, a love which gives me no guarantee that it will not turn into hatred; ... Christian love has not overcome hell, because it has not overcome faith. Love is in itself unbelieving, faith unloving.[47]

Yet why, one might well ask, should faith in God, even a self-subsistent God (who is, after all, described as 'love'), cause the faithful to commit acts of wickedness? This question would appear to be connected with an idea which we have already mentioned in relation to Feuerbach's *Thoughts on Death and Immortality*, namely that Christianity encourages individualism, and hence selfishness, through its doctrine of a transcendent God. For this God absorbs the individual's deepest energies, and thus deflects his interest from the earth and from his fellow human beings. We might note, in passing, that this aspect of Feuerbach's thought must be in some kind of contradiction with the idea, which he also expounds, that Christianity's 'God' was really, in substance, human nature. But, picking up a theme we have already noted in Hegel's writings, he

45 *Ibid.*
46 *Ibid.*, p. 265.
47 *Ibid.*

clearly also believed that Christianity fostered the exaltation of the individual over the species, a mistake avoided by the ancients:

> Christianity ... cared nothing for the species, and had only the individual in its eye and mind. Christianity – not, certainly, the Christianity of the present day, which has incorporated with itself the culture of heathenism, and has preserved only the name and some general positions of Christianity – is the direct opposite of heathenism, and only when it is regarded as such is it truly comprehended, ... The ancients sacrificed the individual to the species; the Christians sacrificed the species to the individual.[48]

Herein, for Feuerbach, lies the source of the poison Christianity has poured into history, through its depreciation of earthly, natural, and sexual life – an attitude clearly reflected in its extolling of asceticism and monasticism[49] – and through its false understanding of death itself. These ideas, as we shall see, reappear, sharpened and intensified, in the thought of Nietzsche. To heal the wounds Christianity has inflicted on the human race Feuerbach recommends in his best-known work what could almost paradoxically be termed a sort of 'Christian neo-paganism' or secular love-mysticism.

Contemporary critiques

In *The Essence of Christianity* Feuerbach described the true meaning of humanity: it was simply the essence of divinity, now finally recognised for what it genuinely was. But while humanity, so understood, seemed to be an unproblematic and fairly straightforward reality for Feuerbach, it was not interpreted as such for very long. Even before Darwin's theory of evolution challenged the very notion of humanity's special status, Marx's critique of Feuerbach had attacked the abstract nature of his philosophy. For – like Freud later – Feuerbach saw religion as produced by the unchanging structures of human nature, whereas Marx saw these structures, and hence religion itself, as a reflection of specific economic and social conditions that produced alienated human beings.[50] 'Life', he

---

48 *Ibid.*, pp. 151f., quoted in Harvey, *Feuerbach and the Interpretation of Religion*, p. 111. See also Harvey's useful comments in this theme, *ibid.*, pp. 111f.

49 See Harvey, *ibid.*, p. 112. Cf. also above, Chapter 7, n.17.

50 Cf. Harvey in N. Smart et al. (eds.), *op. cit.*, pp. 291f.

wrote, 'is not determined by consciousness, but consciousness by life.'[51] Marx therefore, writing in 1844, found Feuerbach's thought too abstract despite the latter's protestation of materialism, relayed in the famous pun: 'Der Mensch ist, was er isst.'[52] So while welcoming Feuerbach's unmasking of religion as a purely human construct, Marx criticised him for overlooking 'that vale of tears of which religion is the halo,'[53] i.e. the concrete, historical conditions in which people were condemned to live out their alienated existence. For Marx Feuerbach presented the individual as a being 'squatting outside the world'.[54] The abolition of religion must therefore be carried through, Marx argued, by the abolition of the economic, social and political structures of which religion was the 'inverted consciousness'.[55]

It is debatable whether Marx's criticism of Feuerbach is entirely justified. Certainly Feuerbach never inspired the kind of revolutionary political changes with which Marx can be legitimately associated. But he was a resolutely 'this-worldly' philosopher who at least claimed that his philosophy possessed 'an essentially practical – and indeed in the highest sense practical – tendency.'[56] He was also of an almost 'existential' cast of mind, with a near-dread of pure thought's inadequacy in the face of real 'flesh and blood' living. 'If the starting-point of the *old philosophy*', he wrote, 'was the proposition: *I am an abstract, a thinking being only, the body does not belong to my essence*, then, on the contrary, the *new philosophy* begins with the proposition: *I am a real, a material being: The body belongs to my essence; indeed the body in its totality is my self* [ego], *my very essence.*'[57] Feuerbach wanted to create then not so much a 'philosophy of man' as a 'philosophy for man'.[58] In the 'Preface' to his

---

51 Karl Marx, and Friedrich Engels, *The German Ideology, Part I*, ed. with intro. by C. J. Arthur (New York, 1976), p. 47, quoted by Harvey in N. Smart et al. (eds.), *op. cit.*, p. 307.
52 'Man is (*ist*) what he eats (*isst*).'
53 Quoted by Harvey in N. Smart et al, *op. cit.*, p. 302.
54 Quoted by Harvey, *ibid.*, pp. 301f.
55 *Ibid.*, p. 302.
56 L. Feuerbach, *Principles of the Philosophy of the Future*, tr., with an intro., by Manfred H. Vogel (Indianapolis, 1966), pp. 72f.
57 L. Feuerbach, *Werke in sechs Bänden*, ed. E. Thies (Frankfurt a/M, 1975), vol. 3, p. 302, quoted in F. Fellmann (ed.), *Geschichte der Philosophie im 19. Jahrhundert* (Reinbek, 1996), p. 107. (See Feuerbach, *Principles of the Philosophy of the Future*, p. 54.)
58 Feuerbach, *Principles of the Philosophy of the Future*, p. 72.

Principles of the Philosophy of the Future, published in 1843, he set out his down-to-earth humanist credentials:

> The philosophy of the future has the task of leading philosophy from the realm of 'departed souls' back into the realm of embodied and living souls; of pulling philosophy down from the divine, self-sufficient bliss in the realm of ideas into human misery.[59]

Furthermore, Feuerbach had a keen sense of the social nature of the self, and even anticipated what one might term the 'dialogical principle', associated with the thought of Martin Buber, i.e. the view that an 'I' can only truly emerge in relation to a 'Thou'. Indeed, in the work just referred to, he develops the claim made in *The Essence of Christianity* regarding the identity of divinity and humanity by describing 'God' as the interrelatedness of human beings with each other:

> Solitude is finiteness and limitation; community is freedom and infinity. Man for himself is man (in the ordinary sense); man with man – the unity of I and thou – is God... The true dialectic is not a monologue of a solitary thinker with himself; it is a dialogue between I and thou.[60]

Feuerbach, like Hegel, reviewed the past, and saw the shortcomings of former modes of thought. The 'absolute philosopher', for example, identified truth with himself, just as the 'absolute monarch' identified the state with himself, and just as the religious consciousness identified 'the absolute God' with pure 'being'. 'The human philosopher, on the other hand, says: even in thinking and in being a philosopher, I am a man among men.'[61] In arriving at the 'new philosophy', which coincides with his own thought, Feuerbach does not, however, simply dismiss the efforts of the past. But where Hegel had raised up the figurative truth of religious faith to the higher level of conceptual truth, Feuerbach sought to bring down the hidden truth of religious consciousness to the real world of human existence. The mysteries of Christianity are therefore not to be dismissed as foolish superstition but revealed in all their deep human significance. The highest Christian mystery of all, the doctrine of the Trinity, can be 'de-theologised' and shown to harbour profound truths about the social nature of man:

---

59 *Ibid.*, p. 3.
60 *Ibid.*, pp. 71f.
61 *Ibid.*, pp. 71f.

... [T]he secret of the Trinity is the secret of communal and social life; it is the secret of the necessity of the 'thou' for an 'I'; it is the truth that no being – be it man, God, mind, or ego – is for itself alone a true, perfect, and absolute being, that truth and perfection are only the connection and unity of beings equal in their essence. The highest and the last principle of philosophy is, therefore, the unity of man with man.[62]

Even on the evidence so far adduced, then, Marx's criticism that Feuerbach's philosophy is still too abstract, is, surely, scarcely sustainable. Even his famous 'Thesis XI on Feuerbach' (1845): 'The philosophers have only *interpreted* the world, in various ways; the point is to *change* it,' is itself one more intellectual statement on 'the world'. And if the practical consequences of the implementation of a philosopher's ideas are to be taken into account in any assessment of his philosophy, Marx may be in deeper 'practical' trouble than Feuerbach. In any case, what is slightly more worrying about Feuerbach than his possible political naïveté is, it seems to me, his conviction of having reached the end of the philosophical road, reached the final truth about the human condition (cf. the 'highest and last principle of philosophy'). It is, I think, legitimate to be suspicious of all 'last words', and not just for their possibly disastrous practical implications or consequences. For how can one underwrite the validity of such words? An acceptance of the incomprehensibility of God can at least corroborate all suspicion concerning philosophical 'last words'.

After Marx's critique of Feuerbach's philosophy, another 'Young Hegelian', Max Stirner,[63] also criticised Feuerbach for the abstract nature of his thought. For Stirner, a somewhat eccentric figure, Feuerbach's thought is still 'thoroughly theological'.[64] Feuerbach had simply replaced the abstraction of divinity, in the guise of Hegel's Absolute, with that of humanity:

I am neither God nor *Man*, neither the supreme essence nor my essence, and therefore it is all one in the main whether I think of the essence as in me or outside me... To God, who is spirit, Feuerbach gives the name 'Our Essence'. Can we put up with

---

62 *Ibid.*, p. 72.
63 On Stirner (pseudonym of Johann Kaspar Schmidt [1806–1856]) see *The Young Hegelians. An Anthology*, intro. and ed. by Lawrence S. Stepelevich (Cambridge, 1983), pp. 325ff.; David McLellan, *The Young Hegelians and Karl Marx* (Aldershot, 1993), pp. 117ff.
64 Quoted by D. McLellan, *op. cit.*, p. 121.

this, that 'Our Essence' is brought into opposition to us – that we are split into an essential and an unessential self? Do we not therewith go back into the dreary misery of seeing ourselves banished out of ourselves?[65]

Having attacked the basic thesis of Feuerbach's *Essence of Christianity*, finding the new god of humanism as irrelevant to his own situation as the traditional God of Christianity, Stirner turned on Feuerbach's favourite theme of love, and found it wanting too:

> After the annihilation of faith Feuerbach thinks to put in to the supposedly safe harbour of *love*. 'The first and highest law must be the love of man to man. *Homo homini Deus ist* – this is the supreme practical maxim, this is the turning point of the world's history.' But, properly speaking, only the god is changed – the *deus*; love has remained: there love to the superhuman God, here love to the human God, to *homo* as *Deus*. Therefore man is to me – sacred. And everything 'truly human' is to me – sacred! ... Haven't we the priest again there? Who is his God? Man with a capital M! What is the divine? The human! Then the predicate has indeed only been changed into the subject, and, instead of the sentence 'God is love', they say 'love is divine'; instead of 'God has become man', 'Man has become God', etc. It is nothing more or less than a new–*religion*. ... Feuerbach's proposition, 'Theology is anthropology,' means only 'religion must be ethics, ethics alone is religion.' ... How could he hope to turn men away from God when he left them the divine?[66]

Stirner's point is that love only makes sense if applied to an individual for *that* individual's own sake, not if applied to the individual for the sake of the individual's 'humanity', which is as vague as anything formerly proposed by religion. And he adds: 'It is not how I realise the *generally human* that needs to be my task, but how I satisfy myself.'[67] Stirner's anarchistic individualism is impervious to Feuerbach's fine-sounding assertions. But if Stirner thought Feuerbach was still too much in love with abstraction, Marx accused Stirner of precisely the same crime, arguing 'that "ego" was also an abstraction, the product of a certain type of social system.'[68] Thus, from Hegel to Feuerbach to Stirner to Marx one sees

---

65 Max Stirner, *The Ego and His Own* [*Der Einzige und sein Eigenthum*], ed. John Carroll (London, 1971), pp. 52f.

66 Stirner, *The Ego and His Own*, pp. 53f.

67 *Ibid.*, p. 55.

68 Baumer, *op. cit.*, p. 320.

the wide range of possibilities with which German Idealism was pregnant. Provisionally the movement ended in two diametrically opposed destinations: extreme individualism and extreme communism, both – like Hegel's own position – based on the merely asserted power and validity of human thought.

But Feuerbach's exaltation of 'humanity' received more comprehensive blows in the second half of the century. The first came from Darwin's theory of evolution, and the second from Nietzsche's undermining of the premises on which any Idealist thought – including his own? – could claim to be important. In *Daybreak*, for instance, we read:

> '*Humanity*'. – We do not regard the animals as moral beings. But do you suppose that the animals regard us as moral beings? – An animal which could speak said: 'Humanity is a prejudice of which we animals at least are free.'[69]

In such passages Nietzsche undercuts provocatively the glorious distinction Idealism had always made between man and the animals, and in so doing forces his readers to ask once again, no longer simply: 'Does God exist?', a question with which atheists could be relatively at ease, since their own humanity was not immediately or obviously under threat by it, but more subversively: 'Does man exist?' Nietzsche brings out more powerfully than Feuerbach the implications of the 'death of God' in modern culture, because he shows that God's demise evacuates humanity of its traditional meaning, which Feuerbach thought could still be saved. But both Feuerbach and Nietzsche are undeniably part of the Judaeo-Christian tradition, which always speaks about God together with the human condition. Inevitably therefore, when 'God' disappears, the status of man is under threat. In more recent times this consequence has been more forthrightly drawn by, for instance, the structuralist anthropologist Claude Lévi-Strauss ('We believe that the ultimate aim of the human sciences is not to constitute man but to dissolve him'[70]) and the philosopher Michel Foucault ('In our day one can only think in the void of man who has disappeared. One can only utter a philosophical laugh at all those who still want man, his reign or his liberation, at all those who ask "What is man?"').[71]

---

69 *Daybreak* §333, tr. R.J. Hollingdale (Cambridge, 1983), p. 162.
70 Quoted by Dominique Morin, *How to Understand God*, tr. John Bowden (London, 1990), p. 61.
71 *Ibid.*

Evaluation

Feuerbach's critique of the Christian God as a projection of an ideal humanity or of a purified, idealised human nature would appear to rest on the assumption of the fundamental, intrinsic goodness of human beings, and indeed of life as such. Such optimism was certainly 'in the air' in Feuerbach's day, although, as the massive counter-example of Schopenhauer indicates, it was not universally shared. But Strauss, for instance, described mankind as 'the Sinless One',[72] and around the same period Auguste Comte who, as we have already seen, tried to develop his own 'Religion of Humanity', was preaching the virtue of *altruism*, a term he himself actually coined.[73] Emphasis on the species (which was also to be a hallmark of Darwin's thought) may have been to some extent a reaction against the perception that traditional, transcendental Christianity had encouraged a 'religious selfishness' among its followers, urging them to think first and foremost of their own individual salvation.[74] On the other hand, one might argue that the theoretical questioning of individualism may also have had something to do with doubt about the wisdom of the Romantic cult of the hero, living in superior isolation to the conventional masses.

In any case, the danger of excessive individualism and selfishness is one to which traditional Christianity itself draws attention. Indeed the paradox of finally losing one's life by trying to preserve it, is part of, though of course not exclusive to, Christian teaching. And even as individualistic a thinker as Luther himself realised that religion could be exploited for selfish reasons. 'Hence,' as B.A. Gerrish writes, 'at his most provocative, he can assure us that they are damned who want to escape from damnation.'[75]

In a more general sense – and again from within the Christian fold itself – Malebranche (1638–1715) was aware that one could 'project', as we now say, a false image of God, without thereby destroying God: 'This word "God" is equivocal, and infinitely more so than one believes ... And so people think that they are loving God when in fact they are only loving a huge phantom which they

---

72 Quoted by H. R. Mackintosh, *Types of Modern Theology* (London and Glasgow, 1969), p. 119; cf. Baumer, *op. cit.*, p. 323.
73 See Baumer, *ibid.*, p. 320. Comte was also the first to use the term 'sociology'.
74 See Baumer, *ibid.*, p. 315; cf. above, pp. 203f.
75 Gerrish, *op. cit.*, p. 167. See also above, Chapter 2, n.36.

have created for themselves.'[76] Already in antiquity Xenophanes had criticised too anthropomorphic a view of the divine precisely in order to reassert real divine transcendence. To have a false image of God is clearly then not to prove there is no God.

Moreover, Feuerbach's unmasking of theology as a projection of human desires and ideals and needs, is not an explanation of why people keep falling into the temptation of wanting to create a God and a divine realm out of their own imagination. Neither indeed before Feuerbach was the Enlightenment able to explain why human beings, if they are supposed to be essentially rational, created religions that clearly go beyond rationality and the so-called real world of our earthly experience. It would seem then that humanity's concern with God – documented in the religions of the world – can be as validly explained as a series of responses to, or tokens of, the reality of God perceived in human existence, as it can be explained away as a series of projections of humanity's needs on to a non-existent deity. Both explanations are compatible with the evidence.

Logically, therefore, Feuerbach's challenge to religion can be resisted. What is intrinsically corruptible (religion) need not be on that account also intrinsically corrupt. Similarly, even though we may wish to believe that God exists, such wishing will not actually disprove the existence of God (cf. above, p. 150).

However, for Christianity the problem is that Feuerbach's challenge cannot be dealt with exclusively at the level of strict logic, because that is not the most important level at which he makes his challenge. Feuerbach did not attack the human corruption of religion but religion as the corruption of humanity. In his psychological analysis of human needs he did not only point to the possible source of religion, but plausibly suggested that such needs could never shake off their earthly origin and hence could never find anything other than a purely earthly satisfaction. One may, of course, complain that he was so interested in psychology that he forgot about the question of Being, which is allegedly the realm where the 'real' religious question must be asked. No doubt. Yet while Being may indeed be superior to becoming, becoming is what we experience. Redemption, similarly, may be superior to suffering, but suffering is what we experience or, as Feuerbach himself expresses it: '[T]he history of Christianity is the history of the Passion of Humanity... [T]he imperfect tense in which the fact of suffering is

---

76 Quoted by Dominique Morin, *How to Understand God*, tr. John Bowden (London, 1990), p. 6.

expressed makes a deeper, more enduring impression, than the perfect tense which expresses the fact of redemption.'[77] It seems to me, therefore, that Feuerbach's questions can only be answered, if at all, on the same terrain as he himself asks them. And that terrain is the human condition, if this expression is (still) permissible. The reservation is now necessary, because the nineteenth-century critique of religion has thrown into doubt not just the question of God, but the related question of the status of 'humanity', and the meaning of humanity's trials.

Feuerbach was himself unquestionably aware of suffering. Indeed he saw his critical philosophy as aimed at freeing man from the 'hellish torments of contradiction',[78] inflicted on him 'by the despairing, suffering consciousness of his distance from the divine absolute self.'[79] He also had experience of loss in one of its most poignant and 'meaningless' forms – his young daughter Mathilde died in 1844, aged three years.[80] But he nevertheless appears to have continued to believe that the 'God' projected as an ideal humanity by generations of human beings was fundamentally good and even that the nature, on which human beings depended, was 'holy'.[81] Thus, in a passage which occurs towards the end of *The Essence of Christianity*, Feuerbach proclaims in tones of quasi-religious enthusiasm:

> If in water we declare: Man can do nothing without Nature; by bread and wine we declare: Nature needs man, as man needs Nature...The sacrament of Baptism inspires us with thankfulness towards Nature, the sacrament of bread and wine with thankfulness towards man.[82]

Like Hegel, therefore, and in line with the main Judaeo-Christian tradition, Feuerbach's outlook was life-affirming, despite the reality of suffering. But unlike Hegel, Robert Tucker argues, he did not try to justify the suffering of the human race in view of the final goal it might help to achieve:

> He sees no justification for the suffering. He sees only that man is oppressing himself. Morally speaking, Feuerbach turns

---

77 *Essence*, pp. 61f.
78 *Kleine Philosophische Schriften*, p. 159, quoted in Tucker, *op. cit.*, p. 90.
79 Tucker, *op. cit.*, p. 90.
80 See Volker Spierling, *Kleine Geschichte der Philosophie* (Munich, 1996), p. 259.
81 *Essence*, p. 277.
82 *Essence*, pp. 276f.

against the Absolute and takes the part of suffering man. He rebels against the misery that self-deifying man inflicts upon himself ... His philosophy is, therefore, imbued with a profound compassion, perhaps one might even say a Christian compassion, for man conceived as a being historically divided against himself in 'religion'.[83]

It is nevertheless remarkable that for Feuerbach the human mind had produced an agreeable 'God', now revealed as having been all along really the projected perfection of human nature, whereas for thinkers and artists like Schopenhauer and Goya human reason revealed a vision of horror. It is curious to reflect that almost at the same time as Feuerbach[84] and Comte were singing the praises of humanity, Schopenhauer was indignantly anatomising the distinctive features of *Weltschmerz*, and Kierkegaard, a more specifically Christian thinker, was tormenting himself over the exasperating dimensions of the human condition.[85] And more recently, as Van Harvey grimly reminds us, for the cultural anthropologist Ernest Becker, 'as for Elias Canetti, "each organism raises its head over a field of corpses, smiles into the sun, and declares life good."'[86] One might conclude that world views are perhaps as much a matter of temperament as of actual evidence. However, the final truth of the world must surely include what no single temperament can exhaustively embrace; or, in other words, it must transcend what any single temperament can absorb.

It might be worth recalling that traditional Christianity only ever decreed 'paradise' to be unambiguously good, whereas history it saw as a *selva oscura*. It thus kept alive the tension between the reality of the essential goodness of creation, which only God can see, and the reality of history's imperfection. Christian faith never finally abolished this tension in favour, exclusively, of one of the two poles. In

---

83 Tucker, *op. cit.*, p. 92.

84 Harvey, *Feuerbach and the Interpretation of Religion*, pp. 118–120, shows convincingly that Feuerbach is not at his best when talking about 'original sin'.

85 See Baumer, *op. cit.*, p. 323. Baumer includes even Ritschlianism within the great wave of optimism that swept through the nineteenth-century New Enlightenment. Like Pelagius of old, Ritschl 'rejected the doctrine of original sin, substituting for it a "kingdom of sin," which ... originated ... in habit, imitation, and the wrong use of free will' (*ibid.*).

86 Harvey, *Feuerbach and the Interpretation of Religion*, p. 296; the quotation from Becker is from E. Becker, *Escape from Evil* (New York, 1975), p. 2.

recent centuries, for example, Christianity has refused to abandon its belief in 'original sin', even though this was the doctrine, apart from the claim to special revelation, with which the *Aufklärung* most reproached the Christian church.

Baumer interestingly entitles the chapter of his book which deals with the new 'Religion of Humanity', *The New Enlightenment*. This captures nicely the point at issue, which is that thinkers like Feuerbach or Comte, or later Marx, would appear to have assumed that the human condition was in principle improvable from within its own resources and those of nature. They therefore repudiated the Christian notion that historical humanity was so flawed at source that only an 'external provider' for its ultimate needs was conceivable.[87] The Promethean project of the 'New Enlightenment' has not yet delivered the goods, but then neither of course has anyone else. Somewhat ironically, therefore, both the secular religion of the 'New Enlightenment' and traditional Christianity find themselves in the same boat. But both are still able, or perhaps condemned, to hope. The exceptional figure of Nietzsche escapes this predicament by rejecting, like the ancient Greeks he so admired,[88] the possibility of hope, and simply rejoicing in whatever happens.

Faced with Feuerbach's provocative, disturbing, but also somehow bizarre ideas, one is tempted to ask: Is he, unwittingly, using 'God' as a scapegoat for human shortcomings? And in so doing, is he seeking an explanation for the reality of evil? If so, is this a plausible explanation of evil? In other words, is it plausible to locate the cause of human evil (cf. 'the horrors of Christian religious history') in false consciousness ('faith')? Feuerbach's attempt to explain the fact of evil in this way is ingenious and no doubt honestly meant. But his starting-point, here as elsewhere, appears to be the tacit assumption that reason can illuminate everything, and can explain even evil. In the light of this problematic, it seems to me, one can see that the strength and weakness of German Idealism have the same

---

87 The correspondence between the 'existential' and the intellectual side of the question of humanity's destiny is worth noting: those who think the world needs a saviour from without usually also think the world is not self-explanatory, whereas those who reject salvation from without usually also think the world is a self-contained and self-sustaining system – and to that extent self-explanatory.

88 Cf. Jürgen Moltmann: 'According to the Greek Promethean myth, hope is an evil that comes out of Pandora's box to confuse the human spirit.' Quoted in D. W. Musser and J. L. Price (eds.), *A New Handbook of Christian Theology*, Cambridge, 1992, p. 239.

root, namely belief in the omnicompetence of reason. Without such a belief philosophical Idealism could not have achieved so much, and without it, equally, it could not have made such great mistakes. Despite thinking that he had turned Hegel upside down, despite breaking officially with Hegelianism in the work *Zur Kritik der Hegelschen Philosophie* (1839), there is a sense in which Feuerbach did not really break the spell that Hegel's Idealism cast over his own thought. Feuerbach's world is, in Robert Tucker's phrase, 'a world of *naturalised Hegelianism*.'[89]

Idealism notoriously has difficulty dealing with particularity and otherness, to say nothing of the problem of evil. It is, consequently, not surprising to find that, for Feuerbach, Christian love, by its very particularity, is a contradiction in terms, since true love must be universal.[90] Hence to be truly love, Christian love must abandon its 'qualification of Christian.'[91] In short, all heteronomy, all recognition of genuine 'otherness' appears inimical to Feuerbach. Yet this claim may appear strange. For one of Feuerbach's strengths as a thinker is precisely his sense of the 'other'. Martin Buber, after all, hailed Feuerbach's discovery of the 'Thou' as one of the great breakthroughs of modern thought. And Feuerbach specifically stated: 'The being of man is given only in communion, in the unity of man with man, a unity resting on the reality of the distinction between the I and the Thou.'[92] However this can surely remain only an arbitrary assertion, if it rests solely on the authority of the one who makes it. Can Feuerbach, with only a belief in the value of human beings' common nature to guide him, make good his claim that the 'being of man is given only ... in the unity of man with man'? Is belief or hope in a communion between an 'I' and a 'Thou' not simply one more human 'projection', mere wishful thinking? And if it is, then is Feuerbach hoist with his own projectionist petard?

Feuerbach could always, of course, respond that his belief in the 'being of man' is as valid as a theist's belief in God, indeed more so, in that he can experience directly the object of his faith, whereas a theist cannot see God. This is true. But in reply, it seems to me, a believer in God can say that, certainly, the value of human beings is intrinsic to them; it is not, however, their creation or possession, as

---

89 Tucker, *op. cit.*, p. 82.
90 *Essence*, pp. 265f.
91 *Ibid.*, p. 265.
92 *Kleine Philosophische Schriften*, p. 169, quoted in Tucker, *op. cit.*, p. 91.

birth, transience and death teach us. Hence, the paradox of religious belief is that the value of life, which is not an illusion, must have its source beyond us. So it is 'beyond us, yet ourselves'. And this 'beyond' is what some people call 'God'. But far from this leading to alienation, it rather strengthens our sense that life is not a dream.

Feuerbach's disbelief in God would appear to have been partly due to the instinctive dislike of heteronomy that we have already noted in his philosophy. Hence he asks: '[H]ow could [man] find consolation and peace in God if God were an essentially different being? How can I share the peace of a being if I am not of the same nature with him? If his nature is different from mine, his peace is essentially different, – it is no peace for me.'[93] The idea that divinity might have a real 'otherness' that cannot be captured or absorbed by human thought seems anathema to Feuerbach.

Not surprisingly, German Idealism has had its opponents. One trenchant critic, Robert Tucker, sees in Feuerbach's *Essence of Christianity* a revelation of the true meaning of Hegel, rather than a revelation of the true meaning of Christianity: 'What he has disclosed is not the "mystery of religion" but the secret of Hegel.'[94] And that secret, according to Tucker, is not a good one. For Tucker, Feuerbach was misled by Hegel into misunderstanding Christianity, which he also mistakenly assumed to be virtually synonymous with 'religion': 'He took the Hegelian religion of the self as God to be the key to the meaning of Christianity as the prototype of religion in general.'[95] In consequence, Tucker contends, what Feuerbach analyses in *The Essence of Christianity* 'is a reality of human experience, but is not properly described as "Christianity" or "religion". It is the neurotic phenomenon of human self-glorification or pride, and the estrangement from the self that results from it.'[96] By an almost perverse irony, then, Feuerbach has located the essence of Christianity, for Tucker, precisely in that which Christianity itself 'regards as the essence of evil.'[97] At the basis of Feuerbach's work is undoubtedly awareness of a form of religious experience, but it is 'the peculiar Hegelian form of religious experi-

---

93 *Ibid.*, p. 45. Cf. Feuerbach's question: 'If God is really a different being from myself, why should his perfection trouble me?' Quoted in Tucker, *op. cit.*, p. 89.

94 Tucker, *op. cit.*, p. 93.

95 *Ibid.*

96 *Ibid.*

97 *Ibid.*

ence, which is pride become theological, [taken] as the paradigm of all religion.'[98] Hence, Tucker concludes, in rejecting this false form of 'religion', Feuerbach is in effect rejecting Hegelianism only, but not real Christianity. His work has, indeed, a certain moral value, which Hegel's lacks: 'Feuerbach's opposition to religion is more anti-Hegelian than genuinely anti-Christian. Morally speaking, it expresses a revulsion against the supreme form of human pride.'[99]

Yet Tucker's stern judgment on Feuerbach's precursor Hegel – he is clearly not so severe on Feuerbach himself – strikes me as rather harsh. It is no doubt difficult to keep moral and intellectual issues separate, but it is maybe more necessary to try to see where Hegel or Feuerbach can be criticised intellectually than to see where they possibly went wrong morally. At least a mainly intellectual approach to their work may permit a more sympathetic encounter with their ideas, if one grants that they were primarily men of ideas.

Perhaps it is in the character of Idealist thought to be monistic, and to swallow up everything into its capacious mind, obliterating in the process all real differences. And on this account, Idealist thought can legitimately be criticised, because – as previously intimated – it cannot do justice, ultimately, to real 'difference' or 'otherness' in human experience. Thus, as regards the value of human life, which Feuerbach was obsessed with, one might have to conclude, against Feuerbach, that it is not enough simply to talk of 'humanity' in order to reach a genuine recognition of human beings. The real, inviolable worth of human beings is perhaps only guaranteed if it is seen as a reflection of the real inviolability of God. And inviolability means acceptance of, or belief in, the true 'otherness', or the true irreducibility to any intellectual formula, of either God or us. In short, inviolability and incomprehensibility or unknowability belong together, both for God and for us. Philosophical Idealism does not seem to share this belief. Hence it is hazardous to try to convey Christian truth by means of it. For, as in Hegel and Feuerbach, its inner dynamic leads to a coalescence of God and man, indeed to an acceptance of their ultimate sameness.

It is significant that in speaking of what might be called divine 'otherness' Feuerbach does not use this (now) attractive term; he talks rather of 'egoistical independence':

'God is love,' means, God is nothing by himself: he who loves,

---

98 *Ibid.*
99 *Ibid.*

gives up his egoistical independence; he makes what he loves indispensable, essential to his existence.[100]

This no doubt can have a non-threatening, 'caring' meaning, and was surely so intended; but it could also be interpreted in a possessive sense, thereby adding an ominous dimension to the idea that *omnia vincit amor* ('Love conquers all'). Human love can be possessive and destructive, possibly because of the transient nature of existence. But because the 'being' of God is believed to be not transient like ours, that very difference allows divine love to be non-possessive. So Christianity, through its doctrine of the incarnation, can respect the similarity (in love) between God and us; this was the aspect of the question that interested Feuerbach, and without it God would indeed be of no attraction to human beings. But it can also respect the difference between God and us, without which God would be an oppressive presence (a difference respected, paradoxically, by the very humanity of Christ). It is this difference that is meant when reference is made to the incomprehensibility or hiddenness of God. Ironically, in identifying this difference with alienation and trying then to overcome it, Idealism worked against human freedom, undermining its foundations, placed burdens on human shoulders that they were never designed to carry, and intensified the very suffering it had set out to alleviate.

As Tucker rightly indicates,[101] one cannot overlook the deep sense of something being amiss in the human condition that animates Feuerbach's thought and drives him to seek a solution to human suffering in human love. In a sense his philosophy is a philosophy of redemption. This underlines its relationship to Christian teaching, but also its profound difference, since for Christianity redemption comes from beyond us, not from within us.

The need for emancipation from religious faith for which Feuerbach argued, and which he saw as a prelude to 'man's reconciliation with his humanity,'[102] was undoubtedly part of the same, general Western emancipation from the power of the Christian church which in the century before Feuerbach had been carried through in France. But in Germany the intellectual struggle over the meaning and possible future role of Christianity in a modern society was more complex than in France. For in Germany, rather than simply trying to annihilate the religious tradition (*Écrasez l'infâme*),

---

100 *Essence*, p. 264.
101 Tucker, *op. cit.*, p. 94.
102 *Ibid.*

an attempt was made, from Schleiermacher and Hegel onwards, to transform it. Hegel saw faith as fundamentally good, but believed that its content needed to be raised up to the level of knowledge. Feuerbach, on the other hand, sees faith itself as intrinsically almost a disease of the human mind which attacks the power of love. It needs therefore to be excised so that love may reign supreme. Faith in its Christian form, he concedes, may have had a role to play in the past in popularising the idea of love and of human solidarity,[103] but now such an expedient is no longer necessary. The idea of universal love can stand on its own two feet. Feuerbach's philosophy can be seen then as a therapy to help people overcome the alienation Christianity, he believes, introduced into human existence. The therapy consists in transferring belief in the self-subsistence of God to belief in the self-subsistence of human love, i.e. to belief in the self-subsistence of humanity.

In decreeing, rather than acknowledging (believing in), what is ultimately valuable in human existence, Feuerbach committed, from the point of view of the Judaeo-Christian tradition, the primal religious error. In wishing to abolish faith in order to make room for love alone, Feuerbach wished to abolish 'God' in order to put man in his place. This can, however, only be done by an act of self-assertion, which is yet so close to the religious act of faith that it is entirely understandable. But, it may be noted, Feuerbach has simply changed the object towards which human faith is now to be directed; he has not abolished the reality of faith.

And indeed, at the heart of Feuerbach's thought there is an act of faith which assumes that that on which we find ourselves dependent – which Feuerbach himself calls Nature, indeed 'holy Nature'[104] – is ultimately not the transcendent God of Christian tradition but the purely natural, immanent forces of the world itself. As he wrote in the *Essence of Religion*:

> Man's feeling of dependence is the basis of religion; the object of this feeling of dependence, that on which man is dependent and feels himself dependent, is, however, nothing other than nature.[105]

---

103 Cf.: 'Christ is nothing but an image, under which the unity of the species has impressed itself on the popular consciousness ... Christ, as the consciousness of love, is the consciousness of the species' (*Essence*, pp. 268f.).

104 *Essence*, p. 277.

105 L. Feuerbach, *Das Wesen der Religion*, ed. A. Esser (Heidelberg, 1983), p. 229, quoted in F. Fellmann (ed.), *op. cit.*, p. 122.

Such an assumption, however, will always run up against the immovable rock of human freedom which cannot be subsumed under any naturalistic system of thought, and short of being dismissed as an illusion (and even then it remains a submerged rock of an illusion), would seem to have no other cogent explanation than that of being the created reflection of the transcendent God.

Feuerbach maintained that his teaching represented a turning-point in world history. In this he was mistaken and as deluded perhaps as he claimed were those he himself criticised. The claim to have discovered the 'secret' of God or reality or humanity, should perhaps always be treated with a grain of salt. The fact that the world still remains opaque and messy, despite all the enlightened revelations about its 'real' meaning that have been proposed in modern times, gives pause for thought. Feuerbach's conviction that he had unravelled the secret of existence could perhaps be interpreted as a secularised form of eschatology. Christian eschatology teaches, contrary to Feuerbach, that God lies beyond even the future of history. Hence there can be no definitive, eschatological solutions, no 'Final Solutions', to any ultimate human question within history itself, least of all to the question of God. For God *is* the 'Final Solution'. Any purely human 'Final Solution' will therefore be, in religious terms, idolatrous. In intellectual terms, there can be no final understanding, just as there can be no final end to ambiguity and conflict within human beings while history lasts. That at least is what the Christian doctrine of 'original sin' implies. But Feuerbach's inability to uproot the eschatological instinct in himself is an indication of how 'trapped' he in fact remained in the religion of his upbringing. The question of God which Feuerbach considered he had definitively settled, remains still an ambiguous, and hence still an open, question.

However, Feuerbach's intellectual integrity and his search for existentially relevant truth cannot but be admired. It is also important to remember that those who suffered for their honest thinking in the last century were not the guardians of various orthodoxies, but the questioners and enquirers who, time and again, lost their academic positions or never reached them to begin with. Strauss, Feuerbach, Bauer, Marx, to name a few, were *personae non gratae* with the established powers in state and church, as was Heinrich Heine. Nietzsche was academically 'dead' once he published *The Birth of Tragedy*. As Van Harvey points out: 'It is not surprising that the professorship, which was once their ideal, became an object of scorn and ridicule.'[106] Indeed not only the professorship. But while Feuerbach's integrity is beyond doubt, it could on the other hand be asked whether or not the high value placed on such integrity and on truth is itself a fruit of the Christian tradition, and difficult perhaps to maintain once that tradition has been repudiated and replaced with a thoroughgoing materialism or naturalism. Nietzsche's response to the 'death of God' is much more intense, not to say distraught, than Feuerbach's rather starry-eyed humanism.

Neo-orthodoxy and Feuerbach

Even a brief examination of Feuerbach's influence on the modern God-question should make some reference to neo-orthodoxy's exploitation of his atheist critique of religion in the first half of the twentieth century. This was an exploitation that seems ultimately however to have backfired.

Neo-orthodoxy is also known as 'dialectical theology', so-called because it sought to transcend the difference between the affirmative (*via dogmatica*) and the negative (*via negativa*) approaches to the apprehension of God.[107] Neo-orthodoxy saw God's presence indicated paradoxically by his painfully felt absence from the human condition. Dominated by the towering figure of Karl Barth, it was completely out of sympathy with the proposal that Christian theology should take religious experience as its starting-point. Yet this defiant disavowal of modern theology's own attempt at overcoming the Enlightenment's critique of Christianity has itself been criticised by Pannenberg, on the grounds that neo-orthodoxy's much-vaunted distinction between religion, which atheist criticism *à la Feuerbach* had unsettled, and revelation, which Barth claimed was immune from such criticism, was entirely specious. For is not neo-orthodox talk of revelation subject to precisely the same Feuerbachian criticism as was the 'liberal' modernisation of Christianity? Is it not just one more unsubstantiated theological assertion? Thus, to have taken its stand on the atheist critique of religion which it then claimed to be able to 'trump' by 'a radical belief in revelation,'[108] is neo-orthodoxy's fatal flaw, representing not the overcoming of, but in Pannenberg's view, 'the cheapest form of modernity.'[109] Somewhat ironically, therefore, neo-ortho-

---

106   Harvey, in N. Smart et al. (eds.), *op. cit.*, pp. 294f.
107   Cf. *The Oxford Dictionary of the Christian Church* (London, 1974), p. 399.
108   *Basic Questions in Theology*, vol. 3 (London, 1973), p. 87.
109   *Ibid.*, p. 88.

doxy's hostility towards religious experience as a basis for theological discourse, is ultimately self-destructive: proof, if proof were needed, that theology is a two-edged sword.

Excursus: Modernism in the Catholic church[110]

Modernism was an intellectual effort within the Catholic church just before and after 1900 to rethink the meaning of Christianity in the modern world. The Modernists took seriously the challenges presented to traditional Christianity both by Kantian and post-Kantian philosophy and by the critical historical study of the bible and of the Christian doctrinal tradition. They were dissatisfied with the Neo-Scholastic[111] expression of orthodoxy prevailing in the Catholic church in the latter part of the nineteenth century which they saw as an attempt to prop up Christian faith in an 'extrinsicist', 'intellectualist' way with a discredited philosophy that no modern person could take seriously. The Modernists believed it was pointless to insist any longer, as the Neo-Scholastic theologians did, that the grounds for faith were purely objective.

The Neo-Scholastics, in harmony with Vatican I, and developing arguments based mainly on the 'five ways' of St Thomas, taught that the existence of God 'can be known with certainty from the things that were created through the natural light of human reason.' Faith was interpreted as the assent of mind and will to a body of true propositions revealed by God, for which objective supporting reasons – e.g. miracles, especially the resurrection, the fulfilment of prophecies, the continuity of the witness itself of the church – could, the Neo-Scholastics claimed, be adduced. The Modernists, on the other hand, understood faith as an internal, subjective, experiential appropriation of the divine spirit in one's life.

The French Modernist Alfred Loisy – perhaps the most important figure in the movement – had a developmental sense of truth and thus saw the church as the evolutionary expression of the original gospel. All the Modernists, whatever their differences, believed

---

110 Cf. B. M. G. Reardon, *Roman Catholic Modernism* (Stanford, 1970); id., 'Roman Catholic Modernism', in Ninian Smart et al. (eds.), *Nineteenth Century Religious Thought in the West*, Vol. II, Chapter 5 (Cambridge, 1985).

111 Neo-Scholasticism is sometimes dated from the appearance of Pope Leo XIII's encyclical *Aeterni Patris* in 1879 which had recommended that scholasticism, and especially the works of St Thomas Aquinas, be the only philosophy and theology used in Catholic seminaries.

that for the Christian religion to continue to make sense to people, it had to be related to their own experience.

Modernism was formally condemned by Pope Pius X in 1907 by the decree *Lamentabili* and the encyclical *Pascendi*. Loisy was excommunicated in 1908 and steps were taken to eradicate all traces of Modernism from the Catholic church. Modernism was considered to be a threat to, if not an outright denial of, the objectivity of the Christian faith because of its view of faith as subjective and experiential and because of its view of the relativity of truth to any given historical context.

However, while one may disagree with the Modernists' solution to the problem of Christianity and modernity, to ignore the problem entirely would be to admit that Christianity is now merely a fossil, an interesting remnant of a vanished world, of no real human concern for the present or the future.

CHAPTER NINE

The Nietzsche factor

... [I]n five main points of his [Spinoza's] doctrine I recognise myself; this most singular and loneliest thinker is closest to me in precisely these things: he denies the freedom of the will –; ends –; the moral world order – ; the unegoistic – ; evil – ...

... I hold up before myself the images of Dante and Spinoza, who were better at accepting the lot of solitude. Of course, their way of thinking, compared to mine, was one which made solitude bearable; and in the end, for all those who somehow still had a 'God' for company, what I experience as 'solitude' really did not yet exist. My life now consists in the wish that it might be otherwise with all things than I comprehend, and that somebody might make my 'truths' appear incredible to me....   — Friedrich Nietzsche

What is divinity if it can come
Only in silent shadows and in dreams?   — Wallace Stevens

Introduction

Nietzsche's name occurs many times in this book, a fact which may strike some as odd. For how, many may wonder, can an avowed atheist have anything interesting to say about God? In reply one could say, first of all, that not all those who say 'Lord, Lord' are necessarily already inside the Kingdom of Heaven, and by the same token, that not all those who are outside the pale are ignorant of what goes on inside it. Hostility, even hatred, which, humanly speaking, comes from the same source as love,[1] can sharpen the

---

1   An old idea: 'The Duc de Saint-Simon said long ago that love and hate were fed by a single nerve' (Saul Bellow, *It All Adds Up*, Harmondsworth, 1995, p. 45). And the spurned Hermione's famous line about Pyrrhus in Racine's *Andromaque* has become almost a proverbial statement of love's ability to turn into its opposite, given the right condi-

wits. And obsession with an enemy can make one become like him. Since Christianity not only presents an image of God, but also an image of man made in the image of that God, it can continue to irritate former believers who have only consciously shed Christianity's image of God. Such seems to have been at least part of the explanation of Nietzsche's spiritual odyssey.

It is undeniable, even if many find it hard to swallow, that Nietzsche with his sense of the 'unreality of God', and the looming nihilism[2] that was to engulf modern Western culture, is one of the prophets, indeed creators, of the modern world. For its part, Christianity in its history has never sought to live in an ivory tower, since it came into the world claiming to be the salt of the earth, not a substitute for the earth or a retreat from the earth. One of the salient features of the Christian intellectual tradition is that it has not been 'isolationist', but has sought to see how its truth can be articulated with respect (in both senses of the term) to the world's own self-understanding. To take Nietzsche seriously is simply to return the compliment he paid Christianity in taking it seriously enough to criticise and, at times, to abhor it. In the realm of thought at least (and in what other realm can theology sensibly claim to operate?), attention, which according to Malebranche is 'the natural prayer of the soul,'[3] is surely preferable to, or at least ultimately more fruitful than, indifference. One may add that this is so even if the attention is antagonistic, as with Nietzsche's attention to Christianity. To ignore Nietzsche as alien is of course possible. But then how can we continue to accept the 'otherness' of God that we do not see, while not taking seriously the 'otherness' of a Nietzsche that we do see?

Nietzsche, then, cannot, or at least should not, be ignored. Nor should one think he wished to drown out all other voices. His friend Franz Overbeck (1837–1905) said of him that he was the per-

---

tions: 'Ah! je l'ai trop aimé, pour ne le point haïr' ('Ah! I have loved him too much, not to hate him').

2 R. J. Hollingdale, *Nietzsche. The Man and His Philosophy* (London, 1965), p. 90, following Walter Kaufmann, sees a parallel between Nietzsche's response to Darwinian evolutionary theory and Kant's response to Hume's scepticism: in both cases the German thinkers were provoked into 'creating a new picture of man in reply to the "true but deadly" nihilism from beyond the Channel' (W. Kaufmann, *Nietzsche. Philosopher, Psychologist, Antichrist*, New Jersey, 1974, p. 167).

3 Quoted by Paul Celan with reference to poetry; see P. Celan, *Selected Poems*, tr. and intro. by M. Hamburger (Harmondsworth, 1990), p. 31.

son in whose presence he breathed most freely – an enviable compliment. Nietzsche's stridency can certainly be off-putting, and the power of his rhetoric intoxicating: as Wallace Stevens wrote in a letter of 8 December 1942 to Henry Church: 'Nietzsche is as perfect a means of getting out of focus as a little bit too much to drink.'[4] However as a bracing antidote to cant, as a writer who can engage the attentions of his readers through provocation and anticipation, and as a thinker who thought against but somehow also with Christianity, he is really a unique figure.

The drawback about reading Nietzsche in English should also be adverted to, as he is one of the supreme masters of German prose, a fact which clearly cannot be conveyed by any translation. Wallace Stevens noted, writing to the same correspondent on 10 March 1944, with regard specifically to the first volume of *Human, All Too Human*, that he 'felt the vast difference between reading the thing in English with its total lack of voice and reading it in German with all of the sharp edges and intensity of speech that one feels in reading Nietzsche.'[5]

This chapter has merely the modest aim of introducing Nietzsche to those especially who might be inclined to dismiss him unread, because of the whiff of brimstone that still wafts about his reputation. It is also meant to serve as an introduction to the following chapter on postmodernism, of which Nietzsche is often seen as one of the forerunners. The biographical details included are unavoidable if one wishes to have a feel for this most intensely personal of thinkers.

The man

Nietzsche was born on October 15, 1844 in the little village of Röcken in Saxony. His father was the local Lutheran pastor and his mother was herself the daughter of a Saxon country pastor. On both sides of his family, in fact, Nietzsche was descended from a long line of Lutheran clergymen. His claim to Polish ancestry, made in *Ecce Homo*, a kind of intellectual and spiritual autobiography, should not be taken too seriously: it was Nietzsche's high-spirited way of ticking off the Germans ('the mere presence of a German hinders my digestion') for failing to respond to his books during the course of his life. 'I seek … in vain,' he wrote in *Ecce Homo*, 'for a sin-

---

4   Quoted in Patrick Bridgwater, *Nietzsche in Anglosaxony* (Leicester University Press, 1972), p. 192.
5   *Ibid.*, p. 193.

gle sign of tact, of *délicatesse* towards me. From Jews yes, never yet from Germans.'[6]

Nietzsche's father died in 1849 as the result of a brain injury after a fall. His early death and the manner of it have led some to speculate on its exact causes, and to suggest that it was in fact due to a hereditary brain disease.[7] If this were so, it might give grounds for believing that Nietzsche's own insanity, which overtook him in 1889 and from which he never recovered, was hereditary. Such theories, however, are extremely difficult to substantiate, especially since Nietzsche's father's brain disorder may have occurred quite fortuitously, as a result of the fall from which he suffered a severe concussion.

In January 1850 Nietzsche's mother moved with her family to Naumburg. The household here included young Friedrich ('the little pastor'), his mother (who lived until 1897), his sister Elisabeth, his father's mother and two maiden aunts. In view of the fact that Nietzsche grew up surrounded by women, it is perhaps strange that his adult life should have been marked by an extraordinary shyness and timidity towards them. Or possibly over-exposure in his early years induced in him a lifelong suspicion and distrust of women.

In any case, even in his early years Nietzsche revealed the quality that his closest, or at least his most loyal friend, the Basel theology professor Franz Overbeck, singled out as contributing most profoundly and most intensely to his greatness, namely his ambition. We are told that when he was a mere eight years old, his sister, who was two years younger than him, was already filing away his literary productions. At the age of ten he wrote his first poems. By the time he was twelve he would rise before dawn and study far into the night, and at fourteen he was already reviewing his intellectual development which he divided into three phases ...

In 1858 Nietzsche went to the famous Protestant boarding-school, Schulpforta, which had previously been attended by such

---

6 Tr. R. J. Hollingdale (Harmondsworth, 1980), p. 124; (p. 60 for the previous quotation).

7 In his recollections on Nietzsche, Overbeck considered his madness had resulted from his mode of life, and was certainly not the result of any *inherited* condition. Nietzsche himself, in Overbeck's dealings with him, had never evinced any fear of madness from this source, even though he was well aware of the cause of his own father's death. See F. Overbeck, 'Erinnerungen an Friedrich Nietzsche', *Die Neue Rundschau*, 1906, p. 215.

famous figures in German literature and philosophy as Novalis, Fichte and the two Schlegel brothers. Here he acquired a strict classical education, and not surprisingly distinguished himself academically, being often at the head of his class. In 1861 he wrote an enthusiastic essay on Hölderlin, whom he called his 'favourite poet'. At that time Hölderlin was little known in Germany. Although praising the essay, Nietzsche's teacher also wrote: 'But I must give the author the friendly advice to attach himself to a healthier, clearer, and *more German* poet.'[8] Nietzsche's enthusiasm for Hölderlin, who had died insane, is perhaps an early sign of his instinctive, unremitting engagement with the dangerous depths of human existence. 'For believe me: the secret for harvesting from existence the greatest fruitfulness and the greatest enjoyment is – to *live dangerously*,' he was later (1882) to write in *The Gay Science* (IV, 283).[9]

The medical records of Nietzsche's school show that in 1862 he was short-sighted and often plagued by migraine. This is an early indication of the chronic ill health that was to plague him in the 1870s and 1880s when he produced his greatest works against appalling odds. But as he wrote, defiantly, in *Twilight of the Idols* (1888): 'What does not kill me makes me stronger.'[10]

It was also while he was at Schulpforta that another major influence in his life first began, namely his infatuation with the music of Richard Wagner. When he was introduced through piano transcriptions to Wagner's opera *Tristan und Isolde*, he fell immediately and completely under its spell. Later, as we shall see, he was to become closely attached to the master and his circle (in the early 1870s), before eventually breaking violently and irrevocably with him in 1878 soon after the Bayreuth Festival had been established. Subsequently he had very harsh and dismissive things to say about Wagner and his operas ('To listen to Wagner I need pastilles Gérandel') and even affected to admire Bizet's opera *Carmen*, in opposition, as it were, to Wagner. But in a letter to the music critic Carl Fuchs, dated 27 December 1888, less than a fortnight before his breakdown, he stated: 'You must not take seriously what I say about Bizet; for someone like me, he is completely out of the question. But he provides a very effective, ironic *antithesis* to Wagner ... You certainly cannot avoid *Tristan*: it is the *supreme* masterpiece and

---

8   See Hollingdale, *Nietzsche. The Man and His Philosophy*, p. 28.
9   Tr. W. Kaufmann (New York, 1974), p. 228.
10 Tr. R. J. Hollingdale (Harmondsworth, 1990), p. 33.

casts a spell which is unmatched not only in music but in all the arts.' In almost the same terms he wrote in *Ecce Homo*: 'But I still today seek a work of a dangerous fascination, of a sweet and shuddery infinity equal to that of Tristan – I seek in all the arts in vain.' Thus, although Nietzsche found it impossible to remain a disciple of Wagner's, he never denied that he owed to him some of the greatest experiences of his life ('All in all I could not have endured my youth without Wagnerian music'[11]). And but for Wagner would he ever have written: 'Without music life would be a mistake'?[12]

In 1864 Nietzsche graduated from Schulpforta with a thesis on Theognis, and went on to the university of Bonn where he studied theology (briefly) and classics. He remained there for only one year, moving in 1865 to Leipzig where he studied only classics, having decided, much to his mother's displeasure, to give up theology. It was while he was a student at Bonn that he is reported to have contracted syphilis, after a visit to a brothel in Cologne. However the evidence for this is inconclusive. That he visited a brothel during his student days in Bonn seems certain, but there is evidence to suggest that he was taken there by a cab-driver by mistake and left hurriedly after playing a few bars of music on the ladies' piano.[13] There is something almost symbolic for Nietzsche's life about this story: all of his dealings with women were awkward, often strained, sometimes – as in his relationship with Lou Andreas-Salomé – even pathetically inept.

At Leipzig, where the famous philologist Professor Ritschl taught, Nietzsche continued his brilliant academic career, working on Aeschylus, publishing papers on Theognis and a prize-winning essay on Diogenes Laërtius. The move from Bonn seemed to have been successful, as he wrote somewhat snootily to his friend Carl von Gersdorff in October 1866: 'Whereas there [Bonn] I had to submit to silly rules and regulations, amusements were forced on me which I found repugnant, and an idle existence among rather crude

---

11 *Ecce Homo*, tr. R. J. Hollingdale (Harmondsworth, 1979), p. 61, (for the last two quotations). Cf. *ibid.*, p. 59 ('at no price would I relinquish from my life the Tribschen days').

12 *Twilight of the Idols/The Anti-Christ*, tr. R.J. Hollingdale (Harmondsworth, 1990), p. 36, (henceforth cited according to which of the two works is being quoted).

13 See Hollingdale, *Nietzsche. The Man and His Philosophy*, pp. 36–38; Crane Brinton, *Nietzsche* (New York, 1965), pp. 15f.

people kept me in a very sour mood, in Leipzig everything did an
about turn in an unexpected way.'

But even at this stage of his academic career, Nietzsche's ambition, his impatience with purely academic work, and his driving
need to transcend any intellectual position he might arrive at, are
clearly in evidence. He confided to his friend and fellow-student
Erwin Rohde (who was himself to go on to become a highly distinguished classical scholar) that he found his prize essay 'repulsive'
and completely inadequate (Kaufmann). 'What is Diogenes Laërtius?'
he wrote. 'Nobody would lose a word over the philistine physiog-
nomy of this scribbler if he were not by accident the clumsy watchman guarding treasures of which he does not know the value. He is
the night watchman of the history of Greek philosophy: one cannot
enter it without obtaining the key from him.'

Nietzsche interrupted his studies at Leipzig to begin his military
service in October 1867. A year later, after a painful riding accident,
he was discharged formally from the army, and resumed his philological studies at Leipzig. Almost immediately upon the resump-
tion of his studies he began complaining again about the inadequa-
cies of the academic life. In a letter to Rohde of November 1868 he
wrote: 'I am forced again to see the swarming philologists' breed of
our day from close-up, and have to observe daily the whole mole-
like business, the full pouchy cheeks and blind eyes, the delight at
having caught a worm, and indifference toward the real and urgent
problems of life.'

Nietzsche found, for the moment, important relief from the
mediocrity of his environment at Leipzig in the music of Wagner,[14]
with which, as we have seen, he was already familiar, and in the
philosophy of Schopenhauer, which he first discovered at this time.
Schopenhauer's philosophy, with its (in Balthasar's rather tetchy
phrase) 'salon-scented nihilism',[15] its indignant, relentless pessimism, caustic wit, and savage indictment of progressive, liberal
thought, came as a revelation and a liberation to Nietzsche at this
period of his life. Though in later years he still looked back on
Schopenhauer as one of his educators in the business of living, he
was eventually to outgrow this influence too in his frantic search for
a more positive, affirmative philosophy of life.

---

14 'If one wants to get free from an unendurable pressure one needs
   hashish. Very well, I needed Wagner' (*Ecce Homo*, p. 61).
15 *Herrlichkeit*, III, 1, Part 2 (Einsiedeln, 1965), p. 929.

In 1869 Nietzsche's career took a decisive turn when in April, as Professor Ritschl's star pupil, the like of whom Ritschl had never seen in all his thirty-nine years of teaching, he was appointed professor of classical philology at Basel at the exceptionally young age of twenty-four, even though he had not yet written a doctoral dissertation.

At Basel Nietzsche came in contact with the great historian of the Italian Renaissance, Jacob Burckhardt, who shared his enthusiasm for Greek antiquity and for Schopenhauer, and sympathised warmly – though not too warmly – with his growing concern for the cultural malaise of modern Europe. To both men Europe was now definitively post-Christian without positively being anything very much else. Burckhardt, however, was always careful to keep Nietzsche at a distance. He clearly found the younger man too radical and too subversive for his taste. 'Living dangerously' is hard to combine with emotional equilibrium. Nietzsche, for his part, longed to find a positive echo of his ideas in Burckhardt, and continued to send him copies of his new books, as they appeared, but his hope for an enthusiastic human response to his writings, based on a deep understanding of them, was not, could not, be fulfilled by Burckhardt. Nietzsche's craving on this score always remained unsatisfied.

A final important new friendship in Nietzsche's life at this time was that of the radical theology professor Franz Overbeck, who came to Basel in 1870 as professor of New Testament and early church history. Temperamentally, Overbeck was of a much milder disposition than Nietzsche, but he shared Nietzsche's concern with the state of modern European culture and was also a keen admirer of Schopenhauer. The two new professors, as chance would have it, shared lodgings in the same house in Basel for about five years, and soon became close friends. Overbeck's theology was certainly radicalised by his contact with Nietzsche, and Nietzsche, for his part, consulted Overbeck on many points of church history in the course of his protracted and indeed never-ending debate with the Christian tradition. Overbeck was the last person with whom Nietzsche came to be on intimate terms, i.e. they used the German 'Du'-form of address to one another. When Nietzsche collapsed in Turin in early January 1889, it was Overbeck, alerted by Burckhardt, who went to rescue him and brought him back to Basel. Their correspondence was published in 1916.

As was mentioned earlier, Nietzsche's personal acquaintance with Wagner dates from his time as professor in Basel. Wagner was

then living in Switzerland, at Tribschen, not too far from Basel, with
Franz Liszt's daughter, Cosima, the wife of his conductor Hans von
Bülow. Nietzsche soon became a member of Wagner's intimate circle
of disciples and an ardent propagandist for the master's cause. As
the 1870s advanced, however, Nietzsche found his relationship
with Wagner becoming more and more strained, until eventually
he broke with him definitively in 1878. In a letter of July 1878 to
Mathilde Maier he stated his reasons for the break:

> That metaphysical obfuscation of everything true and simple,
> reason's struggle *against* reason to see wonders and absurdities
> in everything, and a correspondingly baroque art full of over-
> excitement and glorified extravagance – I mean Wagner's art – ,
> it was these two things that finally made me ill and more ill ... I
> am immeasurably nearer the Greeks than before. Now in every
> way I *myself live* striving for wisdom, whereas before I only
> idolised *wise men* ... You see, I have reached a level of honesty
> where I can endure only the purest of human relations. I shun
> half-friendships, and especially partisanships; I have no use for
> disciples. Let everyone be his (and *her*) *own* true follower!

The final sentiments here illustrate convictions that remained dear
to Nietzsche. In *Twilight of the Idols*, for instance, he writes: 'What?
... you want to multiply yourself by ten, by a hundred? you are
seeking followers? – Seek zeros!' And in *The Anti-Christ*: '[T]he party
man necessarily becomes a liar.'[16]

It certainly would appear from the letter just quoted, that
Nietzsche's break with Wagner was provoked to an important
extent by a growing impatience at being himself a mere disciple,
even of a genius like Wagner. But he also considered that Wagner
was abusing his genius for ignoble purposes, simply to win popularity and influence over the Germans. Wagner wished – Nietzsche
suspected – to become Germany's cultural leader and was willing
to exploit any opportunity in order to achieve this position, even if
it meant re-embracing Christianity for which he, Wagner, had hitherto expressed contempt. Wagner's allegedly Christian opera *Parsifal*
(which Wagner discussed with Nietzsche in Sorrento in the autumn

---

16 *Twilight of the Idols/The Anti-Christ*, pp. 34, 183. In passing we may note
how Nietzsche always saw the snags in any forthright position he
would ever adopt, such as love of honesty. For he can also write: ' ... let
us see to it that through honesty we do not finally become saints and
bores!' (*Beyond Good and Evil* §226, p. 157).

of 1876, the last time the two met) was therefore anathema to Nietzsche, since he found its inspiration to be in bad taste, to say nothing of bad faith. There may also have been an element of jealousy in his rejection of Wagner. For he himself had tried to compose music, though never successfully. One composition which he had sent to Hans von Bülow was returned with the comment that it constituted an act of rape on Euterpe (the muse in antiquity associated with flute-playing) ...[17]

Yet while rejecting Wagner's *décadence*[18] – an important term in Nietzsche's writings, signifying the antithesis of his own unreserved affirmation of existence (*amor fati*): perhaps an echo in a Nietzschean register of the Christian distinction between 'Fall' and 'Redemption'? – he himself was unclear about what a renewed, revitalised European culture would actually look like. He had difficulties in defining what he once termed[19] the 'image of man' in any conclusive way. It is somewhat ironic that Nietzsche himself, like the religion and the theology he rejected, was always much more successful in stating clearly what he thought was wrong with the world, than in outlining how it might look, if all were well. In a similar way, theology is usually stronger on saying what God is not, than what he is. Yet it is part of Nietzsche's genius that he can occasionally suggest how life on earth could be a cause for envy even among the 'gods',[20] or as William Blake has it: 'Eternity is in love with the productions of time.'

Apart from becoming estranged from Wagner in the course of the 1870s Nietzsche also found his health growing steadily worse, and he finally had to resign his professorship in Basel in 1879. From that year on he spent his time moving about restlessly between Italy, the French Riviera and Switzerland, spending many summers in Sils-Maria. Part of the reason for his ill health can no doubt be attributed to the intensity of his intellectual activity, and the equally intense pitch at which he conducted his friendships.

One revealing incident may illustrate this. When one of his friends in Basel, the *Privatdozent* Heinrich Romundt, whom he had known since his Leipzig days, began to have serious doubts about living as a pure rationalist, and indeed began to speak about returning to Christianity and even becoming a Catholic priest in

17 Cf. *Ecce Homo*, 'Why I am so Clever', §4.
18 See *The Case of Wagner* (1888).
19 *Human, All Too Human*, II, 1, 99, p. 236.
20 See *Human, All Too Human*, II, 2, 160.

Germany, Nietzsche was deeply upset and, in a letter of April 17, 1875 to Gersdorff, described Romundt's departure from Basel in the following terms:

> It was horribly sad. Romundt knew, repeated endlessly that henceforward he had lived the better and the happier part of his life. He wept and asked our forgiveness… At the last moment I was seized with a veritable terror; the porters were shutting the doors, and Romundt, wishing to continue to speak to us, wanted to let down the window, but it stuck; he redoubled his efforts, and while he tormented himself, trying in vain to make himself heard, the train went slowly off, and we were reduced to making signs to each other. The awful symbolism of the whole scene upset me terribly, and Overbeck as much as it did me: it was hardly endurable. I stayed in bed the next day with a bad headache that lasted thirty hours, and much vomiting of bile.[21]

In February of the same year Nietzsche had written to Rohde about Romundt's predicament, revealing, interestingly, his strong sense of what freedom of thought owes to the Protestant tradition:

> Our good clean Protestant air! I have never until now felt just how profoundly I am indebted to the spirit of Luther; I have never felt this more strongly than I do now, and the unfortunate Romundt wants to turn his back on all these liberating geniuses. I ask myself, has he taken leave of his senses and whether he should not be treated with cold baths; it is absolutely incomprehensible that this spectre should arise right beside me, after Romundt had been an intimate friend of mine for eight years. And finally, and even worse, it is *I* who am besmirched by the stain of this conversion. God knows, I am not saying this out of a selfish concern for my own reputation; but I too consider that I am defending something sacred, and I am deeply ashamed to think that I might be open to the suspicion of having anything to do with Catholicism which I find so thoroughly detestable. As my friend, try to understand how dreadful this whole business is for me, and send me a few words of consolation.

Nietzsche's dislike of Catholicism[22] is rooted, of course, in his

---

21 Translated in Brinton, *Nietzsche*, p. 34.
22 J. P. Stern's insinuation (*A Study of Nietzsche*, Cambridge, 1981, p. 12) that Nietzsche broke – ironically enough – with Gersdorff in December of 1877 over 'the latter's engagement to a Catholic Italian girl', because of the girl's Catholicism, is not borne out by the evidence of the relevant letter.

uncompromising attachment to freedom of thought, to which he felt Catholicism was inimical.

From 1879 until his breakdown in January 1889 in Turin, Nietzsche produced a stream of important works: *Human, All Too Human* (completed 1880), *Daybreak* (1881), *The Gay Science* (1882), *Thus Spoke Zarathustra* (1883/85), *Beyond Good and Evil* (1886), *On the Genealogy of Morals* (1887), and in 1888 *The Case of Wagner*, *The Twilight of the Idols*, *The Anti-Christ*, *Ecce Homo* and *Nietzsche Contra Wagner*. After his collapse he spent the last eleven years of his life in psychiatric hospitals or being cared for by his mother and sister. He died in August 1900.

Nietzsche's dramatic and permanent collapse in 1889 has prompted many to speculate on the causes of his eventual insanity. Above all, because his final breakdown was diagnosed as the result of a form of syphilis, the question, alluded to already, of whether or not Nietzsche did in fact contract syphilis as a student, has been much debated. Thomas Mann's novel *Dr Faustus*, which is partly inspired by and based on Nietzsche's life, brought this whole question into further prominence after its publication in 1947. Yet whatever the medical reason for his madness, it is not essentially relevant to a reading of Nietzsche's works, if it be accepted that a significant distinction can be made between a completed work and its genesis. The fact that Nietzsche did ultimately become insane has, however, sometimes been used as an invitation to see all of his writings, especially his later books, which became increasingly shrill, as evidence of a steadily developing personal instability, and hence to dismiss them as the products of a madman, of interest only to pathology.

This would be an unfortunate way to approach Nietzsche's *oeuvre*. Those who were closest to him accepted that as time went on Nietzsche worked under intensifying pressure, but they never thought of him as insane, until he finally collapsed. The final books themselves, works of concentrated power, precision, ironic humour, lucidity and beauty are the best argument against any cheap attempt to view them reductively as tokens of a progressively more insane mind. In Freud's view, Nietzsche's psychological history could not be reconstructed. Indeed he implied there would be a certain impertinence involved in any attempt to do so, given that, in his view, Nietzsche 'had a more penetrating knowledge of himself than any other man who ever lived or was ever likely to live.'[23]

---

23 Reported by Freud's biographer, Ernest Jones; cf. W. Kaufmann in *The Encyclopedia of Philosophy*, ed. P. Edwards (New York, 1967), vol. 5, p. 505.

Overbeck, who was his most loyal friend, especially in the final years before 1889, wrote in his reminiscences of Nietzsche that he had turned his brilliant gifts of psychological analysis (*Seelenanalyse*) most ruthlessly and relentlessly on himself and thus destroyed himself. ('Whoever goes to the foundations, founders', as Nietzsche himself once put it ...)

Early writings

In the light of what has so far been indicated of Nietzsche's personality, it is perhaps not very surprising to observe that his first book, published during his Basel professorship, was no ordinary work of classical scholarship. The book, *The Birth of Tragedy* (1872), dedicated to Wagner, was a revolutionary re-interpretation of the genesis, meaning and demise of Greek Tragedy, unaccompanied by such reassuring, traditional trappings of classical scholarship as footnotes or Greek quotations. The final sections of the book were an extended piece of propaganda on behalf of Wagner's music, which Nietzsche tried to present as the rebirth of Tragedy, seemingly – in part at least – to keep the great man happy. Nietzsche's analysis of Greek Tragedy focused on a discussion of two tendencies he discerned within Greek culture, the 'Apollinian' and the 'Dionysian', corresponding roughly to 'form-imposing' and 'turbulent'. In 1888 he returned to the problem of defining these two terms in notes that were published posthumously as part of the *Will to Power*, a book prepared at the instigation of his sister Elisabeth. The content of the *Will to Power* is from Nietzsche's own unpublished writings, but the structure of the book was determined by the editors. Nevertheless Nietzsche's final thoughts on the subject in question are probably accurately reproduced, in so far as they echo, as we shall see, the typical expression of his late philosophy:

> The word '*Dionysian*' means: an urge to unity, a reaching out beyond personality, the everyday, society, reality, across the abyss of transitoriness: a passionate-painful overflowing into darker, fuller, more floating states; an ecstatic affirmation of the total character of life as that which remains the same, just as powerful, just as blissful, through all change; the great pantheistic sharing of joy and sorrow that sanctifies and calls good even the most terrible and questionable qualities of life; the eternal will to procreation, to fruitfulness, to recurrence; the feeling of the necessary unity of creation and destruction.

> The word '*Apollinian*' means: the urge to perfect self-suffi-

ciency, to the typical 'individual,' to all that simplifies, distinguishes, makes strong, clear, unambiguous, typical: freedom
under the law.[24]

Between 1873 and 1876 Nietzsche published four short works, the
Untimely Meditations, in which he turned his critical gaze on different aspects of contemporary culture. The first of these four pieces,
'David Strauss, the confessor and the writer', was really, under the
guise of an attack on D. F. Strauss, author of the famous *Life of Jesus*
(1835/36), who had just written *The Old Faith and the New* (1872), an
onslaught on the triumphalistic, complacent, bourgeois attitudes of
the new German *Reich*, that had just been established after the
defeat of France in 1870-71. In this work Nietzsche established the
significance of the term 'culture-philistine' to describe disparagingly the smug, educated Germans of his day who, to his mind, were
blind to the deep moral and cultural issues of the times. In his late
work *Ecce Homo* Nietzsche described Strauss 'as the type of a
German culture-philistine and *satisfait*, in short as the author of an
ale-house gospel of "old faith and new" ...'

In the second of the *Untimely Meditations* ('On the uses and dis-
advantages of history for life') he dealt with the problem that an
excessive concentration on the past can cause for the present, which
is where people actually live. Nietzsche begins by discussing a form
of historiography he calls 'monumental'. This approach to history
focuses on heroic, stirring events, personages and achievements of
the past. These can act as a stimulation and consolation to later generations in times of despondency and mediocrity by bringing to
light what, even in difficult, unpromising circumstances, was once
possible. The second type, 'antiquarian' history, concentrates on the
continuity between past and present, nourishing the present's feelings of pride in, and piety towards, its own tradition. As long as a
tradition is still genuinely alive, and people are not affecting, in def-
erence to the past, a way of life in which they no longer believe,
such history is useful. Once, however, the living force of a tradition
has dried up, antiquarian history becomes a matter of searching the
past indiscriminately and futilely. Finally, 'critical' history concentrates on the need to make a break with a long tradition, and, as
Nietzsche puts it, to replace a tradition, which had become one's
'first nature', with a new 'nature', which will at first be a 'second
nature', but will grow, if successful culturally, into another 'first

---

24 *The Will to Power*, tr. W. Kaufmann and R. J. Hollingdale (London, 1968),
    p. 539.

nature'. 'Critical' history will be of use to man as 'one who is suffering and in need of liberation' (i.e. from his tradition). That is to say, it will help him to break free from the burden of a past whose values he can no longer endorse.

Nietzsche thus raises in this *Untimely Meditation* the central question of modernity, namely the relation between what might be called tradition and reason, or faith and reason. Great cultures only thrive, he argues, if the faith or vision that inspires them succeeds in resisting the acids of critical reason. Once, however, knowledge reveals the faith in question to be a life-sustaining, but merely human, all too human illusion, the faith in question crumbles and the culture on which it is based collapses. 'Man is a king when he dreams, a beggar when he reflects,' as Hölderlin had put it in his day. The implications for Christian culture are obvious. If the faith that is its foundation is destroyed by rational analysis, what remains? Nietzsche's answer will be: 'nihilism'.

Yet Nietzsche, it is hardly necessary to point out, is never a simple-minded writer ('I am a *nuance*'[25]). For, contradictory though it may appear in one who ostensibly rejected any moral world order[26] (cf. the first epigraph to this chapter), there is a moral, even – paradoxically – a theological, reason why Nietzsche finds the traditional Christian view of reality impossible to accept, a reason that betrays the heritage, from which he never entirely escaped. As expressions like 'the thorough *immorality* of nature and history'[27] indicate, Nietzsche always remained acutely aware of the impossibility of reconciling rationally the Christian notion of God with the undeniable presence of evil in history. In this regard he differed sharply from Hegel,[28] and was initially closer to Schopenhauer, although on

---

25 *Ecce Homo*, p. 124.
26 For Nietzsche the problem of getting from 'is' to 'ought' is non-existent, since there is no 'ought' to get to, only the 'is', the eternally recurring and inescapable 'is' of life itself. In Nietzsche's world 'ought' leads a shadowy existence; it can be recognised only as a linguistic relic from former times. Nietzsche is, so to speak, the wizard of 'is'.
27 From the 'Preface' to *Daybreak*, tr. R. J. Hollingdale (Cambridge, 1983), p. 3.
28 Cf. Hegel's oft-quoted statement in the 'Preface' to *Elements of the Philosophy of Right*: 'To recognise reason as the rose in the cross of the present and thereby to delight in the present – this rational insight is the *reconciliation* with actuality which philosophy grants ...' (tr. H. B. Nisbet, Cambridge, 1991, p. 22).

this decisive question he gradually reached a unique conclusion of his own. Already in the second *Untimely Meditation* he writes:

> If he is to live, man must possess and from time to time employ the strength to break up and dissolve a part of the past: he does this by bringing it before the tribunal, scrupulously examining it and finally condemning it; every past, however, is worthy to be condemned – for that is the nature of human things: human violence and weakness have always played a mighty role in them. It is not justice which here sits in judgment; it is even less mercy which pronounces the verdict: it is life alone, that dark, driving power that insatiably thirsts for itself. Its sentence is always unmerciful, always unjust, because it has never proceeded out of a pure well of knowledge; but in most cases the sentence would be the same even if it were pronounced by justice itself. 'For all that exists is *worthy* of perishing. So it would be better if nothing existed [Goethe].' It requires a great deal of strength to be able to live and to forget the extent to which to live and to be unjust is one and the same thing. Luther himself once opined that the world existed only through a piece of forgetful negligence on God's part: for if God had foreseen 'heavy artillery' he would not have created the world.[29]

One might try to summarise Nietzsche's point, by saying that he has anticipated Walter Benjamin's well-known and depressing insight: 'There is no document of civilisation which is not at the same time a document of barbarism.'[30] Yet why does Nietzsche find the reality of evil difficult to deal with, if not because he still operates with the tacit assumption of a *good* God? ...

Later writings

In the books he wrote in the 1880s Nietzsche attempted to develop a statement of his philosophy in a world from which truth, moral order and religion had vanished, leaving only what he termed 'nihilism' in their wake. Many, such as Strauss, had left Christianity behind, but thought that everything would remain standing as before. Nietzsche was thus by no means the first nineteenth-century thinker to abandon belief in the Christian religion, but unlike many liberal atheists he sought to face up with ruthless honesty to the

---

29 *Untimely Meditations*, tr. R. J. Hollingdale (Cambridge, 1983), pp. 75f.
30 From 'Theses on the Philosophy of History', in *Illuminations*, tr. H. Zohn (Fontana, 1982), p. 258; cf. *The Portable Nietzsche* (1981), p. 39.

consequences of living in a nihilistic universe. Now that Nietzsche's late works in which he confronted nihilism undoubtedly abound in contradictions, he knew as well as anyone, but it might nevertheless be interesting to mention some of the more glaring ones.

Nietzsche, for example, called himself a great 'Yea-sayer', but had to spend much of his time saying: 'No!' He believed that absolute truth was a great delusion, but he was fired by an ethic of truthfulness. He knew that he had declared the moral world order to be an illusion, a fiction imposed on reality to give it a semblance of order: 'One day', he wrote, '[the *ethical significance* ascribed to the world] will have as much value, and no more, than the belief in the masculinity or femininity of the sun has today.'[31] And yet he constantly railed against the immorality and dishonesty of various kinds of human behaviour. On the question of redemption he asserted: 'To redeem the past and to transform every "It was" into an "I wanted it thus!" – that alone do I call redemption!'[32] And he constantly spoke about the world process as 'the innocence of becoming' (*die Unschuld des Werdens*), free of all moral values. Yet he also continually criticised the false values, the 'herd morality' of Christianity ('morality is herd instinct in the individual'),[33] with its nurturing of *ressentiment* among its adherents. In disgust he denounces 'faith' as meaning 'not *wanting* to know what is true,'[34] and yet thinks 'truth' is a fiction. How is it possible to endorse 'everything'[35] and yet grow indignant over so much? How can one say 'Yes' and 'No' simultaneously? It is as if one were to say that there is no truth and Nietzsche is its prophet. In appearing so often to have things both ways, is Nietzsche unwittingly following in Christianity's own footsteps?

---

31 *Daybreak*, I, 3; cf. R. J. Hollingdale, *Nietzsche* (1965), p. 160.

32 *Thus Spoke Zarathustra*, Part 2, tr. R. J. Hollingdale (Harmondsworth, 1986), p. 161. Although this passage refers ostensibly only to the past, it surely implies a vision of redemption as an unquestioning, willing acceptance of the way things were, are and ever will be, *in saecula saeculorum*. One might note also that what Nietzsche achieves by an act of will (acceptance of the past and indeed of all history), Hegel accomplishes by an act of comprehension (the past and – although this is more ambiguous – the present, summed up in thought).

33 *The Gay Science*, III, 116, p. 175.

34 *The Anti-Christ* , p. 179.

35 'I do not want in the slightest that anything should become other than it is; I do not want myself to become other than I am ... But that is how I have always lived' (*Ecce Homo*, pp. 65f.).

Perhaps the simplest way to illustrate the complexities alluded to in the previous paragraph is to cite two passages from Nietzsche's writings which show the strength of his passion, but at the same time his own almost helpless awareness of its 'unjustifiability'. In the first passage, from *Beyond Good and Evil*, Nietzsche asserts the value of showing man honestly just what he considered him now, in a world without God, to be, and yet at the same time Nietzsche knows that he can find no conclusive reason why he judges this task to be so important:

> To translate man back into nature; to become master over the many vain and overly enthusiastic interpretations and connotations that have so far been scrawled and painted over that eternal basic text of *homo natura*; to see to it that man henceforth stands before man as even today, hardened in the discipline of science, he stands before the *rest* of nature, with intrepid Oedipus eyes and sealed Odysseus ears, deaf to the siren songs of old metaphysical bird catchers who have been piping at him all too long, 'you are more, you are higher, you are of a different origin!' – that may be a strange and insane task, but it is a task – who would deny that? Why did we choose this insane task? Or, putting it differently: 'why have knowledge at all?'
>
> Everybody will ask us that. And we, pressed this way, we who have put the same question to ourselves a hundred times, we have found and find no better answer – [36]

The second example, from *Daybreak*, contains a typically Nietzschean onslaught on the dishonesty of Christian scholars. On Nietzsche's own terms, however, he would not have been able to find clinching reasons for attacking such dishonesty, since moral values are, in his view, illusory. Not only that, but he constantly has to presuppose the validity of the very values like love of truth and justice, in which he has no longer any 'official' belief, to make his point, which in this passage he does with force, indignation and wit:

> *The philology of Christianity.* – How little Christianity educates the sense of honesty and justice can be gauged fairly well from the character of its scholars' writings: they present their conjectures as boldly as if they were dogmas and are rarely in any honest perplexity over the interpretation of a passage in the Bible.

---

36 *Beyond Good and Evil* §230, tr. W. Kaufmann, *Basic Writings of Nietzsche* (New York, 1968), pp. 351f.

Again and again they say 'I am right, for it is written – ' and then follows an interpretation of such impudent arbitrariness that a philologist who hears it is caught between rage and laughter and asks himself: is it possible? Is this honourable? Is it even decent? – How much dishonesty in this matter is still practised in Protestant pulpits, how grossly the preacher exploits the advantage that no one is going to interrupt him here, how the Bible is pummelled and punched and the *art of reading badly* is in all due form imparted to the people: only he who never goes to church or never goes anywhere else will underestimate that. But after all, what can one expect from the effects of a religion which in the centuries of its foundation perpetrated that unheard-of philological farce concerning the Old Testament: I mean the attempt to pull the Old Testament from under the feet of the Jews with the assertion it contained nothing but Christian teaching and *belonged* to the Christians as the *true* people of Israel, the Jews being only usurpers. And then there followed a fury of interpretation and construction that cannot possibly be associated with a good conscience ... [37]

Here, as elsewhere in his writings, Nietzsche uses humour to provoke. We recall the epigraph he placed at the beginning of *The Case of Wagner*: 'ridendo dicere *severum*—' ('Through what is laughable say what is somber').[38] In this case he raises the difficult and tricky questions for Christians of how they should now interpret the bible, and even more so perhaps, 'What is or what should be the relationship between Christianity and its mother religion, Judaism?'

Finally, in this review of Nietzsche's later writings, we must mention what was his final vision of life. This can be summed up simply as one of total, unconditional affirmation of the course of all reality, no matter how painful[39] – the antithesis of any *gran rifiuto* in the face of an inescapable and potentially excruciating destiny. To express this outlook, Nietzsche used terms like *amor fati* (love of fate) to which reference has already been made, 'the will to power' and 'eternal recurrence'. Through such expressions he wished to assert his affirmation of all existence, and his sense that such affir-

---

37 *Daybreak*, I, 84, (pp. 49f.).

38 Tr. W. Kaufmann, *Basic Writings of Nietzsche*, p. 609; Kaufmann adds that this is a 'variation of Horace's *ridentem dicere verum, quid vetat* ('What forbids us to tell the truth, laughing?') *Satires* I,1.24.'

39 'Pain does *not* count as an objection to life ... ' (*Ecce Homo*, p. 100).

mation was the most humanly admirable stance to adopt in the face of existence: 'My formula for greatness in a human being is *amor fati*: that one wants nothing to be other than it is, not in the future, not in the past, not in all eternity. Not merely to endure that which happens of necessity, still less to dissemble it – all idealism is untruthfulness in the face of necessity – but to *love* it ... '[40] The rather daunting expression 'will to power' I take to mean, in Nietzsche's writings, the amoral 'life force' which manifests itself in all existence and which is unquenchable. As for the idea of 'eternal recurrence', this indicates an emotional attitude towards, rather than a purely intellectual assessment of, life. To wish that everything that happens should have happened an infinite number of times in the past, and will happen an infinite number of times in the future, exactly as it is now happening, with no addition or subtraction, is to give one's most totally unreserved assent to the way things are.[41] It is hard to imagine a more forthright rejection of the pessimism contained in Kant's question in the *Critique of Judgement*: '[W]ho would be willing to enter upon life anew under the same conditions?'[42]

Yeats uses the Nietzschean idea of an unreserved acceptance of life in a poem like 'A Dialogue of Self and Soul' ('I am content to live it all again/And yet again ...') or 'Lapis Lazuli' ('Gaiety transfiguring all that dread'). This prompts the question – despite Nietzsche's conviction that dying for something, being a martyr for it, adds nothing to its truth – of what value, if any, is added to an idea if it extracts the ultimate price from the holder, as it seems to have done in Nietzsche's case, making him literally a martyr to his cause. Nietzsche certainly thought of himself as more than just a writer or a thinker, he was a destiny. One can only imagine what he meant if one is not prepared oneself to live and suffer as he did. Maybe there is, again, a parallel here with Christianity, and Nietzsche's sense that there has only ever been one Christian. And how then can anyone write 'Christian' theology if ... ? It is rather like enjoying a luxury with little idea of how much it costs, and an ambiguous attitude towards paying for it.

But to return to Nietzsche's ideas, why it should be important to affirm existence in all its moods and tenses, he does not say, nor

---

40 *Ecce Homo*, p. 68.
41 Cf. *Twilight of the Idols*, 'What I Owe to the Ancients', §5; *Beyond Good and Evil*, §56.
42 Quoted in the 'Introduction' to I. Kant, *Religion within the Limits of Reason Alone* (New York, 1960), p. LX.

does he leave much philosophical room for justifying any possible resistance to the way things are. This all could give rise to the suspicion that his sense of the perpetual ambiguity of existence coupled with his determination to affirm it, is possibly a secularised account of the Lutheran idea of *simul justus et peccator*. That is to say, for Luther historical man is inherently corrupt and will remain so, but God chooses to justify him nonetheless. For Nietzsche the world is inherently 'unjust' from man's point of view, but it has nonetheless to be affirmed (or 'justified'). Life he views as a never-ending, hence eternally recurring, series of often painful phenomena from which there is and can never be nor, for Nietzsche, ever should be any escape, either into a Platonic, metaphysical other world or a Christian heaven. Despite all his criticism of Kant, Nietzsche appears, ironically, half-Kantian, for he accepts that all knowledge is only human, all too human knowledge of appearances, but unlike Kant[43] he is unwilling to deny this knowledge in order to make room for (religious) faith, unless perhaps his *amor fati* itself be considered a kind of faith. He recapitulated his awesome vision in notes written in 1885 but first published in the *Will to Power*:

> And do you know what 'the world' is to me? Shall I show it to you in my mirror? This world: a monster of energy, without beginning, without end; a firm, iron magnitude of force that does not grow bigger or smaller, that does not extend itself but only transforms itself; ... a sea of forces flowing and rushing together, eternally changing, eternally flooding back, with tremendous years of recurrence, with an ebb and a flood of its forms; ... blessing itself as that which must return eternally, as a becoming that knows no satiety, no disgust, no weariness: this, my *Dionysian* world of the eternally self-creating, the eternally self-destroying, this mystery world of the twofold voluptuous delight, my 'beyond good and evil,' without goal, unless the joy of the circle is itself a goal; without will, unless a ring feels good will toward itself – do you want a *name* for this world? A *solution* for all its riddles? A *light* for you, too, you best-concealed, strongest, most intrepid, most midnightly men? –*This world is the will to power – and nothing besides!* And you yourselves are also this will to power – and nothing besides![44]

One final comment: it was claimed earlier that, on the assessment of reason's competence, Nietzsche and Hegel are opposites. Yet,

---

43 Cf. the 'Preface' to Kant's *Critique of Pure Reason*, B xxx.
44 *The Will to Power*, §1067, pp. 549f.

superficially at least, they could in other ways appear to be very alike: both, for example, endorse reality in its entirety. Where, then, lies the essential difference? The difference, it seems to me, is that Hegel was convinced that the endorsement he gave reality could be justified rationally, whereas Nietzsche was not, and so fell back on an act of will, a heroically willed act of acceptance of all existence, in order to bridge the gap between himself and the rest of reality, thus reconciling himself to 'life' and 'overcoming' nihilism.[45] Whether one calls that an act of faith or not – though in what, finally? – is immaterial. It certainly was not an act of pure reason, any more of course than was Hegel's use of reason an act of pure reason. Whatever their differences, however, both are at one in lacking a doctrine of grace, in the Christian sense. This is understandable in Nietzsche's case; its lack in Hegel's would seem to underline the old truism, adverted to earlier, that from a Christian point of view there is no appreciable difference between atheism and pantheism.

Nietzsche and Christianity

The question of Nietzsche's final relationship to the religion he rejected rises spontaneously from his writings. While clearly not wishing to re-baptise Nietzsche, it is important, nevertheless, not to imagine that his anti-Christianity was crudely or facilely reached. Despite such witty aphorisms as: 'What is now decisive against Christianity is our taste, no longer our reasons,'[46] Nietzsche struggled with and against Christianity for all of his life in a way that now scarcely seems credible, and as the second epigraph at the beginning of this chapter suggests, his 'victory' over Christianity was won at the cost of incalculable suffering. Moreover, how inconclusive that 'victory' may have been, Overbeck hinted when he described Nietzsche's 'optimism' as that 'of a desperado', and concluded that his projected 'remaking' of humanity was conceived in the shadow of desperation.

The inadequacy of all human existence, the notion that 'happiness is an escape from reality,'[47] is undoubtedly part of Christian teaching. Despite such defiant asides as: 'Man does *not* strive after happiness; only the Englishman does that,'[48] Nietzsche did not want to accept this melancholy message about the human condi-

---

45 Cf. above n. 32.
46 *The Gay Science*, III, §132.
47 Kolakowski, *Religion*, p. 41.
48 *Twilight of the Idols*, p. 33.

tion, yet it seems, despite his own heroic efforts, to have finally
impressed itself upon him. Nietzsche clearly wished to be able to
deny the 'ontological permanence' of 'human infirmity,'[49] to borrow Kolakowski's terms, and he even forced himself into endorsing
all of reality, but his ultimate position was one that at heart he did
not, I think, 'believe in'.

'Belief makes blessed: *consequently* it lies ... '[50] Half-truths, wishful thinking, make-believe, all such short cuts to 'truth' Nietzsche
abhorred, and in so doing remained 'true' to his own sense of honesty, which was always probing itself, mistrusting itself, tormenting itself.[51] Nietzsche is like a latter-day Job who has inflicted all his
misfortunes on himself, and refuses to part with them if he can find
no good reason why he should. He is often seen as a champion of
freethinking, but how many freethinkers have his endurance, or
subtlety (he once told Lou Andreas-Salomé: 'First one needs to
emancipate oneself from one's chains, and then one must free oneself from this emancipation'), or awareness of the cost of freedom?

To have a sense of the man Nietzsche's personal debate with
Christianity, it is perhaps worth observing that in a letter to Heinrich
Köselitz[52] of 21 July 1881 he had stated: 'It occurred to me, dear
friend, that for you the constant inner struggle with Christianity in
my book [*Daybreak*] must be strange, even distressing; but it is still
the best piece of ideal life which I have become really familiar with
... I am after all the descendant of whole generations of Christian
ministers – forgive me this narrowness!' And on 23 June 1881 he
had written to Overbeck: 'As far as Christianity is concerned, I hope
you will believe this much: in my heart I have never held it in contempt and, ever since childhood, have often struggled with myself
on behalf of its ideals. In the end, to be sure, the result has always
been the sheerest impossibility.' Yet despite rejecting Christianity

---

49 Kolakowski, *Religion*, p. 202.
50 *The Anti-Christ*, §50.
51 This preference for truth over comfort goes back a long way in
   Nietzsche's biography. In a letter to his sister of 11 June 1865, replying
   to her attempt to defend the Christian faith, he wrote: '[I]f you wish to
   strive for peace of soul and happiness, then believe; if you wish to be a
   disciple of truth, then inquire ...' (quoted in Hollingdale, *Nietzsche. The
   Man and His Philosophy*, p. 39).
52 The composer Heinrich Köselitz (1854–1918), who also used the pseudonym 'Peter Gast', was a student, friend and sometime secretary of
   Nietzsche's. He was associated with the 'Nietzsche-Archiv' in Weimar
   from 1900 until 1908.

as a possibility for himself, he did write in *The Anti-Christ* (§39) that 'genuine, primitive Christianity will be possible at all times.'

Nietzsche's case is at one level not unique, in that from the time of Goethe onwards in nineteenth-century Germany, open rejection of, and even hostility towards, Christianity by the intelligentsia were quite common. Even Hegel,[53] whom many subsequently saw as the intellectual saviour of Christianity in the modern world, shared this Enlightenment-inspired aversion to Christianity in his early works. And it is interesting to see that one of the means of expressing such aversion was to contrast Christianity adversely with the religion and culture of ancient Greece, a contrast that of course is vehemently exploited in Nietzsche's writings. With reference to Hegel, Claud Sutton points out that: 'Like Schiller, he contrasted Christianity unfavourably with the life-affirming religion of the Greeks. This was no novelty at the time, but Hegel was the first person, as far as is known, actually to criticise the character of Jesus, contrasting him unfavourably with Socrates.'[54]

However, Nietzsche's uniqueness lies in the way he retained, despite his hostility towards Christianity, so much of its form and content, but without 'God', without 'grace'. For he wished to re-determine what had hitherto passed for 'values', thus re-defining the meaning of 'humanity', and re-creating the world. There is a sense in which Nietzsche could not, any more than his creation

---

53 Cf. J. C. Livingston, *Modern Christian Thought: From the Enlightenment to Vatican II*, p. 145: 'What the young Hegel found lacking in Christianity was that, unlike the *Volksreligion* of the Greeks, it did not reflect the spirit and genius of a people. Christianity appeared to the young Hegel as something imposed and alien, lacking a sense of beauty and joy.'

54 Sutton, Claud, *The German Tradition in Philosophy* (London, 1974), p. 59. Before Hegel, Giordano Bruno (1548–1600), from Nola near Naples, had excoriated Jesus for denigrating learning and science, and generally preferring plebeian to aristocratic values (cf. art. by H. J. Fischer, *Frankfurter Allgemeine Zeitung*, 15 August 1995). On the more philosophical front, Bruno's extreme pantheistic views, through Spinoza's mediation, influenced German figures like Herder, Goethe and Hegel, and through them perhaps Nietzsche also: cf. H. Urs von Balthasar, *Herrlichkeit* III,1, Teil 2 (Einsiedeln, 1965), pp. 605, 749; W. Kasper, *The God of Jesus Christ*, tr. M.J. O'Connell (London, 1984), pp. 22f., 153. Given the Hegelian texture of Joyce's mind it is not surprising to find the claim that Bruno 'has reappeared in contemporary consciousness ... largely through *Finnegans Wake*, across which he flits as "Mr. Brown," "Bruno Nolan," "the firm of Brown and Nolan," and many other travesties, for he is a central figure in the thought of James Joyce' (Giorgio de Santillana (ed.), *The Age of Adventure*, New York, 1956, p. 244).

'Zarathustra' (who himself speaks in a pseudo-biblical style, as a
new deity), be 'merely a believer', but had to be one 'who first *creates* truth, a *world-ruling* spirit, a destiny.'[55] Nietzsche's life and
thought also resembles a pattern discernible in the drama of Jesus'
life, in that Nietzsche pushes inexorably for a decision about existence, for a resolution of its tensions, just as in the trial and crucifixion of Jesus the resolution of the tensions he had generated within
his society was enacted. Whether that resolution or dénouement
was provoked by Jesus or those who opposed him, must remain
historically ambiguous, because an answer to this question
involves faith. That is to say it involves a decision on the part of any
onlooker about the meaning of Jesus' life and the source of his
identity. The final resolution of Nietzsche's own life is not, it seems
to me, so profoundly ambiguous because he was not so obviously
destroyed by others as was Jesus. In Jesus' drama there were simply
more wills or freedoms involved. It was ironically, given
Nietzsche's passionate commitment to this-worldliness, a more
political, a more 'incarnate' drama than Nietzsche's, which was
played out in the theatre of his own extraordinary mind.

It might be going too far to speak of an almost 'divine' (or
Luciferian?) rivalry with Jesus on Nietzsche's part,[56] but how else
can one interpret statements claiming that his thought will split the
history of humanity into two halves?[57] Or that, in a letter to his
mother and sister of July 1881, he was now 'hatching the future of
mankind'; or that, as he wrote to Overbeck on 21 May 1884: 'if I do
not succeed in having whole millennia taking their highest vows in
my name, in my eyes I shall have achieved nothing;'[58] or that, in
another letter to Overbeck of 12 November 1887, a piece of music
('The Hymn to Life') he had composed would be sung in a distant

55 *Ecce Homo*, p. 106.
56 Christianity itself, of course, has always been good at spotting rivals,
    vying for possession of the supposedly same psychic space as
    Christianity itself was thought to occupy. So was Nietzsche, in his
    opposition to Christianity, remaining ironically, almost perversely,
    true to his Christian upbringing?
57 For example, in letters to Overbeck: 10 March 1884 (where he also uses
    the expression 'courage to *carry* that thought!', reminiscent of the
    Christian notion of 'carrying one's cross'), and 18 October 1888 ('I fear I
    am shooting the history of humanity into two halves'); to Paul Deussen,
    14 September 1888; to August Strindberg, 7 December 1888.
58 Cf. the similar expression used in a letter of 22 May 1884 to Heinrich
    von Stein. See also *Ecce Homo*, p. 69: 'One day or other institutions will

future, when he had been finally understood, 'in memory of me' – a clear echo of the Christian Eucharist;[59] or that, in a letter to Carl Fuchs of 18 December 1888, he should write: 'In the coming years the world will be in utter turmoil: since the old God has abdicated, *I* shall rule the world from now on;' or that, shortly before his breakdown, when his mind was, admittedly, clearly unhinged, he should have begun notes to Cardinal Mariani in Rome and to King Umberto of Italy with the greeting: 'My peace be with you'? Finally, the title 'Ecce Homo', with its obvious Christological overtones, to say nothing of 'The Anti-Christ', would appear to indicate that Nietzsche wished to stake his own claim to significance in the history of culture in terms of, and of course in rivalry with, the magnitude of the importance attaching to Jesus Christ in human history. Why did he not take his cue from, or pit himself against, say, a great philosopher, artist or poet? Even allowing for the fact that Nietzsche often indulged in outrageous irony and jokes at his own expense (in *Ecce Homo*, for instance), the conclusion seems unavoidable that Christianity always remained 'under his skin', or rather that he wished to get under the skin of Christianity to provide it with a new substance: himself. Small wonder that Overbeck saw 'burning ambition'[60] as Nietzsche's innermost quality, and remarked that Nietzsche had, as an individual, always taken himself with religious seriousness.[61] Yet, should one be entirely surprised by this, granted that Christianity has always taught that God became man so that man could become God? ...

However, in suggesting that Nietzsche can be viewed as a

---

be needed in which people live and teach as I understand living and teaching: perhaps even chairs for the interpretation of Zarathustra will be established.' *Ibid.*, pp. 116f: 'Only I have the standard for "truths" in my hand, only I *can* decide... only after me are there again hopes, tasks, prescribable paths of culture – *I am the bringer of the good tidings of these* [*ich bin deren froher Botschafter*] ... Precisely therewith am I a destiny. –'

59 Cf. *Ecce Homo*, p. 100, which also mentions the *Hymn to Life*, 'the score of which was published two years ago ... a perhaps not insignificant symptom of the condition of this year, when I was possessed to the highest degree by the *affirmative* pathos *par excellence*, which I call the tragic pathos. It will one day be sung in memory of me [*zu meinem Gedächtnis*].'

60 F. Overbeck, 'Erinnerungen an Friedrich Nietzsche', *Die Neue Rundschau*, 1906, p. 214; cf. *ibid.*, pp. 209, 320.

61 See Arnold Pfeiffer, *Franz Overbecks Kritik des Christentums* (Göttingen, 1975), p. 60, n.175.

thinker who, in a sense, tried to turn Christianity inside out, one is, of course, speaking always 'from the outside'. It would be presumptuous, not to say ungracious, to suggest that this is also how things must appear to the divine eye. What human being can judge such matters with finality? One of Nietzsche's supreme gifts is to be able to convey how impossible it is ever to speak the full truth, because 'reality' – what we traditionally call 'God' and 'creation' and 'redemption' – and, hence, the 'truth' about reality, lie always beyond the bounds of any intellectual and, consequently, any linguistic expression (even though Christianity will of course claim, in the tradition of 'negative theology', that certain things can be definitely ruled out, even if it will always be impossible to say positively what should be 'ruled in'). Hence Nietzsche's undying mistrust of any 'system' of thought (such as Hegel's, for instance) that claims to explain everything, 'without remainder': 'I mistrust all systematisers and avoid them. The will to a system is a lack of integrity.'[62] In fact, Nietzsche does leave the 'last word' always unspoken, thus intimating obliquely, by contrast with the magnificent but, on his own terms, the still inadequate *oeuvre* that he created, how incomprehensible, how unknowable, how wonderful that 'last word' might be ...

Nietzsche's indebtedness to the Judaeo-Christian tradition has, as is well known, often been adverted to, not always in the most flattering terms. Wyndham Lewis, for example, wrote of Nietzsche that he 'had very little in his composition of the health, balance, measure, and fine sense of the antique world (of Spengler's "Classical" and Goethe's before him) towards which he turned so often; he had much more of the frantic, intolerant fanaticism of a genevan reformer or an Old Testament prophet.'[63] Less hostilely, T. S. Eliot claimed: 'An individual European may not believe that the Christian Faith is true, and yet what he says, and makes, and does, will all spring out of his heritage of Christian culture and depend upon that culture for its meaning. Only a Christian culture could have produced a Voltaire or a Nietzsche.'[64]

Even the shape of Nietzsche's impassioned attack on otherworldly religion, his stress on being loyal to the earth (why should one? why not just destroy it, since it is ultimately 'nothing'?), seems unimaginable without the Christian doctrine of the incarnation,

---

62 *Twilight of the Idols*, p. 35.
63 *Time and Western Man* (London 1927), pp. 375f.
64 *Notes towards the Definition of Culture*, (London 1972) p. 122.

which brings God and man so dangerously close together, and which also keeps both sides of the human reality in tension: the reality of our embodied existence, and – and here's the rub – the reality of its inviolable status as made in the image of God. If these are split apart, either only matter remains, and why should some matter be considered more important than any other? Or else only a phoney 'spirituality' is regarded as what most matters, and on this Nietzsche's comment is better than most: 'Pure spirit is pure lie.'[65]

His rejection of Christianity, like his aversion to Platonism, was grounded in a conviction that both are forms of escaping from rugged reality. The courageous man, for Nietzsche, accepts the facts of existence, and does not have the bad taste to shrink from life as it is.[66] 'No amount of pain,' he wrote to Malwida von Meysenbug on 14 January 1880, 'has been or will be able to betray me into bearing false witness to life *as I know it.*' This seems to be almost a moral issue for Nietzsche. The coward looks for a refuge from life in Idealism (in the philosophical sense). The truly human response to life is, for him, to accept and live it, boldly, without moaning or whimpering. This sounds like stoicism, but on Nietzsche's lips it has a completely different tone.

Nietzsche's renunciation of Christianity had, however, another important root. This was his revulsion at the 'slave-morality' he thought Christianity fostered, and which he considered to be motivated by hatred and resentment (Nietzsche uses the French term *ressentiment*). In this he develops a theme taken up before him by the poet Heinrich Heine who had described the new gods, who replaced the old gods of Greece, as 'the new, ruling, sad gods – malicious ones in the sheep's clothing of humility'. Nietzsche himself wrote in *Daybreak* (IV, 411): 'The soul of the Christian who has freed himself from sin is usually afterwards ruined by hatred of sin. Regard the faces of great Christians! They are the faces of great haters.' And in a powerful passage in *On the Genealogy of Morals* (I,15) he raises the question of how the Christian paradise has been conceived and writes:

---

65 *The Anti-Christ*, p. 130.
66 As well as the idea that Christianity amounts to cowardice in the face of 'real life', the notion that belief in God steals human energies (cf. Rimbaud: 'Christ! ô Christ, éternel voleur des énergies') and prevents people from experiencing and enjoying life as it 'really is', also became quite popular after Nietzsche, as one can judge from the almost offhand way in which, for example, Jacques Prévert begins his poem 'Pater Noster': 'Our Father who art in heaven/Stay there/And we'll stay here on earth …'

We might even guess, but it is better to have it expressly described for us by an authority not to be underestimated in such matters, Thomas Aquinas, the great teacher and saint. *'Beati in regno coelesti,'* he says, meek as a lamb, *'videbunt poenas damnatorum, ut beatitudo illis magis complaceat* (The blessed in the kingdom of heaven will see the punishments of the damned, in order that their bliss be more delightful for them).'[67]

While one can readily appreciate what disgusted Nietzsche and his Enlightenment forbears in the typical attitudes adopted by 'official' Christians against their 'enemies' (whom they were 'officially' supposed to love), it is probably the case that the clash between a Christian and a so-called heroic or aristocratic morality is older than the nineteenth century and that it reflects an underlying and perhaps even insoluble conflict between a naturalistic view of existence (with no doctrine of creation) and a view that considers existence to derive – as a created reality – from a transcendent source. Lichtenberg, for example, saw an interesting, almost proto-Nietzschean difference between the way ancient and (Christian) modern poets treated their heroes:

> The heroes of the poets of antiquity are very different from those in, e.g., Milton. They are brave, shrewd and wise, but seldom amiable or compassionate in the sense of our morality. Milton took his from the Bible. Does our Christian morality perhaps have its origin in a certain weakness, in a Jewish cowardice, while the other is founded on strength? Universal acceptability is perhaps only a fair chimera and something that will never be attained.[68]

Perhaps rather oddly, Nietzsche exempts Jesus himself from the strictures he freely pours on the Christian centuries ('in reality there has been only one Christian, and he died on the Cross').[69] Overbeck noted that Christianity had in *The Anti-Christ* received much the same treatment from Nietzsche as Marsyas from Apollo (who,

---

67 Tr. W. Kaufmann, *Basic Writings of Nietzsche*, p. 485, with changed typography. The reference to Aquinas [*STh*. III, Supplementum, Q. 94, Art. 1] is not quite accurate, but the sentiment in both cases is the same.
68 *Aphorisms*, p. 107.
69 *The Anti-Christ*, p. 161. Of the followers of Christ down through the ages Nietzsche appears to have had deep respect for only one: Pascal, whom he once referred to, in a letter to Georg Brandes (20 November 1888), as 'the only *logical* Christian.'

according to legend, flayed him alive). Jesus, however, he remarked, was spared in the general onslaught. Indeed on Nietzsche's portrait of Jesus, Overbeck commented that 'all previous attempts to make a human figure out of [Jesus] seem absurdly abstract and aimed only at illustrating some rationalistic dogmatics, compared with Nietzsche's achievement and the way in which both the originality and the humanity of the person [of Jesus] come across.'[70] Nietzsche sees Jesus as in fact completely free of resentment, but only out of an incapacity for enduring guilt through even the slightest inflicting of pain.[71] However, whether this 'historical Jesus' is the real one, or a hypersensitive reflection of the Jesus of German Pietism at the bottom of a deep Nietzschean well – to adapt Tyrrell's celebrated phrase – is at least open to debate.

Conclusion

In trying to grapple with Nietzsche's challenge to Christianity, one could begin by recalling his jibe: 'this pitiable God of Christian monotono-theism!'[72] Or again: 'Be a philosopher, be a mummy, represent monotono-theism by a gravedigger-mimicry!'[73] The point Nietzsche is making in both passages is that 'God', at least in theological Christianity, has been reduced to a mere rationally conceived, lifeless ghost, with no longer any existential bite in human affairs. It is also in *The Anti-Christ* that Nietzsche makes the rather sinister statement: 'One has as much need of the evil God as of the good God: for one does not owe one's existence to philanthropy or

---

70 In a letter to H. Köselitz, 13 March 1889; see C. A. Bernoulli, *Franz Overbeck und Friedrich Nietzsche. Eine Freundschaft* (Jena, 1908), vol. 2, p. 250.

71 Cf. *The Anti-Christ* §30. (It is perhaps instructive to compare this view of Jesus with Newman's remark: 'It is almost a definition of a gentleman to say that he is one who never inflicts pain.') Nietzsche, it is surmised (see Hollingdale's comments in *Twilight of the Idols/The Anti-Christ*, p. 200), may have been confirmed in his interpretation of Jesus as 'an idiot' (or 'Holy Fool') by Dostoevsky's creation of the 'idiot-figure', (the reference is to Prince Myshkin in the novel *The Idiot*); cf. F. Nietzsche, *Nachgelassene Fragmente 1887–1889*, ed. G. Colli and M. Montinari (Munich/Berlin/New York, 1988), p. 409, (in this passage Nietzsche mentions Russia as the only place where a 'Christ', as he interprets the term, was still a psychological possibility: 'wo ein Christus jeden Augenblick entstehen kann ...').

72 *The Anti-Christ*, p. 139.

73 *Twilight of the Idols*, p. 45.

tolerance precisely. ... There is in fact no other alternative for Gods: *either* they are the will to power – and so long as they are that they will be national Gods – *or* else the impotence for power – and then they necessarily become *good* ...'[74] In other words, belief in the goodness of God is a projection of believers' inability (or fear?) to do evil.

Gods, in Nietzsche's view, have only ever been truly believed in when their nature was mixed, not simple (purely good). It is indeed astonishing, as René Girard points out,[75] that Nietzsche saw more clearly than anyone else in the nineteenth century (including, needless to say, the theologians) where the heart of Christianity lay, but he interpreted the crucial evidence in a way diametrically opposed to the Christian faith. For according to this faith Jesus endures the pain and suffering of the world as an innocent victim, whose death was undeserved and unjustified, whose innocence cannot therefore be undermined by any power in the world, and thus is other than the world. Nietzsche, on the contrary, sees the world as a given, immutable mixture of 'good' and 'evil', all of which must be endorsed and affirmed if one is to be 'true to life' and to accept it in its entirety. This is the (inevitably?) dark side of believing, to quote Wallace Stevens, ' ... that if nothing/Was divine then all things were, the world itself,/And that if nothing was the truth, then all/Things were the truth, the world itself was the truth.'[76]

In Nietzsche's world, then, the only 'innocence' is that of 'becoming', i.e. the 'innocence' of the natural world-process itself. Hence his affirmation of the world must include also an endorsement of what Christian faith calls 'evil'. (We recall that it only makes sense to refer to evil as 'the problem of evil' in a theistic context.) Nietzsche has simply no way, one might say 'metaphysically speaking', of 'refusing' the evil of this world. For he cannot invoke or appeal to any other 'world' (beyond this one),[77] in terms of which such a 'refusal' would make sense and would be justified, and where such a 'refusal' would be, so to speak, fully 'at home'. Hence he agrees with Heraclitus who 'will always be right in this, that being is an empty fiction. The "apparent" world is the only one: the

---

74 *The Anti-Christ*, pp. 136f.
75 *Quand Ces Choses Commenceront* ... (Paris, 1994), pp. 197ff.
76 From 'Landscape With Boat', *The Collected Poems of Wallace Stevens* (New York, 1978), p. 242.
77 Cf. *The Gay Science* §344, pp. 282f.: '[T]he question "Why science" leads back to the moral problem: *Why have morality at all* when life, nature,

"real" world has only been *lyingly added* ...'[78] Nietzsche cannot, in short, 'believe' in any other world whose reality might encourage him to deny to the evil and to the evil-instigated suffering of this world any kind of legitimacy.

But Christianity sees its belief in God unmistakably evoked at precisely this point. Jesus, in enduring his agony innocently – thus refusing it any moral or final justification, though obviously not denying its reality – reveals, beyond, but also *in and through*, the suffering that can be inflicted by evil in this world, the existence of a reality, which we can call 'God', that guarantees unreservedly, indeed that *is* the truth for which – and because of which (this is the humanly frightening part of the story) – he was killed, and thus preserves unblemished and forever indestructible what evil thought it had destroyed. Thus both backwards and forwards in history the death of Jesus affirms, or rather enacts the real, indeed the divinely sanctioned superiority of suffering humanity (and hence life itself: suffering as such is not what is good, but life for whose sake suffering is endured) over the powers of evil and death, which are thereby robbed of any ultimate legitimacy or authority, though clearly not of their penultimate virulence. Yet 'how' this can be we can

---

and history are "not moral"? No doubt, those who are truthful in that audacious and ultimate sense that is presupposed by the faith in science *thus affirm another world* than the world of life, nature, and history; and insofar as they affirm this "other world" – look, must they not by the same token negate its counterpart, this world, *our* world? – But you will have gathered what I am driving at, namely, that it is still a *metaphysical faith* upon which our faith in science rests – that even we seekers after knowledge today, we godless anti-metaphysicians still take our fire, too, from the flame lit by a faith that is thousands of years old, that Christian faith which was also the faith of Plato, that God is the truth, that truth is divine. – But what if this should become more and more incredible, if nothing should prove to be divine any more unless it were error, blindness, the lie – if God himself should prove to be our most enduring lie? –' (This is a theme to which Nietzsche returned in *On the Genealogy of Morals*, III, 24.) One can see with particular clarity from this passage how Nietzsche constantly had to presuppose the validity of a system of thought (based on such solid notions as 'true' and 'false') that he was bent on dismantling. He is thus obliged to try to cajole the reader somewhat, to take him into his confidence, to persuade him to agree with what is manifestly false but somehow also true to the 'impossible possibility' that we are, as contingent creatures who cannot guarantee the validity of our perceptions ...

78 *Twilight of the Idols*, p. 46.

never know or understand: this is the mystery of redemption, tied permanently to the person and the sacrifice of Jesus.

What makes Nietzsche, from a Christian point of view, a fascinating figure is that, he was of course, in an absolutely primordial sense, right! It was said above that, from his own perspective, Nietzsche had no way 'metaphysically speaking' of 'refusing' the evil of this world. If 'refusing' here means, as it must do to be humanly meaningful in this world, to 'take away' or to 'redeem' the evil of the world, then Nietzsche was right not to 'refuse' it, because who can take away evil, but God alone? What is at stake here is not, in other words, whether one believes or not in the existence of a transcendent world. What is at stake, rather, is whether or not one has at one's disposal the reality or the power of that world, and of course no human being has such power at his or her disposal – except, Christian faith confesses, Jesus, because he is both human *and* divine. In refusing to arrogate such divine power to himself, Nietzsche remains, in an exemplary sense, human. But in denying that such power is real or that it could be received as grace by human beings, and in attempting to replace that divine power with his own humanity, Nietzsche confused two orders of reality, collapsing, in theological language, grace into nature, and must now be seen as demanding, ironically, from all who would want to be consistent in the acceptance of his message, the surrender of their humanity in their endorsement of evil.

The life-giving truth of Christianity, which guarantees and defends the inviolable worth of life *in* this world, is, therefore, paradoxically but irrefutably, as its classical exponents have always insisted, not *of* this world: it cannot be, for as Nietzsche saw more clearly than most, this world is not a place of unalloyed goodness. Christianity can therefore never abandon belief in the transcendence of God, *propter nos homines et propter nostram salutem*. It is, however, also historically undeniable that Christianity's otherworldly anchorage has been frequently (deliberately? for less than heavenly motives?) misinterpreted in order to provide a would-be escape-hatch out of a world perceived as radically evil and irredeemable (and such dualism cannot but issue in an inhuman 'spirituality'), or in order to deflect people's interests away from worldly affairs so as to control those affairs better oneself.

How tantalisingly close Nietzsche is to the heart of Christianity, how like an identical twin of Christianity his lived vision of existence actually is, is revealed in his unambiguous affirmation of the fundamental goodness of life, in his refusal to wish to escape from the suffering inseparable from life in this world as it in fact is, and in his so movingly (and no doubt unintentionally) ambiguous statement that Jesus died 'not to "redeem mankind" but to demonstrate how one ought to live.'[79]

If however one chooses to refuse the interpretation of existence enacted by Jesus and subsequently proclaimed by the Christian church, what is the alternative? Nietzsche tells us:

> Dionysus versus the 'Crucified': there you have the antithesis. It is *not* a difference in regard to their martyrdom – it is a difference in the meaning of it. Life itself, its eternal fruitfulness and recurrence, creates torment, destruction, the will to annihilation. In the other case, suffering – the 'Crucified as the innocent one'– counts as an objection to this life, as a formula for its condemnation. – One will see that the problem is that of the meaning of suffering: whether a Christian meaning or a tragic meaning. In the former case, it is supposed to be the path to a holy existence; in the latter case, being is counted as *holy enough* to justify even a monstrous amount of suffering. The tragic man affirms even the harshest suffering: he is sufficiently strong, rich, and capable of deifying to do so. The Christian denies even the happiest lot on earth: he is sufficiently weak, poor, disinherited to suffer from life in whatever form he meets it. The god on the cross is a curse on life, a signpost to seek redemption from life; Dionysus cut to pieces is a *promise* of life: it will be eternally reborn and return again from destruction.[80]

There is, to sum up, the way of Jesus, which is to endure suffering to the end, but not to endorse the evil that inflicts it, and the way of Nietzsche, which is not only to endure but to 'justify even a monstrous amount of suffering,' because life, he is convinced, can only be truly and unconditionally affirmed, when it is affirmed without ifs or buts, in *all* its manifestations. The first way believes in a real, indissoluble difference between good and evil; the second can find or believe in no basis for maintaining this distinction. There is, as Nietzsche with utter lucidity and unflinching honesty discerned, no third possibility, unless one rejects the world of matter altogether as some kind of illusion, like Buddhism, or embraces the dualist option of gnosticism.[81] But Nietzsche was attracted by neither of

---

79 *The Anti-Christ*, p. 157.
80 *The Will to Power* §1052, pp. 542f.
81 'Gnosticism' I use loosely to refer to dualist views of reality (especially

these paths. Since evil, however, will not do anyone the favour of disappearing, those who wish to affirm, and not to escape from, earthly existence have to make the choice (or the act of faith) between the two ways represented by Jesus and by Nietzsche. As Borges says in his deadpan way, 'the world, unfortunately, is real ...'[82]

Jesus' crucifixion, however, far from being a denial of life as Nietzsche so poignantly misunderstood, is in fact life's highest, indeed its eternal affirmation as *good*. Even though he himself absorbed life's pain until it finally destroyed him, Nietzsche, who could only believe in the reality of this world, could not logically accept the God of Jesus, perhaps finally because 'believing in God' and 'being God' were, or would have had to be, for him the same thing. From early on Nietzsche accepted that a serious belief in God could not be a mere mental act or be confined to a state of consciousness, but was bound up with how one lived life, a conviction that is not alien to Christianity. Thus he saw at once the religious significance of the downgrading of Christ, represented by Strauss' *Life of Jesus*. In 1865 he wrote to his friend Deussen: '[I]f you give up Christ, you will have to give up God as well.'[83] Nietzsche's ultimate failure to defeat and supplant his great rival – despite the intensity

---

popular in the Mediterranean area in the early centuries of Christianity), in which existence is seen as blighted from the beginning, even before the beginning (as in the title of Beckett's piece 'I Gave up Before Birth' ...), because it is the product of an evil god, who is hostile to man. A spark of divine consciousness in man was supposed, however, to enable him to seek union with the true God (who had no hand in making the world), and in this way escape the misery of earthly existence for which no hope of redemption was possible. Schopenhauer's philosophy which shares these ancient systems' pessimism about material reality has been aptly described as an 'atheistic gnosis' (M. Brumlik. *Die Gnostiker*, Frankfurt a/M, 1992, p. 266). In rejecting Schopenhauer, Nietzsche repudiated implicitly this very old, prestigious rival to Christianity, without of course returning to Christianity, or its crude and popular nineteenth-century transformation into a belief in inevitable evolutionary progress (cf. John Passmore, *The Perfectibility of Man*, London, 1972, p. 249). Indeed as regards evolution, Nietzsche impishly suggested: '[P]erhaps at the end [mankind] will stand even lower than at the beginning!' (*Daybreak*, I, 49, p. 32). – For a brief, sympathetic characterisation of gnosticism, see Jacques Lacarrière, *The Gnostics*, tr. N. Rootes (London, 1977).

82 In 'A New Refutation of Time', in J. L. Borges, *Labyrinths*, ed. D. A. Yates and J. E. Irby (Harmondsworth, 1972), p. 269.

83 See R. J. Hollingdale, *Nietzsche*, p. 40.

of his heroic challenge – casts a perhaps unexpected but uniquely powerful light on what differentiates them: the divinity of Jesus. Yet Jesus' victory (which is not really the right word: 'divinity', here, is more appropriate) does not belittle, still less patronise or attempt to appropriate, the immensity of Nietzsche's struggle; nor does it devalue the seriousness and the passion and the almost unbearable, complete vulnerability with which he lived that struggle. If redemption means the preservation or salvation of human worth, healed from evil, then Jesus' unambiguously pure 'victory' ('than which nothing greater can be thought'), is paradoxically the true and invincible source of that affirmation and redemption of life (and not, as Nietzsche feared, its humiliation or its betrayal), which Nietzsche himself sought to reach, against Christianity, in and through the tragic and searingly self-destructive greatness of his own humanity.

Before insanity overwhelmed him,[84] or before he resigned from the human race, or before the unstoppable dynamism of his own tragic error propelled him relentlessly towards a truly awesome dénouement – depending on one's interpretation – Nietzsche wrote a final, exuberant and unnerving letter to his former colleague in Basel, Jacob Burckhardt, in which he mentioned that he had recently gone up to complete strangers in Turin, tapped them on the shoulder, and asked them: *'Siamo contenti? Son Dio, ho fatto questa caricatura'* (Are we happy? I am God, I have made this caricature).[85] The pathos of Nietzsche's last, still lucid though crazed, declarations in his final letters, signed in some cases *Dionysus*, in others *The Crucified*, movingly testifies to the inescapably religious character of his thought and its tormentedly close relationship to Christianity.

---

84 Nietzsche perhaps anticipated his fate in the Prologue (§5) to *Thus Spoke Zarathustra*, where Zarathustra sees the only option for whoever refuses to abandon his difference from the nihilistic herd, is to go 'voluntarily into the madhouse.'

85 Cf. W. Kaufmann, *The Portable Nietzsche* (Harmondsworth, 1981), p. 687. In a *Nachlass* fragment from July/August 1882 one finds a foreshadowing of this sentiment. It reflects Nietzsche's sense (despite his scornful dismissal of Idealism) that real or actual life cannot be the full truth about human existence: 'Whoever has seen the ideal of a man, feels the actual man [*den wirklichen Menschen*] to be its *caricature*' (F. Nietzsche, *Nachgelassene Fragmente 1882-1884*, ed. G. Colli and M. Montinari Munich, 1988, p. 24).

CHAPTER TEN

God in postmodernity

*[T]ry as we may we cannot get behind things to the reality. And the
terrible reason may be that there is no reality in things apart from
their appearances.* — Oscar Wilde

*The passage beyond philosophy does not consist in turning the page
of philosophy (which usually amounts to philosophising badly), but
in continuing to read philosophers* in a certain way.
— Jacques Derrida

How can we be sure that we are not impostors? — Jacques Lacan

The aim of this chapter is to suggest that the notoriously vague
terms 'postmodernism' and 'postmodernity' can in fact plausibly
be construed as referring to one aspect of the secularisation of
Christian theological ideas, including of course the idea of God,
that has been in progress since the Enlightenment, if not before.
This interpretation, which some may judge tendentious, is advanced
briefly towards the end of the chapter, but an attempt is first made
to situate postmodernism historically in the contemporary world.

Introduction: modernity and modernism

In trying to understand the term 'postmodernism', it may be useful
to take it in conjunction with 'postmodernity', a closely related but
distinct concept. The two terms 'postmodernism' and 'postmodernity' must in turn be seen in relation to the correlative or parallel
expressions, 'modernism' and 'modernity'. For it is against modernism and modernity that postmodernism and postmodernity
appear to define themselves. And indeed that fact alone – if it is a
fact – should alert us to the possibility that when cultural theorists
describe modernism and modernity, it may not be, so to speak, an
innocent description that is given, but a description covertly
weighted against modernism and modernity and in favour of postmodernism and postmodernity.

Be that as it may, one should perhaps begin by attempting to

261

describe what is meant by modernity and modernism. Putting it rather crudely, modernity may be seen as designating various social, political, scientific, economic and legal realities, i.e. concrete historical facts, whereas the term 'modernism' has an intellectual and cultural reference. The two are evidently closely interconnected. Modernity – in the sense of the 'modern age' – refers to the post-mediaeval world,[1] to the period when in the West life began to be characterised by a gradually intensifying process of secularisation. Secularisation involved the organisation of the life of this world according to rational, ordered principles, and a relegation of religious matters increasingly to the sphere of individual choice and responsibility.

The factors contributing to the emergence of the recognisably modern world certainly include the scientific revolution of the seventeenth century. The essence of that revolution was the dual conviction that 'there are no privileged or a priori *substantive* truths' and that 'the laws to which this world is subject are symmetrical.'[2] In the course of time this conviction produced what Max Weber was to call the 'disenchantment of the world.' For where everything had to happen according to laws that could not admit of exceptions, there could no longer be any possibility of special events, divine interventions or miracles. Any 'knowledge' acquired by circumventing the scientific method was not real knowledge at all. In the wake of the seventeenth-century scientific revolution came the Enlightenment of the eighteenth century, the industrial revolution, and the spectacular growth of historical consciousness in the nineteenth century, followed by the emergence of a post-industrial, highly technological civilisation in the twentieth century.

This entire development is sometimes referred to as the 'project of modernity', i.e. the attempt to expand human power and mastery over the world in a rationally controlled fashion. In its own way, it was a quasi-religious, or at least a teleologically inspired, i.e. goal-directed, total vision of reality, for it sought through constant progress to bring about the perfection, or the maximisation, of

---

1   When the mediaeval world ended is, of course, a much-disputed question, and depends on which country – or segment of a country – one is talking about. Voltaire is alleged to have said on one occasion that the Middle Ages were a few hundred yards down the road from where he himself was staying... Luis Buñuel once mentioned that in his native village in Aragón, the Middle Ages ended in 1914 ...

2   E. Gellner, *Postmodernism, Reason and Religion* (London, 1992), pp. 80-81.

human dominance over the environment. The project of modernity was thus, in theological parlance, a Pelagian project, aimed at self-sufficiency, and at least implicitly repudiating the traditional Christian doctrine of 'original sin', according to which there is a humanly irremovable weakness in the human condition. This whole modern development clearly defined itself in opposition to the older experience of the West in the Middle Ages and antiquity. The immediate predecessor of the modern age, namely the mediaeval period, was perceived as other-worldly, religion-dominated, feudal and communitarian; the modern age was this-worldly, rationalist, increasingly democratic, individualist, and profoundly marked by the growth of capitalism.

Now, while modernity can be seen as covering quite a long period of time, from about the fifteenth century onwards, that period's awareness of itself is a much later development. By that is meant simply that any wide use of 'modernity' as a theoretical concept is not, as far as this writer can ascertain, to be found before the nineteenth century.[3] The French poet Rimbaud's use of the term ('Il faut être absolument moderne')[4] is an example of its recently acquired cultural significance. That is to say, it was only relatively late in the day that 'modern' Westerners began to suspect that their own cultural reality was something very different from that of their ancient and mediaeval forbears, and appeared to involve a radical break with what their predecessors had believed to be eternally and universally true about the human condition.

Once this realisation began to sink in, it was reflected in the intellectual, literary and artistic life of the West: i.e. in the cultural movement known now as 'modernism', which could be dated very roughly, following M. Bradbury and J. McFarlane,[5] from 1890 to 1930. This 'movement' was a reaction against realist modes of rep-

---

3 The actual terms 'modernus' and 'modernitas' (in opposition to 'antiquus' and 'antiquitas') can be found in Latin as far back as the fifth and twelfth centuries respectively (cf. Niklaus Peter, *Im Schatten der Modernität*, Stuttgart and Weimar, 1992, p. 6); according to others (e.g. Jencks), the term goes back even further, to the third century. 'Modern' was used to refer to recent, as opposed to older, phenomena. But the connotation of the present's radical difference from the past, and a sense even of its superiority with regard to the past, only began to attach to the term 'modern' from the Enlightenment onwards.

4 At the end of *Une Saison en Enfer*.

5 Authors of the volume *Modernism* in the *Pelican Guides to European Literature*.

resentation in the arts and in literature, and up to the start of this century was communicated by tendencies like Symbolism, Impressionism and Decadence. From the early part of the twentieth century up to the First World War, 'modernism' was expressed by Fauvism, Cubism, Post-Impressionism, Futurism, Imagism and Vorticism. Finally, during and following the First World War Expressionism, Dada, and Surrealism came to the fore. Modernism would thus include: atonalism in music, anti-representationalism in art (i.e. abstract art), free verse in poetry, fragmentation and 'stream of consciousness' in the novel, functionalism in architecture (*Bauhaus*) and the general move away from linear or representational forms and towards the use of new spatial configurations in the arts (e.g. in the technique known as 'collage').

Modernism should however be seen in more than purely formal or artistic terms. That is to say, it was about more than a search for new forms in the arts and in literature, for it was, more profoundly, an often frenetic reaction to the political, social, military and ideological upheavals of the times. It represented, among other things, a sustained attempt at giving a radically new interpretation of space and time as the coordinates, if that is the right word, by which to plot the movement of human life.[6] This fact is probably not unconnected with contemporary developments in the sciences, especially in physics, which overturned the Newtonian picture of reality, and more disturbingly overturned long-held assumptions about the relative solidity and stability of the material world.[7]

Modernity indeed, in its late phase, witnessed such a violent overthrow of traditional patterns of interpreting and trying to manage the human condition, that for some theorists (cf. the phrase used by Marx and Engels in *The Communist Manifesto*: 'all that is solid melts into air'[8]) it already contained implicitly within itself the flux and uncertainty associated with the postmodern mood.[9]

---

6   For the above information on modernism in the arts and literature I am indebted to the entry 'modernism' in *The Fontana Dictionary of Modern Thought*, ed. A. Bullock and O. Stallybrass (London, 1977), pp. 395f.

7   Cf. William McNeill, *The Rise of the West* (Chicago, 1963), p. 753: 'By 1917, leading painters had rejected the perspective frame within which European artistic vision had operated since the fifteenth century. Physicists had modified the Newtonian laws of motion within which European scientific thought had moved since the seventeenth century.'

8   An allusion to Prospero's words from *The Tempest*, Act 4. Sc.1, l.150, quoted by David Lyon, *Postmodernity* (Buckingham, 1995), p. 8.

9   Cf. the article 'modernity' in *Collins Dictionary of Sociology*, ed. D. Jary and J. Jary (Glasgow, 1995), p. 421.

To summarise this first part of the discussion: one could say that
when the modern age achieved self-consciousness as the 'modern
age', 'modernity' was born, and that in turn provoked the cultural
response known as 'modernism'. Then, when a self-conscious
modernity became self-critical and self-doubting, postmodernity
and its corresponding cultural and intellectual expression, postmodernism, appeared. It should, however, be pointed out that
there are disputes about whether postmodernism can be properly
described as the culture of postmodernity.

Postmodernity: Hegel, Benjamin and Wittgenstein

I now propose to take up three quotations, which cast significant
light, in my judgement, on what has been said so far, and which can
also serve to set the scene for what has still to be said about postmodernity and postmodernism proper. The first is from the
'Preface' to Hegel's *Elements of the Philosophy of Right or Natural Law
and Political Science in Outline* (first published 1821). This work was
Hegel's attempt to set out his philosophy of law and his understanding of the modern state within the framework of his overall
philosophy of history. Towards the end of the 'Preface' there is a
famous passage that reads:

> A further word on the subject of *issuing instructions* on how the
> world ought to be: philosophy, at any rate, always comes too
> late to perform this function. As the *thought* of the world, it
> appears only at a time when actuality has gone through its for-
> mative process and attained its completed state. This lesson of
> the concept is necessarily also apparent from history, namely
> that it is only when actuality has reached maturity that the ideal
> appears opposite the real and reconstructs this real world,
> which it has grasped in its substance, in the shape of an intellec-
> tual realm. When philosophy paints its grey in grey, a shape of
> life has grown old, and it cannot be rejuvenated, but only recog-
> nized, by the grey in grey of philosophy; the owl of Minerva
> begins its flight only with the onset of dusk.[10]

The final sentence of this passage has been interpreted as meaning
that 'a culture's philosophical understanding [i.e. its self-under-
standing] reaches its peak only when the culture enters its
decline'.[11] Or, to put the matter in a slightly different way, once a

---

10 Hegel, *Elements of the Philosophy of Right*, ed. A. W. Wood, tr. H. B.
    Nisbet (Cambridge, 1991), p. 23.
11 *Ibid.*, p. 392 (comment of A. W. Wood's).

historical era has been understood, it has ceased to be truly alive, and a new era has begun. This, it seems to me, is what the term 'postmodern' is trying to articulate with respect to the period in which we are now living. For what is perceived as dead or dying is modernity itself, and until a new understanding emerges of where or what we are now, cultural commentators have to make do with describing the present time as the age of postmodernity.

Some indeed would eschew even a term like 'age' or 'period' as being too redolent of an assumption of linear, progressive development within history. For such assumptions are, from a postmodernist perspective, incompatible with the perceived demise of all 'metanarratives', about which more will be said later. However, if Hegel is correct, presumably the real understanding of our own age – the age of the postmodern, if we agree to call it that – will only emerge when our age itself will have ceased to live. Until then it cannot, in Hegelian terms, be understood. That, in turn, would seem to imply that so long as you are not sure about what contemporary experience means, you are at least still alive, which is some consolation perhaps.

The second quotation comes from Walter Benjamin (1892–1940), who was both a philosopher and a major literary critic. Benjamin's rather apocalyptic vision of history, in which he had a keen eye for, as he put it, 'the image of history . . . in its rejects', i.e. the casualties or 'victims of progress' (Merquior), is evident in the following passage from his *Theses on the Philosophy of History* § IX, a work completed in 1940, though not published until 1950:

> A Klee[12] painting named 'Angelus Novus' shows an angel looking as though he is about to move away from something he is fixedly contemplating. His eyes are staring, his mouth is open, his wings are spread. This is how one pictures the angel of history. His face is turned toward the past. Where we perceive a chain of events, he sees one single catastrophe which keeps piling wreckage upon wreckage and hurls it in front of his feet. The angel would like to stay, awaken the dead, and make whole what has been smashed. But a storm is blowing from Paradise; it has got caught in his wings with such violence that the angel can no longer close them. This storm irresistibly propels him into the

---

12 Swiss-born modernist painter (1879-1940). See article by J. G. Merquior in J. Wintle (ed.), *Dictionary of Modern Culture* (London, 1984).

future to which his back is turned, while the pile of debris before him grows skyward. This storm is what we call progress.[13]

Benjamin's prophetic and pessimistic view of history can reasonably be interpreted as a symptom of the collapse of faith in modernity's ideal of progress through the sustained application of Enlightenment rationalist principles to the organisation of human life. The optimism of the Enlightenment had already received a body-blow from the carnage of the First World War. The rise of fascism in the turmoil of the interwar period, followed by the destruction of European Jewry, the invention and utilisation of atomic bombs, and all the other catastrophes of the Second World War, together with a growing historical awareness of past, quite elaborate Western crimes (such as, for example, the post-mediaeval slave-trade): all of this helped to spread an attitude of scepticism towards the great project of modernity. More recently the breaching of the Berlin Wall in 1989, marking the collapse of the Soviet Empire in Eastern Europe, appeared to underline irrefutably yet another failure – after precisely two centuries – of the grand experiment, launched in 1789, to create a rationally based political system, initially for Europe, but aimed at encompassing the whole world in due time.

The belief in rationality as a universal feature of human nature, and in the ability of rational thought to control social, political, and economic life has thus suffered serious set-backs in this century. Even the belief in a relatively stable human self, often referred to as the 'autonomous self' of the Enlightenment, has met with increasing scepticism. 'Our ready-made individuality, our identity,' wrote D. H. Lawrence, 'is no more than an accidental cohesion in the flux of time'.[14] Since the end of the Second World War, apprehension and uncertainty about where poverty, ecological imbalance, and political instability on the one hand, and humanity's highly developed technological power, on the other hand, – anxiety about where this is all leading, only serves to underscore still further the illusory quality of the Enlightenment's dream of controlled progress. The 'key psychological mood of postmodern culture' has been characterised as one of 'panic' (Arthur Kroker, in Baudrillard's

---

13 Walter Benjamin, *Illuminations*, Edited and with an Introduction by Hannah Arendt, tr. Harry Zohn (London, 1982), pp. 259f.

14 See C. Taylor, *Sources of the Self. The Making of the Modern Identity* (Cambridge, 1992), p. 463, citing Quiñones, *Mapping Literary Modernism*, p. 93.

wake).[15] Such radical disenchantment ushers in the end of modernity – and the beginning of what? We shall look presently at what followed the collapse of confidence in the project of modernity.

But before that, the third quotation referred to above must be mentioned. This is a brief passage (written in 1930) from Wittgenstein's posthumously published book, *Culture and Value*, where he remarks:

> I once said, perhaps rightly: The earlier culture will become a heap of rubble, and finally a heap of ashes, but spirits will hover over the ashes.[16]

Wittgenstein conveys memorably in these few words his sense of living in a period of fragmentation, dissolution, and decline. He shared the cultural pessimism of Oswald Spengler (*The Decline of the West*) that the world in which he had grown up was doomed, and so he, too, like Benjamin, can be seen as a kind of prophet of postmodernity – a term he would no doubt have recoiled from, but perhaps valid to the extent that Wittgenstein among others marks the end of an era, which we may call the era of modernity, and communicates, in such remarks as those just quoted, the sense of a civilisation in crisis. All that the West had built up over long centuries – on the three pillars of Judaeo-Christian religion, Greek philosophy and Roman organisational, political and legal know-how – that enormous cultural edifice seemed to be disintegrating.[17]

---

15 D. Lyon, *op. cit.*, p. 16.

16 L. Wittgenstein, *Culture and Value*, ed. G. H. von Wright in collaboration with H. Nyman, tr. P. Winch (Oxford, 1980), p. 3e.

17 It should be added, however, that Wittgenstein did not equate what he felt was a cultural decline with a decline in the value of human existence as such. In the same year (1930) in which the previous short passage was written he also wrote that, although modern civilisation 'in its industry, architecture and music' and 'in its fascism and socialism' was 'alien and uncongenial' to him, this was not 'a value judgement'. For what he took to be 'the disappearance of the arts' did not 'justify judging disparagingly the human beings who make up this civilisation.' He added 'that the disappearance of a culture does not signify the disappearance of human value, but simply of certain means of expressing this value' (*Culture and Value*, p. 6e).

Postmodern: a working definition

As for the term 'postmodern' itself, its first use goes back, according to Charles Jencks,[18] a writer on postmodern architecture and art, to the 1870s, when it was used by the British artist John Watkins Chapman. The popularity of the prefix 'post-' dates also from the end of the nineteenth century. 'Post-impressionism' can be found in the 1880s, and 'post-industrial' in the period during and immediately following the First World War. By the 1960s the prefix had become attached to studies of literature, social thought and even religion (post-Christian). According to Jencks, the notion of posteriority ('the negative feeling of coming after a creative age or, conversely, the positive feeling of transcending a negative ideology') became much more prevalent in the 1970s, in architecture and literature.

In architecture the term stands for a rejection of architectural modernism, i.e. the tradition represented by, say, Walter Gropius (*Bauhaus*) or Le Corbusier ('A house is a living-machine'). In postmodern architecture the modernist principles of abstraction, simplicity, geometric purity and functionality are discarded in favour of a 'renewed interest in buildings as signs and signifiers and in their referential potential and resources.'[19] 'Deconstructive postmodernism' became an influential movement when the French post-structuralists (Lyotard, Derrida and Baudrillard) were accepted in the United States in the late 1970s. Jencks plausibly suggests that the attraction of the term 'postmodern' lies in the way it captures the thought that we have outgrown modernity and modernism, but without knowing really where we are heading.

The term 'postmodern' attempts, thus, to hold together a number of different ideas and attitudes. Intellectually, postmodernist thought represents a reaction to many aspects of modern philoso-

---

18 In a letter to the *TLS* reprinted in R. Appignanesi and C. Garratt, *Postmodernism for Beginners* (Cambridge, 1995), p. 3.

19 Art. 'postmodern' in *The Cambridge Dictionary of Philosophy*, 1995, p. 635. Cf. Robert B. Pippin, *Modernism as a Philosophical Problem* (Oxford 1991), p. 199: 'The general relation between assumptions inherent in architecture of all historical epochs and broad philosophical issues is not limited to the modernism/postmodernism controversy. The relation between the idea of self-sufficiency and architecture goes back at least to the Tower of Babel story'. The symbol of the Tower of Babel has indeed, fittingly, come to signify – again – the confusions of the contemporary scene.

phy and to the assumptions underlying that philosophy. It is a movement that, rather than outlining or adhering to a particular set of beliefs on specific philosophical issues, radically calls into question the fundamental presuppositions of modern philosophy itself. (One should perhaps note that in attempting to see more precisely what 'postmodernism' 'means' within contemporary thought, one is adopting, strictly speaking, a non-postmodern perspective, for one of the salient features of philosophical postmodernism is the idea that there is no such thing as a fixed meaning to anything, neither world, nor word, nor text, nor individual human subject.) Yet as a reactive movement, postmodernism is – somewhat ironically – also deeply traditional, in that it re-enacts one of the most deep-seated tendencies in Western thought. One has only to think of the Reformation or the French Revolution, to say nothing of other upheavals, to see how ingrained the inclination actually is in Western history to call received wisdom into question, and to strike out in new directions.

There will certainly be disagreement on what precisely are the fundamental assumptions of modern (i.e. post-mediaeval) philosophy, which postmodernism calls into question, but the main targets of postmodern thought would appear to include two central issues that can be dealt with quite briefly. These are, firstly, the notion of an autonomous, clearly defined self, and, secondly, foundationalism.

To begin with the fate of the human self in postmodernism, here there is a noticeable difference from modernism. A modernist poet, like Yeats, could take the experience of dislocation (cf. 'Things fall apart; the centre cannot hold') as a spur to create his own 'subjective centre,' as 'an autonomous self-defining artist,'[20] but 'for postmodernism there is no center at all, the subject itself is "de-centered," no longer an origin or source, but itself a result, a product of multiple social and psychological forces.'[21]

What is this 'decentred self' which crops up frequently in discussions of postmodernism? The expression refers to 'a conception of the self, i.e. of the thinking and acting subject, in which the self is no longer regarded as providing the kind of ultimate grounding for epistemological thinking that is often assumed in traditional forms of philosophy.'[22] Three different sources seem to have contributed

---

20 Pippin, *op. cit.*, p. 156.
21 *Ibid.*, pp. 156f.
22 Article 'decentred self or decentred subject' in *Collins Dictionary of Sociology*, p. 147, on which the rest of the above paragraph is based.

to the emergence of this view: (a) from psychoanalysis has come the
idea that the 'ego' is not in charge of the individual's life, but is in
various, ultimately unaccountable ways affected by the subcon-
scious; (b) from the influence of Saussurean linguistics has come the
notion that, just as in language each element or sign only makes
sense in relation to, and differentiated from, the other elements or
signs in the overall system, so the self ('I') does not make sense in
isolation, but only in relation to, and differentiated from, such terms
as 'you', 'she', they', 'we', etc.; hence the 'self' does not enjoy any
real autonomy or discrete identity;[23] and finally (c) a belief that
autonomy belongs, if anywhere, to culture as such, or, in the case of
a writer, to the text, from which the notion of an author has been
banished, has also played a significant role in this process. In struc-
turalism meaning was at least preserved in a total system of which
the self was one element, even if the self was decentred and thus no
longer centre-stage. But in post-structuralist thought, which feeds
into postmodernism, neither the self nor the system in which the
self is embedded is seen as providing a secure foundation for any
final meaning or truth about the human condition.

This brings us to the second target of the postmodernist critique
of Western thought mentioned above: foundationalism. Postmodernism is associated with the alleged end of foundationalism,
foundationalism being the view that for such intellectual activities
as science or philosophy solid bases do exist, in empirically observable facts, for instance, or self-evident ideas or a priori truths.
Foundationalism is thus an epistemological position that attempts
to justify our beliefs by giving or finding foundations for them that
cannot be doubted.[24]

As a prime example of a foundationalist thinker Descartes, for
one, finds no favour with the postmodernists. For Descartes moved
from what he himself was convinced was indubitable first-person
knowledge to knowledge of the objective (external) world, a move
relying on first-person knowledge (knowledge of the self) as the
foundation of all other knowledge. But, barely a century after
Descartes, the Scottish Enlightenment philosopher David Hume is
sceptical of such Cartesian moves and, curiously enough, already
very close to a postmodern position (if position is not too definite a

---

23 Cf. at the start of Samuel Beckett's novel, *The Unnamable*: 'I, say I.
    Unbelieving.'
24 Cf. R. Scruton, *Modern Philosophy* (London, 1994), p. 47.

term). Roger Scruton remarks that 'Hume was inclined to say that the self is a kind of illusion, as are all the conundrums which derive from it.'[25] Hume himself once confessed that 'whenever I look inside myself, there is no self to be found.'[26] Elsewhere he describes the self as 'only a heap of perceptions.'[27] Indeed the line that goes from Hume via Bertrand Russell to the modern American philosopher Quine ends up at the same point as the conclusions of the post-structuralists, Foucault and Derrida. That is to say, 'the notion of the self' is eliminated 'as the source of consciousness, the arbiter of meaning, the unifying *thing* that thinks. Foucault's remark that "It is not man who takes the place of God, but anonymous thinking, thinking without a subject" sounds like an unconscious echo of Russell's statement in *The Analysis of Mind* that instead of saying "I think" "It would be better to say 'it thinks in me' or better still …'there is a thought in me'".'[28]

Now if, as one spokesman for postmodernism, the American philosopher Richard Rorty, urges, we set aside the foundationalist assumptions shared by the major philosophers of the sixteenth, seventeenth, and eighteenth centuries, we are left free-floating, as it were, with no basis on which to establish hierarchies of intellectual or moral or aesthetic value or truth that would be universally binding. This is one of the consequences to flow from the nihilism diagnosed so ruthlessly in the nineteenth century by Nietzsche, and enacted, according to some observers, in the twentieth.

The forsaking of universal values and canons of taste combines naturally enough, however, with a renewal of interest in local and minority concerns, which many would regard as a plus for postmodernism. This may help to explain, or alternatively, it may be a reflection of, the increased social and political weight now attaching to 'minority' issues in such areas as race (ethnicity), religion, sex, culture and language.[29] (A similar concern for minority interests can be observed in the period of Romanticism, which in its day

---

25 *Op. cit.*, p. 43.
26 Cited in R. C. Solomon, *Continental Philosophy since 1750* (Oxford, 1988), p. 1.
27 William Barrett, *Death of the Soul* (Oxford, 1987), p. 46.
28 Brenda Almond, *Philosophy* (Harmondsworth, 1988), p. 130; the reference to Foucault is to M. Foucault, *The Order of Things* and the reference to Russell is to B. Russell, *The Analysis of Mind*, p. 18.
29 Cf. Pippin, *op. cit.*, p. 157.

rejected the universalising claims or pretensions of the Enlightenment.)[30]

The 'flux and fragmentation' that postmodernism celebrates is notoriously difficult to pin down, as may be becoming clear, so perhaps one way of trying to find our way tentatively, if not through, then at least into the ever-changing world of postmodernism, might be to deal with some of the theorists whose names have become almost synonymous with the movement, rather ironically perhaps, in view of what postmodernism is supposed to believe about the death of the old (Cartesian) self. In what follows it is important to bear in mind, however, that not all those mentioned would accept the label 'postmodern'.

Jean François Lyotard

We may begin with Lyotard (b. 1924) since he has been credited with having popularised the term 'postmodern' through his book *The Postmodern Condition*.[31] 'Simplifying to the extreme', he says, 'I define *postmodern* as incredulity towards metanarratives'. According to one writer 'the main "metanarrative" in question follows the Enlightenment line that science legitimates itself as the bearer of emancipation ... '[32] However all the grand narratives or metanarratives, such as the Myth of Progress, Marxism (an important case for Lyotard, who had been a Marxist himself), Emancipation through Science, and, of course, older metanarratives like the Judaeo-Christian narrative of 'God, Creation, Fall, Redemption and

---

30 Romanticism revolted against the notion that reality has an objective, unchanging structure existing independently of human beings. For the Romantics truth is not discovered, but created by us. They repudiated the idea of a priori (pre-existent), universally valid truths that only needed to be discovered, and substituted instead the ideal of creating truth as an artist might create a work of art. A corollary of this attitude is a new respect for minorities, whose authentically expressed 'truth' may run contrary to traditional, accepted, 'objective', conventional wisdom. On this question see I. Berlin, 'Preface' to H. G. Schenk, *The Mind of the European Romantics* (Oxford, 1966). The attitude of the Romantics is exacerbated in postmodernism, which can thus perhaps be interpreted as an extreme form of neo-Romanticism, but with this important difference: that faith in the autonomy and coherence of the self, which the Romantics retained, has (officially, at any rate) disappeared with the postmodernists.

31 French edition 1979, ET 1984.

32 D. Lyon, *op. cit.*, p. 12.

Eschatological Fulfilment', all of these metanarratives have, according to Lyotard, collapsed. Borrowing an idea from Wittgenstein, Lyotard regards even modern science as now at best to be accepted as one particular language-game, i.e. bereft of any universalist pretensions.

In speaking of the end of metanarratives Lyotard and other theorists of postmodernism are giving voice to a widely perceived lack of any overall vision of reality in the contemporary world. That is to say, no one, according to Lyotard's diagnosis, can any longer see the wood for the trees, for the very simple reason that there is no 'wood' to see, just as there is no 'God', hence no 'God's eye' (over)view of things ...

Thus for Lyotard the idea that any state of affairs, or view of reality, can be legitimated through a metanarrative has foundered in the postmodern world. Fragmentation and the atomisation of social life are the result. It should be noted however that Lyotard's announcement of 'the end of politics' has led some (e.g. Jürgen Habermas) to accuse him of neo-conservatism, since he lacks 'all theoretical justification of an alternative to the social status quo in advanced capitalism.'[33] Habermas' own refusal to abandon, as Lyotard appears to do, the moral imperative of seeking a rationale for any political course of action, is, one may suggest, surely preferable to the alternative of dismissing as an Enlightenment prejudice the need to work out a theoretical legitimation for one's actions. The fact that, as Lenin was fond of pointing out, one is often faced with the need to act in the absence of a completely satisfactory theoretical justification for one's course of action, hardly makes the search for such justification – even if it cannot ever be definitively found within history – redundant, or humanly irrelevant.

Jean Baudrillard

Another influential theorist of the postmodern condition is the French sociologist Jean Baudrillard (b. 1929), who is associated above all with the idea that, through the influence of the mass media, the consumer society is being transformed into a kind of madhouse of ever-proliferating signs which end up by blurring or effacing the distinction between image and reality. Baudrillard caused a bit of a stir by declaring that the Gulf War did not happen, which obviously was something of an exaggeration, but drew attention to the way the material and human substance of life is in danger of being trans-

33 J. G. Merquior, *Foucault* (London, 1985), p. 148.

muted into electronically reproduced images (*simulacra*), thereby losing its specificity and its depth.[34] It is this simulated, humanly empty, world that Baudrillard seems to have in mind by his use of a term like 'hyperreality'. Hyperreality is a condition 'in which the alleged "real" is no more real than the thing which feigns [or reproduces] it.'[35] The overall effect of postmodernity for Baudrillard is thus to produce a 'loss of stable meaning.'[36] Clearly Baudrillard has raised Marx's sense of 'everything solid melting into air' to an almost apocalyptic level.

Michel Foucault

We come, lastly, to two other important theorists of the postmodern situation, both also French like Lyotard and Baudrillard, but whose influence outside France has perhaps been more pervasive than theirs: Michel Foucault and Jacques Derrida.

Firstly, Michel Foucault (1926–1984). Foucault was a French philosopher and historian who worked mainly in Paris, the home of 'radical rhetoric'[37] for the French intelligentsia. Foucault has been an important voice in the twentieth-century French philosophical debate on reason, language, knowledge and power. He has become well known for his historical studies of madness, imprisonment, medicine and sexuality, which are not carried through in the tradition of studies in the 'history of ideas', but seek rather to uncover the linkages between knowledge and power within various societies and institutions. In this endeavour Foucault acknowledges his indebtedness to Nietzsche who, in his own works, had traced connections between the human will to power and belief systems (notably Christianity), suspecting the latter of being merely rationalisations of the former.

The drawback with such a radically sceptical approach to knowledge as Foucault espouses is that if all 'discourse' is assumed to be a more or less sophisticated justification of a set of power-

---

34 These complaints may, arguably, have been anticipated in general terms by Feuerbach when he wrote (in 1843): '... [T]he present age ... prefers the sign to the thing signified, the copy to the original, fancy to reality, the appearance to the essence ...' ('Preface' to *The Essence of Christianity*, tr. George Eliot, New York, 1957, p. xxxix; cf. G. Debord, *La Société du Spectacle*, Paris, 1992, p. 13).

35 *Collins Dictionary of Sociology*, p. 301.

36 *Ibid.*, p. 39.

37 J. G. Merquior, *Foucault*, p. 159.

structures, what exempts the critic's own 'discourse' from a similarly radical scepticism? The rather pessimistic conclusion that all discourse only has the 'authority' of the epoch it reflects to support it, is only true, paradoxically, if it is false.[38] Nietzsche, in fairness, was at least more worried about this problem than Foucault, who seemed content to deny any abiding value to his own critique of what were, from his perspective, false 'discursive practices', exerting power over human bodies at different times and places.

Foucault is unlike Nietzsche too in his revolt against Enlightenment rationalism, and in the absence from his work of anything resembling Nietzsche's 'dionysian' affirmation of 'life', for all his (Nietzsche's) critique of *décadence*. Foucault, as the – or at least one – *enfant terrible* of late twentieth-century French philosophy, combines what appears to be a slightly self-indulgent intellectual anarchism with an extremely bleak view of human prospects; he once spoke of his 'hyperactive pessimism'. In Foucault, postmodernity looks like the second, definitive, 'Fall of man', from which there can be no redemption, unless perhaps one were to see a glimmer of hope in his assertion of a moral value in philosophy's readiness to 'think the unthought', which is also, he claims, a willingness to 'refuse what we are.'[39]

Jacques Derrida

The final postmodernist key-figure I shall discuss is Jacques Derrida, born in Algeria in 1930, but now resident in France. He is perhaps best known for his radical mode of thought, known as 'deconstruction.'

Derrida has argued that philosophers have simply been on the wrong tack in looking for underlying 'essences' or 'first principles' in reality. He himself, drawing on the Swiss linguist Saussure and the German philosopher Heidegger, holds that language, as a system that functions because of the differences inherent in it, cannot be, as traditionally conceived, the unambiguous bearer of truth. Even structuralists like the social anthropologist Lévi-Strauss had still held to this latter, for Derrida untenable, position. Derrida regards the sign (signifier) – which is in any case arbitrary both as an acoustic (spoken) and a visible (written) image – as having no stable semantic relation to that which is signified. For a linguistic

---

38 Cf. R. Scruton, *Modern Philosophy*, p. 6.
39 *Encyclopedia of Western Philosophy and Philosophers*, ed. J. O. Urmson and J. Rée (London, 1991), p. 112.

sign gains its signification from the fact that it is differentiated from other signs within a system (e.g., fat, cat, mat, bat, sat, etc.). Hence its meaning depends on its relation to other (absent) signs and must consequently always be deferred (postponed). Derrida plays on the two meanings of the French verb 'différer' (meaning 'to differ' and 'to defer' or ' to postpone') to make his point, coining the neologism 'différance' to drive it home. What is true at the relatively humble level of phonetics Derrida takes to be transferable or applicable to the altogether higher and more complex level of meaning itself.

Strictly speaking, the 'absent' signs on which the meaning of any specific sign depends are not actually absent, but, in Derrida's terminology, 'self-effacing'. Thus, as one commentator has put it:

> [I]n any spoken or written utterance, the seeming signification is the result only of a 'self-effacing' trace – self-effacing because one is not aware of it – which consists of all the nonpresent meanings whose differences from the present instance are the sole factor which invests the utterance with its 'effect' of having a meaning in itself. The consequence, according to Derrida, is that we can never have a determinate, or decidable, present meaning; he asserts, however, that the differential play of language does produce illusory 'effects' of determinable meanings.
>
> ... [T]here is indeed an 'effect' of meaning in an utterance which is produced by its difference from other meanings, but ... on the other hand, since this meaning can never come to rest in an actual presence, or 'transcendental signified,' its determinate specification is deferred from one substitutive linguistic interpretation to another, in a movement, or 'play,' without end. The meaning of any spoken or written utterance, as Derrida puts it in another of his coinages, is disseminated – a term which includes, among its deliberately contradictory significations, that of having an effect of meaning (a 'semantic' effect), of dispersing meanings among innumerable alternatives, and of negating any specific meaning. There is thus no ground, in the incessant play of différance that constitutes language, for attributing a decidable meaning, or even a finite set of determinately multiple meanings (which he calls 'polysemism'), to any utterance that we speak or write. As Derrida puts it in *Writing and Difference*, p. 280: 'The absence of a transcendental signified extends the domain and the play of signification infinitely.'[40]

---

40 M. H. Abrams, *A Glossary of Literary Terms*, (Orlando, 1988), pp. 204f.

Moreover, just as meaning is not transparently and exhaustively present in any sign, neither can the author of a text any longer be thought of as 'authoritatively' present in that text. The author has no command of a text, and cannot impose meaning on it. As Derrida put it in an interview given a few years ago: the author 'is not in the situation of the creator god *before* his text.'[41] Texts, therefore, as linguistic artefacts do not belong to their authors, for a linguistic system precedes and eludes the full grasp of any author.

The technical Derridean term 'dissemination', mentioned in the above quotation, is relevant to this notion. For Derrida, 'Dissemination is something which no longer belongs to the regime of meaning; it exceeds not only the multiplicity of meaning, but also meaning itself. I attempt to read the movement of this dissemination in the text, in writing; it can't be dominated by either the semantic or the thematic field.'[42] Dissemination seems, thus, to be a sort of irresistible 'supra-semantic' flux, the course of whose finally unspecifiable movement the critic attempts, always unsuccessfully, to chart. For the critic, like everyone and everything else, lives in an infinite multiplicity ('the Many'), from which all possibility of ultimate, transcendent, unitary comprehension ('the One') has been banished. This flux is, however, irresistible in the sense that it is the element in which alone the critic can live, just as a fish can live only in its element of water.

In such circumstances texts themselves can at best only be provisionally interpreted in relation to other texts (this seems to be what is meant by *intertextuality*) and not in relation to any 'truth' outside the text ('il n'y a pas de hors-texte'),[43] whether that 'truth' be the author's mind, or some other 'objective' standard existing allegedly in independence of the text.

It is also in this context that the notion of 'logocentrism' can be located. For Derrida logocentrism is 'the belief that the Word of the *transcendental signifier* (e.g. God, the World Spirit) may provide a foundation for a whole system of thought.'[44] It is 'an attempt which can only ever fail, an attempt to trace the sense of being to the logos, to discourse or reason ... and which considers writing or technique to be secondary to logos. The forms which this has taken in the west are of course influenced by Greek philosophy.'[45] As this comment

---

41 R. Mortley, *French Philosophers in Conversation* (London, 1991), p. 98.
42 *Ibid*.
43 From *De la grammatologie*, quoted in M.H. Abrams, *op. cit.*, p. 203.
44 *Collins Dictionary of Sociology*, p. 148.
45 Mortley, *op. cit.*, p. 104.

prepares us to see, the demise of logocentrism is closely connected in Derrida's mind with the startling claim that the written word takes precedence over the spoken word.

The target at which this claim is aimed is the traditional privileging in the West of the 'notion of speech as the voice or "presence" of consciousness,' which in Derrida's terminology is labelled 'phonocentrism.'[46] In making his claim about the untenability of 'phonocentrism', Derrida is espousing or endorsing the idea that it is 'with writing that language takes on the appearance of what Foucault called "autonomous discourse", without an author, without intention or interpretation, and outside of space, time and context'.[47] In affirming this Derrida is taking up a so-called anti-transcendental stance with regard to truth. 'For Derrida, as for Lévi-Strauss and Foucault, there is no constitution of meaning by a transcendental subject, a point which he makes with characteristic hyperbole by insisting that "texts have no author". Consequently texts do not and cannot express universal meanings, and the point of deconstruction is to do away with "the transcendental signified". He too accepts the fact that one cannot escape from one's historical and cultural context, but he turns this even against Foucault, who could not possibly understand the madness he describes in his work (Foucault, in return, dubbed Derrida *"le petit pédagogue"*).'[48]

Derrida is thus systematically critical of all metaphysical thought, and one might say almost neurotically aware of how our language is shot through with philosophical assumptions which he claims must always be called into question. His thought contains a consistent critique of the main Western tradition in philosophy going back at least to Plato, whom Nietzsche once referred to as 'das grösste Malheur Europas!' (Europe's greatest calamity!)[49] This tradition is, in Derrida's eyes, based on an erroneous desire for, and belief in, some fundamental certainty conveyed by, or rather betrayed in, such philosophical concepts as substance, essence, origin, identity, truth. In *Twilight of the Idols* Nietzsche had already written: 'Today ... we see ourselves as it were entangled in error, *necessitated* to error, to precisely the extent that our prejudice in favour of reason compels us to posit unity, identity, duration, substance, cause, materiality, being ...'[50] Derrida's philosophical 'strat-

---

46 *Collins Dictionary of Sociology*, p. 148.
47 Solomon, *op. cit.*, p. 201.
48 *Ibid.*
49 In a letter to Franz Overbeck (written in Nice, 9 January 1887).
50 *Twilight of the Idols/The Anti-Christ*, tr. R.J. Hollingdale, p. 47.

egy' (as he prefers to call it, rather than 'method') of deconstruction is aimed at uncovering and laying bare such hidden philosophical assumptions in the texts of Western philosophy, even in thinkers like Nietzsche who was himself, of course, already pathologically suspicious of metaphysics.

Deconstruction is therefore a 'project ... to reveal the ambivalence of all texts, which can only be understood in relation to other texts ... and *not* in relation to any "literal meaning" or normative truth.'[51] Putting it slightly differently and more simply, deconstruction can also perhaps essentially be seen as a strategy for puncturing the illusions of philosophers whose claims for their own philosophy cannot be made good and are thus, for Derrida, pretentious. The heart of the supreme Western metaphysical claim is what Derrida 'calls (following Heidegger) ... "the myth of presence", whether this takes the form of the immanent presence of God, or the world as a determinate entity, or the self as an "inner" certainty.'[52] This myth Derrida wishes to subvert. He knows, however, that 'it is an illusion to suppose that one can escape altogether from the pervasive metaphysics of presence, since to put oneself "outside" metaphysics is an indirect way of affirming it;' thus 'he suggests that one has to think in terms which neither affirm nor oppose but *resist* metaphysical concepts.'[53]

Derrida is reminiscent of Nietzsche in his realisation of how difficult it is to subvert a tradition while still operating within it, and having to work quite consciously and, as it were, parasitically with its assumptions (of truth, order, etc.). As Nietzsche once said in a famous remark: 'I fear we are not getting rid of God because we still believe in grammar ... '[54] However in a wider or longer perspective Derrida's thought, like Nietzsche's, might perhaps be seen as being ultimately dependent upon a tradition of radical, and essentially religious, scepticism, a tradition which is aware of the difference, but simultaneously of the connection, between 'truth' and its verbalised, codified, fixed, written expression, or, in more conventional terms, between the 'spirit' and the 'letter' (as in the paradigmatic Western case of the difference, but also the connection, between God and Holy Writ, *the* textual trace – to use a Derridean term – of the deity).

---

51 *Collins Dictionary of Sociology*, p. 148.
52 Solomon, *op. cit.*, p. 200.
53 J. Wintle (ed.), *Dictionary of Modern Culture*, p. 91.
54 *Twilight of the Idols/The Anti-Christ*, p. 48.

Conclusions

A conspicuous feature of postmodernism is that it is a Western (and not, for instance, an Islamic) phenomenon, and can, perhaps, be interpreted as an extreme form of secularisation. The Enlightenment project, or the 'project of modernity', with its belief in Progress, is itself often regarded as a secularised form of the Christian notion of Providence.[55] But how can postmodernism be seen as a secularised form of Western (and hence, Judaeo-Christian) thought?

One might first of all suggest that the postmodernist notion of the decentred self is a version of a very ancient religious notion, that places God and not the self, or even the whole created order, at the centre of reality. In postmodernism, admittedly, the self does not yield to God but to infinite multiplicity. One might therefore not wish to place too much weight on the possible religious genealogy of the decentred self.

However, one is on firmer ground, in my view, in seeing postmodernism as dialectically related to Judaeo-Christianity, if one bears in mind the traditional Judaeo-Christian doctrine of creation. According to this doctrine the world is God's creation, and hence is not intrinsically divine. The world thus enjoys a certain relative autonomy or independence or 'reality', but it is an autonomy ultimately related to, or dependent upon, the deity.

If belief in God falls out of the picture, one is still left with a world, but it is now a world whose giver and guarantor of 'reality' no longer exists. Hence the world's intrinsic value collapses into a void and one ends in nihilism, which in postmodernism translates into such concepts as: loss of the 'transcendental signifier', or absence of 'a transcendental signified' or of any determinate meaning. Similarly, human beings have been traditionally understood by our culture to be made in the image of God, but if there is no God, that image fades away, leaving behind an unidentified, and perhaps unidentifiable, 'humanity'.

But the nihilism just mentioned is a nihilism which is still dialectically related to a now non-existent God. Is it, however, not strange that the world should in these circumstances be interpreted nihilistically, rather than as 'naturally' meaningful and valuable by and in itself? It seems, therefore, plausible to suggest that the concept of nihilism – and thus of postmodernism – itself still moves within the

---

55 For instance, by David Lyon, *op. cit.*, p. 5.

shadow of theism, or within the orbit of religious discourse, that it is in fact, despite its name, an intrinsically, even if parasitically, Judaeo-Christian religious concept.

Related to this thesis is the further consideration that in Christianity the 'word' or 'logos', as the expression of God, has, as the doctrine of the incarnation reveals, never been exhaustively identified with pure thought or pure intellect, nor has the expression of the 'logos' in history been identified with a text (the bible), as in, say, Islam. It is perhaps not too surprising then that, if written texts are – contrary to the deepest instincts of our civilisation, if one may so express it, – given priority (as in Derrida) over the unwritten 'word', no amount of intellectual probing of any text ever yields a satisfactory, final solution as to its 'meaning'. This, a postmodernist might of course retort, is precisely how things are and should be: meaning is never fully accessible in this world, it is always deferred ... But as against this objection, one could argue that the search for meaning or understanding (except in a purely functional or pragmatic sense) is rather futile and literally pointless, if there is, finally, no 'point'. And yet the undeniable attraction of trying to decipher the meaning of texts is emphasised by our seeming inability to resist it,[56] as if, again somewhat instinctively, we assumed that there was a genuine connection (not, however, amounting to an identification) between linguistically expressed meaning, and the most abiding, ultimate explanation of reality that traditionally has been called 'God'.

---

56 Cf. Kant's idea that although thought cannot grasp the a priori conditions of our existence, neither can it resist the desire to do so. See Alastair Hannay, *Kierkegaard* (London, 1991), pp. 23f.

PART IV
Locating God

CHAPTER ELEVEN

Where is God?

*Cry aloud, for he is a god; either he is musing, or he has gone aside,
or he is on a journey, or perhaps he is asleep and must be awakened.*
— 1Kings 18:27

*If God were suddenly condemned to live the life which He has
inflicted on men, He would kill Himself.*

— Alexandre Dumas fils

*The major poetic idea in the world is and always has been the idea of
God.*   — Wallace Stevens

The simulating obscurity of the world

A sceptic looking for indications of God's existence might be forgiven for thinking that, if God exists, he has managed to keep the secret of his whereabouts well-guarded until now. Especially at times of great crisis, people often wonder why God will not speak up, declare his hand and put the world out of its misery. On the other hand, from the religious tradition comes, as it were, the opposite sentiment: that, if God were to reveal himself unambiguously, the world would not be able to withstand the experience, or as the bible puts it: man cannot look on the face of God and live.

A vital distance between God and man must seemingly then be maintained if we are to exist. Hence faith – our vital connection with God through which we search for our own identity and meaning – must always be different from, or other than, sight. And, consequently, trying to 'prove' faith must involve one in either circular argument or infinite regress. For to verify any alleged experience of or 'sighting' of God, one must appeal finally to some a priori notion of divinity, thus assuming what one had to prove. Such a procedure is clearly circular or, if one persists in it, can at best lead one to question one's basic notion of divinity backwards *ad infinitum*. Thus, as just said, faith must always be something other than direct vision or perception, and hence intellectual enquiry can never force anyone to adopt or abandon a faith, as if one had no option but, as the French say, to 'surrender' to the evidence.

For if the intellectual illumination or penetration of existence were so powerful as to make all reality irresistibly clear, then the ultimate answers to life's questions would be available to us within some conceptual framework, such as Hegel's dialectic. The latter would itself then necessarily be more ultimate than the 'ultimate answers', it would usurp their place, rendering them in fact 'penultimate'. Faith resists such a surrender. Any intellectual system that 'accommodates the mess' of existence, in Beckett's phrase, is always suspect. As Schopenhauer, Hegel's implacable antagonist, writes somewhere: 'Was dem Herzen widerstrebt, lässt der Kopf nicht ein' (What the heart is reluctant to accept, the head will not admit). First principles and ultimate answers must then be that beyond which one cannot go, to echo Anselm, conceptually or in any other way. Ultimate answers or beliefs can therefore only be believed in, witnessed to, pointed to, or affirmed, but they cannot be held in the palm of our hands; rather it is we who are, as it were, held in the palm of their hands.

Kolakowski, in agreement with Pascal, argues that to expect clear answers from God in the midst of the world is to 'beg the question', the question being that in the universe of faith the notion of evidence is entirely different from the empirical evidence demanded by the sciences. He continues:

> Whoever believes in God's presence in the world, has to admit that empirically His presence is ambiguous. Clearly, there would be no need of faith if the course of world affairs followed directly and unmistakably the norms of justice; this would mean that we live in Paradise... Life in exile is bound to be ambiguous, God's signs are never clear, trusting Him is inevitably to defy the limits of natural knowledge.[1]

Kolakowski raises this matter again at the end of *Metaphysical Horror* only to repeat that the question is 'wrongly asked',[2] for two reasons. Firstly, we have no means of knowing the difference between the world we have and a hypothetical other world where all would be clear. Thus, presumably, the question why do we not have another, clearer world is ultimately no different from and just as unanswerable as the question: why do we have this one?

1   L. Kolakowski, *Religion*, p. 49.
2   *Metaphysical Horror*, p. 119.

Secondly, if we knew the reason why the meaning of the world is hidden or indecipherable, it would possibly no longer be so. Hence part of the indecipherability of the world consists precisely in our failure to understand why it should be indecipherable. The world's indecipherability is also, I suspect, its saving grace, saving it from ever having to surrender all its secrets. 'Nature loves to hide,' as Heraclitus put it. And Gracián reminds us: 'secrecy has something of the lustre of the divine about it.'[3] Whereas Socratic questioning is finally indistinguishable from torture.[4]

Yet the stimulating obscurity of the world, which seems to be at the root of all religion and all metaphysics,[5] once felt, is a kind of nagging revelation that never fades, and bears out a saying of Paul Valéry's: 'A difficulty is a light... An insurmountable difficulty is a sun.'[6] To regard religion from this angle might make one more open to the suggestion that the real religious question is not whether God exists, but why we do, indeed why anything at all apart from God exists, when no reason can be found for why it should. In this perspective, the real mystery to which religion seeks to draw our attention, may not be God after all, but ourselves and the universe into which we appear to have stumbled.

To put the same idea somewhat differently, religion is not something we have but it is something we are. We do not have a religious problem, we are a religious problem, or in St Augustine's pithy formulation: life is not a spectacle but a predicament.[7] Christianity has accommodated man's precarious, ambiguous, 'unsettled' or 'undecided' status in the world in its doctrine of the transcendence and immanence of God in whose image we exist and who is in the world but radically other than it, like ourselves in our own created way. The 'unsettled' nature of human existence has been variously described in the history of Christianity. The theologians of the early church spoke of man as being *capax Dei* (literally: 'capable of God'). To take two examples from the twentieth century, the expressions 'supernatural existential' (Rahner) and 'praecogni-

---

3   Baltasar Gracián, *The Oracle* §160, tr. L. B. Walton (London, 1953), p. 171.

4   'The Socratic method *intensified* – I mean *torture*' (Lichtenberg, *Aphorisms*, p. 178).

5   Cf. Pascal Quignard, *Le sexe et l'effroi* (Paris, 1994), p. 10: 'l'homme est un regard désirant qui cherche une autre image derrière tout ce qu'il voit' (in man there is the desire to look for another image behind everything he sees).

6   Quoted in W. V. O. Quine, *Quiddities: an intermittently Philosophical Dictionary* (Harmondsworth, 1987) p. 6.

7   Mentioned by Ernest Gellner, *Thought and Change* (London, 1972), p. 31.

tio inchoativa' (Balthasar) both refer to the real but not completely definable human capacity for transcendence. Christian tradition interprets this transcendence as being directed towards union with God. However, clearly, not all interpretations of human indeterminacy are favourable to theism. One thinks of Nietzsche, whose thought is atheistic, but who sees man as 'the animal *whose nature has not yet been fixed.*'[8]

Literature in particular – though not only literature – lives, it seems to me, from the 'undecided' or 'unclarified' quality of human existence, whose intriguing mixture of the unfathomable and the coherent makes it at once frustrating and beautiful, an apt projection of the transcendent God. When Rimbaud wrote: 'I is another' (*Je est un autre*) he evoked the elusive immanence of transcendence. For transcendence is what makes an 'I' possible, partly intelligible but finally enigmatic, 'unpossessible'. In a sense one does not even have a self to call one's own[9] (cf. Borges' famous short 'parable' 'Borges and I'). Kant put it in his own terms, contrasting appearance and reality: 'I have no *knowledge* of myself as I am, but merely as I appear to myself.'[10] Nothing that can be said about the reality of human subjectivity will ever exhaust it. Here volubility and silence can finally coincide, another happy *coincidentia oppositorum*. Transcendence is thus not merely an aspect of human subjectivity. Rather it is both immanent in every human subjectivity and also that against, or in relation to, which a human subjectivity can provisionally (mis)understand itself. The Greek adage 'Know thyself' may have been meant as a joke.[11]

However the question of divine transcendence arises in a more directly accessible way when one considers the contingency of life, discussed in a previous chapter. Yet it is not so much that the universe should exist at all which really moves us; but – *tua res agitur* – the fact that our personal arrival on earth in a somewhat eerie universe has more than a touch of the gratuitous about it, *that* is per-

---

8 *Beyond Good and Evil*, §62.
9 Cf. Kafka's pun on the German *sein*, mentioned in Chapter 3.
10 *Critique of Pure Reason*, tr. N. Kemp Smith, B 158.
11 Cf., however, the following sombre observation of Cioran's: 'He who sees himself *as he is* rises above him who raises the dead. The saying comes from a saint. Not to know oneself is the law for everyone, a law which it is dangerous to infringe. The truth is that no one has the courage to infringe it, and that is what explains the saint's exaggeration' (E. M. Cioran, *Aveux et anathèmes*, p. 28).

plexing, not to say frightening.[12] We never feel quite at home here. To human beings the universe often seems, in the revealing German term, *unheimlich*. This ancient, indeed archaic experience has fostered the sense of life on earth as an exile of sorts and not man's final home. To an innocent eye the evidence is of course – how could it be otherwise? – ambiguous. For it is compatible with seeing the human race as simply a blind alley on the evolutionary map, rather than, as Herder once put it, 'God's risk' – the hazard-laden consequence of a gracious (and gratuitous) divine act, which is still being played out.

Regarding the first of those two possibilities, it may be that the human mind – at least in some cases – is reluctant to entertain the conclusion, especially when there exists for it no finally decisive evidence, that the whole process of the universe is an entire absurdity with no beginning or end, no meaning, no order, no truth, no goal. Final absurdity may be difficult to countenance but it may nonetheless be true (whatever *that* could then mean), even if we cannot see how or why.

Yet should we not suspect that the very possibility of a notion like the 'truth' or 'meaning' of the whole cosmic process makes no sense, could not even enter into the human mind, if in fact there is no transcendent source of such truth or meaning? ('[God] has put eternity into man's mind, yet so that he cannot find out what God has done from the beginning to the end,' as Ecclesiastes has it.) For, as was stressed in a previous chapter, the very concept of 'totality' is, surely, intellectually unattainable and thus, strictly speaking, unthinkable from within the cosmos itself. How can the part conceive of the totality with its putative beginning, middle and end? For as individuals we find ourselves always already in the middle of things, before any reflection, still less any decision on our part, can occur. We have thus no say in our beginning or in our end, though we may wriggle around on life's hook in the period in between. However, even when applied to 'creation', to say nothing of 'God', notions like 'beginning', 'end' and 'totality' are literally 'off limits'. They are inconceivable to us, and, if applied to the cosmic process, may only be used analogically, i.e. by extrapolation from limited human ventures which do have a beginning, middle and end. The best we can do is to be aware of our cognitive limits

---

12 Cf. Pascal's much-quoted *Pensées* (fr. 201): 'Le silence éternel de ces espaces infinis m'effraie' (The eternal silence of those infinite spaces frightens me).

and imagine that something must lie beyond them, to constitute them as limits.

Hence if one must talk about all of existence or 'existence as such' – an impulse which it is humanly difficult to resist for good – it cannot be because one seriously hopes to comprehend the whole of even one's own experience, let alone the whole of reality. It can, realistically speaking, only be to register a sense of wonderment, mingled with unease (the *mysterium tremendum et fascinans*) at the opacity of a world transcending the individual so comprehensively.

This dual reaction to existence is evidenced in modern times – to take just two examples – in the way contemplation of the widely extending horizons of the universe (outwards and inwards) opened up by the modern physical sciences can lead to competing conclusions: an awareness of the sheer grandeur and irreducible complexity of the material world balanced against a suspicion that any individual's role within it must be insignificant. Small wonder that Saint-John Perse believed science and poetry 'put the same question to the same abyss.'[13] And similarly, the discoveries of the historical and social sciences can vastly increase understanding of the ways in which major world-shaping cultural traditions are forged by the activities of anonymous millions guided, as Hegel would have it, by the 'cunning of reason', but at the same time such knowledge can also heighten the feeling of the individual's almost total unimportance.

One may of course object that this is a crudely materialistic or quantitative way of looking at human existence. As Pascal noted a long time ago: 'Through space the universe grasps me and swallows me up like a speck; through thought I grasp it'.[14] And as St Leo the Great indicated, an even longer time ago, in a Christmas sermon: 'For if we are the temple of God and the Spirit of God dwells within us, what each of the faithful has in his soul is greater than what can be seen in the heavens.'[15] But while a believer may certainly rest assured that God will not be moved to neglect us by either the physical immensity of the universe or the comparative puniness of humanity, how on the other hand can one argue against a suspicion of our final insignificance and meaninglessness, once it has taken root in a human consciousness? Elias Canetti described

---

13 Quoted by Michael Hamburger, *The Truth of Poetry* (Harmondsworth, 1972), p. 333.

14 *Pensées* (fr. 113), tr. A. J. Krailsheimer, p. 59.

15 *Sermon Nativ.* 7, 2. 6.

Angst as 'God's heartbeat within us.'[16] J. G. Hamann (1730–1788) remarked that *Angst* was the only sign of our difference from the world. But what is gained even if all, including those not religiously inclined, agree that the 'self-conscious' or 'spiritual' dimension of human existence makes it unquestionably of a different kind from the existence of purely physical matter? Different, yes; but where can one go with this difference? All 'differed up' and nowhere to go … And does humanity just not know where to go, or is there finally nowhere to go? Is difference then simply its own reward?

While it is difficult to dispel suspicions of meaninglessness by argument, one may still hope that they will finally be discovered to be unfounded. Indeed were they well founded, they would constitute paradoxically an expression of truth or meaning, irreconcilable surely with outright absurdity. When however we realise that our sun is expected to die eventually, and that any life still left on this planet will die with it,[17] this may well give rise to some anxious questions: if life as we know it on earth will one day cease to exist, what will have become of the life on earth that preceded our planet's extinction? If cosmic evolution made possible and prepared the way for biological evolution, which in turn made possible human evolution, will the whole process have been for nothing? Has it no ultimate future, no ultimate meaning? However, to say that the slow evolution which has characterised the life of the universe is a futile process, rather than one that has value, but whose full understanding lies in the future, is surely to make an act of faith in meaninglessness. And what guarantees the superiority of such a faith over that of traditional Christianity?

God and evil

The ancient dilemma, mentioned at the end of the last section – meaning or meaninglessness? – can of course simply be refused and killed off, but it has a way of rising from the dead. One may say: 'Sufficient unto the day is the passing thereof' – the banality of the daily routine from daybreak till nightfall, followed by the recurrent encounter with the long hours of darkness, hauntingly evoked by Beckett in '… *but the clouds* …' However out of 'the deepening

---

16 *Die Fliegenpein* (Frankfurt a/M, 1995), p. 61.
17 Cf. Theodosius Dobzhansky, *The Biology of Ultimate Concern* (London 1971), p. 40.

shades' the old questions, like the owl of Minerva but not so wise, inexorably arise.

What brings them back on a fairly regular basis is the pain of existence, natural and, perhaps even more so, moral suffering, for which no adequate pain-killer has yet been invented. 'If there were no death,' Feuerbach said, 'there would be no religion.' But why draw the line at death? If there were no suffering, there would probably be no religion either. Yet it is a delicate matter to try to relate human suffering to God without seeming to exploit the former, or the latter. Since the most intense human suffering often has a moral source, the question of the relation between suffering and God usually turns on the question of God's relation to evil, and hence to morality. This question I now propose to look at.

Morality has since time immemorial been interwoven with religion, until that is to say the emergence of mass atheism in the modern world. But yet even here, the old connection persists in new ways. Since the Enlightenment, which tended to sideline purely metaphysical 'proofs' for God's existence, the role of morality in religious apologetics for example has increased, not always or necessarily one imagines for their mutual benefit. The so-called moral argument for theism has indeed often been wielded to great emotional effect. Dostoevsky's ambiguous pronouncement: 'If there is no God, everything is permissible,' can certainly possess a shock-value in forcing the question of the source and sanction of morality on the attention of a possibly uninterested public. But even the less dramatic and less menacing fact that moral experience is a universal human phenomenon leads many to assume that the source of humanity's moral sense must ultimately be connected with an unconditional principle of goodness, i.e. with the transcendent God. What is at stake here is not any specific moral system, but rather the fact that human beings experience a moral dimension in life, regardless of how they try to structure it in different cultures. According to this argument, those committed to respect moral values as exercising an unconditional claim on them, must by implication believe in the reality of a more than human source and foundation for these values, which we call 'God'. 'Thus, Immanuel Kant argues that both immortality and the existence of God are "postulates" of the moral life, i.e. beliefs which can legitimately be affirmed as presuppositions by one who recognizes duty as rightfully laying upon one an unconditional claim.'[18]

---

18 J. Hick, *Philosophy of Religion*, p. 29.

There seems to be some force in this argument: if we acknowledge moral claims as transcending other interests – as the notion of
'unconditionality' implies – this is in fact to believe in the existence
of a reality beyond or other than the natural world, a reality moreover that attracts us and whose attention we find undeniable,
indeed on occasion irresistible. However, the weakness of the moral
argument for God's existence, at least as Kant promotes it, is
twofold. In the first place, as Schleiermacher argued implicitly
against Kant in his *Speeches on Religion*, 'to resort to "postulating"
God as a demand of practical reason in effect compromised the
principle of autonomy itself'[19] which Kant was keen to safeguard
for morality. For Kant's assumption that only God could bring
about the coincidence of duty and happiness eventually for human
beings surely undermined belief in the total autonomy and purity
of moral endeavour. In Schleiermacher's own words: 'If the desire
for happiness is foreign to morality, later happiness can be no more
valid than earlier ...'[20] And in the second place the whole concept of
the unconditional authority of moral obligation can be called into
question, and so the historical experience of moral values and oblig-
ations cannot be proved to point conclusively to the existence of a
transcendent moral reality and authority, which religion tends to
identify with God. For many, what theists call the unconditional
authority of moral obligation is simply the awareness of claims that
are relative to the specific needs, interests and ambitions of a particular society at a given period, hence claims that have only a pragmatic, not an absolute status, claims that do not therefore point very
far beyond the specific reality of the time and place where they
manifest themselves. In short, in a reductionist interpretation
morality is understood simply as preserving or on occasion even
making human existence 'richer' and hence more 'liveable' than it
might otherwise be. It is a purely human arrangement.

Were one to try to stiffen the moral argument for theism, one
might point out that for example the human desire for moral perfection, though not one that can be fulfilled on earth, nevertheless
refuses to disappear. And if human beings were to die like wasps,
this desire would seem difficult to account for. Does this not strongly suggest that we are in fact destined to transcend death and reach
moral fulfilment elsewhere? However, here again, those who
choose to see the phenomenon of morality as only a question of the

19 B. M. G. Reardon, *Religion in the Age of Romanticism*, p. 33.
20 *On Religion*, p. 20; cf. Reardon, *op. cit.*, pp. 33f.

human organism's ability to adapt itself ever more adequately to its environment, who see in morality only a kind of biological *tour de force*, will presumably not be inclined to read into it any kind of religious or transcendental significance. They will be able to give, from their own point of view, a perfectly (if that is not an odd word in the circumstances) satisfactory explanation even of the desire for moral perfection, by seeing in it for instance an evolutionary drive that saves us from ever becoming complacent.

If one does insist on giving a purely this-worldly account of moral experience, one does of course have a point. For what *difference* to one's sense of morality, or indeed more seriously to one's actual conduct, is made by a belief that the ultimate source of moral value is God, and that moral fulfilment is to be reached only after death? As against that, of course, one can always ask why should belief in God as the ultimate explanation for moral experience have to have any practical or, as it were, utilitarian consequences? Is truth not its own reward? And may not the best things in life be free?

There is however a further complication in the moral argument for theism that is, from, say, a Kantian perspective, not without a certain piquancy. This lies in the fact that, for reasons they might be inclined to term 'moral', many would reject any invitation to partake in divine company, because God is seen as the monstrous creator of the world. Here God is not *not* believed in, but the world of pain and suffering he is believed to have created is judged to be the ultimate argument against having any voluntary contact with him. No matter what end God might be able to arrange for his creation, the means necessary for its implementation are deemed immoral, hence unjustifiable. As George Santayana put it: 'To remove an evil is not to remove the fact that it has existed... And the case is much worse if we are expected to make our heaven out of the foolish and cruel pleasures of contrast, or out of the pathetic obfuscation produced by a great relief. Such a heaven would be a lie, like the sardonic heavens of Calvin and Hegel. The existence of any evil anywhere at any time absolutely ruins a total optimism.'[21] (Christianity, wisely or shrewdly, has, it should be said, usually tended to avoid the word 'optimism', speaking rather of 'hope', which of course is not a human attitude or emotion, but a theological virtue. At least the immensity of the problem is thus respected. And from the human side hope is perhaps – as with so many other theological terms – best described negatively as, in Manès Sperber's words, 'the categorical refusal of discouragement, hence a *resistance to resignation*'.)[22] In short, judged by a venerable moral principle, the end, even if that End be the Eschaton, does not justify the means. This, as is well known, is the position of Dostoevsky's creation, Ivan Karamazov. It incorporates, however, an objection to belief in a good God that, in Christian tradition, goes back at least as far as the second century heresiarch Marcion.

Marcion's objection is summarised in an ancient gnostic story, retold concisely by Cioran:

> When Christ descended into hell, the just of the old law, Abel, Enoch and Noah, were suspicious of his teaching and did not respond to his call. They took him to be an emissary of the Tempter whose snares they feared. Only Cain and his like embraced his doctrine or pretended to, followed him and left hell with him. – That is what Marcion the heresiarch taught.
>
> 'The happiness of the evil man' – who, more than Marcion, has consolidated this old objection to the idea of a merciful or at least an honourable Creator, who else has seen, with such penetrating insight, how unanswerable it is?[23]

The problem of evil has returned to haunt monotheism with unparalleled virulence in this century. One of the most eloquent and powerful voices to express the challenge of evil to any belief in a just God is that of the Jewish writer Primo Levi, a survivor of Auschwitz. In *The Drowned and the Saved* he writes:

> Like [Jean] Améry, I too entered the Lager as a non-believer, and as a non-believer I was liberated and have lived to this day; actually, the experience of the Lager with its frightful iniquity has confirmed me in my laity. It has prevented me, and still prevents me, from conceiving of any form of providence or transcendent justice.[24]

Levi's inability to countenance belief in a just providential order is unforgettably conveyed in his confession of how he resisted the

---

22 M. Sperber, *Nur eine Brücke zwischen Gestern und Morgen* (Munich, 1983), p. 109.

23 E. M. Cioran, *Aveux et Anathèmes* (Paris, 1987), p. 9.

24 Primo Levi, *The Drowned and the Saved*, tr. R. Rosenthal (London, 1989) p. 117. Jean Améry, the name taken in the 1930s by the Austrian Jewish intellectual Hans Mayer, also survived the Nazi death camps and also, like Primo Levi, committed suicide a few years ago.

temptation to pray in his place of torment. His words, which show how he kept faith with his own unbelief, are a harrowing but wonderfully human witness to one man's sublime integrity against unimaginable odds:

> I must nevertheless admit that I experienced (and again only once) the temptation to yield, to seek refuge in prayer. This happened in the October of 1944, in the one moment in which I lucidly perceived the imminence of death. Naked and compressed among my naked companions with my personal index card in hand, I was waiting to file past the 'commission' that with one glance would decide whether I should immediately go into the gas chamber or was instead strong enough to go on working. For one instant I felt the need to ask for help and asylum; then, despite my anguish, equanimity prevailed: you do not change the rules of the game at the end of the match, nor when you are losing. A prayer under these conditions would have been not only absurd (what rights could I claim? and from whom?) but blasphemous, obscene, laden with the greatest impiety of which a non-believer is capable. I rejected that temptation: I knew that otherwise were I to survive, I would have to be ashamed of it.[25]

Such a testimony gives the lie to the glib remark, found on the lips of some 'believers', more one suspects for their own comfort than that of those in danger (if not out of resentment against those who refuse to 'toe the metaphysical line'), that 'there are no atheists in a lifeboat.' There are. (Moreover, just to temper the disputed remark with an innocent question: 'How many theists in a lifeboat really believe in God?')

There is in the Jewish tradition an attitude manifested quintessentially in the Book of Job where the believer, pushed beyond endurance, vents his anger on God and seeks an explanation for his sufferings. (Rather than rebels Christianity appears to produce apostates who are fired by something more akin to contempt and even hatred for their former Divinity than pure anger.)[26] Paul Celan the German-speaking Jewish Romanian poet who lost his family in the Nazi death camps, and like Levi and Améry ended his own life, finds a way of saying the unsayable when he goes beyond an atti-

---

25 Ibid., pp. 117f.
26 Cf. George Orwell's remark about 'the sort of atheist who does not so much disbelieve God as personally dislike Him,' quoted in M. Parris, Scorn, p. 251.

tude of anger, and in a stark reversal of traditional roles invites God in the terse poem *Tenebrae* to pray to history's suffering victims. With infinite ambiguity and poignantly ironic echoes of Hölderlin's famous poem 'Patmos', Celan suggests that God is being called inexorably to account by life's victims for the anguish of the world.

Any form of monotheism is thus confronted inescapably with the problem of evil and suffering, however reluctant it may be to walk on such holy ground, the place above all others in the modern world where the *mysterium tremendum et fascinans* speaks unmistakably to us. The indescribable human degradation of the twentieth century appals and fascinates, as only human horror can, because humanity is indivisible, a truth taught over and over again to the world by the Jews in their writings and even more so in the language of their own flesh and blood. This truth shines forth most agonisingly, most undeniably and with a divine irony in the form of its most explicit denial.

Faced with the reality of evil and suffering, Christianity has no intellectual message to offer the world. For the doctrine of the incarnation and belief in the redemptive sacrifice of the God-man Jesus Christ obviously do not 'solve' the problem of evil. Even though Christians may believe and hope that one day 'all shall be well,' this is a belief and a hope that relate to the End of Time, which we cannot yet see. And equally, even though Christians may believe that Christ's sacrifice has in some incomprehensible way 'atoned for' the evils of history, and 'taken away the sins of the world,' there is no way of saying how this can be so. Such a vision of reality does not even have an unambiguously clear point of contact with moral experience. For, while someone may freely and meritoriously endure evil and suffering in the place of another, what can we say about the undeserved suffering inflicted on unwilling victims since the dawn of history? Can their suffering be justified? We have no answer to this question. And we do not even know whether that is because there is no answer; or because the answer is one to which we have no access.

Even were we to say that suffering, willingly borne, can reveal the reality of a power that is even more 'real' than suffering, and that this power radiates from the passion, death, and resurrection of Jesus, would that not be to take a Pelagian step and make of Jesus 'merely' an exemplar of human resilience, whom we could try to imitate, but in whom we could no longer see a divine redeemer? Perhaps it is sufficient for Christian faith to say that what differentiates Jesus from us and makes him uniquely the redeemer, is 'simply' that he triumphed over evil in the resurrection, as his first followers claimed. As a result the subsequent followers of Jesus have in him not only an example of a power that is more 'real' than evil – which many other victims of evil could also show – but they also have in Jesus contact with a power that emerged from the encounter with evil mysteriously enriched and transfigured, a power that eventually was declared to be divine. Yet no attempt to 'explain' the Christian mystery of redemption can be other than ham-fisted. Since for Christian faith redemption is explicitly tied to the reality of the living God, it must always be more than any con-figuration of ideas can suggest.

However, to return directly to the problem of evil, it should be observed, once again, that it cannot, curiously enough, be a 'prob-lem' for many who would certainly not wish to deny the reality of what is normally called evil, but who could not describe it as the 'problem of evil'. For the expression 'problem of evil' is in fact a reli-gious expression, and to use it at all is to be irretrievably locked into a religious view of the world. That is to say, unless one is a gnostic dualist, 'evil' only becomes the 'problem of evil' for those who believe in a good and omnipotent God. For those who do not, 'evil' can only be part of human experience and to pure reason can consti-tute no more a 'problem' than the reality of good. For unrepentant rationalists, life is a variable mixture of good and bad. 'Evil' is not a problem, but simply a brute fact. Thus to see 'evil' as a 'problem' is, to repeat, the mark of a religious person. No matter how hard or impossible it might seem to reconcile evil with God, the two seem inseparable, and both would appear to stand or fall together. At least, evil cannot stand alone, although our hope is that good can.

That is to say, were one to try to solve the 'problem of evil' by concluding that it makes belief in God impossible, as the Marquis de Sade insisted in his *Dialogue entre un prêtre et un moribond*, if one were to cut the Gordian knot in this manner, then in taking the step of abolishing God one would at the same stroke also have abolished evil, for evil can only be regarded as evil in relation to God. In a nat-uralistically conceived world, vice and virtue are, in the words of Taine, 'products like sulphuric acid and sugar.' For if there is no God, then neither is there any evil, only facts, what Nietzsche as we have seen called 'the innocence of becoming', life conceived as a stream of morally neutral, value-free, valueless phenomena, beyond the distinction we call good and evil. For Nietzsche all human interpretations of the world are fictional: we impose on things and events the meanings we wish them to have; there is no *logos* to make the facticity of the world comprehensible in intellectual or moral terms. This is, if pressed even slightly, of course a self-destructing position, but it is more important to see it as a desperate, distraught, almost frenetic solution to the problem of evil: what cannot be understood or redeemed must be simply endorsed, including evil, and then said to be thus redeemed. Such a 'solution' to the 'problem of evil' seems however to leave an even greater problem in its wake. The Nietzschean price for redemption is unpayable. The cure is worse than the problem.

To sum up this part of the discussion, the argument for the existence of God from moral experience is at best inconclusive but, what is more worrying, it can even be double-edged. For while moral experience may well be seen to point beyond itself to a transcendent source, for Christian faith what is at stake is the nature of that source. And for some people moral reasons speak powerfully *against* believing in the goodness of such a source, and hence against believing in God altogether. Those on the other hand to whom the idea of a transcendent God is meaningless to start with, can point to 'nature, red in tooth and claw', at the whole process euphemistically termed 'evolution' which reveals tremendous violence perpetrated by animals on each other, and worse still, the moral wickedness of man and the suffering inflicted on human beings by natural disasters — and conclude, with Stendhal, that 'God's only excuse is that he does not exist.'[27] If belief in God is nevertheless still maintained in the teeth of such difficulties, it might be then, paradoxically, not because of, but in spite of, the tug of our ordinary moral instincts. What might stop us taking the drastic and dramatic step of pushing our sense of outrage to the point of abolishing God altogether, is an awareness of the question: what would this do for the world and its horrors? Moreover if belief in God collapsed, could those horrors still retain their soul-destroying meaning? Our sense of good's superiority over evil can, it seems to me, despite all our mixed moral feelings, only in the end be intensified by the pressure of enormous evil.

---

27 Cf. J. Hick, *Evil and the God of Love* (London, 1970), p. ix. This quip is used also, not unexpectedly, by Nietzsche (*Ecce Homo*, 'Why I am so Clever', §3, p. 58).

What to choose?

Still, however one tries to deal with the problem of evil, the least that can be said about it is that it continues to be an embarrassment for theistic belief. It is the perpetually open wound in the body of theism. It even leads some to conclude that good and evil are equal ontological first principles, and others, like Schopenhauer, to believe that 'ultimate reality' is evil. Such possible reactions to the problem of evil show that belief in God is not merely a question of the existence, but even more so, of the moral nature of God. Is God, the creator of the world, benevolent or malevolent?

One possible answer to this worrying question may be suggested by the common human assumption that good is how things ought to be, or how they will eventually work out ('Oh yet we trust that somehow good/Will be the final goal of ill', as Tennyson has it), and that evil is an intruder in the divine scheme of things, the snake in the grass (but how did it get there?). Furthermore the notion of creative, and in some obscure sense, even necessary suffering can be found in the testimony of many civilisations. Thus the great tragedians of ancient Greece or of seventeenth-century France reveal through the sufferings of the characters in their plays that man belongs to a moral universe in fact: he may try to break out of his proper sphere, thus bringing great suffering, even disaster, upon himself and others, but ultimately he must fail to do so. We, the onlookers, realise with awe and relief (the true *catharsis*) – *not* the relief Santayana had in mind in the quotation given above, which I take to be the 'cavalry to the rescue' kind of relief – that the moral order of life cannot in fact be destroyed, but is always restored after every human violation. Reality always ultimately reasserts itself.

Not all, of course, will accept such a reading of Tragedy, or – more to the point – accept that it relates us in any redemptive or salvific sense to God. For not all will accept the potentially redemptive value of 'Tragic relief'. A fairly widespread, pessimistic reading of the human condition, going back in its typically modern expression to the Romantic period, though with much older roots in human experience, does not deny the pain of existence. Indeed it almost seems to revel with exuberant indignation in it. Hence the last thing it craves for is immortality. This represents a complete reversal of the Judaeo-Christian attitude to human existence, for which life, though historically flawed, is fundamentally good. Human fulfilment is sought in God through, not in isolation from, the vicissitudes of this earthly life. However for a thinker like the French aphorist Chamfort (1741–1794), 'Living is an illness to which sleep provides relief every sixteen hours. It's a palliative. The remedy is death.' The equally dispiriting outlook on life evoked by an unknown author in the early nineteenth-century German work *The Nightwatches of Bonaventura* (1804) is symptomatic of a mood that is still prevalent in the contemporary world:

> Life, or man's life in the world, at any rate, is a delusion, a series of masks thrown over a core of chaotic meaninglessness. Life is not only transitory, ending in death; it is so meaningless that an after-life would be a prospect horrible beyond description. The loving, all-wise, trustworthy God of the Judaeo-Christian tradition is gone; in his place is a fumbler who has spoiled his creation, which harbours also the devil, with his malicious laughter. In the midst of this howling chaos cowers the ego, consuming itself to no purpose, and able to retain its integrity by calling attention constantly to the true condition of reality.[28]

From such a perspective it is clear, as was said at the beginning of this section, that it is not so much God's existence that is the problem of modernity but the moral nature of 'ultimate reality'. That is to say, is God good or evil? Or is God perhaps somehow both good and evil? And indeed is it even possibly immoral for orthodox religious believers to believe in a good God, given the evidence of history? On this precise question, surely part of the tension generated by Job's struggle with God over his own personal fate, or by Abraham's debate with God on the fate of Sodom and Gomorrah (Genesis 18), can be attributed to the unspoken fear of both Abraham and Job that God might possibly be evil, and hence no longer worthy of belief or trust?

Human beings, who may wonder about God's nature, can of course make a choice in this regard and act upon it. One could believe, and hope, that God is good, and try to behave accordingly. But one's belief and actions will not of course make God good, if he is not already good intrinsically. Yet the alternative possibility is, one must concede, emotionally hard to swallow. For to assume that the supreme, transcendent reality on which all else depends is itself a force for evil, as it appears to be for Schopenhauer, seems

---

28 J. L. Sammons, *Die Nachtwachen von Bonaventura. A Structural Interpretation* (The Hague, 1965), p. 78, quoted in S. Prawer (ed.), *The Romantic Period in Germany* (London, 1970), p. 8.

inevitably to invite that one imitate such an evil god. And why not, if everything began with, and will ultimately end up in, evil?

However, despite the intellectual confusion about God, many evaluate their experience almost intuitively, that is to say, without any systematic reflection, and they live out responses to the grand questions of existence in their daily routine. They sometimes even reach a kind of wisdom or serenity, at peace in a bemused kind of way with life's inscrutabilities.

What is the secret of their happiness? And what indeed is to be gained by pondering on the contingency, insecurity, restlessness of man, on his search for meaning? Why continue the search? There is perhaps what might be termed in innate element of contradiction in such a line of questioning however. And it relates to the suspicion that our right to ask questions and expect answers – which morally no one would, I think, wish to deny or suppress – may be nevertheless finally incompatible with the very contingency we are trying to understand. Perhaps what is centrally at issue here, is how to find the right *tone* in which to speak about God. While questions should certainly be permitted, even they should maybe not be taken too seriously. For surely one of the drawbacks of writers associated with 'existentialism', like Camus and Sartre after the Second World War, is that they took the ultimate questions of human existence so deadly seriously, and themselves too in the process, that they became rather didactic. Not that the question of human happiness is, as a nineteenth-century Archbishop of Dublin, Richard Whately, pointed out, any 'laughing matter', but contingent creatures like ourselves cannot, without remainder as it were, assume responsibility for the existence of the cosmos. When the Austrian writer Robert Musil was asked what was the purpose of living, he replied, cryptically: 'I live, in order to smoke.' This apparently frivolous reply conveys, nevertheless, with admirable economy, how silly it is to think that ultimate questions can ever receive from us ultimate intellectual answers.

But if we will never get to the bottom of the questions (to say nothing of the answers), we should nevertheless be concerned with the specifically Western mode of posing the ultimate question. For could the human restlessness which triggers off the search for transcendence in its typically Western form simply be a creation of Christianity, as Heidegger implied?[29] Would we ever have known

---

29 'Heidegger remarks that "the idea of 'transcendence' – that man is something that reaches beyond himself – is rooted in Christian dogmatics"' (J. Macquarrie, *In Search of Humanity*, London, 1982, p. 32).

about man's 'restless heart' if we had never been told about it? Or seen man as an 'incomprehensible monster', the 'greatness and garbage of the universe', if Pascal had not been egged on by Augustine to speak thus? Or does this way of interpreting human existence interest us because it really accounts for the facts of experience, and because it also seems to mesh with a Christian view of human existence as fallen, but redeemed?

Who is not to say, however, that an affirmative answer to these questions is tantamount to a tautology? For will a Pascal not naturally see his experience as supporting the Christian interpretation of existence? That is to say, did Pascal not (naively?) accept a way of interpreting human existence which Christianity had long fostered in the West, and then assume that it was universally valid and true even apart from its basis in Christian culture? In other words, did Pascal simply see in life what Christianity first put there and then, not surprisingly, find a perfect fit between Christian teaching and human experience? Is the logical nature of his Christianity for which Nietzsche admired him perhaps circular?

Without wanting to digress too long on this difficult question which is suggested by Franz Overbeck's interpretation of Pascal,[30] it seems to me, that once again Christianity can have things both ways. Overbeck is right in thinking that there is something in Christianity that is specific. Its whole interpretation of existence is surely unthinkable without the historical reality and particularity of Jesus. That is to say, the truth of Christianity is not simply the intellectual expression of an ever available historical possibility for humanity; it is not an interpretation of human existence that was, in principle, open to anyone to decipher at any time, in any place. It is rather tied to the unique and – because beyond our control – 'impossible', divine possibility of Jesus: 'beyond us, yet ourselves', to echo Wallace Stevens. So of course Pascal found in life what Christianity first put there. But Christian faith would say it could not have got there any other way. To go from that, however, to saying that Christianity's specificity invalidates necessarily its universal relevance, as Overbeck feared,[31] seems in strict logic untenable.

---

30 See *Christentum und Kultur*, pp. 126–134, especially p. 128.

31 Overbeck is right, I think, to see mankind as unchanging: *'What is eternal about us has always been in us and did not come to us belatedly at a particular moment in the life of mankind.* Our experience of Christianity cannot overturn this conception of history, it can only confirm it' (*Christentum und Kultur*, p. 73). However why should this be incompatible with the

Which is not to say it makes it necessarily true either, of course. But the question is at least still open. Perhaps one could compromise and see Pascal's logic as not circular but elliptical, revolving round the two fixed points of the human condition and Jesus Christ.

As was said earlier, however, these kinds of questions do not interest everyone, and many believers manage to exist without them. This prompts however for someone who may wish to think about them, the following question: If belief in the transcendent is mainly affirmed by those who are not by nature or training inclined to reflect systematically on their experience, could it be that any attempt to legitimate the validity of such belief is a false move? Is it not simply the case that belief in God expresses that than which nothing better, nobler, more hopeful or more coherent can be conceived, both as an explanation of life, and as an encouragement to affirming rather than deploring it? Those for whom such belief is real will presumably concur with the assertion that 'everything is grace' (Georges Bernanos, borrowing a St Thérèse of Lisieux saying).[32] Such a belief is not melodramatic or simplistic, nor of course is it foolproof. It does not see such basic issues as good and evil, to say nothing of religion, as being clearly defined. It is a belief that lives with the inevitable, irresolvable ambiguities of life, but that regards meaning rather than absurdity or blind chance as the final word on life's rich, incomprehensible web, but a final word that we listen out for, rather than speak ourselves.

For faith, since it may ultimately be mistaken (in which case, however, who would ever know?), cannot be the creator of meaning – *pace* Unamuno's punning affirmation that 'to believe is to create' (*creer es crear*) – it can only be one response to the human condition, a response that presupposes but cannot prove that 'life' is ultimately meaningful, or – what amounts to the same thing – that it is, notwithstanding the pain of existence, good rather than evil, that it is worth living. To that extent – being elicited by and reactive to existence – the primordial movement of faith is not unlike the

---

belief that in Jesus the redemption of the whole human race was accomplished? In fact if humanity did radically change in the course of its history, precisely *that* would render the Christian notion of redemption questionable, because the unity of mankind which the Judaeo-Christianity tradition affirms and the Christian doctrine of redemption presupposes would then be broken.

32 *Journal d'un Curé de Campagne*, in *Oeuvres Romanesques*, Bibliothèque de la Pléiade (Paris, 1961), p. 1259, cf. p. 1851.

already mentioned urge to philosophise, referred to by Aristotle as 'wonderment'. Theology is perhaps more like curiosity: not as valuable, and deeply ambiguous, but for some – like a temptation – irresistible.

Belief

To believe, therefore, that 'God is', or to see in the existence of the incomprehensible God the 'object' of faith, if one may so put it, and to believe that the world is his creation, will entail, surely, seeing the world as a projection of God's incomprehensibility. The unfathomability of the world not only fits this description, but also means that it will never yield an unambiguous clue as to the *nature* of God. But who is the projection of whom? a Feuerbach might well ask. Or, as Nietzsche wrote: 'Which is it? is man only God's mistake or God only man's mistake? –'[33] Why, that is, give precedence to God's incomprehensibility over that of the world? Why not simply say that there is, so to speak, an internal solution to the problem of the world, that the world can be understood 'without external reference', to borrow a phrase from Wallace Stevens? Here, it seems to me, the problem of evil can be the turning-point in the debate. For the world's incomprehensibility includes its undeniable *mélange* of good and evil, whereas God's incomprehensibility does not extend to the accommodation of a morally mixed divine nature. At least that is our faith. Thus it makes sense to accord precedence to God over his creation (or, in biblical terms, to have 'no other gods' before 'the Lord your God', Ex 20:2–3, cf. Mt 22:37–38), for in that way hope in the ultimate reality of goodness, and in the goodness of ultimate reality, can stay alive. If, like both Nietzsche and Christianity, one rules out any gnostic dualism, the only other option, is – as Nietzsche clearly saw – to give precedence to the world, which thereby becomes 'God', warts and all, and the old 'God' of Christianity becomes, in such a Nietzschean scenario, simply irrelevant to human existence.

Faith in God, then, accords God precedence over creation. However it does so not in some vacuum but from within the world that is God's free creation and that is thus inescapably dependent on an incomprehensible God who cannot *not* exist. Faith also sees life as worthwhile in this world because this is the only place from where we can affirm (believe in) God. But we will never fully understand why it is worthwhile to live and to believe in God

---

33 *Twilight of the Idols*, p. 33.

because we are not God, and we do not know and possibly never will know why God created us. There is however no clash, no conflict, no tragic split between loving God and loving the world, as Nietzsche thought, and as has become a cliché since his day. We affirm the world, as the only place where we have the possibility of affirming God. Even our freedom to do so is itself part of our created status. God, for Christian faith, is a condition of, not a threat to, human freedom. And we wish to affirm God because God has brought this world into being out of nothing, keeps it in being and, according to Christian teaching, has become part of this world in Jesus to take its evil on himself and thereby to make life desirable forever: it would not be worth having forever if it were to be blighted eternally. Our interest in God is thus not without self-interest. Does this cheapen our faith? Hardly, if the life we wish to maintain and enjoy is God's way of expressing himself to us. The two motives for religion – to enjoy being alive and to give thanks to God – simply reinforce one another.

The exhilarating futility of life is consonant with the suspicion that human being is rooted firmly in created reality and always will be, but that that reality will eventually be transfigured in its entirety, when in traditional Christian language God will be 'all in all.' In the meantime the world's 'flowers of evil' are a token or a promise of what is possible, since even terrible human suffering and mistakes can be transmuted into works of beauty. Nietzsche once spoke of transforming by sheer will-power ('the tyrant in me') his experience of intense physical and spiritual suffering into 'gold'.[34] This may be Pelagian, but it seems to me to err in the right direction. Christianity which sees redemption stemming from human evil lives from the faith that divine power can even somehow absorb evil, and bring unimagined good from it. But it brings good out of evil, it does not make evil go away or pretend that it never existed or put a pretty covering over it or 'make up for it' in some facile sense by, as it were, compensation on the good side.

Faith in God thus includes, to put it in slightly different terms, a possible answer, not to the question: 'Why is there something, rather than nothing?', which is a philosophical question, but to the – dare one say? – theological question: 'Is that which exists, despite the evil that now mars it, worth affirming and taking care of, as the creation of a good God, or is it the, in human terms, amoral manifestation of an inexhaustible and awe-inspiring source of energy

---

34 See his letter to Overbeck, summer 1883.

(Nietzsche), or, finally, might it even represent a 'gnostic' catastrophe, perpetrated by a wicked deity, whose action must be endured, since it cannot be avoided? In saying that faith *includes* an affirmation of the world as the creation of a good God, one is simply emphasising that such an affirmation does not exhaust the meaning of faith. Being in Christian tradition a grace, faith cannot be completely understood but only ever tentatively elucidated in its human dimension.

Conclusion

The Christian doctrine of God has always officially recognised both divine transcendence and divine immanence, God's absence from the world and his presence in it, even if, historically, one-sided emphases have occasionally occurred. For instance the deism of the Enlightenment could arguably be seen as springing at least in part from too exclusive a concern for divine transcendence, which was itself a reaction against the excessive stress on divine immanence at the Renaissance and especially during the Reformation period. Enlightenment deism in its turn provoked the reaction of the European – especially the German – Romantics (e.g. Schleiermacher and Hegel as we have seen) who put God firmly back into the world.

It is important to observe that when a secularising process of religious ideas takes place (as in the modern West), it is always a specific notion of God that gets secularised. Thus the phase of the secularisation of Christianity that started with the Young Hegelians in Germany, beginning in the 1830s, was as it happened the intellectualisation of an immanentist conception of God. This led to the identification of God with the historical process as such in Marx, and produced that vivid and powerful sense of the pathos of history in so much of what Nietzsche wrote.

The Christian doctrine of God is not compatible with seeing history as an absolute (hence the doctrines of Christ's resurrection and ascension and the eschatological doctrines, like the Last Judgement) and therefore rejects all utopias, just as it refuses to see in history only an illusion (*maya*) hiding true reality from our gaze. Christian teaching on God, which stresses both God's transcendence of history, and his immanence within the historical process, like a composer in his music, helps us see that we are real, that history is not an illusion, but a place where questions of good and evil have to be faced in the here and now and not postponed to a vague future.

Christianity sees history, in other words, as a place from which we cannot escape into some cloud-cuckoo-land. But it also teaches that, because of God's transcendence, the history he has called into existence can, if he so wishes, be redeemed from evil. It is the teaching of the New Testament that God has in fact redeemed the world from evil in Jesus Christ.

The connection between God and history can be summed up by saying that history is nothing without God, and yet history is radically other than God. History has thus a real, though limited, autonomy or independence of God. Hence evil is a possibility in history, but not in God. Moreover, because God transcends history, it is possible for people in history to show no conscious awareness of or interest in God, because the link between history and God is not one of identity or – and this amounts to the same thing – necessity (according to Christian teaching God did not *have* to create the world). If it were, the reality of God would be inescapably present to every human consciousness, and in that case we would not be free. We can only be free, to the extent that God remains in part hidden, thus allowing us – literally – a breathing-space.

The importance, to repeat, of the doctrine of divine transcendence is that it permits us to make a firm distinction between creator and creature, and to believe that evil is not part of God, even though it is clearly an aspect of a contingent creation. We can *believe* that evil is not within God, because we do not *know* the nature of God: the substance of God cannot be conceived by the human mind. While we can make the judgement *that* God exists, Aquinas taught – as we have already mentioned – that we cannot know *what* God is in himself. Hence, those for whom God must, in order to be God, be conceivable as God by the human mind, will sooner or later incline to atheism. Atheism, as an intellectual outlook, is a powerful sign of the mind's inability to satisfy itself about the possibility of conceiving God.

Yet the challenge of evil to the continuation of belief would be completely unanswerable (as was mentioned in Chapter Three) if one did not have a doctrine of divine transcendence. For were the link between God and the world one of identity, what we call evil would be an aspect of God himself and thus, assuming God to be essentially good, it would have to be declared to be also a form of the good. Alternatively – and perhaps this comes to the same thing – the difference between good and evil would have to be abolished. If 'evil' were to be thus whisked away, it would at least of course cease being an absurdity.

However, if we do see evil as an absurdity that defies our reason, just as God transcends our reason, why do we not say that evil itself is an ontological principle of equal power with God himself, or even – as dualists, from the Manichees onwards, have always taught – that matter, the whole physical and material world, is the product of an evil creator? Assuming there is nothing inherently self-contradictory in believing in two equal ultimate principles, are God and evil simply two co-equal principles, between which the world is destined to be pulled to and fro in a kind of never-ending cosmic tug of war? Or do we give priority to God over the force of evil? And if so why, granted that both God and evil transcend our understanding? For if God gives the peace, evil equally can give the anguish, that surpasses all understanding. The God-question is, therefore, not a question of which of the two we prefer, peace or anguish, but which (if either) of the two is the final truth, and why.

A transient process like history which reveals absolutely evil happenings and also an indestructible force of good, can surely only make sense, if we believe that a transcendent God is involved in it actively or redemptively, and not simply in a sustaining, creative way. For only an absolute force of good, which God is believed to be, can resist destruction by absolute evil. History reveals both. It reveals not only the reality of total evil, but also the presence of incorruptible good that survives the challenge of evil. However if God is to resist destruction by evil, he must also transcend history. If he does not, if he is confined to the historical process, then either he is himself implicated in the evil of history, or else he is a helpless bystander, manifestly unable to put an end to evil. In neither case can he be a saving God.

If however one accepts that there is a real difference between good and evil, and if furthermore one admits that it is impossible to *know* how a transcendent good God can redeem the world from evil, and yet if finally one wishes to accord priority to either good or evil, it would seem that this can only be done by an act of will, by a choice perhaps guided ultimately by taste, but an act of will or a choice that is also essentially a response to an uncontrollable attraction. In traditional Christian terms the attraction and the free yielding to it are known, in the case of the 'good', as grace.

Choosing between good and evil – or 'believing in God' in the terms of the argument being suggested here – is thus not in the final analysis, oddly enough, a moral dilemma. It is somewhat more like the comparison between happiness and misery. Happiness is obviously a more desirable commodity than misery, but it is also, sadly, much rarer. Lost love lasts longer. However both happiness and misery are passions we suffer, we cannot actively *decide* to experience them. Does the rarity of the precious metal of happiness also confer a metaphysical or ontological superiority on it? This is one of those questions to which we cannot *know* the answer. We can of course, without being charged with obvious irrationality, believe and hope that it does, and even hope that the best wine is being reserved for the End. Likewise we can believe and hope that the beautiful (which Stendhal described as *une promesse de bonheur*)[35] is superior to the ugly. And similarly, we can hope that 'belief in God', which is not self-evidently irrational, is ultimately more 'true' to the way things are and to the way 'all manner of thing' shall be, and is thus finally more persuasive, more compelling than 'unbelief', perhaps like Nietzsche's sense that 'joy' is 'deeper than heart's agony.'[36] But from our perspective, which is always 'in transit', belief can never be more than a human possibility which is and which will always remain ineluctably obscure, because we cannot see things as they really are. For this reason, faith must be unconditional, for otherwise it could or would be eroded by the infinite possible objections anyone may care to raise against it.

Faith affirms that God (the origin and goal of our existence) is good, not evil. In practice this boils down to accepting (*not* proving) that life, with all its woes, is – not, of course, literally – better than nothing ('nothing' being – like God in this respect – inconceivable), that it is good to live, rather than never to have been born, and that evil is an aberration, a perpetual problem for faith, rather than the other way round. Faith thus, finally, parts company with, though should never forget, the pessimism one finds expressed in European thought from ancient times onwards as, for example, in Sophocles ('not to be born is, past all prizing, best' [tr. R.W. Jebb]), Calderón ('man's greatest crime is to have been born'), Goethe ('for all that comes to birth/Is fit for overthrow, as nothing worth;/Wherefore the world were better sterilised' [tr. P. Wayne]) or Beckett ('Birth was the death of him'). 'Good' is admittedly no more comprehensible than 'evil'. Its ultimate source is not within our grasp, and cer-

---

35 Quoted (without reference) by Nietzsche, *On the Genealogy of Morals*, III, 6.
36 *Thus Spoke Zarathustra*, p. 333.

tainly not of our making, but its reality is undeniable.[37] Faith lives
with the sense that goodness is more thoughtful, more considerate,
more understanding, more intelligent and, finally, more interesting[38] than evil, agreeing implicitly with Oscar Wilde that: 'There is
no sin except stupidity,' against which, alas, 'the gods themselves
struggle in vain' (Schiller). Faith, thus, prefers to see evil as a problem we have to put up with, and goodness as a welcome guest.

---

37 Cf. the final lines from Gottfried Benn's late poem ('People Met'):
    'Often I have asked myself, but found no answer,/Where gentleness
    and goodness can possibly come from;/Even today I can't tell, and it's
    time to be gone' (tr. Christopher Middleton).
38 Cf. Paul Claudel: 'Le bien est plus intéressant que le mal parce qu'il est
    plus difficile (Good is more interesting than evil because it is more diffi-
    cult)' (*Journal*, vol. 1, intro. and ed. F. Varillon and J. Petit, Paris, 1968,
    p. 616).

God and Death[1]

Deathlessness is no blessing but only a weariness if grace does not transfigure it. — St Ambrose

Death is not a God. He is only the servant of the gods. — Oscar Wilde

To be immortal is commonplace; except for man, all creatures are immortal, for they are ignorant of death; what is divine, terrible, incomprehensible, is to know that one is immortal. I have noted that, in spite of religions, this conviction is very rare. Israelites, Christians and Moslems profess immortality, but the veneration they render this world proves they believe only in it, since they destine all other worlds, in infinite number, to be its reward or punishment. — Jorge Luis Borges

It is very difficult to speak about death because there is nothing else quite like it. In fact the only comparison you can find or make for death is with the whole of life itself. In one of Victor Hugo's poems – if my memory serves me right – he made the striking remark that when a person dies, the whole universe is decapitated. No single one of us is of course the centre of the universe, but when each one of us dies, a particular way of looking at and experiencing the world that was unique to us will cease. What Tomás Ó Criomhthain wrote about his own people of the Great Blasket island applies, for those who are willing and perceptive enough to see it, to all human beings: ' … the like of us will never be again.' For, as Borges wrote in one of his 'fictions': 'Death (or mention of it) makes men precious and pathetic … Everything among the mortals has the value of the irretrievable and the perilous.'[2]

---

1   A version of this short piece was published in the December 1992 issue of *The Furrow*. It is reprinted with kind permission of the Editor.

2   From 'The Immortal', in J. L. Borges, *Labyrinths* (Harmondsworth, 1972), p. 146 (amended).

For the *living* who suffer the death of someone they love there is no ritual, no explanation, no consolation that can dissolve the mystery of loss and restore the *status quo*, because the one who died was unique and after his or her death, life can and will never be the same again.

We all know this, people have known it from the dawn of history and yet we still have not got used to it, even when and maybe especially when we make death a taboo-subject. It just does not seem fair that this miracle of life and the people we know and love in it should be taken away from us; it seems even less fair that life is often taken away from people in the most brutal, inhuman, murderous and degrading ways. Human beings instinctively ask: 'Why must the gift of life end up for so many in unspeakable misery and squalid death, and for all of us in some form of death?' Job can stand here as a symbol of the human refusal to sweep such questions under the carpet or to be browbeaten by pious bullying into not asking them.

But the fact that we instinctively and continually rebel against the idea that injustice and death should have the last word about life is a hint to us that the way we experience reality here and now is not the way reality will ultimately be. We are not here on earth what we will finally be, even though what we will finally be, we do not yet know, for – as St John wrote – it has not yet been revealed to us.

We live by faith which, if it is genuine, can take ignorance about the ways of God in its stride. Our faith tells us that injustice and death do not have the last word about life, just as they did not have the first one either. In the beginning was not injustice and death, nor even the world itself, but in the beginning was the *Word* through whom the world was made and who in Jesus Christ became the world's redeemer. Job's faith in a living redeemer was vindicated in Jesus Christ in whom God's love is active towards us in a way that nothing can ever undermine.

Thinking and brooding about death and its undoubted terrors can however sometimes tempt us into being more concerned with what Christ has saved us from here on earth, than with the glory which his victory over death in the resurrection has made possible for us. In this world, we should perhaps remind ourselves from time to time, we are only being prepared for heaven, even though of course without this world we would never get to heaven. Our faith in God teaches us that what matters most here on earth is not the experience we may think we have or do not have of God before death, but the experience God has of us. Experience in its root meaning is concerned with testing and trying. God's experience of us is the testing we must go through in order to reach heaven. If we have faith in God, any pain we have to suffer in life can be out-reached by the joy of knowing that our lives, painful and finite though they are, are being tested by God and hence they are in God's hands. That is the secret of religious peace, and likewise the liberating truth and relief of Tragedy, for Tragedy always brings us up sharply against the limits of the human condition and in so doing allows us painfully to learn something of the power that set those limits and thus created meaning for our world.

We moderns seem however sometimes more keen to want to experience and thus test God, than to allow ourselves to be tested and experienced by God. In trying to take religion seriously in this way, in making ourselves responsible for it, we confuse our role with God's and the result cannot but be slightly ridiculous. Bishops worry about their pastoral responsibilities, priests worry about run-ning their parishes, theologians worry about their relevance. Could this ever be the case, if we really believed our redemption was an accomplished fact that no worldly power could ever undo? A reli-gion with human beings and their problems at the centre of the stage is not true religion, at least it is not, I think, true Christianity.

It is interesting to look back sometimes at our forbears in the faith and see how they responded to the great truths of Christianity. 'We possess a Ritual from Besançon for the year 1582 which gives the following directions for Vespers on [Easter] day: "After the end-ing of None the dances take place in the cloisters, or if the weather is wet, in the centre of the nave. During these are to be sung the chants found in the processional. And when the dance is ended drinks of red and white wine will be served in the chapter house." We possess an even more exact account of this Easter custom in the case of the cathedral of Auxerre. There the dance, combined with a sacral ball game, took place in the cathedral choir and ... upon the so-called "labyrinth" which decorated the floor in the form of a mosaic... To the melody and rhythm of the Easter sequence, *Victimae paschali*, bishop and clerks moved in a carefully regulated dance order over the pattern of the labyrinth, throwing ... the Easter ball to one another, rejoicing like children in their redemption, for this was the evening of the day which had celebrated the victorious sun of Easter.'[3]

---

3   Hugo Rahner, *Man At Play* (New York, 1972), pp. 84-86.

We may smile or even laugh at such practices. They may strike us nowadays as childish or mind-boggling or not serious enough in religion. But surely they are the practices of people who believed that God and the redemption won for them by God in Christ were at the centre of religion and rejoiced in this fact. They are not the practices of people taking the weight of the world's problems on their shoulders, but the practices of people who find Christ's burden light and his yoke easy.

We of course are not sixteenth-century people, but the faith we have inherited from our forbears must not be allowed to be weighed down and choked by the cares and anxieties of this world. It must be what it has fundamentally been down through the centuries: a joyful act of thanksgiving to God who has called us out of nothingness into being and who – even beyond death – offers us and all the faithful departed a share in everlasting glory.

Bibliography

REFERENCE WORKS

Abrams, M. H. *A Glossary of Literary Terms*, (Orlando, 1988[5])
Audi, R. (ed)*The Cambridge Dictionary of Philosophy* (Cambridge, 1995)
Ayer, A. J. and O'Grady, J. (eds) *A Dictionary of Philosophical Quotations* (Oxford, 1994)
Barth, K. *Protestant Theology in the Nineteenth Century*, tr. B. Cozens and J. Bowden (London, 1972)
Baumer, F. L. *Modern European Thought* (New York and London, 1977)
Bradbury, M. and McFarlane, J. (eds) *Modernism* in the *Pelican Guides to European Literature* (Harmondsworth, 1976)
Bullock, A. and Stallybrass, O. (eds) *The Fontana Dictionary of Modern Thought* (London, 1977)
Edwards, P. (ed.) *The Encyclopedia of Philosophy*, 8 vols. (New York, 1967)
Fellmann, F. (ed.) *Geschichte der Philosophie im 19. Jahrhundert* (Reinbek, 1996)
Flew, A. (ed.) *A Dictionary of Philosophy*, (London, 1984)
Ford, D. F. (ed.) *The Modern Theologians*, (Oxford, 1996[2])
Grenz, S. J. and Olson, R. E. *Twentieth-Century Theology. God and the World in a Transitional Age* (Downers Grove, 1992)
Harvey, V. A. *A Handbook of Theological Terms* (London, 1964)
Hick, J. *Philosophy of Religion* (Englewood Cliffs, N. J., 1983)
Hinnells, J. R. (ed.) *Dictionary of Religions* (Harmondsworth, 1984)
Hodgson, P. and King, R. (eds) *Christian Theology. An Introduction to its Traditions and Tasks* (London, 1983)
Inwood, M. *A Hegel Dictionary* (Oxford, 1992)
Jary, D. and Jary, J. (eds) *Collins Dictionary of Sociology* (Glasgow, 1995)
Livingston, J. C. *Modern Christian Thought. From the Enlightenment to Vatican II* (New York and London, 1971)
Lutz B. (ed.) *Metzler Philosophen Lexikon* (Stuttgart and Weimar, 1995[2])
Mackintosh, H. R. *Types of Modern Theology* (London and Glasgow, 1969)
Macquarrie, J. *Twentieth-Century Religious Thought* (London, 1989[4])
McGrath, A. (ed.) *The Blackwell Encyclopedia of Modern Christian Thought* (Oxford, 1993)
Musser, D. W. and Price, J. L. (eds) *A New Handbook of Christian Theology* (Cambridge, 1992)
Neuner, J., SJ and Dupuis, J., SJ (eds) *The Christian Faith* (Dublin and Cork, 1973)
O'Connor, D. J. (ed.) *A Critical History of Western Philosophy* (New York, 1985)
Pelikan, J. *The Melody of Theology. A Philosophical Dictionary* (Cambridge, Mass., 1988)
Richardson, A. and Bowden, J. (eds) *A New Dictionary of Christian Theology* (London, 1983)
Scruton, R. *Modern Philosophy* (London, 1994)
Seymour-Smith, M. *Guide to Modern World Literature* (London, 1986)
Smart, N. *The World's Religions* (Cambridge, 1993)
Solomon, R. C. *Continental Philosophy since 1750* (Oxford, 1988)
Spierling, V. *Kleine Geschichte der Philosophie* (Munich, 1996)
Störig, H. J. *Kleine Weltgeschichte der Philosophie* (Frankfurt a/M, 1995)

Tanner, N.P., S.J. (ed.) *Decrees of the Ecumenical Councils*, 2 vols. (London, 1990)
The Catechism of the Catholic Church (Dublin, 1994)
The Young Hegelians. An Anthology, intro. and (ed) by L. S. Stepelevich
    (Cambridge, 1983)
Urban, L. *A Short History of Christian Thought* (Oxford, 1986)
Urmson, J. O. and Rée, J. (eds) *The Concise Encyclopedia of Western Philosophy and
    Philosophers* (London and New York, 1991)
Wintle, J. (ed.) *Dictionary of Modern Culture* (London, 1984)

THEOLOGICAL AND PHILOSOPHICAL WRITINGS

Albrektson, B. *History and the Gods* (Lund, 1967)
Almond, B. *Philosophy* (Harmondsworth, 1988)
Anselm, St, *Basic Writings*, tr. S. N. Deane (La Salle, Illinois, 1974)
Armstrong, A. H. 'On Not Knowing Too Much About God' in G. Vesey (ed)*The
    Philosophy in Christianity* (Cambridge, 1989)
Armstrong, A. H. and Markus, R. A. *Christian Faith and Greek Philosophy*, (London,
    1964)
Balthasar, H. Urs von, *Herrlichkeit* III,1, Teil 2 (Einsiedeln, 1965)
— *Love Alone: the Way of Revelation*, ed. A. Dru (London, 1977)
Barnes, J. *Aristotle* (Oxford, 1986)
Barr, J. *Biblical Words for Time* (London, 1969)
— *Explorations in Theology 7* (London, 1980)
— *Holy Scripture: Canon, Authority, Criticism* (Oxford, 1983)
— *Old and New in Interpretation* (New York, 1966)
— *The Bible in the Modern World* (London, 1973)
— *The Semantics of Biblical Language* (Oxford, 1961)
Barrett, W. *Death of the Soul. Philosophical Thought from Descartes to the Computer*
    (Oxford, 1987)
Barth, K. *The Humanity of God* (London and Glasgow, 1971)
Beeck, F. J. van, *God Encountered: A Contemporary Catholic Systematic Theology*, Vol, 2/1
    (Collegeville, Minnesota, 1993)
Benjamin, W. 'Theses on the Philosophy of History', in *Illuminations*, ed. and with an
    intro. by H. Arendt, tr. H. Zohn (London, 1982)
Bernoulli, C. A. *Franz Overbeck und Friedrich Nietzsche. Eine Freundschaft*, 2 vols.
    (Jena, 1908)
Bottéro, J. *Babylone et la Bible* (Paris, 1994)
— *Naissance de Dieu* (Paris, 1992)
Bridgwater, P. *Nietzsche in Anglosaxony* (Leicester University Press, 1972)
Brinton, C. *Nietzsche* (New York, 1965)
Buber, M. *Eclipse of God: Studies in the Relation Between Religion and Philosophy* (New
    Jersey, 1979)
Chadwick, H. *Lessing's Theological Writings* (London, 1956)
Dupré, L. *Kierkegaard as Theologian* (London, 1964)
— *The Deeper Life. An Introduction to Christian Mysticism* (New York, 1981)
Farrelly, M. J. *Belief in God in Our Time* (Collegeville, Minnesota, 1992)
Feuerbach, L. *Das Wesen des Christentums* (Stuttgart, 1974)
— *Principles of the Philosophy of the Future*, tr. with an intro. by M. H. Vogel
    (Indianapolis, 1966)
— *The Essence of Christianity*, tr. George Eliot (New York, 1957)
Frei, H. *The Eclipse of Biblical Narrative* (Yale, 1974)
Gellner, E. *Postmodernism, Reason and Religion* (London, 1992)

— *Thought and Change* (London, 1964)

Gerrish, B. A. *Tradition and the Modern World. Reformed Theology in the Nineteenth Century* (Chicago and London, 1978)

Gilson, É. *God and Philosophy* (New Haven and London, 1969)

Hannay, A. *Kierkegaard* (London, 1991)

Harvey, V.A. 'Ludwig Feuerbach and Karl Marx', in Ninian Smart et al. (eds) *Nineteenth Century Religious Thought in the West*, vol. I (Cambridge, 1985)

— *Feuerbach and the Interpretation of Religion* (Cambridge, 1995)

— *The Historian and the Believer* (London, 1967)

Hegel, G. W. F. *Elements of the Philosophy of Right*, ed. A. W. Wood, tr. H. B. Nisbet (Cambridge, 1991)

— *Lectures on the Philosophy of Religion*, ed. P. C. Hodgson (Berkeley and Los Angeles, 1988)

— *On Christianity: Early Theological Writings*, tr. T.M. Knox, intro. R. Kroner (Gloucester, Mass., 1970)

— *Phenomenology of Spirit*, tr. A.V. Miller, with analysis of the text and foreword by J. N. Findlay (Oxford, 1979)

— *The Encyclopaedia Logic*. Part I of the *Encyclopaedia of Philosophical Sciences* with the Zusätze. A new translation with intro. and notes by T. F. Geraets, W. A. Suchting, and H. S. Harris (Indianapolis, 1991)

— *The Logic of Hegel*, tr. from the *Encyclopaedia of the Philosophical Sciences*, with Prolegomena, by W. Wallace (Oxford, 1874)

— *The Philosophy of History*, tr. J. Sibree (New York, 1956)

— *Werke in zwanzig Bänden*, ed. E. Moldenhauer and K. M. Michel (Frankfurt a/M, 1969–71); *Register*, ed. H. Reinicke (1979)

Henry, M. *Franz Overbeck: Theologian? Religion and History in the Thought of Franz Overbeck* (Frankfurt a/M, 1995)

Hersch, J. *L'étonnement philosophique. Une histoire de la philosophie* (Paris, 1993)

Hick, J. *Evil and the God of Love* (London, 1970)

Hollingdale, R. J. *Nietzsche* (London and Boston, 1973)

— *Nietzsche. The Man and His Philosophy* (London, 1965)

Janaway, C. *Schopenhauer* (Oxford, 1994)

Kasper, W. *The God of Jesus Christ*, tr. M. J. O'Connell (London, 1983)

Kaufmann, W. (ed. and tr.) *Basic Writings of Nietzsche* (New York, 1968): includes *The Birth of Tragedy, Beyond Good and Evil, On the Genealogy of Morals, The Case of Wagner, Ecce Homo*

— (ed and tr.) *The Portable Nietzsche* (Harmondsworth, 1981): includes *Thus Spoke Zarathustra, Twilight of the Idols, The Antichrist, Nietzsche contra Wagner*

— *Nietzsche. Philosopher, Psychologist, Antichrist* (Princeton, N. J., 1974)

Kolakowski, L. *Main Currents of Marxism* , vol. I (Oxford, 1978)

— *Metaphysical Horror* (Oxford, 1988)

— *Modernity on Endless Trial* (Chicago and London, 1990)

— *Religion* (Oxford, 1982)

Lichtenberg, G. Chr. *Aphorisms*, tr. R. J. Hollingdale (Harmondsworth, 1990)

Louth, A. *Discerning the Mystery* (London, 1983)

— *The Origins of the Christian Mystical Tradition* (Oxford, 1983)

Lyon, D. *Postmodernity* (Buckingham, 1995)

Macquarrie, J. *In Search of Deity* (London, 1984)

— *In Search of Humanity* (London, 1982)

Marsh, T. *The Triune God: A biblical, historical and theological study* (Dublin, 1994)

McLellan, D. *The Young Hegelians and Karl Marx* (Aldershot, 1993)

Merquior, J. G. *Foucault* (London, 1985)

Milet, J. *God or Christ?* tr. J. Bowden (London, 1981)

Moltmann, J. *God in Creation* (London, 1985)

Morin, D. *How to Understand God*, tr. J. Bowden (London, 1990)

Newman, J.H. *Apologia Pro Vita Sua* (London and Glasgow, 1972)

Nietzsche, F. *Beyond Good and Evil*, tr. R.J. Hollingdale with an intro. by M. Tanner (Harmondsworth, 1990)

— *Daybreak*, tr. R. J. Hollingdale (Cambridge, 1983)

— *Ecce Homo*, tr. R. J. Hollingdale (Harmondsworth, 1980)

— *Human, All Too Human*, tr. R. J. Hollingdale, intro. E. Heller (Cambridge, 1986)

— *Kritische Studienausgabe*, ed. G. Colli and M Montinari, 15 vols. (Munich, 1988)

— *Sämtliche Briefe. Kritische Studienausgabe*, ed. G. Colli and M. Montinari, 8 vols. (Munich, 1986)

— *The Gay Science*, tr. W. Kaufmann (New York, 1974)

— *The Will to Power*, tr. W. Kaufmann and R. J. Hollingdale (London, 1968)

— *Thus Spoke Zarathustra*, tr. R. J. Hollingdale (Harmondsworth, 1986)

— *Twilight of the Idols/The Anti-Christ*, tr. R. J. Hollingdale (Harmondsworth, 1990)

— *Untimely Meditations*, tr. R. J. Hollingdale (Cambridge, 1983)

Oehler, R. and Bernoulli, C. A. *Friedrich Nietzsches Briefwechsel mit Franz Overbeck* (Leipzig, 1916)

Overbeck, F. 'Erinnerungen an Friedrich Nietzsche', *Die Neue Rundschau*, I (1906), 209–231, 320–330

— *Christentum und Kultur*, ed. C. A. Bernoulli (Darmstadt, 1963)

— *Über die Anfänge der patristischen Literatur* (Darmstadt, 1966)

— *Über die Christlichkeit unserer heutigen Theologie* (Darmstadt, 1974)

— *Vorgeschichte und Jugend der mittelalterlichen Scholastik*, ed. C. A. Bernoulli (Darmstadt, 1971)

— *Werke und Nachlass*, ed. E. W. Stegemann et al., 9 vols. projected (Stuttgart and Weimar, 1994ff.)

Owen, H. P. *Christian Theism* (Edinburgh, 1984)

Pannenberg, W. *An Introduction to Systematic Theology* (Edinburgh, 1991)

— *Basic Questions in Theology*, vols. 2, 3 (London, 1971, 1973)

Pascal, B. *Pensées*, tr. A. J. Krailsheimer (Harmondsworth, 1983)

Passmore, J. *The Perfectibility of Man* (London, 1972)

Pawlowsky, P. *Christianity*, tr. J. Bowden (London, 1994)

Peter, N. *Im Schatten der Modernität – Franz Overbecks Weg zur 'Christlichkeit unserer heutigen Theologie'* (Stuttgart and Weimar, 1992)

Pfeiffer, A. *Franz Overbecks Kritik des Christentums* (Göttingen, 1975)

Pippin, R. B. *Modernism as a Philosophical Problem* (Oxford, 1991)

Popper, K. *The Open Society and Its Enemies*, vol. 2 (London, 1969)

Rahner, H. *Man At Play* (New York, 1972)

Ratzinger, J. *Introduction to Christianity* tr. J. R. Foster (London, 1968)

Reardon, B. M. G. 'Roman Catholic Modernism', in Ninian Smart et al. (eds) *Nineteenth Century Religious Thought in the West*, Vol. II, (Cambridge, 1985)

— *Hegel's Philosophy of Religion* (London, 1977)

— *Religion in the Age of Romanticism* (Cambridge, 1985)

— *Roman Catholic Modernism* (Stanford, 1970)

Ritschl, A. *Justification and Reconciliation*, tr. H. R. Mackintosh and A. B. Macauley (Edinburgh, 1900)

Schleiermacher, F. *On Religion: Speeches to Its Cultured Despisers*, intro., tr., and notes by R. Crouter (Cambridge, 1988)

— *On Religion: Speeches to Its Cultured Despisers*, tr. J. Oman, with an intro. by R. Otto (New York, 1958)

— *The Christian Faith*, ed. H. R. Mackintosh and J. S. Stewart (Edinburgh, 1968)
Schopenhauer, A. *Werke* 5 vols., ed. W. Frhr. von Löhneysen (Darmstadt, 1974ff.)
Scruton, R. *Kant* (Oxford, 1982)
Sokolowski, R. *The God of Faith and Reason* (Notre Dame, Indiana, 1982)
Sprigge, T. L. S. *Santayana* (London, 1995)
Stern, J. P. *A Study of Nietzsche* (Cambridge, 1981)
Stirner, M. *The Ego and His Own* , ed. J. Carroll (London, 1971)
Sutton, C. *The German Tradition in Philosophy* (London, 1974)
Sykes, S. *Friedrich Schleiermacher* (London, 1971)
Taylor, C. *Hegel* (Cambridge, 1977)
— *Sources of the Self. The Making of the Modern Identity* (Cambridge, 1992)
Theissen, G. *On Having a Critical Faith*, tr. J. Bowden (London, 1979)
Thomas Aquinas, St, *Summa Theologiae*, Ia. 1–26 (vols. 1–5, Blackfriars ed., 1964–67)
Tracy, D. *Plurality and Ambiguity* (London, 1988)
— *The Analogical Imagination* (London, 1981)
Tucker, R. *Philosophy and Myth in Karl Marx* (Cambridge, 1972)
Watson, G. *Greek Philosophy and the Christian Notion of God* (Dublin, 1994)
Wittgenstein, L. *Culture and Value*, ed. G. H. von Wright in collaboration with
    H. Nyman, tr. P. Winch (Oxford, 1980)

LITERARY SOURCES

Borges, J. L. *Labyrinths. Selected Stories and Other Writings*, ed. D. A. Yates and
    J. E. Irby (Harmondsworth, 1970)
Brodsky, J. *Less Than One. Selected Essays* (Harmondsworth, 1987)
Buñuel, L. *My Last Breath*, tr. A. Israel (Vintage Books, 1994)
Calder, J. *A Samuel Beckett Reader* (London, 1983)
Canetti, E. *Die Fliegenpein* (Frankfurt a/M, 1995)
Celan, P. *Selected Poems*, tr. and intro. by M. Hamburger (Harmondsworth, 1990)
Cioran, E. M. *Aveux et Anathèmes*, (Paris, 1987)
— *La chute dans le temps* (Paris, 1964)
Cohen, J. M. (ed) *The Penguin Book of Spanish Verse* (Harmondsworth, 1988)
Constant, B. *Oeuvres*, (ed) A. Roulin (Paris, 1957)
Ellmann, R. *The Identity of Yeats* (London, 1968)
Gracián, B. *The Oracle*, tr. L. B. Walton (London, 1953)
Hamburger, M. *The Truth of Poetry* (Harmondsworth, 1972)
Hesse, H. *Lektüre für Minuten* 2 (Frankfurt a./M, 1976)
Hone, J. *W.B. Yeats* (Harmondsworth, 1971)
Jean Paul, *Siebenkäs*, in *Werke*, vol. I, (ed) P. Stapf (Die Tempel-Klassiker, n.d.)
Kundera, M. *The Art of the Novel* (London, 1990)
Levi, P. *The Drowned and the Saved*, tr. R. Rosenthal (London, 1989)
Sperber, M. *Nur eine Brücke zwischen Gestern und Morgen* (Munich, 1983)
—*Sein letztes Jahr*, ed. H. Friedrich (Munich, 1985)
Stevens, W. *The Collected Poems of Wallace Stevens* (New York, 1978)

CULTURAL HISTORY AND MISCELLANEOUS

Arendt, H. 'The Concept of History: Ancient and Modern', in *Between Past and
    Future* (Harmondsworth, 1977)
Brown, P. *Augustine of Hippo* (London, 1969)
Brumlik, M. *Die Gnostiker* (Frankfurt a/M, 1992)
Debord, G. *La Société du Spectacle* (Paris, 1992)
Dodds, E. R. *Missing Persons* (Oxford, 1978)

— *Pagan and Christian in an Age of Anxiety: Some Aspects of Religious Experience from Marcus Aurelius to Constantine* (Cambridge, 1965).

Frankfort H. et al. *Before Philosophy: The Intellectual Adventure of Ancient Man* (Harmondsworth, 1971)

Girard, R. *Quand Ces Choses Commenceront...* (Paris, 1994)

Glover, J. I: *the Philosophy and Psychology of Personal Identity*, (Harmondsworth, 1991)

Johnson, P. *Intellectuals* (London, 1993)

Lacarrière, J. *The Gnostics*, tr. N. Rootes (London, 1977)

Liiceanu, G. *Itinéraires d'une vie: E.M. Cioran, suivi de 'les continents de l'insomnie' entretien avec E M. Cioran*, tr. A. Laignel-Lavastine (Paris, 1995)

Lovejoy, A. O. *The Great Chain of Being* (Cambridge, Mass., 1974)

McNeill, W. *The Rise of the West* (Chicago, 1963)

Mehta, V. *The New Theologian* (London, 1966)

Momigliano, A. *Alien Wisdom: The Limits of Hellenization* (Cambridge and New York, 1975)

— *Essays in Ancient and Modern Historiography* (Oxford, 1977)

Mortley, R. *French Philosophers in Conversation* (London, 1991)

Parris, M. *Scorn: With Added Vitriol* (Harmondsworth, 1996)

Prawer, S. (ed.) *The Romantic Period in Germany* (London, 1970)

Quignard, P. *Le sexe et l'effroi* (Paris, 1994)

Schenk, H. G. *The Mind of the European Romantics* (Oxford, 1966)

Stern, F. *The Politics of Cultural Despair: A Study in the Rise of the Germanic Ideology* (Berkeley and Los Angeles, 1974)

Whitehead, A. N. *Adventures of Ideas* (Cambridge, 1943)

Wilken, R. L. *The Christians as the Romans Saw Them* (Yale, 1984)